Australian Literature in the German Democratic Republic

Anthem Studies in Australian Literature and Culture

Anthem Studies in Australian Literature and Culture specialises in quality, innovative research in Australian literary studies. The series publishes work that advances contemporary scholarship on Australian literature conceived historically, thematically and/or conceptually. We welcome well-researched and incisive analyses on a broad range of topics: from individual authors or texts to considerations of the field as a whole, including in comparative or transnational frames.

Series Editors

Katherine Bode – Australian National University, Australia
Nicole Moore – University of New South Wales, Australia

Editorial Board

Tanya Dalziell – University of Western Australia, Australia
Delia Falconer – University of Technology, Sydney, Australia
John Frow – University of Sydney, Australia
Wang Guanglin – Shanghai University of International Business and Economics, China
Ian Henderson – King's College London, UK
Tony Hughes-D'Aeth – University of Western Australia, Australia
Ivor Indyk – University of Western Sydney, Australia
Nicholas Jose – University of Adelaide, Australia
James Ley – *Sydney Review of Books*, Australia
Andrew McCann – Dartmouth College, USA
Lyn McCredden – Deakin University, Australia
Elizabeth McMahon – University of New South Wales, Australia
Susan Martin – La Trobe University, Australia
Brigitta Olubas – University of New South Wales, Australia
Anne Pender – University of New England, Australia
Fiona Polack – Memorial University of Newfoundland, Canada
Sue Sheridan – University of Adelaide, Australia
Ann Vickery – Deakin University, Australia
Russell West-Pavlov – Eberhard-Karls-Universität Tübingen, Germany
Lydia Wevers – Victoria University of Wellington, New Zealand
Gillian Whitlock – University of Queensland, Australia

Australian Literature in the German Democratic Republic

Reading through the Iron Curtain

Edited by Nicole Moore and Christina Spittel

ANTHEM PRESS

Anthem Press
An imprint of Wimbledon Publishing Company
www.anthempress.com

This edition first published in UK and USA 2019
by ANTHEM PRESS
75–76 Blackfriars Road, London SE1 8HA, UK
or PO Box 9779, London SW19 7ZG, UK
and
244 Madison Ave #116, New York, NY 10016, USA

First published in the UK and USA by Anthem Press 2016

© 2019 Nicole Moore and Christina Spittel, editorial matter and selection;
Individual chapters © individual contributors

The moral right of the authors has been asserted.

All rights reserved. Without limiting the rights under copyright reserved above,
no part of this publication may be reproduced, stored or introduced into
a retrieval system, or transmitted, in any form or by any means
(electronic, mechanical, photocopying, recording or otherwise),
without the prior written permission of both the copyright
owner and the above publisher of this book.

British Library Cataloguing-in-Publication Data
A catalogue record for this book is available from the British Library.

ISBN-13: 978-1-78527-179-3 (Pbk)
ISBN-10: 1-78527-179-2 (Pbk)

This title is also available as an e-book.

CONTENTS

List of Figures   vii
List of Tables   ix
Acknowledgements   xi

Introduction. South by East: World Literature's Cold War Compass   1
Nicole Moore and Christina Spittel

Part I.   **CONTEXTS AND FRAMES**

Chapter 1. Censorship, Australian Literature and Foreign-Language Books in East German Publishing History   35
Siegfried Lokatis

Chapter 2. Towards a Cross-Border Canon: Marcus Clarke's *For the Term of His Natural Life* Behind the Wall   51
Russell West-Pavlov

Chapter 3. Community, Difference, Context: (Re)reading the Contact Zone   71
Jennifer Wawrzinek

Part II.   **BOOKS AND WRITERS**

Chapter 4. Sedition as Realism: Frank Hardy's *Power without Glory* Parts the Iron Curtain   93
Nicole Moore

Chapter 5. Katharine Susannah Prichard, Dymphna Cusack and 'Women on the Path of Progress'   117
Camille Barrera

Chapter 6. Walter Kaufmann: Walking the Tightrope   139
Alexandra Ludewig

Chapter 7.	Fictionalizing Australia for the GDR: Adventure Writer Joachim Specht *Patricia F. Blume*	163
Chapter 8.	'To Do Something for Australian Literature': Anthologizing Australia for the German Democratic Republic of the 1970s *Christina Spittel*	187

Part III.	**LITERARY EXCHANGE**	
Chapter 9.	'There I'm a Nobody; Here I'm a Marxian Writer': Australian Writers in the East *Susan Lever*	211
Chapter 10.	Behind the Wall, through Australian Eyes: Anna Funder's *Stasiland* *Leah Gerber*	221
Chapter 11.	'Because It Was Exotic, because It Was So Far Away': Bernhard Scheller in Conversation with Christina Spittel	239

Contributors	249
Index	253

FIGURES

0.1 Permission to print form for Marcus Clarke's *Lebenslänglich* (*For the Term of His Natural Life*) (Berlin: Ministry of Culture, 28 February 1957, BArch DR1/3958a/329–330).   10
0.2 Neon sign of the Leipzig Kommissions- und Großbuchhandel, the single national wholesaler for GDR books; photograph by Christina Spittel, 2015.   12
0.3 Cover of *Australians Have a Word for It*, edited by Gertrude Gelbin, cover design by Lothar Reher (Berlin: Seven Seas, 1964).   18
2.1 Cover of the fourteenth edition of Marcus Clarke's *Lebenslänglich*, a large-format paperback, designed by Dieter Heidenreich (Berlin: Volk und Welt, 1982).   58
3.1 Cover of Fergus Hume's *Das Geheimnis des Fiakers* (Berlin: Verlag Das Neue Berlin, 1984).   72
3.2 Dust jacket for Xavier Herbert's *Capricornia: Die paradiesische Hölle* (Berlin: Verlag der Morgen, 1958).   73
4.1 Cartoon by Noel Counihan for the *World Trade Union Movement*, no. 2 (20 January 1951): 45. (Reproduced by permission of the Counihan Estate.)   96
4.2 Cover of Frank Hardy's *Macht ohne Ruhm*, volume 1 (Berlin: Volk und Welt, 1952).   100
4.3 Cover of Frank Hardy's *Power without Glory*, volume 2 (Leipzig: Paul List/Panther Books, 1956).   109
5.1 Dust jacket for Katharine Susannah Prichard's *Goldrausch* (Berlin: Volk und Welt, 1954).   120
5.2 Dust jacket for Katharine Susannah Prichard's *Die goldene Meile* (Berlin: Volk und Welt, 1954).   121
5.3 Dust jacket for Dymphna Cusack's *Der halbverbrannte Baum* (Berlin: Verlag der Nation, 1972).   121

6.1	Walter Kaufmann signing books in a GDR bookshop; photograph by Klaus Franke, 28 April 1977 (BArch Berlin, Digital Picture Archives 183-S0428-0043).	151
6.2	Walter Kaufmann and Lissy Kaufmann in Brisbane in 1994, personal photograph provided to Alexandra Ludewig.	154
7.1	Joachim Specht at an outdoor reading with teenage apprentices in the late 1970s; photographer unknown (Stadtarchiv Dessau-Roßlau, N 3.13 – Specht – 9, 18).	164
7.2	A group of pupils listening to tales of Australia in a school library; photographer unknown (Stadtarchiv Dessau-Roßlau, N 3.13 – Specht – 10, 62).	164
7.3	Dust jacket of Joachim Specht's *Die Gejagten*, designed by well-respected illustrator Hans Baltzer (Berlin: Verlag der Nation, 1966).	171
7.4	Illustration by Hans Baltzer for the story 'The Encounter' from Joachim Specht's fiction collection *Peterborough Story* (Berlin: Verlag der Nation, 1963), which was judged one of the 'most beautiful books of the GDR' in 1964.	173
7.5	Joachim Specht in a reading, his books in front of him on the table. The poster on the wall translates as 'The GDR my state'; photographer unknown (Stadtarchiv Dessau-Roßlau, N 3.13 – Specht – 10, 179).	175
7.6	Specht in 2011, at his house, in front of hunting boomerangs and spears; photograph by Patricia F. Blume.	181
8.1	Bright orange cover for *Erkundungen: 31 australische Erzähler* (Berlin: Volk und Welt, 1976).	189
10.1	Cover of the Australian edition of *Stasiland* (Melbourne: Text, 2002).	227
10.2	Cover of the second German edition of *Stasiland* (Frankfurt/Main: Fischer Verlag, 2006).	228

TABLES

4.1	East German Editions of Hardy Titles.	110
8.1	Contents of *Erkundungen: 31 australische Erzähler*.	202
10.1	Material Omitted from the Second German Edition of *Stasiland*.	226
10.2	Corrections Made from the English to German Editions of *Stasiland*.	233

ACKNOWLEDGEMENTS

This has been a truly bilingual and collaborative project, with the essays developed in productive and energized face-to-face workshops in Germany and Australia. The editors thank all the contributors for their commitment to this model, which we think has resulted in sustained synergies and suggestive connections among the essays, and properly dual perspectives on cross-cultural exchange. This aspect of the project was enabled by funding from the Deutsche Akademischer Austausch Dienst (German Academic Exchange Service, DAAD), the University of New South Wales, Canberra, and the Freie Universität, Berlin, as well as by enthused support from the Buchwissenschaft department in the Institute of Communication and Media Studies at the University of Leipzig.

The editors also thank the contributors for their work as translators: those writing in English, translating German materials into English, as identified in each chapter, and Siegfried Lokatis and Patricia Blume, both writing in German, working with materials originally in English and then collaborating with the editors, especially Christina Spittel, in rendering their nuanced German into academic English. We thank Niels Blume and Bianca Ross for further assistance with translation, especially of the Frank Hardy materials.

We are grateful to archivists and librarians in three countries. Thanks are due to the Frank Hardy estate for permission to view his papers in the National Library of Australia; archivists at the National Archives of Australia for access to Australian Security Intelligence Organisation (ASIO) files and other material; the Special Collections of the Academy Library at the University of New South Wales (UNSW) Canberra; staff in the manuscripts room and the Petherick Reading Room of the National Library of Australia; staff at the Akademie der Künste Berlin, especially Anja Wolf, in charge of the archives of Volk und Welt; staff at the Bundesarchiv Berlin-Lichterfelde; at the Stadtarchiv Dessau-Roßlau; at the Staatsbibliothek Berlin and the Deutsche Nationalbibliothek, Leipzig, and the special collections archivists in the Cambridge University Library, especially David Lowe and Christian Staufenbiel.

Permissions to reproduce copyrighted illustrations are listed below. Copyright holders for the covers of books published in the German Democratic Republic (GDR) are almost impossible to establish as a great many of those publishers have ceased to exist, but every reasonable effort has been made. The editors welcome any further information if material exceeds fair usage.

For sharing their research expertise and for their guidance through the archives of Reclam Leipzig, we thank Barbara Döhla, Franziska Galek and Ingrid Sonntag. The postgraduates of Leipzig Buchwissenschaft offered feedback on a presentation of the project in its early stages and Professor Jennifer Wawrzinek hosted a paper from Nicole Moore at the Freie Universität Berlin. We could not have proceeded without the bibliographic research of Professor Russell West-Pavlov and Jenz Elze-Volland. For sharing their recollections we thank especially Bernhard Scheller but also Susan Lever and Humphrey McQueen.

Thanks to our colleagues at UNSW Canberra, especially head of school Professor David Lovell, Professor Paul Eggert, school administrator Shirley Ramsay, for her help in hosting the workshops, and Tessa Wooldridge and Jane Rankine of the *AustLit* database. Thanks to Susan Cowan for research assistance, Catriona Lyons for copyediting and Michael Austin for research assistance, copyediting and the index.

At home here in Canberra, Nicole thanks Tim, Nicholas and especially small Ned, and Christina thanks Peter, and in Erfurt, her parents, Ulrich and Christina.

INTRODUCTION

SOUTH BY EAST: WORLD LITERATURE'S COLD WAR COMPASS

Nicole Moore and Christina Spittel

Two small nations, very far apart. Australia, a southern-hemisphere settler country of only 23 million, isolated geographically if yet English-speaking, historically a bastion of European culture in an Asia Pacific cast as its cultural other, with an indigenous population of less than 10 per cent. It is often completely absent from contemporary mappings of world literatures. The German Democratic Republic (GDR), an erstwhile nation, now; for its 40 years in the second half of the twentieth century the intellectual flagship of the former socialist Eastern Bloc, with one of the most surveilled and controlled national populations in contemporary history; a utopic experiment finally sustained through force and coercion. Evoking a German-speaking country now vanished from the middle of Europe, its history pulls between nostalgia, erasure and excoriating exposé. Why bring these two into detailed cultural comparison?

Our reasoning is partly that they *are* polarities, points on a cold war compass long since displaced by an alternative geography, with different claimants to the 'Global South' and an increasingly powerful Asian East. Exploring the imaginative construction of the post-colonial South by the communist East, this book offers a multifaceted, collaborative study of the reception of Australian literature in the GDR. As an account of the fraught and complex, cross-cultural literary exchange between two highly distinct, even uniquely opposed reading contexts, the volume seeks to explore some of the questions basic to each culture in the light of the other. The essays are propelled by opportunities presented through new developments in empirical book history, 'distant reading' methodologies, globalizing cross-cultural theoretical frames and, most compellingly, by the richly exact and reflective reading histories manifest in the GDR's expansive paper trail. The records of the centralized regime of publication control can tell us how many East Germans were expected to read any particular published title and, moreover, exactly *how* the East German nation expected that population to read it, in great detail. Historian of East German book history Siegfried Lokatis opens the collection by observing that 'no other country of the Communist Eastern Bloc has archival records […] that are even remotely as good in quality *and* publicly accessible.'

Australian literature, in turn, forms a perfect case study for this endeavour. Capitalist settler Australia, increasingly urbanized and class conscious, isolated from its Asia Pacific neighbours and proud of its 'white Australia' immigration policy until the 1960s, was conceived and marketed by the GDR as a conundrum: geographically exotic yet politically retrograde. From East Germany, the country appeared a 'paradisiacal hell', as its German publishers subtitled *Capricornia*, Xavier Herbert's breakthrough 1938 novel about the abused rights of mixed-heritage Aborigines, as Jennifer Wawrzinek notes in her chapter for the volume. Australia's historical role as a utopic space for the old world unsurprisingly fuelled much German interest in the literature on both sides of the Wall – the persistent, travel-brochure version of the exotic Australian paradise, with an ideal climate, vast spaces, untrammelled wilderness and unspoiled beaches still sells books today. For East Germans, that appeal had added piquancy given the GDR's injunctions against travel to the West. The East German take on Australian literature, of course, favoured highly critical books from Australia's then disenfranchised cultural left, especially early on, often indicting Australia as an imperial gulag and racist colonizer, exploitative industrialist economy or a sexist slum. From this failed utopia came a string of popular titles, while the ironic parallels for GDR readers were manifest, in their utopic prison state, even when refused and reframed by the authorities.

Australia appeared early on the horizon of the Soviet-occupied zone in post-war Germany. In 1948 newly founded Aufbau Verlag published the first of numerous editions of Czech anti-fascist journalist Egon Kisch's *Landung in Australien* (*Australian Landfall*), a piece of travel journalism about the Australian authorities' refusal to allow him entry in 1934 that had occasioned an 18-foot jump from the deck of his arriving ship.[1] The first edition of venturesome expatriate Australian journalist and sympathiser Wilfred Burchett's *Sonnenaufgang über Asien* (*Democracy with a Tommygun*) appeared in a gigantic print run also in 1948, as Lokatis details in his chapter. This was published by Volk und Welt, which soon became the new state's key publisher of international titles. And not long after the formal establishment of the GDR on 7 October 1949, well before writing from other ex-British colonies such as Canada or South Africa caught East German attention, a surprisingly large number of Australia's most vocal and recognized writers found publishers there. In total, approximately 95 titles by Australians dot the nation's short history.[2] Communist Frank Hardy's explosive *Power without Glory* was released as *Macht ohne Ruhm* less than a year after the 1951 conclusion of its criminal prosecution at the height of the cultural cold war in Australia; it was the first Australian fiction title. Then followed novels and short stories by Marcus Clarke, Katharine Susannah Prichard, Xavier Herbert, Dorothy Hewett, Dymphna Cusack, Walter Kaufmann, Arthur Upfield, Thomas Keneally, Peter Carey, Frank Moorhouse, Nobel Prize winner Patrick White (laggardly, in 1984) and many others. Rewriting Australia's post-war cultural history from behind the iron curtain, this alternative canon of Australian literature spans the 40 years of the GDR's history all the way until the country's final moments: in 1990, just before reunification, a bilingual collection of Judith Wright's poetry was released, reviewed by the *Frankfurter Allgemeine Zeitung* as speaking to Germans in the East and West.[3] Our collection opens up this shadowy literary archive or 'cross-border canon', as Russell West-Pavlov's chapter dubs it, to newly transnational critical perspectives.

In the wake of post-colonialism, contemporary literary studies in Australia has been reconceiving its history via the broadly American-driven recalibration of world literature as global or 'planetary'.[4] Australia is clearly a province in Pascale Casanova's 'metropole-periphery cartography of literary markets', as Australian scholars Robert Dixon and Brigid Rooney cite it, in that the country can be seen to offer 'a less commanding point of vantage' over that planetary system.[5] For scholars thus placed, however, there is an opportunity for rerouting, for provincializing, in a way positively understood by Dixon and Rooney, countering elitist cosmopolitanism and, by Phillip Mead, in different contexts, elaborating the benefits of regionalism and localism.[6] In the same collection, long-term literary comparatist Paul Sharrad is unhappy about the term, however: 'We have spent a long time in both Australian and post-colonial literary studies fighting free of the pejorative use of the term "provincial" by T. S. Eliot, following Arnold's example'.[7] At the same time, David Carter's account of the success of Australian popular fiction in British and American markets (including Fergus Hume's *Mystery of a Hansom Cab* (1886), often credited with inaugurating the crime fiction genre, whose East German career is traced by Jennifer Wawrzinek in her chapter) can conclude that '"Australian literature" (in this view) was international (and not merely imperial) before it was ever national'.[8]

At the heart of Europe, it is hard to conceive of German book markets or readers as provincial, as Dipesh Chakrabarty enjoins us to, but East German regimes were highly distinctive and isolated, even from West Germany, and also, across language barriers, from the Eastern Bloc.[9] And the GDR, in its concerted nation making, as a product of the Cold War and defined by it, always had an eye to the international stakes, although this view varied across its history. By 1980, with the Wall still up, Erich Honecker could declare: '[O]ur socialist national culture in the GDR is open to everything that will be good and valuable here as well. We address ourselves to it with cosmopolitan openness'.[10] This volume's approach is neither provincial nor international; it is closely and intentionally comparative, placing in parallel two highly distinct contexts with a focus on the reception of one country's literature in the other. Cold war conduits for literary production and reception across the Iron Curtain produced alternative canons for the East and the West, and enacted the kind of mutual 'elliptical refraction' that David Damrosch describes for world literatures.[11] They also, arguably, serve as Damrosch's limit case. Produced under the tight control of a centralized market and state censorship, these translations were interested, not 'disengaged', and were overtly ideological, not 'balanced'. The GDR's version of world literature was a highly selective re-making, carried out on ideological as well as cultural grounds, through the powerful forces of pre-publication censorship and industry control, which were supplemented by restrictions on the experiences of readers themselves. If exotic Australian literature was indeed a 'world literature' for the isolated Eastern Bloc, to what kind of world was it perceived to belong?

The 'global turn' in literary studies, pronounced since the publication of Casanova's *La République mondiale des lettres* in 1999 and in English translation in 2004, is usually characterized as a feature of the post-socialist world, the collapse of the former Eastern Bloc a condition of the global model for book publishing, with the fall of the Berlin Wall in 1989 a key triumph of the neo-capitalist world order. It has been a reflex to conjure the Cold War's two worlds as impossibly separate, the Iron Curtain an absolute boundary, the barbed wire of which? no cultural exchange. In his memoirs, Fritz Raddatz (in his twenties, Volk und Welt's deputy editor-in-chief) describes the early 1950s in the GDR as 'Stacheldraht-Zickzack' (a zigzag of barbed wire).[12] But this model forgets, most notably, the degree to which communism had worldly aspirations, not to mention the paranoid exchange of counter-propaganda that characterized the so-called 'soft diplomacy' of the cultural war. It downplays too the profound cultural impact of socialist and left aesthetics in literatures far removed from Soviet-controlled readerships – for example, in the independence movements of Indonesia or South Africa, in critiques of nationalist imperialism in Japan and Korea, or in the leftist cultural nationalism informing settler literatures mid-century in the USA and Australia.[13] No Australian author, publisher or reading city is mentioned in Casanova's survey, nor in David Damrosch's reconsideration of world literature, and Wai Chee Dimock and translation scholar Emily Apter discuss only one Australian writer each,[14] but socialist countries and, indeed, a twentieth-century realist tradition form a much more expansive blind spot.[15]

US critic Michael Denning offers a broad survey of the influence of proletarian literature's aesthetic ideologies across four continents, through the middle decades of the twentieth century, in his 2004 study *Culture in the Age of Three Worlds*. Denning's account reconstructs and reminds us of the inter-war literary 'international', whose expansive influence was crucial but is yet forgotten: 'the aspirations and aesthetics of the novelists' international remain the forgotten, repressed history behind the contemporary globalization of the novel'.[16] He argues that the most significant proletarian movements and, therefore, the most significant cultural expressions of such, 'emerged in four types of situations: those in countries where communist regimes came to power; those in countries where fascist or authoritarian regimes came to power; those in the creole countries of the Americas; and those in colonized regions of Asia and Africa'.[17] These four trajectories form a broad-reaching overview of the interwoven literary *internationale*, from the Bolshevik revolution onward, stretching across those four continents (notably exempting the fifth), and Denning proffers this as a crucial structural scaffold or pre-phenomenon for 'world literature', as it is conceived in contemporary terms by Casanova and others. This huge reading complex had an explicitly internationalist ideology, of course, seeking links across borders and actively fostering translation and cultural exchange, with the ideal not merely workers' anti-nationalist identification or paralleled capitalist critique but, aesthetically, a common form or mode in which to manifest such. Writer Johannes R. Becher, the GDR's first minister of culture, spoke of the 'Internationale des sozialistischen Realismus' in his influential address at the Fourth German Writers' Meeting in January 1956, drawing on pre-war Leninist models but with a decidedly post-war character.[18]

Tellingly, Denning exempts from this complex any country 'with a long-established tradition of the novel – and that did not see overwhelming cultural crises'. In England, for example, he suggests, on this basis, 'the proletarian novel left little mark', but inter-war German writers such as Alfred Döblin and Willi Bredel are key early exemplars.[19] Australia too remains outside his survey, primarily because, one has to impute, the nation's proletarian literary movement was simply too insignificant to figure on this world stage. Australia certainly did not face an overwhelming cultural crisis even during World War II, although the country fought a longer war than the USA, sustained attacks on the mainland and, arguably, was much more disrupted, but neither did it have a long-established tradition of the novel. Denning's interest in the role of the proletarian novel in the mid-century, anti-colonial struggles of Asia and Africa does not extend to the consideration of settler colonies, and one can understand why. National literatures in Australia, New Zealand and Canada have been received as assertively white, especially mid-century, and have been understood to have developed in opposition to the anti-colonial claims of the colonized peoples of those countries, or in appropriative overwriting,[20] seemingly without necessary regard for the economic critique of capitalist colonialism that elsewhere placed the proletarian novel centre stage in anti-colonial struggles for recognition. The settler proletarian novel seems somehow a contradiction. The subaltern model, in particular, renders nonsensical a notion that settler nationalist identity might seek to express itself through identifying with the international workers' movement; through speaking against economic structures of overlordship; or even through grounded realization of localized, working-class solidarity.

Arguably, that was the case in Australia, nevertheless. One of the first twentieth-century novels hailed as genuinely 'Australian' was communist Katharine Susannah Prichard's *Working Bullocks* (1926), an organicist rendering of the interwoven lives of white, West Australian timber workers.[21] Prichard remoulded her internationalist take on working-class identity, learned in London, through a settler nationalist interest in Australian landscape. Simplicity, endurance and loyalty are asserted as working-class qualities grown from Australian conditions that should be lauded, as they had been by Henry Lawson and the influential *Bulletin* school a generation earlier. This construction then served broader nationalist aims for an aspiring, English-language literary culture still powerfully dominated by imperial interests and British cultural hegemony. In some instances, this position built in solidarity with indigenous marginalization and labour rights; in others, it ignored them.

Discussing the Americas, including the USA but not Canada, and drawing on his own history of American left-wing writing, Denning suggests that, while 'at turns bitterly hostile and deeply sympathetic' to the 'New Deals and Estavo Novos' that characterized the inter-war political landscapes, leftist writing from the period 'also inherited the messianic exceptionalism and cultural inferiority complex that characterised settler societies'.[22] 'Messianic exceptionalism' married with a 'cultural inferiority complex': this oxymoronic assertion about the character of settler culture locks the multifaceted and, one should say, ongoing agon of post-colonial settler cultures into a paradoxical coupling, isolating claims to exceptionalism that are themselves produced by cultural cringing. Yet, somehow it is this coupling, for Denning, that effects left cultural nationalism. Thus, he argued, Southern American leftist writers 'like the celebrated Mexican muralists, help to constitute a national imaginary of "the people", and did this by importing European modernisms, reviving American folk traditions and adopting the proletarian musics of the New World metropolises: Jazz, samba, son, and tango'.[23]

An Australian 'national imaginary of "the people"' can certainly be seen in the post-war radical nationalism that spanned left-wing formations in the splits of Australia's cultural Cold War,[24] and it is clearly this that one can see circulating through the appeal of post-war Australian texts for the GDR regime. The success of Katharine Susannah Prichard's work in Soviet contexts seems testament to its legibility in the USSR, although it was the generic, demotic Stalinism of her goldfields trilogy that appealed most strongly, along with her *engagé* short stories. However, as Camille Barrera's chapter outlines, the final volume of that trilogy was never published in East Germany, reflecting distaste among its Ministry of Culture assessors not only for its apparent sentimentalism – a charge laid against more than one Australian book by such assessors – but the genre's predictable orthodoxy. Neither is the first Australian novel published in the GDR, Hardy's *Power without Glory*, a proletarian novel in the sense that Denning conjures it from the inter-war period. Nor is it a strike novel, like Kobayashi Takiji's *Kani Kose* (1929), banned in Japan and translated around the world, as Denning notes, nor quite a metropolitan or ghetto novel. It is a historical novel, in the Lukacsian sense, with claims to universalism. Hardy's three-page author's note printed at the back of the first editions of *Power without Glory* describes its version of 'realism': it presents 'men and women alive in an environment that is peculiarly Australian yet universal, typical of the stage of social history in which we find ourselves'.

It is clear that directed federal customs censorship in Australia was the key factor limiting the development of the proletarian novel, as such, in the inter-war years.[25] In the post-war years, the explosive *Power without Glory* trial in 1951, in the wake of a set of 'show trials' about literary obscenity through 1944 to 1950, functioned as Australia's McCarthyite moment of ideological confrontation and determined, despite Hardy's victory, the decade or almost two of polarized cultural positions and literary political friction that followed.[26] Cold war conduits for transnational literary exchange inherited only aspects of the inter-war internationale, blasted and suppressed by the structures of fascism, Allied victories and the breakdown of US-Soviet relations in the late 1940s. In its turn, Soviet support for, then advancing control over, the Eastern Bloc publishing infrastructure instituted forms of production and distribution that replaced, with powerful regulatory regimes of centralized control, any writer-led, context-generated, literary expression of immediacy that may have characterized the internationale. One key goal of the Soviet-style, worker-led state was to make culture available to all, while carefully directing its role as a force for social transformation (as well as economic redistribution). Literature needed to be remade as a certified and pre-interpreted mass experience, its production and distribution within the Eastern Bloc serving as a key arm of state education, industrial aggregation and cultural control, and outside it, as a crucial aspect of the soft propaganda war against capitalist triumphs internationally.

In this regard, the GDR was at once a flagship state and a distinctive exception. Through its early role as an avant-gardist state, it modelled newly demotic forms of cultural production and consumption, as well as a commitment to an intellectual model of national education with which key expatriate cultural producers, particularly wartime refugees returning from the USA, such as the novelist Stefan Heym, or the communist writer Walter Kaufmann returning from Australia, could affiliate.[27] Indeed, both Heym and Kaufmann remained in the GDR until the very end. At the 1956 Writers' Congress, Heym, later to become the East German writer with the highest number of banned titles and already in trouble over the criticism voiced in his column in the *Berliner Zeitung*, still passionately exclaimed:

> No, we do not have gags, and we do not have censorship here. But the writer has a responsibility for the cause, for the cause of peace and democracy and socialism. The censor, of whom everyone is talking, sits in the writer's heart. And with every sentence, this censor asks, 'Is what you're writing true, in the deepest sense? Does it provoke thought, thought in the right direction? Does it help our cause?'[28]

The Allied victory had marked a 'zero hour' of reading in all four zones of occupied Germany: books were banned and confiscated, librarians retrained, new work screened before imprimatur was granted.[29] In 1946 the Soviet military authorities founded the *Kulturelle Beirat für das Verlagswesen* (Cultural Advisory Committee for the Publishing Trade), an institution mainly charged with monitoring the work of high-profile, Leipzig-based publishers such as Reclam, Insel and Brockhaus, all three then in private ownership.[30] The *Beirat* was succeeded in 1951 by the *Amt für Literatur* (Literature Office), which, after further restructuring, became the *Hauptverwaltung für Verlage und Buchhandel* (Main Administration for Publishing and the Book Trade) on 1 January 1963.[31] A department within the East German Ministry of Culture, the Hauptverwaltung (or HV, as it became known), presided over an East German infrastructure of reading, providing economic and political leadership to publishing houses, printeries, the Leipzig-based wholesaler LKG and the state-owned book trade until autumn 1989. The staff of the HV did not officially censor or ban, but approved publishers' plans, allocated paper stock and foreign currency, and issued the *Druckgenehmigung* (permission to print) on which each newly published title depended. Located in Berlin's Clara-Zetkin Straße (today's Dorotheenstraße), the HV operated under close supervision of the Ministerium für Staatssicherheit (Ministry for State Security), and in collaboration with the Büro für Urheberrechte (Office for Copyright Law),[32] and the publishing houses themselves, as Siegfried Lokatis notes.

> Most of the censorship work on a manuscript – selection, polishing, streamlining, commenting – was undertaken not by the censorship authority but by the publishing houses which only submitted manuscripts to the HV which they themselves considered publishable. Once a manuscript had been submitted to the HV for permission to print, the biggest problems had, as a rule, already been resolved. The publisher had sought the opinion of its readers and had heeded their objections and warnings of its own accord, if they seemed justified […] [At the HV] Explosive or suspicious manuscripts with inadequate reader's reports were scrutinised again, or forwarded to mysterious, anonymous external assessors, whose 'objections' were passed on to the publishers as required changes […] It is only as a result of this successful 'training' that the rejection rate of the censorship authority never exceeded 1–2%.[33]

Thus, when, in early 1974, East German authors Ulrich Plenzdorf, Klaus Schlesinger and Martin Stade invited fellow writers to contribute to an anthology of Berlin stories, to be submitted to a publishing house as a collaboratively edited collection, they were accused of 'wanting to create a platform against our publishing policy', as one report to the Ministerium für Staatssicherheit put it, and the process begun by the Ministry to drive the group apart and cause the project to fail was labelled Operativer Schwerpunkt Selbstverlag (Operational Focus Self-Publishing).[34] As a result, that collection never reached the Hauptverwaltung, which expected to see only full and publishable manuscripts ('nur vollständige und druckreife Manuskripte'), complete with illustrations and afterwords, accompanied by at least one external assessment and a report by the editor-in-charge, all preceded by a carefully completed application form, detailing information pertaining to the title's relationship to the production plan, the print run requested, author, translator, paper stock, printery, date of delivery and so on. In particular, the form provided the following cues for the publisher's statement:

a) Justification for publishing the title.
b) Comments on the author. Where does he work? Has he received awards?
c) Comments on the translator. Where does he work? Which work has he already translated?
d) Comments on the editors – see c).
e) Short summary of the content. Is it planned to include foreword, afterword, footnotes? Is the title part of the curriculum? For which schools?
f) Were there differing opinions about the title?

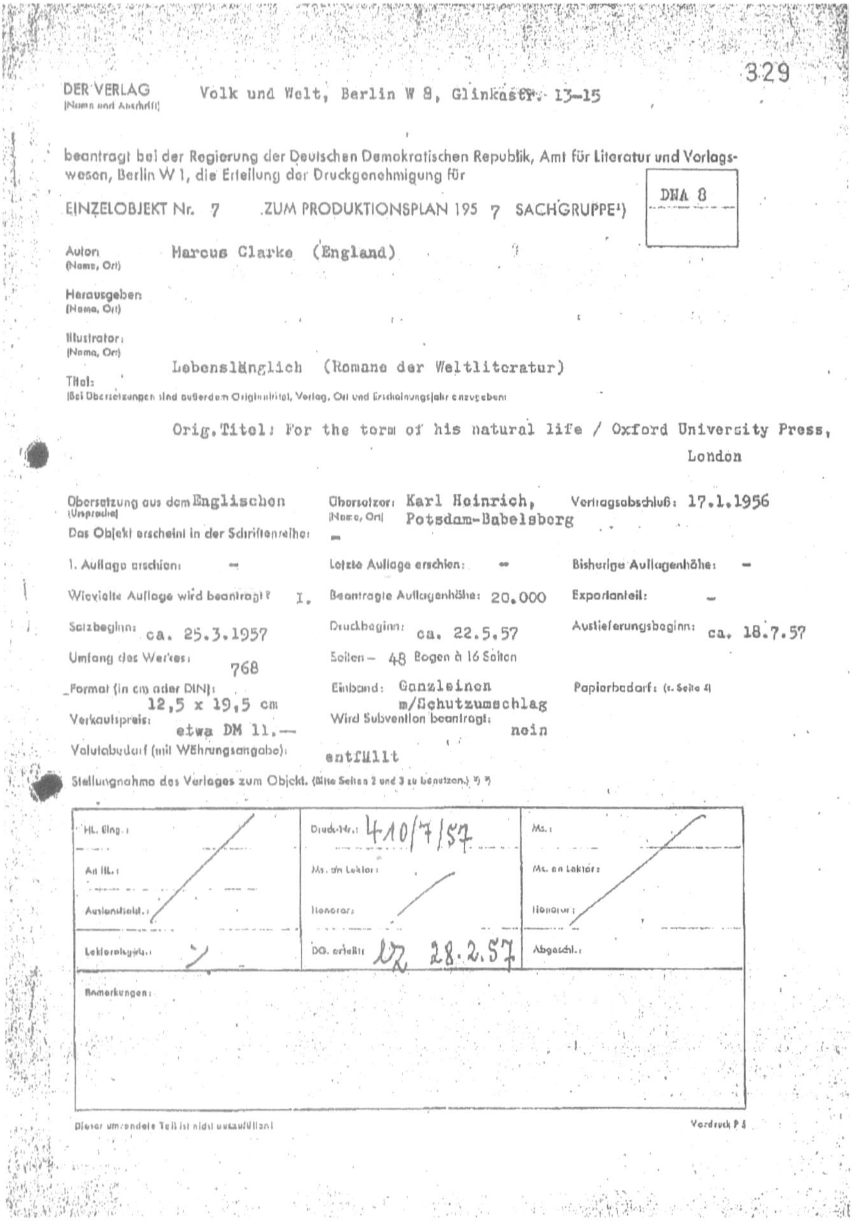

Figure 0.1 Permission to print form for Marcus Clarke's *Lebenslänglich* (*For the Term of His Natural Life*) (Berlin: Ministry of Culture, 28 February 1957, BArch DR1/3958a/ 329–330).

330

Papierbedarf¹)

Inhalt = 768 Seiten : 255 600 Bogen h'fr. Werk
84 x 104 cm, 70 g/qm   =   15,640 t

Umschlag =   =   0,300 t
                                         ─────────────
                                             15,940 t
                                         ═════════════

Druckerei: Karl Marx-Werk, Pößneck

_____ Berlin, den 28.2.1957 VERLAG VOLK UND WELT _Neumann_____
       Ort und Datum   Stempel   Unterschrift der Verlagsleitung
                                                        (Neumann)

Erläuterungen:

¹) In die obere Hälfte des rechts danebenstehenden Feldes ist die Kurzbezeichnung der Bibliographie und in die untere Hälfte die Sachgruppennummer einzusetzen.

Kurzbezeichnungen
  DNA — Deutsche Nationalbibliographie, Reihe A
  DNB — Deutsche Nationalbibliographie, Reihe B
  DM — Deutsche Musikbibliographie
  BdK — Bibliographie der Kunstblätter

²) Die Stellungnahme des Verlages zum Objekt soll enthalten:
  a) Begründung der Herausgabe des Titels
  b) Bemerkungen zum Autor. Wo ist er tätig? Ist er Träger von Auszeichnungen usw.?
  c) Bemerkungen zum Übersetzer. Wo ist er tätig? Welche Werke sind z.B. von ihm bereits übersetzt worden?
  d) Bemerkungen zu den Lektoren — siehe c)
  e) Kurzgefaßte Inhaltsangabe. Sind Vorwort, Nachwort, Fußnoten vorgesehen? Ist der Titel lehrplangebunden? Für welche Schulen?
  f) Bestehen verschiedene Meinungen über den Titel?

³) Es sind möglichst alle vom Verlag eingeholten Gutachten beizufügen, mindestens aber das des verantwortlichen Verlagslektors und das eines weiteren Fachexperten.

⁴) Der genaue Papierbedarf ist für das gesamte Werk einzutragen einschl. Vorsatz, Bezug, Schutzumschlag bzw. Umschlagkarton, z. B.

   Text = 320 Seiten : 160 000 Bogen h/r. weiß Werkdruck A1×64, 70 g/qm = 3,835 t
   Bildteil = 16 Seiten : 3 500 Bogen h/r. weiß Kunstdruck 61×86, 90 g/qm = 0,289 t

Es sind nur vollständige und druckreife Manuskripte einzureichen!
Begleitschreiben für Druckaufträge nicht erforderlich!

Figure 0.1 *Continued*

Figure 0.2 Neon sign of the Leipzig Kommissions- und Großbuchhandel, the single national wholesaler for GDR books; photograph by Christina Spittel, 2015.

Each book published in the GDR bears traces of this process: a file number printed in the impressum and, often, prefaces or afterwords that locate and ground a book for its East German readers, furnishing explanations, justifications and contextualizations not unlike those marshalled in the reports to obtain permission to print.

This endeavour was not merely internal or national, moreover, especially in the early years of the GDR, drawing on Soviet structures in prioritizing control over cultural production – 'experts in the use of culture as a tool of political persuasion, the Soviets did much in [the] early years of the Cold War to establish its central paradigm as a cultural one.'[35] As Frances Saunders's influential 2000 study of the cultural Cold War demonstrated, this war was just as finely pitched as the political one, with both sides investing massively in the soft diplomacy of cultural work. And this was especially true in divided Berlin, that 'traumatic synecdoche of the Cold War', as John Burnham, ex-Trotskyite and public intellectual of American conservatism, described it.[36] 'So it was that an unnaturally elaborate cultural life was dragged to its feet by the occupying powers as they vied with each other to score propaganda points', declared Saunders.[37]

Contemporary interest in the cultural Cold War continues to expand significantly, in the USA in the wake of Saunders' work and in Europe and the UK too, where much of this new interest is in response to the opening-up of the formerly inaccessible archives of the Eastern Bloc and newly declassified records and documents from MI5, the CIA, the Congress for Cultural Freedom and other Western government agencies engaged in the propaganda war, including publishers.[38] Interest in what these records can tell us about the role of books, publishing and writing in the exercise of hostilities on both sides allows us to indeed couch 'books as weapons', as does John Hench in his edited collection about the role of book publishing and distribution in World War II.[39] From the Allied Zone in West Berlin, 'a vast books programme was launched', aimed at countering Soviet efforts by projecting a 'free world' story of cultural vitality, energetic diversity and artistic achievement – and this was an American story, without question. Commercial publishers supplied the occupation government with a constant flow of US titles, without the taint of government-sponsored propaganda. 'But propaganda they were certainly intended to be,' as Saunders notes.[40]

> Translations commissioned by the Psychological Warfare Division of American Military Government alone ran to hundreds of titles, ranging from Howard Fast's *Citizen Tom Paine* to Arthur M. Schlesinger Jr's *The New Deal in Action*, to the Museum of Modern Art's *Built in the USA*. There were also German editions of books 'suitable for children at their most impressionable age', such as Nathaniel Hawthorne's *Wonder Tales*, Mark Twain's *A Connecticut Yankee in King Arthur's Court*, and Laura Ingalls Wilder's *Little Town on the Prairie*.[41]

Literature's role in the soft Cold War instances Casanova's conception of the functions of 'combative literatures', in which competition between national literatures define them as such, but on a polarized and representative global scale.⁴² Australian literature has not registered in the cultural history of anti-communism, however: Philip Deery's work on Australia's laggard use of anti-communist propaganda supplied by MI6's secretive Information Research Department (IRD) details its distribution in Australia, rather than any role for Australian material in the Eastern Bloc.⁴³

On this entrenched cultural terrain, the GDR consciously positioned itself as a *Kulturnation*, a beachhead of committed, democratic reading right at the Western edge of the Eastern Bloc. When the GDR's first minister of culture, Johannes R. Becher, himself a writer returned from a troubled exile in Moscow, developed his much-quoted vision for a *Literaturgesellschaft* ('literary society') at the Fourth German Writers' Congress in 1956, he spoke optimistically about new writers and new readers, but also film-makers, publishers, booksellers and editors, working hand-in-hand to realize the project of a national German literature. This was the project begun by Gottsched and Lessing, figureheads of the German enlightenment, and continued by Goethe and Schiller but reconceived as now, necessarily, a socialist endeavour: 'Bourgeois literature has stopped dreaming, it has nightmares at best.'⁴⁴ As Becher envisioned this humanist literary future, he also referred to the concrete political situation from which it arose: 'An end has been put to German misery, German tragedy within the boundaries of the German Democratic Republic.' Artists in West Germany ('in the West of our Fatherland'), according to this vision, were having their creative energies consumed by a hostility towards art and an art world driven by commerce (*Kunstbetrieb*).⁴⁵

In Becher's eyes, the GDR writer would have a newly conscientious reader – not a mere consumer of his or her wares.⁴⁶ While many of the nuances of Becher's program did not survive its own decade, his notion that East German literary production would work outside the pressures of the marketplace persisted, as the definition for 'publishing house' in the *Kulturpolitisches Wörterbuch* (1978), or dictionary of cultural policy, indicates:

> In the socialist countries, publishing houses are overwhelmingly owned by the people or the [political] parties and organisations; not the pressure to earn profits drives their work but the cultural-political task, set by socialist society, to continue raising the level of political, cultural and technical refinement of the working people.⁴⁷

This dictionary was issued by Dietz Verlag, the official organ of the Sozialistische Einheitspartei Deutschlands (SED), but as Christoph Links has observed, some of the GDR's largest publishing houses really were 'fully grown literary institutes [...] rather than efficient business units'.[48] Links himself spent some of the GDR's final years working for (state-owned) Aufbau Verlag, which could count 180 staff in 1989, including 70 editors, producing 350 titles per year: 'Not a single publishing house in the former Federal Republic had this level of staffing in the literary and creative areas', Links explains. 'There, the emphasis was much more on sales and marketing, whereas the latter was hardly developed in the East.'[49]

Becher's romantic vision of a democratic literary community built on ideas of companionship and sociability was yet nostalgic rather than realistic, even as he was first pronouncing it, seven years into the GDR's history. David Carter has commented that one of the strengths of Casanova's concept of the 'republic of letters' is its ability to bring into view 'the power and violence in play in the game of culture', which the notion of a 'literary community' can neglect, given that a republic is 'designed precisely to regulate the distribution of power and representation'.[50] The GDR was a republic of letters in this political, regulatory, violent sense – 'a book writing "combine" of writers, editors, officials and censors of unprecedented dimensions', as Martina Langermann, Simone Barck and Siegfried Lokatis have put it. Or, rather, a massive 'security area literature' (Sicherheitsbereich Literatur), to use the term employed by the Ministerium für Staatssicherheit, which was founded in 1950 and increasingly interested in monitoring the activities of writers and publishers from the mid-1950s.

To Patrick White in 1975, trying unsuccessfully to persuade him to allow the publication of a number of his short stories in an international collection with Volk und Welt, editor Hans Petersen wrote: 'You will understand that each country has its own way of representing foreign authors to its readers. This is something to do with the readers, but also with the general outlook on life and literature held in each particular country.'[51] In the main, directed by the available data, the volume is a study of the reception of Australian titles in the GDR, so its interest is somewhat uni-directional, but the dissemination of East German titles in English into the Western world is an important aspect of the dynamic, as is the status and reception given to the GDR in Australia. The key publisher in this regard was Panther Books, or Seven Seas, as it became known. From 1953, the independently owned East German publisher Paul List housed an imprint called Panther Books that published only English-language titles sourced from around the world. The imprint was overseen by the redoubtable Gertrude Gelbin, wife of prominent East German writer and later dissident Stefan Heym, whose career as an English-language novelist had been launched when he was a wartime Jewish expatriate in New York, with two high profile novels based on his service as a GI. The older Gelbin was a Jewish New Yorker involved in the book trade there; they moved to the

GDR together in 1952.⁵² In 1958 Gelbin took her list and, with the necessary imprimatur of the Ministry of Culture, established Seven Seas, an East German publisher expressly dedicated to circulating English language works back to their countries of origin and beyond.

'From wherever good books in English are written to wherever good books in English are read',⁵³ was the Seven Seas slogan, and it took the German tradition of publishing English books in a new direction. Publishers like Leipzig's Tauchnitz had an economic agenda but Gelbin's motives were political – as, to some extent, they had to be. She defined Seven Seas' objective as 'saving fine literature from the dustbin'; its list as a 'combination of anti-Fascist, anti-racist and anti-war themes with considerable literary merit'.⁵⁴ In a letter to Erich Wendt, Minister of Culture in August 1961, she termed the publisher unashamedly 'a propaganda project on an international scale'.⁵⁵ Stefan Heym recalled, in his unpublished memoirs of his wife:

> We stressed the ideological and political value of the project. Gertrude pointed out the dire straits in which men like Howard Fast, Alvah Bessie, etc. found themselves. A writer must be published to be able to function and live – what would accrue to the GDR, and we might succeed in bringing progressive literature precisely where it was banned, the USA. From the very beginning, Gertrude considered her work for Panther Books, as the project was first called, and later for Seven Seas as her political duty.⁵⁶

Gelbin's conceived target audience was: 'a vast public in Europe who knew English […] would welcome good books in English at a budget price'.⁵⁷ And indeed, her support for '"left-wing" English-language authors in GDR translation […] was sometimes the only channel through which West Germans could access these literatures'.⁵⁸ From 1960, Seven Seas began to publish East German writers too in English translation, for export internationally, in 'an interesting and significant reversal of the usual publishing relations concerning translated literature', notes Rebecca Jany.⁵⁹ Perhaps inevitably, however, the greatest markets for Seven Seas books were not in Europe or the USA but in the expanding English-language readerships of the former British colonies. India, principally, but also South Africa and Australia formed significant markets where the low-priced, generically covered (a signature green) range of both classic and left-wing books from across the world could find readers through bookshops owned by and affiliated to the organized left, especially the communist parties.

This meant that, as numbers of Australian readers remember, Panther Books or Seven Seas was selling Australian books back to Australians even when those books had fallen out of print in Australia. Gelbin was particularly proud of the Australian list, declaring, with some basis (since Seven Seas acted as an effective agency for European translations of some of its authors' work, such as Dorothy Hewett's[60]), that she had 'discovered' them:

> When I say we 'discovered' the Australians, I mean those Australian authors who have contributed so brilliantly to the literary reputation of our series and whom, we hope we have made favorites among the readers of the world to whom we sell our editions. Frank Hardy's novel *Power without Glory* was the forerunner [published by Panther in 1956]. It seems that every year we have been favored by the right to publish the paperback edition of at least one fine book from Down Under. Chronologically speaking, the list includes *Say No to Death* by Dymphna Cusack, *Bobbin Up* by Dorothy Hewett, *Seven Emus* by Xavier Herbert, two volumes of Australian short stories, *Following the Sun* and *Australians Have a Word For It*, *On Strenuous Wings*, excerpts from the writings of Katharine Susannah Prichard and most recently, for European distribution, *I Can Jump Puddles* by Alan Marshall.[61]

East German writers like Christa Wolf made their way to Australia through this route too, arriving pre-framed and pre-translated.[62] By the late 1960s there had been enough exchange between the two literary cultures for Heym to publish his breakthrough, dissenting essay on left aesthetics, 'The Boredom of Minsk', in Melbourne's *Meanjin* and, in the wake of blacklisting from the GDR authorities, to travel to the Adelaide Writers Festival in 1970, with support from Hewett, Max Harris and Geoffrey Dutton.[63]

This exchange was built and facilitated through the literary institutions of the left in Australia, including, by the mid-1970s, the GDR-Australian Friendship Society, while the conservative government continued to refuse to recognize the GDR through the 1950s and 1960s. The Realist Writers groups fostered by the CPA and the Australasian Book Society (ABS), a member-subscribed publisher also with strong links to the CPA, served as conduits to both Volk und Welt and Seven Seas through the 1950s and 1960s, as well as a range of other Eastern European publishers.[64] Both were dominated by the energies of high-profile communist writer Frank Hardy and reflected the interests of German refugee writer Walter Kaufmann, who would become one of the GDR's most awarded writers after his return. In turn, Hardy's GDR royalties funded the purchase of an East German book-binding machine that seems to have enabled the ABS to produce books independently of the Australian printing industry, as Nicole Moore's chapter in the volume outlines.

Their (highly controlled) positive reception in the Eastern Bloc allowed Australian writers to market and describe themselves as 'internationally

Figure 0.3 Cover of *Australians Have a Word for It*, edited by Gertrude Gelbin, cover design by Lothar Reher (Berlin: Seven Seas, 1964).

acclaimed'. Hardy's defence committee in the *Power without Glory* criminal libel case repeatedly emphasized that eleven countries had accepted the book for publication before the trial, 'including France, Holland, Czechoslovakia and Germany', not specifying the latter as East Germany.[65] By 1967 Dymphna Cusack's books had been published in 26 countries, 'from Albania to Scandinavia and Siberia to the Caribbean', and the William Heinemann London edition of *The Sun Is Not Enough* could report that sales of *Heatwave in Berlin* 'have topped the million mark in Russia alone'. The Eastern Bloc still figured as the world at large for Australian readers – in highly contested ways, of course – but it nevertheless afforded some cachet, in parallel to Australia featuring as part of world literature for the GDR. There could be a significant difference between the critical or official reception of books and their genuine appeal to East German readers, however: the state-controlled regime notoriously produced high volumes of titles that remained unsold in bookshops, while banned titles or those produced in unsupported small print runs could attract great, often clandestine interest, especially for popular and genre fiction. Nicholas Birns's account of the reception of Australian books in the USSR casts them as 'bit players', without a role in any world 'canon':

> Whereas twentieth-century writers like Hemingway and Steinbeck were lauded by an 'official' Soviet writer like Konstantin Simonov, the Australian writers lingered on the back shelves of party propaganda, bit-players to swell a scene in the cavalcade of orchestrated admirers of the Soviet state. For all the differences, it is not unlike the role of the Australian writer in Britain or America at the time: published, yes; reviewed, yes; in bookstores and libraries, yes; but part of the canonicity of self-consciously advanced literary culture, no.[66]

Lokatis is similarly prudent about the importance of Australians for East German readers and literary culture (although he maintains that they took third place after the USA and Britain), while it is clear that Hans Petersen's great passion at Volk und Welt was American writing (with a PhD on Stephen Crane). In a superficial way, Australia and the GDR could both be seen as bit players in this 'canonicity of self-consciously advanced literary culture', if we take this as a version of world literature. But book histories of the Cold War allow us to consider the degree to which such versions differed significantly on both sides of the divide, and even further in more removed polarities like Australia or the smaller Eastern Soviet states. The repeated charge of 'party propaganda' against writers sanctioned by Soviet and communist publishing regimes, without qualification or address to the content, misses moreover the degree to which censorship and aesthetic control were mitigated, nuanced and directed by the efforts of established literary culture, in dynamic interplay with publishing structures.

Like other GDR publishers, Volk und Welt has been shown to have repeatedly deflated print runs, to avoid having to pay hard-currency royalties – a practice born, as Lokatis suggests in his chapter, 'not of necessity, but as the standard routine of habitual criminals'. This counters the notion of a back shelf where Australian books gathered dust, unnoticed by real readers (their often large print runs repeatedly sold out), as does the curious career of the GDR translation of Marcus Clarke's *For the Term of His Natural Life*, by far the most popular foreign-language fiction title published. Even an East German publisher like Volk und Welt, working outside the (immediate) pressures of the capitalist marketplace, could not afford to have books pulped; paper was too scarce a resource and reputations mattered too (Volk und Welt took pride in not having to advertise books).

The East German conception of Australian writing was highly distinct, in fact: different, firstly, from the approach taken by West German publishers, in that it eschewed the increasingly modernist Australian canon, and even from the version of Canadian literature produced in East Germany.[67] Australian books were continuously published from the first years of the GDR's existence, unlike those of other small or post-colonial nations, and proved quite popular. While the translation and publication of communist writers like Hardy and Prichard early in the GDR's history seem predictable, other instances of the reception of Australian literature and cultural concerns in the GDR are surprising or puzzling from an Australian point of view. They offer revealing instances of rereading, misreading or refashioning, as such cross-cultural translations often do – perhaps as evidence of the culturally 'untranslatable' disrupting the smoothed vectors of exchange, as Emily Apter might suggest.[68] Marcus Clarke's great, nineteenth-century convict novel, *For the Term of His Natural Life* (from its 1874 single-volume edition), was published in multiple editions with a new translation and packaging that rendered it as adventure fiction, becoming *the* most popular foreign-language title published in East Germany, as noted. Its foreword suggested that, in the wake of the 'fascist concentration camps', GDR readers were better placed to understand the British colonial convict system than was Clarke himself, supposedly blinkered by his bourgeois class affiliations, as Russell West-Pavlov's chapter elaborates. Such 'classics' were also attractive because they were out of copyright, of course: 'for these titles, author's rights had expired and, in several cases, so had the translator's rights, which made these books cheaper to produce.'[69] East German adventure novelist Joachim Specht spent a few years in South and Western Australia in the immediate post-war period, and used these experiences to publish more than 20 popular titles concerned with Aboriginal themes, crafting these through memory and speculation after being repeatedly denied permission to return. He also drew on the influential work of British/Australian Marxist anthropologist Fred Rose, who had relocated to East Berlin from Australia, to live with his wife's East German family, after being called before the 1954 Petrov Royal Commission on Espionage. Patricia Blume's chapter, based on extensive interviews, is the first complete account of Specht's career in either English or German.[70] Committed Marxist and prominent literary expatriate Christina Stead looked forward to her husband's possible appointment to the University of Leipzig in 1950, as Susan Lever notes in her chapter, but our collection reveals that the GDR did not publish any of her novels, after Aufbau's assessors refused her 1934 modernist collection *The Salzburg Tales*. And we establish that no work by Nobel Prize winner Patrick White was published in the GDR until 1984.

This collection is divided into three simply conceived parts: Contexts and Frames, Books and Writers, and Literary Exchange. The first holds chapters from Siegfried Lokatis, Russell West-Pavlov and Jennifer Wawrzinek that set out, in three quite different ways, historical and conceptual frames through which to approach the book history of the GDR, the practice of comparative literary studies at work in analysing the reception of Australian titles, and the political or communal structures of culture at stake in the relation. The leading German book historian involved in saving some of the archives on which our work is based, Lokatis sketches the broader book-historical contexts for the East German production of Australian literature, with a special focus on Volk und Welt. He traces the beginnings of communist print censorship in the Soviet zone, compares the GDR's regime with other Eastern Bloc countries and charts the ups and downs of East German censorship through its consolidation, moments of liberalization and subsequent icings-over in cultural policy. West-Pavlov's conjuring of a 'cross-border canon' draws on his bibliographic work documenting all Australian titles published in German, in East and West and in other German-speaking countries, couched in broad intercultural frames. He details the East's reception of Clarke's *For the Term of His Natural Life* and extrapolates the reading ironies at work in its revisioning, via the revealing afterword, to *Lebenslänglich*. Wawrzinek's final essay in this section considers the problematic presented by Australian East German works within contemporary theorizations of community and structures of identity and belonging, drawing on the ideas of Jean-Luc Nancy and others, with attention to the reception of the seminal crime fiction novel, *The Mystery of a Hansom Cab*, by Fergus Hume, and Xavier Herbert's interventionist picaresque *Capricornia*.

In the Books and Writers section, chapters range from a full account by Nicole Moore of the publication of *Power without Glory*, as the first Australian novel, through Patricia Blume's chapter on Specht as a rare success story of the Bitterfelder Weg, to an elucidation of the selection processes for a radically revisionist collection released by Volk und Welt in the more open political climate of the early 1970s, from Christina Spittel. Camille Barrera examines the reception in the GDR of widely circulated titles by prominent writers Katharine Susannah Prichard and Dymphna Cusack as 'women's books', addressing the complex question of gender equality in the East German regime post-war, with reference to coeval Australian contexts. Alexandra Ludewig's richly biographical chapter on the key figure of Walter Kaufmann confronts the full complexity of his writing career, from his formative Australian experiences to the question of his complicity or otherwise with the activities of the Stasi, noting his exceptional status as a favoured writer, able to retain his Australian passport in East Berlin, but also his ability to distance himself from the exigencies of the regime (as well as, she suggests, from domestic and marital pressures).

The final section brings together three different essays that thematize the motif of exchange. Reversing the direction of inquiry, Susan Lever's summative chapter details the engagement of Australian literary culture with the Eastern Bloc, singling out particular instances or figures, such as Stead, Cusack and others, within a broader consideration of the ramifications of involvement with those regimes in the light of contemporary knowledge. Leah Gerber's chapter takes up Lever's final interest in the role of current Australian writer Anna Funder's best-selling *Stasiland*, a 2002 account of East German surveillance, drawing on interviews with subjects and victims, that has been acclaimed in English-speaking contexts including Australia. Gerber's chapter analyses the controversially-received German translation of Funder's book, released in 2004, against the English source-text, tracking the points at which the controversy may be in evidence in the text, and considering its reception in the context of *Ostalgie* films such as *Good Bye, Lenin!* or *The Lives of Others*, pointedly criticized by Funder. In *Stasiland*, Funder's Australianness functions as an authorizing distance; she is positioned as alien and external to East German history, refreshingly naïve and unbiased. Gerber's chapter, at the end of the volume, allows us to see that, while *Stasiland* is conceived very much as an exercise in remembering, witnessing the trauma and conflict of Germany's Cold War, it forgets, or perhaps never knew, the extent of Australia's own engagement with that culture. The collection concludes, finally, with an interview conducted by Christina Spittel with Bernhard Scheller, a lecturer in English at the University of Leipzig until his retirement in 1993. Behind the Wall, Scheller wrote his professorial thesis on Australian drama, and taught and supervised post-graduate theses in the area: his lively recollections map the character of East German critical reception for Australian literature through the 1970s until the *Wende*.

The volume examines not just the reception of Australian books in East German contexts, but the Australian reception and textual construction of East Germany in its turn. John Frow in 2008, in the first article published by the new literary studies journal *Reception*, elucidates the assumptions or conceptual methods behind contemporary study of textual reception (with reference to reception theory's debt to Gadamer and hermeneutics). He sets out a position in which it must be understood that

> textuality is not fixed at a single moment in time; that the ontology of the text is thus historically dynamic; and, most radically, that rather than discrete and fixed texts we can speak only of textual processes, of which every moment is a textual variant […] [M]eaning and value are therefore unpredictable as the textualisation process passes from one regime of reading to another.[71]

The construction 'regimes of reading' comes originally from Frow's 1986 *Marxism and Literary History*, and can serve usefully for our study, perhaps more so than the models offered by complex systems theory, utilized in Russell West-Pavlov's chapter, or Moretti's versions of 'distant reading'. There is a level of literalism in applying its descriptions to the GDR's implementation of communist aesthetic ideology for a newly national population – clearly a reading regime by any measure. And the idea has a useful emphasis on historical and geopolitical dynamism – transformation across time and (although not explicated) place – addressing the geopolitical reformulations of meaning that occur through intercultural shifts in the time and place of a text's reception.

Frow makes a case for the kind of grounded book history many of the chapters employ: 'the great attraction of empirical research into reading practices is that it displays the multifarious reality of uses rather than norms of good practice. These uses may radically displace those norms'.[72] The 'reality of uses' is on display in many instances of reading documented in this volume – Australian fiction's appeal for East Germans can be traced not merely in the detailed responses of official assessments, publishers' decisions, sanctioned reviews and afterwords, but in print runs, reprints, remakes and adaptations, and even, occasionally, in letters from readers. But the multifariousness of these uses is not readily apparent, even from this evidence. Frow goes on: 'Readings are not controlled by the text or by any one regime of reading. The task of reception history is in the first place to describe those readings in all their wildness'.[73] Here the assumption of what we might term 'free reading', or a liberal model of individual cognition for the reading act, and particularly the insistence on a text's necessary agency provoke a number of questions in relation to the forms of cultural dictatorship manifest in the GDR. Where there is measurable control over a text's reception, how much agency can be presumed? What if there is measurably little? An impulse of liberal criticism is to focus on the text or reading's ability to resist and escape forms of controlled reading and reception – its romantic 'wildness' – but do accounts risk underestimating the normative reading power of a regime, in placing the emphasis always on the possibility of resistance, no matter how small? Amanda Anderson has diagnosed the attribution of 'aggrandized agency' in forms of feminist criticism and theory, in which 'incoherence' about the possibility of critical detachment makes for over-investment in the possibility of textual agency and the agency of subjects.[74] What of the GDR's ability to make texts and readers at once and in tandem, including readers whose experience may never have been as simple as accession to a pre-empted reading mode or platform, nor as complex as even attenuated resistance, but instead understood as part of an active, formulated assent, working conscientiously for social formation and coherence, against dissonance, against breakdown, against threat?[75]

And if texts, meaning, and readings change between regimes of reading, as in fact products of those regimes, how much do they change? Completely? Are there residues of sense that transfer between regimes, which is what readers must believe when reading texts from outside their reading contexts, in translation or about highly localized, 'exotic' parts of the world – the appeal of difference couched in sameness? But is this substantially the case? Did GDR and Australian readers actually read anything like the same books? If reading is an identificatory process about recognition, about moving from what one knows to then encounter identifiable otherness, how does this productive dynamic make sense of the necessary difference on which transnational literary production proceeds? Jennifer Wawrzinek's essay in the volume votes for structural incommensurability; Ming Xie's theorizing of comparative literature insists on the centrality of misrecognition to intercultural exchange; Emily Apter's work on the translation 'zone' questions culture's disarticulation from language, identifying its resistance to transference as properly a geopolitical question.[76] Our study is able to closely examine the mechanics of cross-cultural reading at a national level, exposing the institutional vectors that make, effect and parlay translation, manufacturing at once ideological similarity and difference, literary recognition and alterity.

The question of *where* reading happens is foremost in studies of reception – is it, finally, only inside people's heads? Frow declares exactly that:

> Readings happen inside people's heads; to gain access to them we must rely on secondary manifestations most of which consist of one or another form of self report and all of which are dependent on translation of the micro-processes of reading into a particular language [...] [so therefore] where we expect to find the idiosyncrasy of a personal encounter with the text, we find rather the conventions of a historically and culturally specific regime.[77]

Our study does find readings that are actually 'available for scrutiny', as do other forms of reading history. They are not only individual readings, moreover – not expressions of the literary student's singular affective take on a work but clear articulations of the 'conventions of a historically and culturally specific regime', and even expressly such, in Ministry of Culture and publisher assessments of the suitability of titles for publication. These are available as self-consciously styled, administrative or bureaucratic readings, by assessor/censors, or performed, directive readings in the press, or in the books' afterwords, in which aesthetic politics and government become themselves reading entities, voiced, enacted or channelled through an individual assessor or reviewer. Frow notes:

We could, as an alternative to studying individual readings, choose to study readerships; that is, the correlation between a demographic formation and particular modes of encounter with texts. But in the forms that such a study usually takes – particularly the audience studies that are a central component of the study of mass media – readerships become autonomous of texts, ready-formed independent variables which are not themselves shaped by the textual encounter.[78]

This book does choose to study readerships, through book history models rather than those of audience studies, and the autonomy of texts and readers remains a key question. The ability of foreign texts such as these Australian books to shape the GDR reader was an issue for the state, which is why its apparatuses of reading were at once so elaborated and so assertive.

Book historians rewriting the history of book production and reception in East Germany emphasize the need for new positions on its cultural history that are neither unthinkingly triumphalist nor nostalgic, in what has been characterized as a 'post-ideological' frame.[79] 'Ideological' is certainly no longer an adequate descriptor of the character of such directed and programmatic publishing regimes, and perhaps never has been, in their implementation of modelled cultural ideals that looked to undo properly and thoroughly the apparently constitutive link between the literary and liberal capitalism. Literature in this context was more than ideological in the sense that Pierre Macherey and Etienne Balibar articulated, from French into English translation in 1978, describing literature's necessarily ideological work in all societies.[80] The 'utopian horizon' of the GDR, as a 'harmonious pan-German communion of art and people', was literally a literary society or *Literaturgesellschaft*, as envisioned by Becher at the Fourth German Writers' Congress in 1956.[81] The development of a 'collective organism of literature', for Becher, would include all social groups, with the pursuit of art, including the German classics, as a central agent of democratization. As Barck, Langermann and Lokatis note in their study of the GDR as a 'reading nation', however, the deployment of this ideal by 'leading cultural politicians' as an already existing reality saw the process 'congeal into a cultural-political cliché', bypassing the necessary precondition that it develop from 'the convictions of citizens as readers rather than from following the orders of a literary apparatus'.[82] Those citizen readers, especially the 'inside of their heads' as Frow suggests, then are present in highly mediated ways in our documentary evidence of the reading nation – if it is the historical reading subject that is revealed by the records of centralized publishing control, this is through the state's manufacture of such. So what we see, now, is the ideological reading subject, even and in as much as this is the actual reader. In 1965 Volk und Welt forwarded to Dorothy Hewett a letter from one of her GDR readers, written on reading the German edition of *Bobbin Up*, and that reader's embrace of the novel was effusive and unalloyed. 'Sydney is far away', wrote Lieselotte Assmann from Berlin-Weissensee to Hewett, 'but there is no distance between human beings who are feeling the same. If women from all over the world feel like you, there will be more love and less tears in the future.'[83] More generally, the ideal, politically conjured reading community is what remains for history, and even, profoundly as well as explicitly, the technocratic ideation of a *Leseland*, a *reading nation*.

In 1989, the year of the *Wende*, US literary historian Louis Montrose sought to describe the function of ideology as a term:

> Traditionally, 'ideology' has referred to the system of ideas, values, and beliefs common to any social group; in recent years, this vexed but indispensable term has in its most general sense come to be associated with the processes by which social subjects are formed, re-formed and enabled to perform as conscious agents in an apparently meaningful world.[84]

It is clear that it is now no longer 'vexed' nor 'indispensable', even in Montrose's general sense. The retreat or collapse of the term into its older, more limited meanings has been compelled seemingly by the Western left's confrontation with the implications of ideology's directed, technocratic *realpolitik* in the lives of the populations of the Eastern Bloc. And in the wake of 9/11 and the millennial 'end of history', the purchase of ideology as a term in fixing and identifying the making of 'subject positions' in democratic states has been dispersed. Arguably, the concept has disintegrated into a broader, post-Foucauldian consensus about governmental subjection that nuances Gramscian hegemony in its characterization of citizenship and consent in the globalized experience of liberal governance. It is telling, for example, that the contemporary theorist Jacques Rancière does not use the word at all in his 2000 collection on *The Politics of Aesthetics* (translated into English in 2004).

Simon During characterizes this theory's politics post 9/11 as *neo-gauchisme*, sourced in France's May 1968 moment, and indeed we see the global geopolitics of that year playing out still, even in literary theory's compulsive returns to that moment, rather than the Prague Spring, and in other reconceptions of the legacy of communist culture. For During, what the recent theoretical turn responds to is 'the end of hope that capitalism's triumph carries with it'; the fact that it can no longer have productive aims is, paradoxically, what makes the theory 'vivid'.[85] At issue for our project is the problem of how one can come to do such cultural history without merely objectifying 'ideology' into democracy's repellent and inevitable totalitarian other, while at the same time thoroughly investigating the impact on historical readerships and textual reception of cultural regulation as control. There should be room for recording resistant anti-communist reading as well as exploring what were productive cultural formations that have significance not only in their ability to homogenize, silence, repel and suppress, but in their sustained and revealing difference from Western capitalist history.

Notes

1 By 1951 Kinderbuchverlag Berlin had issued a version for young East German readers, with an afterword that explained the book's topicality: 'Just like Egon Erwin Kisch landed in Australia despite all obstacles, we too will prevent the remilitarization of West Germany and together with all peace-loving people, enforce world peace'; Horst Schötzki, in Egon Erwin Kisch, *Landung in Australien* (Berlin: Der Kinderbuchverlag, 1951), 29. Eberhard Brüning, Professor of English at Karl-Marx Universität Leipzig, observed in 1978 that Kisch's book would 'keep alive the interest of the GDR reading public in Australia'; Eberhard Brüning, 'Australische Literatur in der DDR: Ein Überblick', *Zeitschrift für Anglistik und Amerikanistik* 26, no. 2 (1978): 101–114 (105). And the East German genre writer Joachim Specht notes of it, as Patricia Blume's chapter records: 'I read that first, naturally'.
2 We have derived this figure from existing bibliographies, especially the 2010 catalogue of Australian literature in German translation from West-Pavlov and Elze-Volland, as well as Ministry of Culture permission to print files available in the Bundesarchiv, Berlin. The latter also cover the activities of Volk und Welt's English-language publishing arm Seven Seas, which fall outside the remit of West Pavlov's and Elze-Volland's catalogue; Russell West-Pavlov and Jens Elze-Volland, *Australian Literature in German Translation: A Catalogue of Titles, Translators, and Trends 1789–2010* (Berlin: Free University, 2010), http://www.geisteswissenschaften.fu-berlin.de/we06/forschung/forschungsprojekte/2010-03-10_Translation_catalogue.pdf, 2010. A 1986 bibliography, compiled with the help of Birgit Scheps at the University of Leipzig, listed 32 titles; John Fletcher, 'Australian Fiction in the German Democratic Republic', *Outrider* 3, no. 1 (1986): 51–56.
3 Gerhard Schulz, 'Die Zeitlosigkeit der Gegenwart, Sprachlicher Ausdruck Australiens: Die Lyrikerin Judith Wright', *Frankfurter Allgemeine Zeitung*, 19 December 1990, 28.
4 Nicholas Birns argues, interestingly, that the 'transnational turn' being witnessed internationally has been 'particularly pronounced' in the national literatures of Russia and Australia; '"Upon the Airy Ocean": Australia, the Russian Pacific, and the Transnational Imaginary', in *Scenes of Reading: Is Australian Literature a World Literature?*, ed. Robert Dixon and Brigid Rooney (Sydney: Sydney University Press, 2013), 73–85. For further elaboration, see other essays in that collection, as well as Robert Dixon, 'Australian Literature: International Contexts', *Southerly* 67, nos. 1–2 (2007): 15–27.
5 Robert Dixon and Brigid Rooney, 'Introduction', in *Scenes of Reading: Is Australian Literature a World Literature?*, ix–xxxvi (xii, xxii).
6 Phillip Mead, 'Nation, Literature, Location', in *The Cambridge History of Australian Literature*, ed. Peter Pierce (Melbourne and Cambridge: Cambridge University Press, 2009), 549–67.

7 Paul Sharrad, 'Which World, and Why Do We Worry About It?', in *Scenes of Reading: Is Australian Literature a World Literature*, 16–33 (16).
8 David Carter, 'Antipodean Romance, Crime and Sensation: Australian Popular Fiction in British and American Markets 1890–1925', in *Scenes of Reading: Is Australian Literature a World Literature?*, 86–100 (86).
9 Dipesh Chakrabarty, *Provincialising Europe: Postcolonial Thought and Historical Difference* (Princeton: Princeton University Press, 2000).
10 'Unsere sozialistische Nationalkultur der DDR ist offen für alles, was uns hier an Gutem und Wertvollem entgegenkommt. Wir nehmen es mit Weltoffenheit auf' (Erich Honecker, *Aus meinem Leben*, 1980), in Wolfgang Wicht, 'The Disintegration of Stalinist Cultural Dogmatism: James Joyce in East Germany, 1945 to the Present', in *The Reception of James Joyce in Europe*, ed. Geert Lernou (London: Continuum, 2004), 70–88 (80).
11 David Damrosch, *What Is World Literature?* (Princeton: Princeton University Press, 2003), 281.
12 Fritz J. Raddatz, *Unruhestifter: Erinnerungen* (München: Ullstein, 2003), 111.
13 Tony Day, 'Still Stuck in the Mud: Imagining World Literature During the Cold War in Indonesia and Vietnam', in *Cultures at War: The Cold War and Cultural Expression in South East Asia*, ed. T. Day and M. H. T. Liem (Ithaca, NY: Cornell South East Asia Program Publications, 2010), 131–69; Monica Popescu, *South African Literature beyond the Cold War* (New York: Palgrave Macmillan, 2010); Heather Bowen-Struyk, 'Rival Imagined Communities: Class and Nation in Japanese Proletarian Literature', *Positions: East Asia Cultures Critique* 14, no. 2 (2006): 373–404.
14 Emily Apter looks at John Kinsella in *The Translation Zone: A New Comparative Literature* (Princeton: Princeton University Press, 2005), 196–201, and Wai Chee Dimock writes about Joan London in 'Recycling the Epic: Gilgamesh on Three Continents', in *Scenes of Reading: Is Australian Literature a World Literature?*, ed. Robert Dixon and Brigid Rooney (Sydney: Australian Scholarly Publishing, 2013), 3–15. See also Sharrad, 'Which World?' and Dixon and Rooney, 'Introduction', xv.
15 This is even though Damrosch quotes Goethe's definition of Weltliteratur from the 'sumptuous edition' of Goethe's writing produced by the Akademie der Wissenschaften der DDR, East Germany's peak research body. Damrosch attributes the quality of that edition to its cold war contexts: 'Lasting national pride in Goethe [was] only heightened by the need of what was then East Germany to assert its cultural identity over against West Germany' (Damrosch, *What Is World Literature?*, 8, n. 3). East Germany figures briefly in Casanova's book as a potential source for world literature but not one of its destinations: prominent author Christa Wolf surfaces in Casanova's account of the reception of German writing in the UK, as 'an East German writer who has become well known in feminist circles in the United States as well'; Pascale Casanova, *The World Republic of Letters*, trans. M. B. DeBevoise (Cambridge, MA: Harvard University Press, 2004), 167f.
16 Michael Denning, *Culture in the Age of Three Worlds* (London and New York: Verso, 2004); chapter reprinted as 'The Novelists' International', in *The Novel, Vol 1: History, Geography and Culture*, ed. F. Moretti (Princeton and Oxford: Princeton University Press, 2006), 703–25.
17 Denning, *Culture in the Age*, 60.
18 Johannes R. Becher, *Von der Größe unserer Literatur* (Berlin: Aufbau, 1956), 47.
19 Denning, *Culture in the Age*, 60.

20 For the most influential elaboration of this position see Bill Ashcroft, Gareth Griffiths and Helen Tiffin, *The Empire Writes Back: Theory and Practice in Postcolonial Literatures* (London: Routledge, 1989); see also Alan Lawson, 'The Anxious Proximities of Settler (Post)Colonial Relations', in *Literary Theory: An Anthology*, ed. Julie Rivkin and Michael Ryan (Oxford: Blackwell, 2004), 1210–23.
21 *Working Bullocks* was hailed as the end of a literary drought that had stretched back to Joseph Furphy's 1903 *Such is Life* and was praised for its sparse modernism and ease with the Australian environment, as Richard Nile details in *The Making of the Australian Literary Imagination* (St Lucia: University of Queensland Press, 2002), 157–58.
22 Denning, *Culture in the Age*, 62.
23 Ibid., 623.
24 For histories of the politics of Australian writing in the post-war decades, see Susan McKernan, *A Question of Commitment: Australian Literature in the Twenty Years after the War* (Sydney: Allen & Unwin, 1989), and John McLaren, *Writing in Hope and Fear: Literature as Politics in Postwar Australia* (Cambridge and Melbourne: Cambridge University Press, 1996); for a discussion of the role of nationalism in left cultural politics, see David Carter, 'The Story of Our Epoch, A Hero of Our Time: The Communist Novelist in Postwar Australia', in *Frank Hardy and the Literature of Commitment*, ed. Paul Adams and Christopher Lee (Melbourne: Vulgar Press, 2003), 89–111 (94–95).
25 Cf. Nicole Moore, 'Red Love as Seditious Sex: Bans on Proletarian Women's Writing in Australia in the 1930s', in *Red Love Across the Pacific: Political and Sexual Revolutions of the Twentieth Century*, ed. Ruth Barraclough, Heather Bowen-Struyk and Paula Rabinowitz (London: Palgrave, 2015), 39-58; Nicole Moore, *The Censor's Library: Uncovering the Lost History of Australia's Banned Books* (St. Lucia: University of Queensland Press, 2012).
26 McKernan, *A Question of Commitment*; John McLaren, *Writing in Hope and Fear*.
27 Cf. Mary Fulbrook, 'A German Dictatorship: Power Structures and Political Cultures in the GDR', *German Life and Letters* 45, no. 4 (2007): 376–92.
28 Quoted in Dietrich Löffler, *Buch und Lesen in der DDR: Ein literatursoziologischer Überblick* (Berlin: Links, 2011), 136; Siegfried Lokatis, 'Zensur', in *Erinnerungsorte der DDR*, ed. Martin Sabrow (München: Beck, 2009), 109–116 (111).
29 John B. Hench, *Books as Weapons: Propaganda, Publishing, and the Battle for Global Markets in the Era of World War II* (Ithaca: Cornell University Press, 2010), 1.
30 Siegfried Lokatis, 'Vom Amt für Literatur und Verlagswesen zur Hauptverwaltung Verlagswesen im Ministerium für Kultur', in Simone Barck, Martina Langermann and Siegfried Lokatis, *'Jedes Buch ein Abenteuer': Zensursystem und literarische Öffentlichkeit in der DDR bis Ende der sechziger Jahre* (Berlin: Akademie-Verlag, 1998), 19–60 (21).
31 Ibid., 21.
32 Ibid., 23.
33 Siegfried Lokatis, 'Paradoxien der Zensur in der DDR', in *Der geteilte Himmel: Literatur und ihre Grenzen in der DDR*, ed. Martin Sabrow (Leipzig: Akademische Verlagsanstalt, 2004), 75–99 (81).
34 Quoted in Ulrich Plenzdorf, Klaus Schlesinger and Martin Stade, eds., *Berliner Geschichten: Operativer Schwerpunkt Selbstverlag. Eine Autorenanthologie: Wie sie entstand und von der Stasi verhindert wurde* (Suhrpkamp 1995), 14. The collection finally appeared in 1995, with extensive documentation from the files of the Ministerium für Staatssicherheit and the Writers' Union, which demonstrates how closely the Union, the secret service and the party collaborated on the case.

35 Frances Stoner Saunders, *The Cultural Cold War: The CIA and the World of Arts and Letters* (New York: The New Press, 2000), 7 (released as *Who Paid the Piper: The CIA and the Cultural Cold War* in London by Granta in 1999).
36 Cited in Peter Coleman, 'Out of the Ruins of Berlin', *Quadrant* 32, nos. 1–2 (1988): 6–13, and Saunders, *The Cultural Cold War*, 10.
37 Saunders, *The Cultural Cold War*, 7.
38 Cf. Andrew N. Rubin, *Archives of Authority: Empire, Culture, and the Cold War* (Princeton: Princeton University Press, 2012); James Smith, *British Writers and MI5 Surveillance, 1930–1960* (Cambridge: Cambridge University Press, 2013); Timothy Melley, *The Covert Sphere: Secrecy, Fiction and the National Security State* (Ithaca: Cornell University Press, 2012); Joel Whitney, 'Exclusive: *The Paris Review*, the Cold War and the CIA', *Salon*, May 27, 2012, accessed October 2013http://www.salon.com/2012/05/27/exclusive_the_paris_review_the_cold_war_and_the_cia/.
39 John B. Hench, *Books as Weapons: Propaganda, Publishing and the Battle for Global Markets in the Era of World War II* (New York: Cornell University Press, 2010).
40 Saunders, *The Cultural Cold War*, 11.
41 Ibid.
42 Pascale Casanova, 'Combative Literatures', *New Left Review* 72 (November–December 2011): 123–34.
43 Phillip Deery, 'Covert Propaganda and the Cold War: Britain and Australia 1948–1955', *The Round Table: The Commonwealth Journal of International Affairs* 90, no. 361 (2001): 607–21.
44 Becher, *Von der Größe unserer Literatur* (Berlin: Aufbau, 1956), 27 and 23 respectively.
45 Ibid., 36.
46 Ibid., 32.
47 'Verlag', in *Kulturpolitisches Wörterbuch*, ed. Manfred Berger, Helmut Hanke, Franz Hentschel, Hans Koch, Werner Kühn and Heinz Sallmon (Berlin: Dietz, 1978), 720–30.
48 Christoph Links, 'Leseland DDR: Bedingungen, Hintergründe, Veränderungen', in *Friedensstaat, Leseland, Sportnation: DDR Legenden auf dem Prüfstand*, ed. Thomas Großbölting (Berlin: Christoph Links Verlag, 2009), 196–207 (198). See also Siegfried Lokatis's description of Volk und Welt in this volume.
49 Links, 'Leseland DDR', 198.
50 David Carter, 'Modernising Anglocentrism: *Desiderata* and Literary Time', in *Republics of Letters: Literary Communities in Australia*, ed. Peter Kirkpatrick and Robert Dixon (Sydney: Sydney University Press, 2012), 85–98 (85).
51 Hans Petersen to Patrick White, c/o Curtis Brown, 27 October 1975, AdK, Volk und Welt Archive, 1344.
52 Sara Jones, *Complicity, Censorship and Criticism: Negotiating Space in the GDR Literary Sphere* (Berlin: Walter de Gruyter, 2011), 95.
53 Gertrude Gelbin, 'Story of Seven Seas Books', *New World Review* 35, no. 2 (1967): 38–42.
54 Ibid., 39, 42.
55 Quoted in Rebecca Jany, *Rewriting as Cultural Politics: The Role and Function of the Publisher Seven Seas*, MA thesis (Berlin: Freie Universität, 2007), 17.
56 Stefan Heym, *Nachruf* (München, 1988), 112–113. Quoted in Jany, 'Rewriting', 18.
57 Gelbin, 'Story of Seven Seas', 38.
58 Jany, 'Rewriting', 14.
59 Ibid., 5.

60 Nicole Moore and Christina Spittel, '*Bobbin Up* in the *Leseland*: Australian Literature in the German Democratic Republic', in *Republics of Letters: Literary Communities in Australia*, ed. Robert Dixon and Peter Kirkpatrick (Sydney: Sydney University Press, 2012), 113–26 (117).
61 Gelbin, 'Story of Seven Seas', 40.
62 But see Luise von Flotow on the changes made to the Seven Seas version of Wolf's *Divided Heaven*; 'Revealing the "Soul of Which Nation?": Translated Literature as Cultural Diplomacy', in *In Translation: Reflections, Refractions, Transformations*, ed. Paul St-Pierre and Prafulla C. Kar (Amsterdam: John Benjamins, 2007), 187–200 (188–89).
63 Stefan Heym, 'The Boredom of Minsk', *Meanjin* 2 (1996): 196–99; Stefan Heym Papers, University of Cambridge Library, C7/D43; Cf. Nicole Moore and Christina Spittel, '*Bobbin Up* in the *Leseland*: Australian Literature in the German Democratic Republic', in *Republics of Letters*, 113–26.
64 See what is a typical spat in 1963 between an anonymous *Bulletin* columnist, declaring the ABS a 'Red Book Society Flop', in crisis and too dominated by the Communist Party ('latest plans include an attempt to get East German publishers, Seven Seas, to print for the Society') and Hardy countering in a letter to the editor: 'As for my "negotiations" with Seven Seas publishers: these consisted of an unofficial chat with Gertrude Heym and her novelist husband Stefan, in Berlin last February. Seven Seas have already published three ABS books and it is common practice for English publishers, for example, to print in Western or Eastern Europe' – 'A Sydney Correspondent', 'The Red Book Society Flop: Looking to East Germany', *Bulletin* 85, no. 4354 (3 August 1963): 12; Frank Hardy, Letter to the Editor, *Bulletin* 85, no. 4357 (24 August 1963): 33.
65 Pauline Armstrong, *Frank Hardy and the Making of* Power without Glory (Melbourne: Melbourne University Press, 2000), 139.
66 Birns, '"Upon the Airy Ocean"', 81.
67 Cf. West-Pavlov and Elze-Volland, *Australian Literature in German Translation*. cf. Barbara Korte, '"Two Solitudes"? Anglo-Canadian Literature in Translation in the Two Germanies.' In *Translating Canada. Charting the Institutions and Influences of Cultural Transfer: Canadian Writing in Germany*, ed. Luise von Flotow and Reingard Nischik (Ottawa: University of Ottawa Press, 2007), 27–51 (45, 48).
68 Emily Apter, *Against World Literature: On the Politics of Untranslatability* (London and New York: Verso, 2013).
69 Gabriele Thomson-Wohlgemuth, 'Publishing and Editorial Policies of Translated Children's Books from the Viewpoint of the East German Censorship Files', *New Review of Children's Literature and Librarianship* 10, no. 1 (2004): 41–54 (46).
70 Manfred Jurgensen's *Eagle and Emu: German-Australian Writing 1930–1990* (St Lucia: University of Queensland Press, 1992) includes a chapter on 'the GDR connection' that divides its attention between Walter Kaufmann and Joachim Specht, with detailed discussion of 6 of his then 14 books (289–300).
71 John Frow, 'Afterlife: Texts as Usage', *Reception* 1 (2008): 1–23 (1).
72 Ibid., 14.
73 Ibid., 15.
74 Amanda Anderson, *The Way We Argue Now: A Study in the Cultures of Theory* (Princeton and Oxford: Princeton University Press, 2006), 46–47.
75 Historians have adopted a similar model, characterizing the GDR's citizens not so much as victims of a totalitarian state than as 'active participants in a […] complex maze of practices, and inhabit[ing] a […] complex moral and political universe'. Mary

Fulbrook, *The People's State: East German Society from Hitler to Honecker* (New Haven: Yale University Press, 2005), 13.
76 Ming Xie, *Conditions of Comparison: Reflections on Comparative Intercultural Inquiry* (New York: Bloomsbury, 2011); Emily Apter, *Against World Literature*.
77 Frow, 'Afterlife', 15.
78 Ibid.
79 Konrad H. Jarausch, ed., *Dictatorship as Experience: Towards a Socio-Cultural History of the GDR,* trans. Eve Duffy (New York: Berghahn Books, 1999); Sandrine Kott, 'Everyday Communism: New Social History of the German Democratic Republic', *Contemporary European History* 13, no. 2 (2004): 233–47; Michael Geyer, ed., *The Power of Intellectuals in Contemporary Germany* (Chicago: University of Chicago Press, 2001).
80 Pierre Macherey and Etienne Balibar, 'Literature as an Ideological Form: Some Marxist Propositions', *Oxford Literary Review* 3 (1978): 4–12.
81 Simone Barck, Martina Langerman and Siegfried Lokatis, 'The German Democratic Republic as a "Reading Nation": Utopia, Planning, Reality and Ideology', trans. Michael Latham and Devin Pendas, in *The Power of Intellectuals in Contemporary Germany*, ed. M. Geyer (Chicago: University of Chicago Press, 2001), 88–112 (89–90).
82 Barck, Langermann and Lokatis, 'The German Democratic Republic as a "Reading Nation"', 90.
83 Lieselotte Assmann to Volk und Welt, 8 September 1965, enclosed in Czollek to Hewett, 24 September 1965 (Hewett Papers, MS6184, folders 3–4). Cf. Moore and Spittel, '*Bobbin Up* in the Leseland', 121–22.
84 Louis Montrose, *Professing the Renaissance: The Poetics and Politics of Culture* (New York and London: Routledge, 1989), extracted in *Literary Theory: An Anthology*, ed. Julie Rivkin and Michael Ryan (Oxford: Blackwell, 2004), 584–91 (585).
85 Simon During, *Exit Capitalism: Literary Culture, Theory and Post-secular Modernity* (London and New York: Routledge, 2009), 132.

Part I

CONTEXTS AND FRAMES

Chapter 1

CENSORSHIP, AUSTRALIAN LITERATURE AND FOREIGN-LANGUAGE BOOKS IN EAST GERMAN PUBLISHING HISTORY*

Siegfried Lokatis

It is possible to date the beginning of the rule of communist censorship in the Soviet-occupied zone of Germany very precisely: to 20 April 1948. This is the date of the 'Circular Addressed to the National Educational Authorities' ('Rundschreiben an die Volksbildungsämter') that was inserted retrospectively into the *Catalogue of Banned Nazi Books and Military Literature* with which the Soviets tasked East German librarians, publishers and booksellers to clean their holdings after the war.[1] Comprising just a single sheet, the circular's additional list starts with the names of Leon Trotsky, Nikolai Bukharin and Gregory Zinoviev, thus indexing, for the first time, authors of quite a different kind: the 'party enemies', 'dissenters' and dissidents of the left who had been prosecuted by Stalin in show trials.

The symbiosis of the Soviet censorship system with bureaucratic German diligence renders the archival records relating to the publishing history of the German Democratic Republic (GDR) increasingly important internationally, particularly in historical research since 1989. It is quite rare for a country's entire literature to be so thoroughly reflected in censors' and publishers' files, across a period of 40 years. It is certainly true that no other country of the communist Eastern Bloc has archival records covering its censorship history that are even remotely as good in quality *and* as publicly accessible. In part, these records are available even online on the website of the German Federal Archive in Berlin, which now holds the detailed, compulsory applications for print supplied by East German publishers.[2] These files offer a tremendous opportunity for research into the conditions, instruments, difficulties, successes and limits of the literary-political experiment that was the GDR.

Therefore, this chapter is about more than what the GDR, that half country, might have constituted from an Australian perspective: a tiny spot on the other side of the globe. Rather, the book history of the GDR opens a strange window onto a twentieth-century society that followed different rules, revealing the distinctive bureaucratic mechanisms of its ideological control. These rules and mechanisms form the interest of this chapter, which introduces the East German censorship system and its role in constituting the distinctive GDR versions of foreign literatures delivered to readers. The essay also sketches some of the basic conditions of literary import into the GDR, above all the permanent shortage of hard currency, of course, and its effects on literary policy, but also the emergence of a differentiated publishing landscape whose individual players enjoyed quite different degrees of latitude in their dealings with the literary administration.

Which features were common to the systems of literary administration in those countries of the Eastern Bloc that were modelled on the Soviet Union? First of all, in countries such as Poland, the Soviet Union, North Korea, Cuba and China, the censorship authority itself presided over a regime of centrally directed book production, with a relatively small number of large publishers dividing the key tasks amongst themselves, with a central publisher for school textbooks, a party publishing house for political writing, and a few key publishers for the important areas of fiction and poetry, academic and artistic writing. Of course, there was a publisher for agriculture and a military publisher.

In principle, such concentration allowed publishers to profit from sizeable print runs, given well-organized distribution and a commensurate population. Who, then, benefitted from this? Publishing houses either belonged to the state and the people (*volkseigen*, in GDR parlance) or to one of the mass organizations: the party or its youth organization, the trade union, the academy of the sciences or the army. It was quite typical for such organizations to finance themselves through the book trade and this could still leave enough 'fat' to fund the expensive apparatus of pre-publication censorship typical of Soviet-style systems, which insists on sighting almost every manuscript in order to submit it to a more or less extensive process of assessment.

Like the entire socialist economy, publishing was also organized via the principle of centralized planning. Thus a process of annual planning – *Themenplanung* (planning of themes) in the GDR – preceded the censorship of individual texts. Publishing houses presented their plans for future writing, editing and translation projects to the central authority for approval well before final manuscripts reached the censors' desks. During this important pre-selection, publishers requested and received the required paper stock and where international writing was concerned, the hard currency required to buy international rights. Whenever cultural functionaries of the 'socialist brother states' met at international publishers' conferences in Budapest, Warsaw or

Leipzig, they swapped notes about these foundational processes and their potential improvement as well as on national deviations and particularities.

What were these, as far as the GDR was concerned? First of all, the GDR was a successor state to vanquished Nazi Germany. Antifascism was its prime political doctrine, and the re-education of readers the purpose of its literary system. But few communist comrades survived the camps and it proved impossible to get by entirely without the skills of 'bourgeois' elements. The powerful tradition of the book city of Leipzig, centre for German publishing since the fifteenth century, could not be fully eradicated, and this also held for many old, suddenly banned books. The task of 'cleansing' the giant second-hand bookshops and libraries could be likened to tilting at windmills. There was a second, even more important point of difference between the GDR and other countries of the Eastern Bloc: with the exception of their colleagues in North Korea and, for a period of time, North Vietnam, the censors in East Berlin were alone in operating in a divided country and sharing a linguistic space with the *Klassenfeind* (class enemy), in this case, the imperialist Federal Republic. Once the Berlin Wall sealed the German-German border in 1961, subversive literature had to pass customs and the vigilant control of the postal service. Prior to that, the difference in currencies had formed the most reliable protection for the East German state's literary policy: after the Western and Soviet-occupied zones introduced separate currencies in 1948, literature from East Germany was much more affordable for its citizens than writing from the West.

In addition, out of consideration for West Germany and to avoid losing precious licences, the GDR's publishing landscape retained a series of 'bourgeois', privately owned companies, such as Gustav Kiepenheuer, well into the 1970s, quite unlike other socialist countries. These publishers were eyed and ruled with as much suspicion by the censors as the Christian publishing houses and the publishing houses owned by the *Blockparteien*, the satellite parties. There was even a series of famous German publishing houses, such as Brockhaus and Reclam, that effectively ran as separate companies in the two states and led a fraught double life, as alienated brothers, after the defection (*Republikflucht*) of their owners to the West. Indeed, for the entire 40 years of its existence, literary policy in the GDR meant competition with the West, trumping them with better writers, only to watch these writers leave, one by one, for the Federal Republic. East German censorship had also to be wary of the vitriol of West German reviewers, for the enemy was reading along, observing the minutest changes in a text and mocking when a book could not be published.

In the schizophrenic, bracing climate of a divided nation, literature is polarized, its interpretation politically charged on both sides (*hüben wie drüben* (over here as well as over there), as Germans used to say). In the GDR, this held for public literary criticism as much as for the secret assessments made for censorship. Naturally, the criteria for censorship changed over the years, as did the rules according to which they were applied. It is the general aim of censorship to remain as invisible as possible. Censorship in the GDR, however, was subject to substantial scrutiny and criticism from the start. Publishers and booksellers liked to compare it with national socialist *Schrifttumspolitik* (politics of literature) and this comparison, strictly forbidden by East German censorship, was highly revealing because the national socialist system, characterized by the chaos of competing institutions, did not have such systematic, centralized pre-publication control. A whole range of East German literary functionaries changed sides in the 1950s, moreover, offering their knowledge of censorship to the West German class enemy. Small wonder that censorship changed form, adapted, learned from frictions and modernized itself *nolens volens*, even transforming into a driver for reform! From the 1970s, particularly, it protected the critical stance of contemporary GDR writing as a new kind of public sphere, the only possible alternative to the regulated East German press.

This long-term process of obvious modernization, however, was overlaid by the changing seasons typical – even constitutive – of communist systems: the larger political weather systems dominate with their feared changes; then there are the highs and lows of political thawing conducive to reform as well as relapses into icy periods – for example, in 1957, after the Hungarian uprising, and in December 1965, after the infamous *Kahlschlagsplenum*, the 11th plenary session of the Central Committee of the Socialist Unity Party (SED). This would be when 'heads would roll': responsible editors, publishers and censors were demoted, dismissed or even arrested, while spectacular bans raised the bar for future censorial practice.

Clever publishers and editors needed stamina and patience, but they could see when, after such backlashes, the time for a 'challenging' book that they yearned to see in print was finally ripe. The moment might come for censors to close their tired eyes and adopt a milder practice. But more liberal publishing was not just a question of timing; it was also a matter of being in the right place, such as the publishers who were operating in the shadows of political attention, perhaps far away from the central authority in Berlin, like Greifenverlag based in Rudolstadt in the Thuringian mountains, for example, or Hinstorff Verlag based in Rostock on the Baltic Coast. This worked well until there too the lightning flash of censorship hit and rebellious authors had to find themselves a different publisher, a powerful one, perhaps, with particularly good connections to the echelons of political leadership, such as Aufbau Verlag or Verlag Neues Leben (house-publisher of the Free German Youth), where pseudo-feudal structures of patronage could easily establish themselves. With these publishers, paper stock was more easily accessible and lucrative reprints, always a good source of income for writers in the GDR, a real possibility. Those who did not want to offer themselves to the Politburo or the Stasi did well to find a publisher who was heavily exporting: if a book promised to earn hard currency, a censor would regularly close both eyes. And of course, it was the rebellious, critical authors who were feted by West German critics and found a market in the Federal Republic. This was, roughly speaking, the situation for many East German authors, although the fit was never perfect. Rather, their relations with the regime were complex, multiform and sometimes ambiguous.[3]

But who looked after international writing? How could a book from Australia find an advocate to survive in this bureaucratic publishing maze and see the light of some public reception? As discussed, the division of labour is one of the specific features of socialist publishing and this applied to literary writing too. There were publishers for children and young adults; Verlag Neues Berlin was responsible for science fiction and crime; Eulenspiegel-Verlag for humour and satire. Why would there not be a place for a suitable book from Australia? A new generation of authors was raised by Mitteldeutscher Verlag in Halle, whose editors looked after the 'writing workers' in the factories. Why should they not, as Joachim Specht did, write about their experiences in Australia, if they had any? This is where the publishing houses belonging to SED's 'bourgeois' satellite parties played a special role: Union-Verlag (owned by the Christian Democratic Union party), Buchverlag der Morgen (owned by the Liberal-Democratic Party of Germany) and Verlag der Nation (owned by the National Democratic Party of Germany). These publishing houses exerted considerable political influence, on the back of which they pursued their own, ambitious publishing programmes. Hence they produced the odd title with an Australian connection. Buchverlag der Morgen brought out Xavier Herbert's *Capricornia* as early as 1960, while Verlag der Nation took on books by Walter Kaufmann and Joachim Specht. Privately owned Kiepenheuer Verlag in Weimar had published communist authors Anna Seghers and Bertolt Brecht in the 1920s but had to hand them over to the GDR's Aufbau Verlag. Instead, Kiepenheuer turned to Kurt Heyd's *Christophs Abenteuer in Australien: Eine Erzählung aus der Goldgräberzeit* (*Christoph's Adventures in Australia: A Story from the Gold Diggers' Era*, 1935), a book that had also helped the publisher through the Nazi period. 'Distant as it is from any politics', there was 'no direct need to remove the book from trade,' grumbled much-feared censor Carola Gärtner-Scholle in late 1954, 'but just as little need to publish it'.[4] And yet, the book did come out.

All these publishing houses, however, including the world-famous Reclam Verlag in Leipzig, operated in the shadow of the two leading Berlin publishers for fiction and prose – Aufbau and Volk und Welt – and had to content themselves with the crumbs left by these *Leitverlage* (key publishers) as they built their lists. Aufbau Verlag was responsible for leading GDR writers such as Bert Brecht, Anna Seghers and Christa Wolf; the classics Goethe, Heine and Schiller; and the *humanistische bürgerliche Erbe* (humanist bourgeois heritage), with Thomas Mann as its most important representative. Among its most famous migrant authors was iconic reporter Egon Erwin Kisch, whose *Australian Landfall*, a reportage about his 1934 trip to Sydney as a delegate of the World Committee against War and Fascism and his subsequent arrest, with a brief history of Australia, appeared regularly with Aufbau Verlag from 1948 after being first released in German by Amsterdam-based Verlag Allert de Lange in 1937. It is the crucial point of departure for any discourse about Australia in the GDR, and in other Socialist countries, the one text about Australia which every comrade knows and should have read.[5] Aufbau Verlag only published a single Australian title, contracted from West German Goldmann Verlag: Arthur W. Upfield's bush whodunit *Gefahr für Bony* (*Bony and the Mouse*), which appeared in 1975 as a paperback in a print run of 40,000 copies, although the East German Volkspolizei would hardly have approved of Napoleon Bonaparte's spiritualist methods of investigation.

The most significant publishing house for Australian literature was without a doubt Volk und Welt, the leading publisher for 'contemporary international writing' and hence also in charge of Australia. Founded in Berlin in 1947, this was almost the only publisher (aside from Aufbau) which, from the early 1960s, could dispose of the most precious asset in the GDR: hard currency for the necessary licensing agreements with foreign countries. As a *Leitverlag*, Volk und Welt could cherry-pick for its readers. It counted no fewer than 42 Nobel Prize winners among its authors. When, in 1964, the firm amalgamated with Verlag Kultur und Fortschritt (Culture and Progress) – the in-house publisher for the GDR's German-Soviet Friendship Association – this was a successful marriage of two very lucrative, well-funded and well-staffed institutions. Kultur und Fortschritt had already published 45 million books and in 1963 it had raked in profits of 2.5 million Deutsche Mark. Volk und Welt had also exceeded its targets for that year (*Plan übererfüllt*) and earned profits of almost 1.5 million (for the party).[6] By the 1970s, Volk und Welt was organized similarly to a university institute and boasted five large departments – *Lektorate* – exclusively in charge of selecting and editing world literature:

- Lektorat I was by far the largest department and looked after Soviet literature. Roughly half the paper stock accorded to Volk und Welt was used for Russian authors as well as for authors from the various Soviet republics.

- Lektorat II was mostly in charge of the socialist democratic countries – above all Poland, the GDR's most important ally aside from the Soviet Union, and Czechoslovakia – while also publishing literature from Greece and Israel.
- Lektorat III was for German-language and Scandinavian writing and brought books into the country mainly from Switzerland, Austria and Sweden.
- Lektorat IV took care of Romance literatures with France, Italy and Latin America its key preoccupations.
- Lektorat V was concerned with Anglo-American literature and was responsible for English-language writing more broadly, including Australia.

Between them, these five departments, their divisions a legacy of the colonial era, administered the entirety of world literature. Africa was divided between *Romanistik* and *Anglistik*; Asia was looked after by the English department, but largely on the side. Behind each Lektorat was a strong academic support network of proved and tested translators, editors, writers of afterwords, and of course, well-respected and trusted assessors. Hans Petersen's English department consisted of no more than three staff and one of them, editor Marianne Bretschneider, was really a trained sinologist. Within Volk und Welt the scarce paper stock and the even scarcer amounts of hard currency were divvied up according to a rigid quota, and even between editors there was competition, with everyone keenly eyeing who could produce how many books from which country. Not even Leonhard Kossuth, head of the department for Soviet literature, was happy, despite having the lion's share and, at one point, he began to argue that, really, each of the Soviet republics was a nation in its own right, so why should Georgia receive less attention than Denmark?[7] Petersen's tiny department received resources for, at best, 15–16 new titles and 7–8 reprints per annual plan, as he recalled.

> We could easily have produced 20 new titles, and many more reprints too; there were always manuscripts which we would have loved to publish or reprint, but we did not have enough hard currency or paper. And apart from that, the proportions of Volk und Welt's lists were eyed carefully, which simply meant that books from socialist countries came first.[8]

In sum, Volk und Welt published no fewer than 23 titles by Australian authors – as much as from Canada and South Africa combined – but 107 titles from Great Britain and 184 from the USA. At the top of Volk und Welt's Australian statistics sits travelling correspondent Wilfred G. Burchett, with eight of the 23 titles, followed by Frank Hardy and Katharine Susannah Prichard with three titles each; two anthologies (*Erkundungen*, 1976; *Australische*

Erzähler von Marcus Clarke bis Patrick White, 1983); Marcus Clarke's bestselling *Lebenslänglich* and various individual books by Dymphna Cusack (*Auf eigenen Füßen*, 1961), Dorothy Hewett (*Die Mädchen von Sydney*, 1965), Xavier Herbert (*Der vertauschte Traumstein*, 1970), Thomas Keneally (*Australische Ballade*, 1977), a volume of short stories by John Bryson (*Melodram für eine Heldin aus Plast*, 1985) and poetry by Judith Wright (*Schweigen zwischen Wort und Wort*, 1990). A request to print a volume of *Australian Plays* (*Australische Stücke*) was submitted to the Ministry of Culture in summer 1989. Like many others, that volume never appeared, because with reunification in 1990, East German publishers lost their licensing rights, ceding them to West German rights owners. This count excludes several titles by Walter Kaufmann, who was considered a German writer, and Ralph de Boissiere, whose books *Kronjuwel* and *Rum und Coca Cola* were counted as coming from Trinidad, despite having been first released by the leftist Australian cooperative the Australasian Book Society.

It is obvious that the penchant for Burchett had little to do with his Melbourne origins or an interest in Australian literature. Quite apart from the fact that he was a captivating writer, he was often the first on location wherever there was a political hotspot – whether in China, Korea, Vietnam or Cambodia – and always had the best connections to insiders, whether they were peasants and guerrilla fighters or their revolutionary leaders.[9] Even in the most difficult phases of de-Stalinization he proved a loyal friend of the Soviet Union and there, as well as in the GDR, such 'biased' (*parteilich*) witnesses from the West were in demand. *Sonnenaufgang über Asien* (*Democracy with a Tommygun*) appeared in 1948 in a first edition of 50,000 copies. Publisher's reports raved enthusiastically about Burchett's virtues as the author even managed the embarrassing ritual of a trip to the Soviet Union in an exemplary fashion. 'Literally every page and every paragraph' relates 'something of the New, of the momentous upheavals' in the Soviet Union 'whose speed and reach many still have not properly grasped here'. And while editors conceded that he did 'address difficulties directly', he did so 'with the sense of responsibility of a Marxist writer' who 'by setting the right accents, can always clearly show a line of development'. It was a critical 'task to overtake the USA with regards to standards of living' and Burchett resolved this assignment by addressing cultural policy instead of remaining stuck in 'comparisons about refrigerators and vacuum cleaners'. To be sure, some 'minor flaws' would have to be excised with the author's agreement, such as 'his observations about missing crime statistics, the odd occurrence of strikes, the causes for the small number of women in leading positions etc. These comments are all well meant, but should be removed from the German edition nonetheless.'[10] Not even a well-meaning and proven writer like Burchett could get by in the GDR without requests for changes from the censorship authorities. His book about the

Soviet Union, *Land der Verheißung* (*New Life in the New Look*) came out with Volk und Welt in 1962, just under a decade after they had published another Australian's account of his trip to the Soviet Union, Frank Hardy's *Reise in die Zukunft* (*Journey into the Future*).[11]

That Volk und Welt should publish relatively few titles by Australian authors is surely also owed to the fact that their books were by no means guaranteed fast sellers. A list of hard-to-sell Volk und Welt titles dated from 1956 contains Ralph de Boissiere's *Kronjuwel* (*Crown Jewel*), Frank Hardy's *Macht ohne Ruhm* (*Power without Glory*) and Katharine Susannah Prichard's *Die goldene Meile* (*Golden Miles*) – with the exception of Burchett, all of Volk und Welt's Australian authors at the time. One-fifth of a print run of Prichard's *Die goldene Meile* (15,000 copies) remained unsold at that point, as did 3,384 of the 10,000 copies of Hardy's *Macht ohne Ruhm* and a staggering 7,928 of the 10,000 copies printed of Boissiere's *Kronjuwel* – a small humiliation for a publisher as spoilt by success as Volk und Welt.[12] Marcus Clarke's novel *Lebenslänglich*, a GDR best-seller that would reach its 17th imprint in 1990 (731,000 copies), did not appear until 1957.

Between 1965 and 1987 Volk und Welt only published a handful of Australian titles: five years separate Dorothy Hewett's *Die Mädchen von Sydney* (*Bobbin Up*, 1965) from Xavier Herbert's *Der vertauschte Traumstein* (*Seven Emus*, 1970); a further six years later, a volume of Australian short stories appeared in the flagship *Erkundungen* series; one year later, Volk und Welt published Thomas Keneally's *Australische Ballade* (*The Chant of Jimmie Blacksmith*, 1977). In the case of Hewett and Herbert, the impulse to publish originated not with Volk und Welt's English department but with its English-language publishing branch, Seven Seas.[13] Founded in 1953 as Panther Books by GDR writer Stefan Heym and his wife, Gertrude, this series originally belonged to Paul List Verlag in Leipzig, before transferring to Volk und Welt in 1958. After returning from his exile in the USA, Stefan Heym, initially, continued to write in English. Thanks to Seven Seas, his wife could effectively publish him, practically sidelining censorship. Apart from this, Seven Seas helped to improve the export of GDR writers such as Christa Wolf into the English-speaking world and aimed to make left-wing Anglo-American writing available in the original, including back in Australia, as the editors explain in more detail in the Introduction to this volume. Hewett's *Bobbin Up* appeared with Seven Seas four years before it was translated into German; Herbert's *Seven Emus* preceded its German version by a full nine years.

But then came the great success of an Australian short story collection, first published in Volk und Welt's *Erkundungen* series in 1976, and reprinted four times, in 1977, 1980, 1981 and 1982.[14] From 1964 this series featured international short stories from over 40 countries with rich narrative traditions, such as

Argentina, Belgium, Chile, Denmark, England, France, Greece, Italy, Iceland, Spain and Sweden; China and Africa too had their *Erkundungen* volumes. It was small wonder that the series should be so popular as a 'window onto the world': each volume put an entire country – otherwise out of bounds – into the hands of the GDR citizen. Despite this, few volumes were reprinted more than once: the Danish volume, the combined Belgian and Dutch volume, the volume dedicated to the Federal Republic and the volume representing Czechoslovakia saw two reprints each. Ireland, with three reprints, took second place, perhaps because this was the first time that a text by 'arch-nihilist' Samuel Beckett, otherwise banned until 1988, when his plays could finally be published, became available in the GDR. But what explains the uncontested lead of the Australian anthology? Kangaroos can leap across walls.

In any event, Hans Petersen, editor and head of Volk und Welt's English department began another attempt in 1983 with a second anthology, *Australische Erzähler von Marcus Clarke bis Patrick White* (*Australian Story-Tellers from Marcus Clarke to Patrick White*). This time he did not privilege members of the young generation, as the *Erkundungen* had, but authors of the first guard who had already been introduced in the GDR – Prichard, Cusack, Waten, Marshall, Hardy – and older texts published before 1960, thus introducing authors such as Marjorie Barnard, Barbara Baynton, Henry Handel Richardson, Vance Palmer and, at long last, Christina Stead, that 'outsider on both sides of the political divide', as Susan Lever puts it. In the European autumn of 1986 Petersen travelled to Perth, Sydney, Canberra and Brisbane – 'a rare occasion' – to study the Australian market and forge and renew contacts with publishers, agencies, magazines, literary scholars and writers. All those he talked to revealed themselves as 'correct in every regard. There were no political provocations and all conversations were conducted in a friendly, matter-of-fact atmosphere. Interest in GDR publishing was surprising, but the lack of knowledge was disappointing.'[15] Petersen visited Judith Wright in hospital in Canberra to prepare what would be the last Australian book Volk und Welt published in the GDR: a bilingual collection of Judith Wright's poetry. *Schweigen zwischen Wort und Wort* (*Silence between Word and Word*) appeared in 1990, in the prestigious 'white poetry series', clad in a wrapper of expensive white glassine paper (to which the series owed its name). This first volume of Australian poetry was published just as the GDR was nearing its end. Reports had been at pains to emphasise that Wright well deserved to appear on a par with the world's most famous contemporary poets. 'How to best introduce the poetry of Australia and what point of reference to offer for further reading' requires 'careful thinking' they insisted, but this author fulfilled 'key requirements of being representative'. As if through a lens, her work reflected 'the mental, political and sociological tendencies of mid-century Australian society'. While not sharing the 'style of local bush-balladists', she nonetheless embarked 'from the start on a search for the essence of Australia or, put more solemnly, its promise'. A general preoccupation of hers is 'of course the evocation of the bush, this omnipresent theme of Australian literature, the epitome of loneliness'.[16]

Volk und Welt did not have a monopoly on publishing contemporary international literature, including Australian writing. As a 'lead publisher' of the relevant *Literaturarbeitsgemeinschaft* (a bureaucratic planning group or advisory committee that made recommendations to the Ministry about the organization and regulation of publishing), it had a better chance of securing the titles it was particularly interested in. Other publishers could only take what was left over and, in the case of Australian literature, that was a number of important titles. This explains how Reclam Verlag, world famous for its cheap editions of classics, secured Patrick White's *Voß* (*Voss*) for publication in East Germany in 1987. West German publisher Kiepenheuer and Witsch in Cologne had published White's novel in German translation as early as 1958, one year after it had first appeared in English. Reclam justified its choice with the preparations for the bicentenary of white Australian settlement. The 175th anniversary of the historical model for the novel's protagonist, explorer Ludwig Leichhardt, was also pending; Leichhardt had been born in Mecklenburg in 1813, now part of the GDR. Reclam snatched the Australian Nobel Laureate from Volk und Welt: this was possible because, at times, Reclam had extraordinary amounts of foreign currency at its disposal and was quite willing to spend that on such a prestigious title. Volk und Welt, on the other hand, would have operated more economically, perhaps deciding to translate the novel itself, instead of paying for a West German translation with hard currency. And incidentally, Volk und Welt would have manipulated its reporting on the print run.

Interestingly, when compiling the Australian *Erkundungen* volume, Hans Petersen and Volk und Welt refrained from including one desirable author because his origins could not be established. At least this is how Petersen put it in a letter to Reclam Leipzig,[17] which had discovered Bahumir Wongar for the GDR. Reclam invited Wongar to Leipzig in 1980 and published his stories in 1981, as *Der Pfad nach Bralgu* (*The Track to Bralgu*), in Reclam's famous Universal-Bibliothek (Universal Library) series, in an edition decorated with bark paintings by indigenous Australians, sourced from the Leipzig Ethnographic Museum (Museum für Völkerkunde) – a lucrative and politically important project, as it turned out, with an author whose fame spread quickly. In 1985 Aufbau Verlag took on another of Wongar's titles, *Der Schoß* (*The Lap*), but assessors were still agonizing over the author's identity. One opined that Reclam had given 1932 as the year of the author's birth but had been deliberately circumspect about his evident pseudonym. The West German Lamuv-Verlag had 'decisively, but not quite logically' stated that Wongar was born in North Australia in the late 1930s, while a more recent report by an external reader had given 'good, but not necessarily legally sound (*wenn auch juristisch nicht zwingende*) arguments' that the author in question was 'probably a meanwhile naturalized Yugoslav by the name of Sreten Bozic', who identifies with the indigenous cause and has 'possibly been accepted into a tribe, as an honorary Abo [sic]'.[18]

'This obscurity around his person, created at least in part by the author himself' could not be illuminated 'from here', but the assessors argued it wasn't relevant for an appraisal of the author's work. What mattered far more was that he firmly came down on the side of the indigenous people and that his knowledge of the subject was beyond doubt.[19] It is striking, however, that Aufbau should have chosen to print only 6,000 copies of this novel by Wongar, with his established high profile in the GDR, after Reclam had first introduced him to East German readers in a print run of 20,000. Aufbau, however, sourced the novel *Der Schoß* through a license from a West German publisher, and from this we can confidently conclude that this is a typical manipulation, a so-called illegal *Plusauflage* or 'plus-run'. It is highly likely that at least 10,000 copies were printed. While relevant files in the Aufbau archive are not accessible, it is well known that behind the protection of the Wall both Aufbau and Volk und Welt systematically broke licensing agreements from the 1960s onwards by lying about actual print runs. Both authors and licencees for titles were given incorrect lower numbers for print runs in contracts and agreements, repeatedly and illegally. The concentration of hard currency for international writing in these two publishing houses allowed for the number of those in the know to be kept low, limited to a dozen accountants and publishing functionaries. More often than not those responsible were to be found in the central literary apparatus and not in the publishing houses themselves: profits from these exploits went straight into the SED's accounts.

It is possible to illustrate this illegal practice using the example of Australian literature published by Volk und Welt because the publisher's print run statistics are available in the publisher's archive, held at the Akademie der Künste in Berlin. Records show that real print runs regularly exceeded the figures stated on the applications for permission to print and corresponding licensing agreements. Thus, the first edition of the Australian *Erkundungen* volume (1976) was officially printed in a run of 8,000, when the actual print run amounted to 20,000 followed by four reprints. Of its second Australian anthology of short stories, *Australische Erzähler* (1984), Volk und Welt printed not 6,000 but 20,000 copies. Dorothy Hewett's *Die Mädchen von Sydney* appeared not in a print run of 5,000, as agreed, but 10,000; of Xavier Herbert's *Der vertauschte Traumstein* not 6,000, but 8,000 appeared, and Keneally's *Australische Ballade* was published in a run of 12,000 while Keneally received royalties for just 8,000. It is tempting to be lenient in judging this practice and to plead that this was no more than petty theft for literary survival in a system notoriously short of hard currency; but couldn't Volk und Welt have afforded to pay Judith Wright the royalties she was due for the 3,000 volumes actually printed of her poems – such a giant print run is rare for poetry – instead of making her sign a contract for 1,000 copies? These inflated print runs were born not of necessity but as the standard routine of habitual criminals. Viewed from an Australian perspective, is it not also flattering to now discover that the East German interest in Australian literature should have been so great?

In all, Volk und Welt had to pay compensation for 12 million illegally printed books after the *Wende*.[20] Since April 2001, the former *Leitverlag* for international literature has been history; there was no place for it in the newly ordered publishing landscape of a reunified Germany. Aufbau, on the other hand, has survived; its last edition of Kisch's *Landung in Australien*, however, now dates back over 20 years. Priorities have shifted, conditions changed. In the book city of Leipzig, Connewitzer Verlagsbuchhandlung, a small publisher founded in 1990, is currently trying to make Henry Handel Richardson's 1908 novel *Maurice Guest* 'accessible to a German audience once more'. Despite its East German connections, the novel was never published in the GDR. As the publisher writes on its website, however, a new translation of the 800-page novel represents a 'costly project' (*kostenträchtiges Projekt*).[21]

In second-hand bookshops and libraries throughout Germany you can still find the Australian *Erkundungen* volume, Marcus Clarke's *Lebenslänglich* and the many other Australian titles edited in the GDR. Occasionally translated into German for the first time and always carefully justified for the censorship authorities, they often sold out as soon as they hit East German bookshops. Readers in the GDR hardly needed all the arguments proffered in the compulsory afterwords, although they were unavoidable. Every single one of these titles testifies to the effort to offer a closed-in population a window onto the world and to open this window further and further with each period of political thawing. The corresponding censorship files and publishers' records show how, with each publishing effort, the room for manoeuvre within the GDR's literary system was surveyed anew and extended.

Notes

* This chapter was translated by Christina Spittel.

1 'Liste der auszusondernden Literatur. Herausgegeben von der Deutschen Verwaltung für Volksbildung in der sowjetischen Besatzungszone. Vorläufige Ausgabe nach dem Stand vom 1. April 1946' (Berlin: Zentralverlag, 1946). On the role of print culture in the process of post-war re-education, see also Christian Kanig, 'Literature and

Re-education in Occupied Germany, 1945–1949', in *Pressing the Fight: Print, Propaganda and the Cold War*, ed. Greg Barnhise and Catherine Turner (Amherst: University of Massachusetts Press, 2010), 71–88.
2. See the finding aid (in German): Janet Heidschmidt and Johanna Marschall-Reiser, *Ministerium für Kultur* (Ministry of Culture)*Teil 3: Hauptverwaltung Verlage und Buchhandel Druckgenehmigungsvorgänge, DR1 1947–1991* (Berlin: Bundesarchiv (BArch), 2010), accessed 18 January 2014, http://www.argus.bundesarchiv.de/dr1_druck/index.htm.
3. See, for example, Sara Jones, *Complicity, Censorship and Criticism: Negotiating Space in the GDR Literary Sphere* (Berlin: Walter de Gruyter, 2011).
4. Carola Gärtner-Scholle, *Christophs Abenteuer in Australien: Eine Erzählung aus der Goldgräberzeit*, report dated 19 December 1954, BArch DR1/1364/82. Gärtner-Scholle was one of a handful of highly influential censors in the GDR's early days, before, in the early 1960s, the assessment of manuscripts became a matter for scholars. Like her fellow assessors at the time, Gärtner-Scholle too had spent some years in Nazi prisons. But the fact that she was pardoned by Himmler, and even granted a scholarship, caused her to lose her place on the GDR's *Kultureller Beirat*, forcing her to censor freelance from her apartment. Siegfried Lokatis, 'Ein literarisches Quartett: Vier Hauptgutachter der Zensurbehörde', in *Fenster zur Welt: Eine Geschichte des DDR-Verlages Volk und Welt*, ed. Simone Barck and Siegfried Lokatis (Berlin: Christoph Links, 2005), 333–36 (336).
5. See Daniela Ihl, *Egon Erwin Kischs Reportagebuch Landung in Australien* (Frankfurt: Peter Lang, 2010).
6. Simone Barck, 'Der Verlag Kultur und Fortschritt, genannt KuFo (1947–1964)', in *Fenster zur Welt*, 35–43, 22.
7. Siegfried Lokatis, 'Nimm den Elefanten: Konturen einer Verlagsgeschichte', in *Fenster zur Welt*, 15–30, 22.
8. Hans Petersen, 'Über Faulkner und die Erschliessung der amerikanischen Literatur', in *Fenster zur Welt: Eine Geschichte des DDR-Verlages Volk und Welt*, 175–78 (175).
9. Burchett's titles include *Sonnenaufgang über Asien* (*Democracy with a Tommygun*), 1948; *Der Kalte Krieg in Deutschland* (*The Wreckers of Potsdam*), 1950; *China verändert sich* (*China Turns Over*), 1952; *Korea kämpft für den Frieden* (*Battle for Peace in Korea*) 1953; *An den Ufern des Mekong* (*Mekong Upstream*), 1959; *Land der Verheißung* (*New Life in the New Look*), 1962; *Schatten über dem Dschungel: Vietnam und Laos heute* (*The Furtive War: Vietnam and Laos Today*), 1963; *Partisanen contra Generale: Südvietnam* (*Special War, Special Defence: South Vietnam*), 1964.
10. Publisher's report on Burchett, *Land der Verheißung*, BArch DR1/3955/275–278.
11. See Nicole Moore's essay in Chapter 4.
12. BArch DR1/1884, 'Liste "Schwerabsetzbare Objekte"' stamped 17.3.1956. These were reprints following booksellers' requests, however, not original editions.
13. Nicole Moore and Christina Spittel, '*Bobbin Up* in the *Leseland*: Australian Literature in the German Democratic Republic', in *Republics of Letters: Literary Communities in Australia*, ed. Robert Dixon and Peter Kirkpatrick (Sydney: Sydney University Press, 2012), 113–26.
14. See Christina Spittel's essay in chapter 8.
15. Copy of Petersen's travel report dated 6 February 1987, forwarded to Joachim Specht by Goldschmidt of the GDR's Writers' Union with the comment: 'Please find enclosed for your interest a rare occasion: a travel report from Australia.' Stadtarchiv Dessau, N3.13–Specht 68.
16. External reader's report by Karl-Heinz Berger on Judith Wright, *Schweigen zwischen Wort und Wort*, BArch DR1/2396a/398–406.

17 Dr Hans Petersen of Volk und Welt to Elvira Pradel of Verlag Philip Reclam, 1 June 1981. (Universität Leipzig, Reclam-Archiv der Leipziger Buchwissenschaft), 426.
18 The original phrase used in this report for 'honorary Abo' is 'Abo h.c.', meaning 'Aboriginal honoris causa' (Latin, literally: 'for the sake of honour').
19 Report on Bahumir Wongar, *Der Schoß*, Friedrich Banke. BArch DR1/2133a/423–426.
20 Lokatis, 'Nimm den Elefanten', 21.
21 Connewitzer Verlagsbuchhandlung, 'H. H. Richardson: Lesung und Konzert', accessed 17 January 2014, http://www.cvb-leipzig.de/2013/10/20/h-h-richardson-lesung-und-konzert/. See also Henry Handel Richardson Society of Australia, 'November 2013 Newsletter', pdf, accessed 17 January 2014, http://www.henryhandelrichardsonsociety.org.au/documents/HHRNewsNovember13.

Chapter 2

TOWARDS A CROSS-BORDER CANON: MARCUS CLARKE'S *FOR THE TERM OF HIS NATURAL LIFE* BEHIND THE WALL

Russell West-Pavlov

National literatures, like the nations whose identity they are thought to codify, are often understood as having clearly defined borders. This, however, is a fallacious notion. A brief glance at the major European models for the nation-state reveals how fluid their borders can be: the frontiers of France have been blurred for much of its history (the early modern essayist Montaigne spoke, when travelling, not of leaving France but of entering 'the Italian language');[1] Alsace and Lorraine were long disputed territory and the Saar region passed back into German hands as late as 1955. Like France, Germany, which only consolidated itself as a nation in 1871, has seen its frontiers constantly fluctuate ever since, with some of them (the Oder-Neisse line) only definitively recognized as late as 1990. Meanwhile, Britain experienced what was effectively a border war in Ireland until the Good Friday referendum of 1998. Australia is one of the few nations in the world whose stable coastal contours are almost exactly isomorphic with the political boundaries of the nation and thus entirely fixed,[2] though this fixity is belied by the cynical fiddling of the national boundaries to create 'immigration exclusion zones' in the 1990s,[3] and forgets a more or less constant off-shore expatriate population of about 5 per cent at any one time.[4] As a continent, Australia appears to guarantee a reassuring sense of cultural continence.[5]

This Australian psychogeography of the coastal border reposes upon a multiple amnesia. It forgets that alongside the convenient distance of the southern continent, it was its island status that configured the Antipodes a natural prison, able to absorb the overflow from the British penal system.[6] (These paradoxical images resurfaced in the 1990s as the mythical centre of Australia became the locus of internment camps for illegal refugees: a 2004 photograph by Rosemary Laing, ironically titled *Welcome to Australia*, shows the razor-wire compound of the former Woomera Immigration Reception and Processing Centre, as the internment camp was euphemistically known, in a quintessential Outback expanse.[7] Such European Enlightenment origins mean that the paradigms of transportation and continental enclosure, continence and invasion, mobility and closure (in successive degrees of structural abstraction) have been from the outset (meaning in this case the white-Anglo *incipit* of 1788) inextricably intertwined with one another. Later originary narratives of the nation-state (in its geopolitical or strict modern sense) continue to register this ambivalence: the first Act of the newly federated parliament of 1901 aimed to re-establish a putative white-Anglo identity on the continent, but only because there was a non-white presence visible enough to demand legislative action.[8] Indeed, Australia had from time immemorial been a zone of immigration: earlier epochs saw indigenous peoples accessing Australia across a land bridge from the north; for thousands of years there was considerable traffic between indigenous north-east Australia and the Indonesian archipelago and between indigenous northern Australia and the Malaysian archipelago, extending as far as contacts with China.[9]

These ambiguities might be summed up in the notion of a 'translated' nation evoked, for instance, by David Malouf.[10] The notion of translation has the potential to accommodate the discrete outlines of the nation as cultural artefact while allowing its connections with an exterior to become visible to a greater or lesser degree.[11] To the extent that 'translation' is acknowledged as a constitutive operation of the national culture, the amnesia about the aporia of 'in/continence' can possibly be dispelled. It is for that reason, then, that this chapter addresses a case in translation studies in which the closure of the Australian continent and its attractiveness for transportation is explicitly at stake: the 1957 East German translation of Marcus Clarke's classic novel of continental incarceration, *For the Term of His Natural Life*.[12] In that novel and its German translation, the dialectic of openness and closure is not only the subject of the narrative itself; it may also have been the implicit preoccupation many GDR readers projected into their reception of the text. Such a translation also embodies, in its paradoxical invisibility to the original cultural context from which it arose,[13] the amnesia about constitutive processes of translation that may still characterize to some extent the Australian literary system.

Expanding the National Canon

Given these aporia within narratives of the nation and its borders, it should not come as a surprise to discover that some of the great literary epics of Australian national identity, such as Henry Handel Richardson's *The Fortunes of Richard Mahoney* (1917/1925/1929), or George Johnston's David Meredith trilogy *My Brother Jack* (1964), *Clean Straw for Nothing* (1969) and *A Cartload of Clay* (1971), all straddle Australia and Europe; more recent narratives of 'Australianness' have increasingly encompassed Asian contexts (see the fictions of Brian Castro, Lilian Ng or Tsu-Ming Teo). Indeed, as Graham Huggan has pointed out, 'to invoke the national specificity of Australia and/or Australian literature is thus often a conspicuously *trans*national activity'.[14]

This paradox notwithstanding, Australian 'literary scholars remain deeply attached to representations of Australia as a nation apart', as Gillian Whitlock noted more than a decade ago; 'a preference for thinking about Australian literature as a literature on its own remains intact.'[15] However, in the ensuing years, the presence of an 'outside' within the national paradigm has slowly begun to erode persistent notions of national culture as isomorphic with the continent itself. As Huggan also observed, there is a 'widespread feeling that, even if the paradigm of identity itself is not completely exhausted, the corresponding view of Australian literature as a container for *national* identity is increasingly under threat'.[16] As a contribution towards this paradigm shift, Jens Elze and I catalogued German-language translations of Australian literature published between 1789 and 2010.[17] That research project revealed an immense and constantly expanding panorama of Australian fiction (and to a lesser extent drama and poetry) in German translation, with a sum total of almost 3,000 titles when the compilation ceased, 2,000 of which had appeared in the previous decade alone. The aim of this project was to show that Australian literature as a domestic phenomenon was shadowed by a parallel canon of substantial proportions, which was largely unsuspected by domestic literary consumers and critics (and in some cases even by the writers themselves). If the 'translated' bodies of Australian literature around the world were mapped in a similarly thorough fashion, a remarkable polyglot 'other' canon of Australian literature would emerge. This 'other' canon would of course overlap with some of the non-English-language literature being produced within Australia to generate an immense, polylingual, global canon of Australian literature that would cast into question, ultimately, the very notion of the epithet 'Australian' that is attached to this canon.[18] (These comments could, to some extent, hold good for many national canons, whence, for instance, recent moves to insert American literary studies within a world context,[19] but the Australian national literary canon can be seen to have been for many years particularly insular in its self-understanding.) Such a mapping would take considerable but not infinite resources and has already been initiated by the 'Windows on Australia' research dataset within the *AustLit* database.[20]

From 'Off-Shore Canon' to 'Cross-Border Canon'

Elze and I coined the notion of the 'off-shore canon' as a way of thinking about an expanse of Australian literary production that had remained largely unconsidered by the domestic custodians of the national literary legacy. Because the national canon had hitherto been understood, like the national identity, as isomorphic with the coastal profile of the land mass, the phrase 'off-shore canon' helpfully expressed that neglected exteriority. The weakness of such a notion, however, was the flipside of its strength. It remained within the semantic field of coast and ocean, thus conceptually projecting the unknown face of Australian literature into another space, figuratively far beyond the horizon and separated from the known and familiar by a vast expanse of water. This contrasts starkly with the term, for instance, of a translative 'seam' joining by multiple threads 'proximate' translation partners and interwoven systems introduced by the South African critic and translator Leon de Kock.[21] The South African context that determines de Kock's theoretical undertaking foregrounds 'intranational' translation[22] and thus eschews the 'tyranny of distance' that dogged the work done by Elze and myself. To that extent, the idea of an off shore merely underwrote the inaccessibility of the other canon it was supposed to open up. The very fact of that other canon being composed in languages other than English both demanded a language-specific catalogue of the sort we had compiled, and paradoxically locked those other canons into an irreducible foreignness in which the extent of translation could be measured, but the qualitative texture and politics of the translated works themselves remained invisible. Almost by definition, the notion of an off-shore canon precluded the sort of earlier attempts I had made to explain the stylistics and politics of translated works such as Heinrich and Annemarie Böll's translation of Patrick White's *The Tree of Man* in the 1950s and Wolf Koehler's 1997 translation of Robert Dessaix's *Night Letters*.[23]

This problem can be elucidated in more theoretical terms by drawing on the insights of sociological and translational (poly)systems theory. The systems theory elaborated by the German sociologist Niklas Luhmann claims that the making of borders is always a two-stage process.[24] A dividing line between us and them, between here and there, between nation and foreignness (between system and environment' in systems-theory-speak) must be drawn, but the act of demarcation itself must be 'observed'. 'Observation' (*Beobachtung*) is a second-order process by virtue of which the now-established line of demarcation is taken up by the system thus cordoned off and, in a reflexive, self-reinforcing movement, is integrated into the systematicity of the system itself: 'We can conceive of system differentiation as a *replication, within a system, of the difference between a system and its environment.* Differentiation is thus understood as a reflexive and recursive form of system building.'²⁵ In other words, the frontier becomes constitutive of the system, or in this case, the community or nation's identity. The border must be 'observed': not only recorded but re-marked, or observed in the sense that rules or religious practices are observed (the affinity between the German *beobachten* and *achten* is visible but without the felicitous homonym produced by the English translation). The border demands constant observation, because the nation whose identity it facilitates must constantly be reasserted through the re-marking of those borders.

The system, according to Luhmann, always re-marks the border from within. It is incapable of assimilating anything from its environment that is not selected according to the code by which it has constituted itself. The environment remains properly invisible to the system except as a negative factor. What the system cannot contemplate is the presence of other systems outside its border, for which it, in turn, is an invisible environment. Indeed, according to systemic translation theory, national literary systems often ignore each other despite or even via their translative interactions, expressing thereby global geopolitical and economic inequalities.²⁶ It is precisely this systemic blindspot that I address in this chapter. In order to overcome this myopic elision of the other side of the shared border and that side's own processes of systemic observation, I want to suggest here an alternative to the concept of the off-shore canon. In its place, I wish to propose the term of the 'cross-border' canon. By this I mean neither merely a canon that crosses the border in the dynamic, spatial sense of geometrical translation, nor an expanded, polyglot canon that straddles the border(s). I mean also the notion of a canon that is 'across' the border, visible perhaps (on a clear day) from the domestic shore, and visible also, when properly scrutinized, in its own activity of gazing (or observation). Here, Emily Apter's notion of a highly conflicted war or border zone of translation activity may provide an apposite figure for my undertaking.²⁷

It is useful to explore the implications of this shift of terms by examining one of the texts documented in the earlier catalogue of German translations of Australian fiction: Marcus Clarke's *For the Term of His Natural Life* (1874; originally published as *His Natural Life* in serial form 1870–72), first published in 1957 by the East Berlin publisher Volk und Welt in Karl Heinrich's translation under the title of *Lebenslänglich*.²⁸ (Heinrich, a freelancer based in Babelsberg, had translated Katherine Susannah Prichard's *Golden Miles* in 1954 and subsequently translated Frank Hardy's *The Four-Legged Lottery* in 1958.) *Lebenslänglich* was one of a rush of GDR translations from Australia, beginning with Hardy's *Power without Glory* in 1952 and Prichard's novel in 1954, but is particularly interesting for the way its carceral thematics resonated with a central tension within GDR history: imprisonment and escape. Heinrich translated an epic narrative of transportation to an Australian penal colony in the context of a German 'democratic' republic whose external borders, already heavily policed even from 1946 onwards (that is, preceding the transition from Soviet Occupation Zone to Democratic Republic in October 1949), were totally sealed off by the time of the 1957 translation; at that point in time, the definitive closure of the internal border around the porous enclave of West Berlin in 1961 was a mere four years distant.[29] Thus the rhetoric of the prison camps (*Konzentrationslager*) mobilized by the East German afterword and its commentaries on the Australian penal colony (*Strafkolonie*)[30] would resonate with West German propaganda against Berlin's 'concentration-camp boundary fence'. Even the East German politburo was aware of the unpleasant associations of the first-generation barbed-wire Berlin Wall.[31] It is significant, then, that the book version of *For the Term of His Natural Life*, rather than the longer, original serial version of 1870–72, formed the basis for the Heinrich translation. Excluding as it does both the period before and after imprisonment, the book focussed upon a purely carceral universe. In its truncation of all other aspects it perhaps spoke particularly eloquently to a GDR audience aware of its own isolation from neighbours both to the West and East.

In the context of the GDR, the resonances of the term 'cross-border observation' can be made more immediate by evoking a visual topos familiar to anyone who has studied the GDR and its constitutive border structures. The image of the East German border guard gazing back at the photographer/spectator/self through a pair of binoculars (or more disconcertingly, a camera) is a recurring one in the context of photography of the Berlin Wall.[32] In a country whose borders were marked by watch-towers, searchlights, alarm-trip wires, indeed a whole state bureaucracy of surveillance, systemic observation takes on a quite different tenor. According to this visual topos, the other on the far side of the border observes the border and what is beyond it, namely the self. Observation is necessary, for within the psychogeography of the GDR, Western neighbours were direct threats to geopolitical legitimacy (internationally unrecognized until 1972) and to national autopoeisis. Observation was a mode of self-preservation in the face of influences that threatened to unravel the national systemic structure. This, indeed, was precisely the phenomenon experienced by the GDR as millions of its skilled workers and professionals fled in the years leading up to 1961, bringing the economy almost to the point of collapse and leading the East German government to order the overnight construction of what would become the Berlin Wall.[33] What this image of border observation reminds us about the other canon produced by translative activity is the need to pay attention to an agency invisible from the point of view of the domestic canon. It reveals that any frontier has two sides and two populations, in a way that the image of the off-shore canon fails to capture.

Schlösser's Postface

In what follows, I read the 'paratext' that accompanied Heinrich's translation, the *Nachwort* (literally, afterword) or postface provided by the then doyen of East German English studies, Anselm Schlösser. Paratexts, in Genette's conception, are thresholds to the text, aiding or guiding the reader in accessing the textual space; in this case, the paratext also acts as a threshold guiding the text as it enters the zone of surveillance that is the GDR literary field.[34] The postface was intended to 'translate' the translated work for East German readers and, by the same token, closely observe and monitor, not without facilitating it in a limited way, such cross-border traffic. The postface is a paradigmatic example of observation, an autopoetic communicative event designed to reinforce the systemic coherence of the highly regulated East German literary field. This, it would appear, was all the more necessary because the possible analogies between Australia as a penal colony and a prison-like GDR would have been evident to all but the most obtuse of readers. (From 1952 onwards, unmonitored exit, de facto prohibited, was only possible via West Berlin, and that route would be closed in August 1961.) Such heavy policing of the GDR's border was necessary to prevent black-market infiltration of the flagging socialist economy, but even more so, the constant drain of labour power. In this context, it is ironic that Volk und Welt's in-house editorial report on the translation manuscript of *Lebenslänglich* was written, with a positive recommendation for publication, by one Fritz Raddatz, the commissioning editor.[35] By the time the book received its first reviews in 1958, Raddatz himself was leaving the GDR for the Federal Republic, where he went to work for the Rowohlt publishing house in Hamburg.[36] Doubtless this invidious isomorphism between the two carceral nations, socialist East Germany and erstwhile penal colony Australia, was part of the unavowed fascination the convict continent narrative clearly exerted over GDR readers for the half-century of their captivity. For Clarke's novel in translation went through a phenomenal number of reprints, with 11 hardcover editions between 1957 and 1972, and a further six paperback editions between 1979 and 1990.[37] For a small publishing system in which paper was scarce and literary publications subject to quota-like controls, this was an astonishingly successful career for a work of fiction. And indeed, Clarke's *Lebenslänglich* in the Heinrich translation can be assessed as the most popular non-German fiction title sold in the GDR.[38]

The publisher Volk und Welt commissioned a postface to accompany the text from Anselm Schlösser, a leading figure in GDR English studies. Born in Jena in 1910, he had completed his doctorate on German translations of English literature at the University of Jena in the mid-1930s, publishing it as a small pamphlet in 1936 and as a major monograph, as German PhD

Figure 2.1 Cover of the fourteenth edition of Marcus Clarke's *Lebenslänglich*, a large-format paperback, designed by Dieter Heidenreich (Berlin: Volk und Welt, 1982).

regulations required and still do require, in 1937.[39] He published a number of pedagogical and popular literary critical books on Shakespeare from the mid-1960s, and pedagogical handbooks such as an overview of English literature for students of the distance-learning program at the PH Potsdam (Potsdam Teacher Training College, now the University of Potsdam). In this way, he exerted a formative influence on the training of GDR English teachers, at the forefront of one of the institutional inculcations of 'ideological state apparatuses' (to take Althusser's terminology and his interest in the place of education in the reproduction of ideology). From the mid-1950s Schlösser had also produced dozens of introductions or postfaces to editions of selections of English writers such as Shakespeare, Nashe, Pepys, Swift, Goldsmith and Galsworthy (the last in cooperation with his wife, Jutta Schlösser, as translator). This level of productivity was indicative of his prominent role as a public mediator of high-cultural texts from the English literary tradition. Given his doctoral research, a stock taking of the incoming translation patterns of the four decades up to the mid-1930s and evaluation of the German reception of those works, it was fitting that in the era after the war he should play such a role in the active formation of the reception of English literature in the GDR. An indefatigable producer of mediating blurbs, his role was often to monitor the literary boundaries of the German Democratic Republic and those English-language works that traversed them.

In the course of his career Schlösser wielded considerable institutional power, holding such prestigious offices as co-founder and editor of the major GDR English studies journal *Zeitschrift für Anglistik und Amerikanistik*.[40] From 1951 onwards he was a professor of English and until his retirement in the late 1970s, head of the English Department at the Humboldt University in Berlin,[41] a flagship institution whose geographical proximity to the seats of GDR power in the district of Berlin-Mitte reinforced its role in the ideological apparatus of the socialist state. Only a small number of institutions in the GDR offered English studies, and as the language of the class enemy, it was a heavily monitored subject with intense ideological surveillance of those selected for degree programs. These clearly political factors say something about the institutional location of the author of the Clarke postface at the nexus of the GDR publishing 'apparatus' (rather than 'industry' in the Western sense of the word), the highly politicized and policed secondary and tertiary education sectors, and the socialist public sphere. These overlapping positions in turn indicate the function that such a postface was to fulfil with regard to a text translated out of the language of the class enemy – and in connection with a political and cultural zone already familiarized for an East German public by Egon Kisch's not uncritical *Landung in Australien*, which was first published from Dutch exile in 1937 and then extensively republished in the early years of the

GDR.[42] (Emblematically, *Landung in Australien* features a world map placing Europe and Australia in relationship to one another; it also includes a number of chapters dealing with convict history.[43])

Schlösser's piece was clearly intended, at a purely pragmatic level, as an explanatory gloss contextualizing the distant colonial context for a postwar socialist reading public. As Raddatz, the commissioning editor at Volk und Welt, wrote prescriptively: 'Ein ausführliches Nachwort müsste die vielen verschütterten historischen und literarischen Bezüglichkeiten wiederherstellen'[44] (A detailed afterword would have to reconstruct the many buried historical and literary contexts). East German readers needed to understand the context in which early nineteenth-century British society found itself obliged to expel its unwanted elements and transport them around the globe to the Antipodes. (Schlösser would point to the dysfunctional character of the industrial revolution and in particular to political unrest.) Yet the afterword did not merely supplement the unsaid of the text's own implicit contemporary knowledge so as to fill gaps in readerly comprehension (as for instance the sober explanatory notes at the end of the volume sought to do (671–77)). It also performed more interventionist roles, seeking to guide or perhaps even coerce the public apprehension of the text. To that extent it can be read as an index of the text's officially intended reception in the closed space of the GDR. In the jargon of systems theory, it is an act of observation (surveillance) that is intended to enforce observation (docile reception in the sense of religious observation) among its readers.

The opening sections of the postface contain passages that are not merely assessments of the original text but can be read as coded performatives, pre-emptive prophecies that would prove to be self-fulfilling. Thus, when Schlösser writes of Clarke's text, 'Das Echo erstreckte sich über Jahrzehnte' (The echo resounded for decades) (662), he is priming, and thereby accurately predicting, the text's thirty-year publishing trajectory in the GDR, in which an East German version of Clarke would become the 'hervorragender Vertreter der australischen Literatur' (the most prominent representative of Australian literature) (662). And indeed, Schlösser's preface does seem to have steered public reception of the text, with reviews of the novel clearly depending upon it heavily, though this practice appears to have been widespread in GDR literary reviewing. Schlösser's postface was quoted in the review by Annalis Thuemmel of 3 April 1958 in the Dresden *Werk-Echo*.[45] A review of the translation by a D. Hornauf in the Frankfurt-an-der-Oder *Neuer Tag* of 11 December 1958 was even more indebted to Schlösser, silently plagiarising three of its total of four paragraphs from the opening sections of the postface.[46] Such plagiarism is perhaps less an index of a docilely reproductive reception than of the institutional pressures exerted by the GDR literature system.

Those pressures, however, were clearly neither unified nor singular. This is indicated by multiple, and at times mutually irreconcilable, intentions that appear to motivate Schlösser's postface. Schlösser stresses Clarke's importance via a thematic analysis of the novel, arguing that the author's relative neglect as a figure within English literary history was the result of his critical stance: 'Die Vermutung, daß diese Außerachtlassung etwas mit der Thematik des Romans "Lebenslänglich" zu tun hat, liegt nicht allzu fern' (The suspicion that this neglect may have something to do with the theme of the novel ... is not entirely unfounded) (662). He then contrasts the topicality and significance of Clarke's theme – publicizing and denouncing the convict system – with the uneven quality of the picture painted by the author and the varying plausibility of the portraiture ('die ungleiche Qualität der Wiedergabe und die unterschiedliche Echtheit der verwendeten Farben' (662)). This unevenness, however, he justifies by pointing to stereotypical figures (Schlösser speaks of *Schablonenhaftigkeit* – literally, the quality of cheap stencilled images) (662), in other great writers of nineteenth-century English literature, going on to place Clarke, in a highly ambivalent gesture, within the great but equally flawed lineage of Dickens: 'ein Vorwurf, von dem freilich auch Charles Dickens nicht ganz frei zu sprechen ist' (an accusation that even Charles Dickens, it must be admitted, cannot entirely avoid) (663).

Schlösser is at pains to stress that in his opinion the intertextual relationships informing Clarke's work do not lessen its aesthetic value by reducing his originality, but rather place him solidly within a long literary tradition, including Defoe, Fielding, Smollett, Dickens, Collins, Godwin, Hardy, Eliot, Lytton Bulwer, Reade, and even Hugo and Poe (663–65); Schlösser is clearly seeking a residual high-cultural legitimization in a 'workers' and farmers' republic', never quite able to shake off its inherited awe of Enlightenment *Bildung*. Ironically, this was something that Clarke himself, working on the colonial periphery of the British Empire, persistently did; he and others of his ilk sensed a nagging need to reference metropolitan predecessors in an effort to legitimize a literary undertaking in ways that the colonial cultural zone (or its felt absence) did not seem capable of doing.[47] In this respect, the source and target cultures of this act of translation, colonial Australia and socialist East Germany, shared a common cultural tenor – namely, the paradoxical, indeed fraught, status of high culture in a polity often dominated by working-class pragmatism (or philistinism, depending on the point of view).[48] The pressure exerted by this partly marginal status of high culture is exemplified in Schlösser's simultaneous insistence that Clarke's work, if flawed by contrast with the great classics it is nonetheless related to, is not to be condemned for its journalistic quality (664). '[D]okumentarische Wahrheit' (documentary truth (664)) is a term Schlösser uses with approval, for it resonates with the dominant paradigm of socialist realism defended by such scholars of the socialist intelligentsia as Lukács in his later phase,[49] or with the work of more popular writers or journalists such as Kisch, mentioned above. Thus Schlösser's preface oscillates between enumerating weaknesses and strengths, original genius, indeed 'episches' (epic) and 'monumentale[s]' (monumental) quality (663), stereotypical and derivative imitation (662), and empirical realism (he speaks of Clarke's 'exakte Dokumentation' (exact documentation) in the tradition of Comte, or of his 'Ausschnitte aus [der] Wirklichkeit' (snippets of reality) (666)). The newly consecrated East German literary tradition, which needed to assert itself over against that of the other Germany, had to be buttressed as a socialist literary tradition by acquiring eligible writers with a decent critical pedigree and a commitment to realism, as opposed to formalism – whence the praise of Clarke's realist qualities. The East-German counter-canon also needed, however, to be placed within a global socialist tradition. That impetus drove the necessity of translation but also brought with it the danger of politically incorrect liaisons with 'bourgeois' writers. Thus residual traces of 'bourgeois' impurity had to be explained away so the import was not contaminated by its origins. Finally, despite Schlösser's espousal of a worker aesthetic of realism, the postface is reluctant to jettison residual 'bourgeois' liberal notions of content-based analysis and literary quality, entrenched critical values from the pre-war academy, which continued to sit uneasily alongside Marxist terminology (e.g. *die literarische Warenfabrikation* (production of literary commodities) (663)), in East German literature departments. The tensions between the hegemonic political aesthetics of documentary realism and the residual bourgeois aesthetics of the *Bildungsbürger* and their respect for inherited traditions evinced in Schlösser's piece demonstrate how fractured and contradictory the discursive techniques of surveillance and observation could be. All the more reason, then, to fear the potentially refractory reading techniques of the public itself.

Observation and Its Aporias

All these contradictions culminate in one central aporia, namely the tension between what the critic knows and what readers potentially know. If the original text needs to be supplemented in its contextually bound hermeticism, there is another sense, for Schlösser, in which it is limited, determined less by mere historical, cultural and geographical distance, and more by the ideological affiliations of its author. Schlösser points up a final deficit in the text in its blindness to aspects of its own historical moment, which only the later reader, with the benefit of historical-materialist hindsight in particular, is in a position to elucidate. In its 'Schilderung der furchtbaren Kehrseite der kapitalistischen Zivilisation' (depiction of the awful shadow side of capitalist civilization) (669), the text can be placed within a historical continuity that connects it to today's realities: 'Sie ist trotzdem nicht überholt. Denn wenn auch die damaligen lokalen Erscheinungsformen abgelöst worden sind, so ist das dahinterstehende Prinzip der Brutalität der Gesellschaftsordung im Monopolkapitalismus nur noch schärfer hervorgetreten' (The text is nonetheless very contemporary. For, although the specific local manifestations of the time have disappeared, the underlying principle of the brutality of the social order of monopoly capitalism has become more evident than ever before) (669). Indeed, in a final, hyperbolic analogy, Schlösser argues that the text can be seen as a forerunner of the GDR's own critique of a German fascism whose redeemed successor the new East German socialism claimed to be:

> In mehr als einer Hinsicht waren die Strafkolonien die Vorläufer der faschistischen Konzentrationslager. Sie waren es insofern, als zu den Deportierten eine nicht geringe Zahl politischer Gefangener gehörte – namentlich irische Aufständische von 1798 und Führer der Chartistenbewegung der 1840er Jahre –, eine Tatsache, die Clarke nicht einmal erwähnt, da seine Kritik bei aller Schärfe doch durch klassenbedingte Hemmungen in bestimmten Grenzen gehalten wurde. (669)

> [In many respects the penal colonies were the predecessors of the fascist concentration camps, to the extent that among the transported convicts were a large number of political prisoners – among others, the rebels of 1798 and leaders of the Chartist movement of the 1840s – a fact that Clarke never once mentions, as his criticisms, for all their acuity, were contained by certain class-defined limits.]

Schlösser implements the standard GDR elision of European Jewry as the main target of the Holocaust so as to bring Clarke's novel into line with an historical teleology which, he claims, Clarke himself could not recognize. Hidebound as he was in a liberal world view, according to Schlösser's narrative, Clarke misguidedly believed society could be changed by humanitarian impulses within the boundaries of the existing system.

> Er mochte als Bürger des 19. Jahrhunderts glauben, daß es innerhalb des bestehenden Systems möglich sei, nicht nur humanitäre Reformen, sondern darüber hinaus das Postulat der Menschlichkeit durchzusetzen, und ahnte wohl kaum, wie stark seine Erfassung der Wirklichkeit ans Grundsätzliche rührte. (669–70)

> [As a citizen of the nineteenth century, he wished to believe that it was possible within the existing system not merely to carry out humanitarian reform, but beyond that, to defend the principle of human dignity, hardly realizing how close he was to essential issues.]

Clarke's ambivalent mix of morally outraged critique and liberal systemic acquiescence – Schlösser speaks explicitly of '[d]ie Zwiespältigkeit Clarkes' (Clarke's ambivalence) (663) – is more accurately mirrored, according to Schlösser, in tortured, ambivalent characters in the novel such as the chaplain, Mr North (669).

By contrast, the later reader, if properly guided by a qualified literary expert, and the translation itself as a recontextualised version of the original, can understand better than the author the original nineteenth-century context. This is because, according to Schlösser, the reader, the commentator, and the translator all have the benefit of supplementary historical experience:

> Dies zu erkennen fällt dem heutigen Leser nach weiteren acht Dezennien kapitalistischer Entwicklung leichter. Man fühlt und begreift die Wesensverwandschaft der Hölle von Macquarie Harbour oder Norfolk Island mit dem Inferno imperialistischer Kriege und versteht die Aussage des Buches in einem weiteren Sinne, als der Verfasser es selbst beabsichtigte. (670)
>
> [It is easier for today's reader to recognize this, after eight decades of capitalist development. One feels and understands the existential resemblance between the hell of Macquarie Harbour or Norfolk Island with the inferno of imperialist wars, and grasps the message of the book in a broader sense than the author himself intended.]

The author's ideological limitations can only be overcome by 80 years of subsequent experiences of capitalism – and by the act of translation, aided by commentary – constituting thereby a double, reinforced supplementarity supplying the lacunae in the original. This position of historical hindsight is performed by the postface itself, looking back upon the translation, which in turn looks back upon the original. In systemic terms, the afterword performs observation of observation, thus laying bare the almost obsessive replication of autopoetic processes never assured of their own effectiveness.

This lack of self-assurance inhabits the fabric of the text itself. Schlösser's final 'Man' ('one') ('Man fühlt und begreift [...]') is, like much of the afterword, a coercive rhetorical gesture in which the commentator corrals the reader into a neutral, collective 'one' by virtue of which potential differences of opinion are elided. The synthesis of the speaking commentator and projected reader positions, in fact, forcibly assimilates the latter to the former. But such a gesture betrays a fundamental mistrust, indeed fear, of the reader. Thus the reader's understanding, although closely monitored and shepherded by the critic, must be observed in a projective act of imagination so as to preemptively perform and thus inculcate observance of socialist dogma – or perhaps, in a paradoxical twist, to prevent the reader observing too much in her or his own way.

This paradox is anticipated in the closing phrases of Raddatz's in-house recommendation to go ahead with publication of the text. Raddatz's report underlines the necessity of an accompanying afterword in apparently contradictory terms:

> Es gibt erstaunlich erbitterte Angriffe auf die englische Gesellschaft, wenig humorig meist, sondern sehr direkt. Ein ausführliches Nachwort müsste die vielen verschütterten historischen und literarischen Bezüglichkeiten wiederherstellen.[50]
>
> [There are astonishingly bitter attacks on English society, mostly unsoftened by humour and very direct. A detailed afterword ought to reconstruct the many buried historical and literary contexts.]

There is a curious contradiction in Raddatz's two sentences. On the one hand, the book is openly critical of the transportation system and the elites that benefit from it; on the other hand, the buried connections necessary to the understanding of the novel in its original context are lacking, both in the text itself, and in its readers. The report assumes a deficit on the part of the text, to make its now-distant context explicit for today's audience, and a matching incapacity of contemporary readers to understand its allusions. At the same time, however, the report may be counteracting not so much a double deficit as a double excess: the potential of the text to produce unruly meanings in collaboration with a public aware of the twists and turns of history.

Both the annotations to the publisher's application for government imprimatur, which makes reference to 'Australian prison camps' and 'commandants',[51] and Schlösser's postface (669–70) make explicit connections with the Nazi concentration camps, whose distant predecessors, they claim, more or less explicitly, were the penal colonies of the Enlightenment. Yet such tenuous and tendentious historical connections could easily escape from their intended teleological lineages. GDR audiences were probably well aware, for instance, that the Sachsenhausen concentration camp on the northern outskirts of Berlin was converted directly into a Soviet internment camp in 1945, even if they had no reliable information about conditions there, which were such that at least 12,000 of its 60,000 inmates died before its closure in 1950.[52] Such audiences would, potentially, have been susceptible to interpreting the novel against the grain. Berlin had seen a workers' uprising in 1953 that was put down with greater difficulty than expected by the Soviet occupation forces; the GDR regime was aware of a need to legitimize its rule, and the reception of literary texts with a critical socialist realist thematic needed to be steered in the right direction. And finally, by the time of the translation, East Germans had been living with borders closed to the Federal Republic for half a decade, even if most of them did not expect the sudden sealing-off of West Berlin in

August 1961. Thus the apparent contradiction in Raddatz's closing statement can be read contextually. It can be understood as expressive of the conflict between politically desired reading and potentially deviant understandings of the text. It expresses approval of literary texts whose critical task could be co-opted by the propagandist program of the GDR, and at the same time, an anxiety that such critique might in turn be wielded against the government by 'lästige Zwischenrufer, dessen Widerhall tunlichst abgedämpft werden sollte' (troublemakers shouting from the audience, whose resonance had to be muffled as much as possible) (662), to turn against its author Schlösser's own description of Clarke's criticism of the British establishment of the day. The task of the postface was to pre-empt such oppositional voices, observing the literary field in advance, as it were, so as to reduce the potential disruptive 'resonance' (*Widerhall*) of a highly unstable literary text bristling with potential analogies between two carceral nations. The notion of a cross-border canon captures just this sense of the dangerous proximity between neighbours, even if geographically, they are off-shore in their real distance – a proximity within a 'translation zone' that necessitated intensive surveillance so as to prevent the transfer of subversive ideas between a fictional Antipodean past and a lived socialist present.

Notes

1. Quoted in John Hale, *The Civilization of Europe in the Renaissance* (London: Harper Collins, 1993), 34.
2. Ien Ang, 'Racial/Spatial Anxiety: "Asia" in the Psychogeography of Australian Whiteness', in *The Future of Australian Multiculturalism: Reflections of the Twentieth Anniversary of Jean Martin's 'The Migrant Presence'*, ed. Ghassan Hage and Roanne Couch (Sydney: The Research Institute for Humanities and Social Sciences, 1999), 189–204.
3. Anja Schwarz and Justine Lloyd, 'The Pacific Solution meets Fortress Europe: Emerging Parallels in Transnational Refugee Regimes', in *Polyculturalism and Discourse*, ed. Russell West-Pavlov and Anja Schwarz (Amsterdam: Rodopi, 2007), 247–70.
4. Nicholas Brown, 'The Changing Resonance of the "International" in Australian Politics and Culture', in *Who's Australia? – Whose Australia? Culture, Society and Politics in Contemporary Australia*, ed. Russell West-Pavlov (Trier: WVT, 2005), 43–64.
5. Laura Joseph, 'Dreaming Phantom and Golems: Elements of the Place beyond Nation in *Carpentaria* and *Dreamhunter*', *Journal of the Association for the Study of Australian Literature (JASAL)*, special issue, 'Australian Literature in a Global World' (2009), vol. 6, accessed 10 May 2012, www.nla.gov.au/openpublish/index.php/jasal/article/view/848/1759.
6. Elizabeth McMahon, 'Encapsulated Space: The Paradise-Prison of Australia's Island Imaginary', *Southerly* 65, no. 1 (2005): 20–29.
7. Rosemary Laing, *Welcome to Australia* (2004), large-format photograph, Bendigo Art Gallery.
8. Pat Grimshaw, 'Federation as a Turning Point in Australian History', *Australian Historical Studies*, special issue, 'Challenging Histories', 33, no. 118 (2002): 25–41.

9 Regina Ganter with Julia Martinez and Gary Lee, *Mixed-Relations: Asian-Aboriginal Contact in North Australia* (Crawley, WA: University of Western Australia Press, 2006); D. J. Mulvaney, *Encounters in Place: Outsiders and Aboriginal Australians 1606–1985* (St Lucia: University of Queensland Press, 1989); Tony Swain, *A Place for Strangers: Towards a History of Australian Indigenous Place* (Cambridge: Cambridge University Press, 1993).
10 See David Malouf interviewed by Jim Davidson, *Meanjin* 39 (1980): 323–34 (327).
11 On the latter option see Lawrence Venuti, *The Translator's Invisibility: A History of Translation* (London: Routledge, 1995).
12 Marcus Clarke, *Lebenslänglich*, trans. Karl Heinrich (Berlin: Volk und Welt, 1957).
13 Stephen Murray-Smith, the editor of the first re-publication of Clarke's novel in unabridged (originally serial) form of *His Natural Life* in 1970, acknowledges only a nineteenth-century German translation of *For the Term of His Natural Life* and appears to be unaware of the 1957 translation – see Introduction, Clarke, *His Natural Life* (Harmondsworth: Penguin, 1970), 7–23 (13). Ironically, he was in Berlin in 1957 on a Peace Council mission at the very moment the translation appeared (biographical entry in the *Australian Dictionary of Biography* online, accessed 11 October 2013, http://adb.anu.edu.au/biography/murray-smith-stephen-14885).
14 Graham Huggan, *Australian Literature: Postcolonialism, Racism, Transnationalism* (Oxford: Oxford University Press, 2007), 2.
15 Gillian Whitlock, 'Australian Literature: Points for Departure', *Australian Literary Studies* 19, no. 2 (1999): 152–62 (153).
16 Huggan, *Australian Literature*, 10.
17 Russell West-Pavlov and Jens Elze-Volland, *Australian Literature in German Translation: A Catalogue of Titles, Translators and Trends 1789–2010* (Berlin: Institut für Englische Philologie, Freie Universität Berlin, 2010); Russell West-Pavlov and Jens Elze, 'Translation-History as a Provocation for Literary Studies: A Case Study on the Translation of Australian Literature into German', *Anglistik: Mitteilungen des deutschen Anglistenverbands* 22, no. 1 (2011): 215–31.
18 See for instance Sneja Gunew, L. Houbein, A. Karakostas-Seda and J. Mahyuddin, eds, *A Bibliography of Australian Multicultural Writers* (Geelong, Vic.: Deakin University Press, 1992).
19 See for instance, David Damrosch, *What is World Literature?* (Princeton: Princeton University Press, 2003), and Wai Chee Dimock, *Through Other Continents: American Literature across Deep Time* (Princeton: Princeton University Press, 2006).
20 'Windows on Australia: Perceptions In and Through Translation' research community (n.d.), www.austlit.edu.au/specialistDatasets/WindowsOnAustralia.
21 See Leon de Kock, 'South Africa in the Global Imaginary: An Introduction', *Poetics Today* 22, no. 2 (2001): 263–98.
22 See for instance Leon de Kock, '"A Change of Tongue": Questions of Translation', in *The Cambridge History of South African Literature*, ed. David Attwell and Derek Attridge (Cambridge: Cambridge University Press, 2012), 739–56.
23 Russell West-Pavlov, *Transcultural Graffiti: Diasporic Writing and the Teaching of Literary Studies* (Amsterdam/New York: Rodopi, 2005), 61–80, 97–109.
24 Luhmann's systems theory, which was immensely influential in the German humanities in the 1980s and 1990s, has never had any sustained reception within the English-speaking academy. Accessible introductions in English to Luhmann's notoriously difficult work and isolated indices of translation into Anglo-American theory are Paul R. Harrison's very clear and concise 'Niklas Luhmann and the Theory of Social

Systems', in *Reconstructing Theory: Gadamer, Habermas, Luhmann*, ed. David Roberts (Carlton, Vic.: Melbourne University Press, 1995), 65–90; William Rasch and Cary Wolfe, eds, *Observing Complexity: Systems Theory and Postmodernity* (Mineapolis: University of Minnesota Press, 2000); and William Rasch, *Niklas Luhmann's Modernity: The Paradoxes of Differentiation* (Stanford: Stanford University Press, 2000).

25 Niklas Luhmann, *The Differentiation of Society*, trans. Stephen Holmes and Charles Larmore (New York: Columbia University Press, 1982), 230–31.

26 See Itamar Even-Zohar, 'Laws of Literary Interference', *Poetics Today* 11, no. 1 (Spring 1990): 53–72 (62); also 'Polysystem Theory', *Poetics Today* 1, no. 1–2 (Autumn 1979): 287–310.

27 Emily Apter, *The Translation Zone: A New Comparative Literature* (Princeton: Princeton University Press, 2006).

28 A three-volume English translation, *Deportiert auf Lebenszeit*, was published in Berlin by Otto Janke in 1876, presumably based on the 1874 George Robertson (Melbourne) and 1875 Richard Bentley (London) first editions titled *His Natural Life*. No German library possesses a copy of the 1874–75 versions, suggesting that this version may have been unavailable in East Germany by the time of Karl Heinrich's translation. The Volk und Welt translations reference *For the Term of His Natural Life*, presumably one of the versions subsequent to the 1884–85 reissues of the novel. The Staatsbibliothek in Berlin, for instance, has a 1926 print (London: Macmillan) and a 1949 print (Melbourne: Hallcraft).

29 Jürgen Ritter and Peter Joachim Lapp, *Die Grenze: Ein deutsches Bauwerk*, 5th rev. ed. (Berlin: Christoph Links, 2006), 13–48.

30 Volk und Welt, 'Antrag auf Druckgenehmigung' ('Application for Permission to Print'), Marcus Clarke, *Lebenslänglich*, 28 February 1957, BArch DR1/3958a/332–337; Anselm Schlösser 'Nachwort', in Marcus Clarke, *Lebenslänglich*, trans. Karl Heinrich (Berlin: Volk und Welt, 1957), 661–70 (669). Subsequent references in the body of the text.

31 Frederick Taylor, *The Berlin Wall: 13 August 1961–9 November 1989* (London: Bloomsbury, 2006), 218, 266.

32 Dieter Hildebrandt, *Es geschah an der Mauer/It Happened at the Wall/...* exhibition catalogue 'Vom 13. August zur modernen Grenze' (Berlin: Haus am Checkpoint Charlie, 1974), 25, 46; Ritter and Lapp, *Die Grenze*, 63, 81, 93, 159.

33 Taylor, *The Berlin Wall*, 150–54.

34 See Gérard Genette, 'Introduction to the Paratext', trans. Marie Maclean, *New Literary History* 22, no. 2 (Spring 1991): 261–72; *Paratexts: Thresholds of Interpretation*, trans. Jane E. Lewin (Cambridge: Cambridge University Press, 1997). Interestingly, the title of the English translation reverses the position of the English subtitle: *Seuils* (Paris: Seuil, 1987). For Genette's interest in literary space, see 'Espace et langage', in *Figures I* (Paris: Seuil, 1966), 101–8, and 'La Littérature et l'espace', in *Figures II: Essais* (Paris: Seuil, 1969), 43–48.

35 Fritz Raddatz, commissioning editor's report for Volk und Welt on translation of *Lebenslänglich* (Berlin: Bundesarchiv, n.d.).

36 Roland Links, 'Fritz J. Raddatz: Eine treibende Kraft der Anfangsjahre', in *Fenster zur Welt: Eine geschichte des DDR-Verlages Volk & Welt*, ed. Simone Barck and Siegfried Lokatis (Berlin: Links, 2003), 337–38 (337).

37 Karl Heinrich's translation of *Lebenslänglich* was published by Volk und Welt in Berlin in hardback in 1957, with 10 subsequent print runs in 1958, 1961, 1962, 1963, 1964 (two print runs), 1965, 1969 and 1972 (two print runs). The six subsequent paperback

editions came out in 1979, 1980, 1982, 1984, 1988 and 1990. These editions are documented in the German digital library databases SWB, GBV, KOBV and BVB, and can be accessed also via the DNB (German National Library) online database.
38 Personal email communication with Siegfried Lokatis, 30 September 2013.
39 Anselm Schlösser, *Die Aufnahme der englischen Literatur in Deutschland von 1895 bis 1934* (Würzburg: Triltsch, 1936).
40 Sandra Schaur, 'Zwischen Nische und Öffentlichkeit – die *ZAA*', in *Britische Literatur in der DDR*, ed. Barbara Korte, Sandra Schaur and Stefan Welz (Würzburg: Königshausen & Neumann, 2008), 159–181, 161.
41 Gerhard Oestreich, ed., *Kürschners deutscher Gelehrten-Kalender 1954* (Berlin: de Gruyter, 1954), 2057–58.
42 Egon Erwin Kisch, *Landung in Australien* (Amsterdam: Allert de Lange, 1937). Aufbau Verlag in Berlin brought out reprints in 1948, 1951 and 1953; Volk und Wissen in Berlin brought out an edition in 1950; and the Verlag der Nation brought out an edition under licence from Aufbau in 1953. Aufbau continued to reprint *Landung in Australien* as part of Volume 4 of Kisch's complete works, with printings in 1962, 1978 and 1984.
43 Egon Erwin Kisch, *Landung in Australien* (Berlin: Verlag der Nation, 1953), 5, 183–91, 196–97.
44 Raddatz, commissioning editor's report, 6.
45 Annalis Thuemmel, '*Lebenslänglich:* Ein lesenswertes Buch', *Werk-Echo* [Dresden], vol. 7 (3 April 1958): n.p.
46 D. Hornauf, '*Lebenslänglich*, Marcus Clarke', *Neuer Tag* [Frankfurt an der Oder] (11 December [?] 1958): n.p.
47 See for instance Simon During, 'Out of England: Literary Subjectivity in the Australian Colonies, 1788–1867', in *Imagining Australia: Literature and Culture in the New World*, ed. Judith Ryan and Chris Wallace-Crabbe (Cambridge: Harvard University Press, 2007), 3–21; Andrew McCann, *Marcus Clarke's Bohemia: Literature and Modernity in Colonial Melbourne* (Melbourne: University of Melbourne Press, 2004), 187; 'Marcus Clarke's *His Natural Life*', in *The Oxford History of the Novel in English: The World Novel to 1950*, ed. Ralph Crane, Jane Stafford and Mark Williams (Oxford University Press, 2016).
48 See for instance Wolfgang Engler, *Die Ostdeutschen: Kunde von einem verlorenen Land* (Berlin: Aufbau, 1999).
49 Georg Lukács, *Ästhetik*, 4 volumes (Neuwied: Luchterhand, 1972 (1963)).
50 Raddatz, commissoning editor's report, 6.
51 Volk und Welt, 'Application for Permission to Print,' 2.
52 See for instance Günter Agde, *Sachsenhausen bei Berlin: Speziallager Nr. 7; 1945–1950* (Berlin: Aufbau, 1994).

Chapter 3

COMMUNITY, DIFFERENCE, CONTEXT: (RE)READING THE CONTACT ZONE

Jennifer Wawrzinek

The majority of Australian novels accepted for publication by the Ministry of Culture were by authors with Communist Party affiliation or by authors dealing with issues of political and/or social oppression and contestation. These novels were often taken up for publication in the German Democratic Republic (GDR) because they illustrated the destructive effects of a capitalist society in which individualism, the commercialization of difference and the dictates of a competitive market economy driven by desire and acquisition could be seen to result in the marginalization of certain sections of society. Yet despite the aims of the GDR to differentiate itself from the capitalist West, and to frame imported literature as a didactic means of reinforcing this differentiation, it nevertheless used the same binary structures of identity constitution as those underwriting nation-states in the West. In this sense both the GDR and Australia had newly established national identities in which notions of self, community, and state were consistently constructed upon dialectical models of identity differentiation that depended upon the subjection and marginalization of otherness.[1]

Two Australian novels approved for publication in the GDR were Fergus Hume's *The Mystery of a Hansom Cab*, first published in Melbourne by Kemp and Boyce in 1886,[2] and Xavier Herbert's *Capricornia*, first published by Angus and Robertson in Sydney in 1938.[3] Hume's *Mystery* tells the story of exploitation, murder and blackmail as it moves between the genteel suburbs of East Melbourne and the inner-city slums of Little Bourke Street. Since its first publication in 1886 and subsequent republication in London the following year, the novel has experienced enormous popularity around the world, appearing in at least 27 editions and several translations, including Swedish (1889), Norwegian (1891), French (1914), Danish (1917) and Spanish (1994). It was translated into German as *Das Geheimnis des Fiakers* in 1895 by the Stuttgart publishing house Lutz and it was this edition that was subsequently reprinted in 1984 by Verlag Das Neue Berlin (Fig. 3.1). Curiously, the German edition relocates the scene of events from Melbourne to the very bourgeois European setting of Vienna, thus necessitating the removal of all descriptive passages particular to Melbourne and its colonial context in the British Empire.[4] Yet the primary narrative of exploitation and blackmail remains as a disturbance of a social space that is heavily regulated and patrolled in order to ensure the class-based hierarchy placing the aristocracy over the working classes.

Xavier Herbert's novel *Capricornia* was published in the GDR three decades earlier than Hume's *Mystery*. In 1958 Verlag der Morgen (Berlin) released a German translation of the novel that had first appeared in 1950 with the Büchergilde Gutenberg (Zurich). It had been subsequently published in a second edition in 1954 by the Hamburg-based publishing house Wolff, which added the evocative subtitle: *Capricornia: Die paradiesische Hölle* (Fig. 3.2). Verlag der Morgen republished the Wolff edition of the novel and by 1961 was already issuing a fourth reprint. It is significant that the novel was

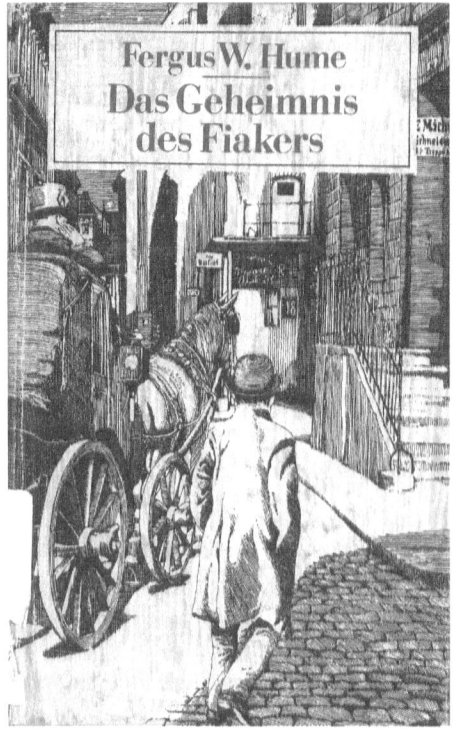

Figure 3.1 Cover of Fergus Hume's *Das Geheimnis des Fiakers* (Berlin: Verlag Das Neue Berlin, 1984).

chosen by Verlag der Morgen and approved by the Ministry of Culture and its freelance publishers' assessors because of its scathing critique of Australia's treatment of its indigenous population. The novel is a brutal and unforgiving account of colonial settlement in Australia's Far North, the dispossession and brutalization of Aboriginal communities, and the world of drunken violence and larrikinism amongst the region's white male settlers.

Although Hume's *Mystery of a Hansom Cab* and Herbert's *Capricornia* were written almost half a century apart, and although their settings and themes

Figure 3.2 Dust jacket for Xavier Herbert's *Capricornia: Die paradiesische Hölle* (Berlin: Verlag der Morgen, 1958).

are quite different (the former set in the aristocratic drawing rooms of late nineteenth-century East Melbourne/Vienna and the latter on cattle stations and homesteads in the mid-twentieth-century Australian Far North), both texts nevertheless depict structures of power underwriting the constitution of selves in community. They are implicitly concerned with the way in which communities (and nations) are formed via the mapping of an imaginary geography onto a group of people who share similar attributes with each other and similar differences from those marked as external to the group. It is for this reason that both novels provide rich material for attempts at nation building.

In the GDR the notion of the individual was consistently placed in opposition to the ideology of the communist state. In the poetry debate of 1966 carried out under the auspices of the literary journal *Forum*, Hans Koch, who was a cultural studies scholar and cultural functionary in the Sozialistische Einheitspartei Deutschlands (SED), criticized what he saw as the trend towards an 'extremely exaggerated egocentricity' in GDR fiction, which he argued was productive of anarchism and which, in moral terms, 'makes the attitude "I am the I" the ethical foundation of the world'.[5] East German writers such as Reiner Kunze and Christa Wolf were singled out for their overt depictions of individuality by Max Walter Schulz, author and secretary of the GDR writers' union, who argued that 'this individualism is ready for action, and it is already collaborating with the malicious distortion of GDR reality and with anti-communism'.[6] These comments emphasize the way in which the individual self was placed in dialectical opposition to the notion of community in GDR discourse. Moreover, they highlight the important role that literature played in the constitution of the GDR social imaginary, through the active and predetermined construction of nationhood, or what Benedict Anderson has famously referred to as 'imagined communities'.[7] According to Anderson, the citizen is constituted as a national subject precisely through the sharing of experience enabled by and engendered through print culture.[8]

In this sense, it is significant that Hume's *Mystery* and Herbert's *Capricornia* have been read as depictions of struggle over social space via the negotiation, contestation and/or re-confirmation of difference. Yet whilst readings of both novels emphasize this struggle, the texts can also be seen to resist being pressed into the service of (imaginary) nation formation. In this sense, Herbert's novel *Capricornia* becomes particularly relevant for its portrayal of the way in which such social space is divided *as* the basis of community. As Persia Campbell noted in her 1943 Australian review of the novel, *Capricornia* demarcates the wild north of 'terra incognita' in the Northern Territory from the 'masses of Australian people, living in the temperate south and east'.[9] Campbell took pains to note that the novel portrays and critiques 'the destruction and degradation which the white man's culture has brought to the natives of this Northern Territory, and particularly the unhappy lot of the half-castes, the "yeller-fellows", acceptable neither to the whites or the blacks'.[10] Brian Kiernan similarly attests to the way in which the novel portrays a microcosm of society that reveals 'at a deeper and more general level the nature of social relationships' in the Australian Far North during colonization.[11] According to Kiernan, *Capricornia* presents a judgement of white civilization as a 'predatory and essentially destructive force' in which a detached viewpoint of 'rational observation' reduces people to 'mere specimens'.[12]

In this essay I therefore want to examine the ways in which the adoption of certain texts, either within the formally organized GDR project of building the East German communist nation, or the implicit project of imagining the (white) Australian nation, resisted, through their reception, all attempts at being 'put to work' in the service of the communal project. My aim here is not to produce new readings of Herbert's *Capricornia* or Hume's *Mystery* but, rather, to explore the ways in which the same texts that were adopted by the GDR as ideologically useful were capable of fissuring its homogenous vision of community, in order to gesture towards a different thinking of community altogether. What is made obvious in the GDR context can also be seen to work within the construction of (white) Australian nationhood. Both nations, either explicitly or implicitly, configure an imagined community based on the premise of similarity and difference.

Literature and the Creation of Community

Books and reading were given a place of prime importance in the GDR. Whether configured as the pre-1956 notion of the *Literaturgesellschaft* or the later, more utopian *Leseland*, literature was consistently placed at the centre of the GDR social imaginary. Although, as Barck, Langermann and Lokatis argue, the development of a specific reading culture in the GDR was never intended as a means of compelling citizens to follow the dictates of an ideological machine,[13] the official rubric of *Kulturpolitik* (cultural policy) in the GDR nevertheless established carefully controlled aesthetic norms for all literary and artistic production. Even though censorship was a term that was forbidden in the GDR, the kind of systematic control exercised over forms of cultural production, publishing and the circulation of imported texts functioned, as David Bathrick has noted, 'to legislate value and social identity as a total discursive system'.[14] Carol Anne Constabile-Heming notes that of the 78 publishing houses in the GDR, a massive 75 per cent were state controlled or state related. The public reception of a text was often guided by official criticism in the form of book reviews that appeared in party-sponsored organs such as *Sinn und Form, neue deutsche literatur, Weimarer Beiträge* and *Neues*

Deutschland. The content of these official reviews was often determined even before the *Druckgenehmigung* (print permission) was granted.[15] These guided 'public' reviews of texts and programmed reception aimed to instruct readers on the appropriate interpretation of a given text. East German writers who engaged actively in critical discourse, thus disturbing such official programmed reception, often became targets of Stasi surveillance.[16] Moreover, the attempt to control and delimit the reception of cultural material began at a much earlier stage in a citizen's public awareness. Promising young teenagers were chosen from the *Freie Deutsche Jugend* (FDJ) and the *Pioniere*, the East German youth organizations, to take on the role of *Propagandist* and thus to disseminate Communist Party ideology, in the form of lectures and presentations, to fellow classmates at school.[17]

If, as Barck, Langermann and Lokatis argue, literature functioned in the GDR as a means of furthering the 'vision of an educated and relatively homogenous society',[18] it was necessarily because the attempted creation (whether prescriptive or descriptive) of an ideal communist society necessitated the regulation of cultural production, in the manner described elsewhere by Jean-Luc Nancy as a secular eschatology, in which the GDR discursive framework of *Kulturpolitik* compelled the world to be known and understood in specific ways. Nancy describes this kind of framework as a 'structuring logos', referring to the manner in which the shared material of our finite existence is organized into a signifying discourse as a series of figures or fictions upon which communal formations and practices can be based.[19] The narratives that form these discourses can be described as mythic and foundational because they enable a political community such as the GDR (or the white Australia nation) to found an existence and to perpetuate that existence *as* the sharing of an identity or an essence. In this way, the perpetuation of the notion of the GDR as *Leseland* and the instrumental approach by the Ministry of Culture to literary texts can be seen to not only comprehend those texts by relating them to known and fixed parameters and values within the structuring logos but also to simultaneously generalize their uniqueness by transforming the performativity of their singularity into a static and useable paradigm. If, as Elizabeth Mittman argues in her article on Christa Wolf, literature was seen in the GDR as an important means of legitimating the state from below,[20] then the articulation of the GDR as an 'imagined community' (either as *Leseland* or as *Literaturgesellschaft*) not only aims to disseminate a top-down ideology of the communist ideal onto its citizens, albeit as one that appears to be generated by its citizens, but also seeks to establish that community as ontology.

Community as Originary Myth

One Australian writer without Communist Party affiliation to be published in the GDR was Fergus Hume. His late nineteenth-century crime novel titled *The Mystery of a Hansom Cab* has been consistently read in its English version as a search for self-renewal in the colonies. As Robert Hughes notes, such concerns were then at the forefront of Australian journalism and literature. He writes that a favourite trope at the time of the Australian Centennial in 1888 was that 'of the nation as a young and vigorous person gazing into the rising sun, turning his or her back on the dark and crouching shadows of the past'.[21] Australian reviews and scholarly essays have reiterated this idea, from Lionel Fredman's suggestion that Hume's success in Australia was due to the novel's setting in a 'young and fast-growing colony whose people […] had been given little opportunity to express their identity',[22] to Vane Lindesay's comparison of Melbourne to London, where 'East Melbourne is the Belgravia of the colony'.[23] For these readers, Hume's *Mystery* is concerned with the expression of an uncertain colonial identity. Yet, as Lindesay points out, it is one that depends on a class hierarchy where 'privileged and mannered people decide matters and solve problems and the lower orders know their place and are kept in it'.[24] But what does this have to do with the concerns of the GDR, a nation-state focussed primarily on the development of socialist principles and supposedly averse to the individuality that seems to be promulgated by this image of self-renewal?

In its German translation, *Das Geheimnis des Fiakers* relocates the scene of events from colonial Melbourne to the more established, aristocratic city of Vienna. In this sense any focus on issues of colonial identity, or on the relation between colonial periphery and imperial centre, comes to be elided in favour of another struggle of difference depicted in the novel: that between the bourgeois subjects of a rich city (in this case Vienna) and its excluded other, the proletarians living in filthy back alleys who are driven to extortion and blackmail through their subjugation. The structures of identity constitution depicted here necessarily hold the excluded other in relation to the identity being depicted, albeit reduced to a field of sameness. Otherness is abstracted into a field of negativity underwriting the construction of bourgeois subjectivity. Nevertheless, the depiction of capitalist vice in the novel serves a similar function for the GDR as it does for a colonial Australia struggling to establish itself as a nation.

The Hegelian language of subject and object, self and other, which is employed both by an Australian nation seeking self-renewal and by the GDR seeking to differentiate itself from a liberal capitalist West and aristocratic past, conceives of otherness and difference not in terms of a radical alterity that cannot be mastered but, rather, as the object of the subject's representation; that is, as a negative reflection of the self. In Hume's hansom cab mystery, tropes of mirroring figure prominently throughout the novel. In the Australian version, various landmarks and spaces are continually positioned in relation to the English motherland. It is suggested, for example, that Mark Frettlby's townhouse in St Kilda 'would have been not unworthy of Park Lane' (39), Collins Street is described as 'to the Southern City what Bond Street and the Row are to London' (67), and an unspecified writer is referenced as having depicted Melbourne 'as Glasgow with the sky of Alexandria' (111). It is perhaps the sparkling figure of Felix as he passes by the Burke and Wills monument, 'looking like an animated diamond' (96), that most encapsulates the work of reflection in this novel. More importantly, however, one cannot help but wonder if these tropes of mirroring function in both Australian colonial and GDR communist contexts as a means for ensuring that the sovereignty of the nation-state remains intact through the injunction to subsume the excess of difference to itself rather than risk the destabilization of a confrontation with that which it cannot master or appropriate.

As Edward Said argues, identity cannot exist by itself without an array of 'opposites, negatives, oppositions'.[25] When Hume writes in *The Mystery of a Hansom Cab* that here, in the space of the novel, is the 'realm of topsy-turveydom, and many things, like dreams, go by in contraries',[26] he is, of course, referring to Melbourne as a negative inversion of the British imperial centre, as evidenced by the examples above. In addition to the world of negative mirror inversions and the sparkling surfaces of aristocratic Melbourne is the filthy underside at the heart of the novel and in the heart of the city, in Bourke Street's Chinatown, where the detective, Kilslip, penetrates the seedy underworld to find Mother Guttersnipe, the inverted queen of the lair (111–19).

The relocation of this structural relation to Europe in the translated version of the novel sets up a curious displacement of the centre/periphery model. An undated reader's report for the Ministry of Culture focusses specifically on the novel's preoccupation with extortion, an act, the reader notes, distinctly associated with the wealth and inequality of capitalist society. This report states that 'this book will be well received, especially as its entertainment value is not small, and through it – perhaps not always according to the direct intentions of the author – can even establish some insights about bourgeois morality and immorality'.[27] It is in statements such as these that it is possible to see the extent to which the construction of the GDR nation-state depended upon an East/West mirroring in which the GDR came to be articulated as both negative inversion of and teleological progression from the capitalist West, and the way it came to construct the West as the undeveloped and primitive state from which the GDR emerged.

Certainly, the depiction of an unruly otherness in both English and German versions of Hume's novel can be seen to provide a means of locating the bourgeois anxiety of the novel's principal characters in an era of rapid capital expansion and shifting boundaries between individual and community, nation and state, bourgeois subject and proletarian other. Indeed, Robert Dixon, writing on the English edition, has pointed to the way in which the novel collocates the 'seething collective body driven by low desires' and a distinct 'fear of contagion'.[28] The genre of crime fiction allows this anxiety to be detected, framed and discursively controlled. When recontextualized within the parameters of the GDR's structuring logos, the otherness that comes to be patrolled, in a bizarre inversion of the topsy-turvy mirroring troped by the novel, is Western bourgeois morality itself. In the first version, the slums of nineteenth-century Melbourne gripped by the hysteria of 'gold rush fever' threaten the disintegration of the bourgeois self via the deregulation of discursive space with forms of crime and disease. When reframed, however, through the mythic structures of the GDR, it is no longer the proletariat that threatens the bourgeois subject. Rather, it is the capitalist West that looms on the horizon of the GDR's imaginary, threatening to destabilize the body of the communist state with dangerous expressions of individuality.

It is important, however, that for a text to speak within the terms described above – that is, as an articulation of a structural process of identity differentiation – it must continue to be pressed into the service of a predetermined end. If Xavier Herbert's novel *Capricornia*, for instance, is to fit into the parameters of SED cultural policy, certain questions must be elided – for instance, those concerning the appropriation of otherness in the service of self and the pregnant silence of the occluded. Whilst both GDR readers' reports and responses from Australian reviewers and scholars have consistently read the novel as a critique of (colonial) power relations because of its brutal depiction of colonial violence and the dispossession of indigenous Australians, the Australian reception of the text is increasingly marked by a growing attention to the structural process of occlusion and silencing that underwrites the sense of (white) Australian mateship depicted in the novel. H. M. Green's review in 1939 complained that Herbert, in his effort to indict the racial prejudice of the Far North, had in fact presented not a human world but, rather, a version of hell.[29] Vincent Buckley echoed this sentiment when he pointed to the chaotic world of disorder presented by a similarly disordered narrative in 1960,[30] and in 1970 Brian Kiernan suggested that such disorder is evidence of a civilization founded on 'exploitation motivated by self-interest and greed', and 'out of harmony with the Nature it seeks to subjugate'.[31] Such discourse was fertile ground for a newly-formed nation such as the GDR, a nation that was seeking to establish an idea of the communist state as the natural outcome of teleological progress.[32] Yet the idea of history as causation and as the natural progression of events in succession necessarily becomes destabilized through a simultaneous attention, by readers both in Australia and, importantly, in the GDR, to the representational limits of the occluded and the silenced in Herbert's text. In *Capricornia*, Aboriginal presence is displaced to the periphery of its narrative world. Yet it remains as an uncomfortable presence, not only in the overly racist descriptions used throughout, but in the use of derogatory terms such as 'wallah', 'lubra' and 'half-caste'. The silencing of Aborigines in Herbert's novel occurs primarily, however, through their reduction to objects. For example, early in the novel, Oscar is described as having taken 'a smelly native from the Compound and converted him into a piece of bright furniture' (11). Later, Tim finds Constance 'lying wrapped in a ragged blanket on a bed of planks in the corner of a dark little earth-floored hovel that stank of phenyle and black bodies' (208), and when Norman goes for a stroll and finds himself at the Compound, instead of engaging with the people he encounters, he merely notes: 'Natives lounging at the doors of huts sat up and stared at him' (259).

In this sense, the reception of *Capricornia* in both Australian and GDR contexts can be read as an interrogation of the very structures of nation building that the ideological apparatus of *Kulturpolitik* sought to establish. By re-reading these reviews and essays with attention to the biopolitical dimension of what has been occluded, exclusionary notions of community as similarity and difference, and of history as teleological progress, can begin to be reconfigured. As such, the reviews can be seen to gesture towards an understanding of community as an act-event of clusters or formations of particular historical moments or spatial locations bound together in this event but not fixed in any particular identity.

The Text as Limit

In her recent essay on Xavier Herbert, Fiona Probyn-Rapsey points to a sense of white illegitimacy in the Australian Northern Territory, suggesting that Herbert's novels articulate a need for white belonging that is not in competition with indigenous Australians but, rather, with other white settlers, in an attempt to define who belongs to the country 'more' than the other.[33] According to Probyn-Rapsey, the biopolitics depicted in Herbert's representations of life in the Far North, where Aboriginality was 'made to work for whiteness, to provide it with roots, heritage, stamina of skin and intelligence', point to an intrinsic directive to maintain life in a particular form. As she writes, 'Herbert's "son of the soil" nationalism was not far removed from Cook's state-sanctioned future vision of a white nation, in that both placed Aboriginal people at the source of white belonging'.[34] These comments on Herbert's writing point to the way in which *Capricornia* has been read in some contemporary Australian circles as an appropriation of Aboriginal belonging in order to secure the basis of a white Australian nation, in effect riding on the back of indigeneity, subsuming otherness in the service of the self. Although Probyn-Rapsey's essay was published more than a decade after the end of the GDR and almost 40 years after the publication of *Capricornia* by Verlag der Morgen in Berlin, these later readings of Herbert's novel are important for the way they draw attention to the possibilities inherent to certain earlier readings, in which the position of the outcast or the liminal figure is either mentioned or alluded to, although not foregrounded. For instance, Sean Monahan, writing seven years earlier on the figure of the Swagman in *Capricornia* as the embodiment of a quintessential (white) Australian notion of freedom from authority and the law, takes care to mention without further extrapolation that 'Herbert's defence of freedom stops short of Aboriginals'.[35]

Almost 30 years earlier, GDR readers' reports might seem at first to confirm the preoccupation with questions of race found in Australian readings of the novel. An unsigned reader's report on *Capricornia* from 1958 emphasizes, for instance, the importance of the novel to the GDR because it 'deals with one of the most urgent problems of the capitalist world: the question of race'.[36] However, the nuances of this critique in the GDR diverge remarkably from the interrogation of marginalization and biopolitical control noted above, in order to foreground these problems as effects of a particular social order. The reader of the unsigned report was not concerned with Herbert's critique of colonial structures of power or with Herbert's presumed appropriation of the 'blackfella mind' but, rather, with the ways in which the brutality and violence depicted in the novel could be harnessed in the GDR as 'a fierce criticism of the capitalist situation in Australia'.[37] What is here appropriated in the service of belonging and for the perpetuation of communal essences to an essentializing 'we', is in effect the same brutality and violence that both the reader's report and Herbert are at pains to criticize. Perhaps, then, at the heart of the violence and degradation depicted by Herbert as intrinsic to colonial settlement (in the Australian view) or capitalist imperial expansion (in the communist view) is the violence enacted on difference when communities are drawn together under the banner of similarity and sameness. In other words, the suffering depicted in Herbert's novel comes to form the basis upon which the GDR enables its own version of community as its dialectical opposite. Difference (racial, gender, class) is elided in the construction of the universal ideal as literature is pressed into the service of the SED's structuring logos.

Yet there is an inherent contradiction in the idea of the GDR as a literary society or reading nation. If the literary work is understood as a product of specific contexts that produce meaning through the mobilization of certain formal properties, meaning must then be something that is taken up within form and, according to its situation, within a nexus of material conditions. As Derek Attridge argues, the literary work is 'the encrypted image of an act-event of invention, waiting to be re-enacted in a reading'.[38] The surplus of meaning inherent to any contextual operation thus ensures that a text necessarily remains more than simply a reflection of a reality outside language. As such, as Attridge notes, 'the question of meaning and referring is kept alive *as a question*' (original emphasis).[39]

The myriad possibilities for re-imagining worlds that become available through understanding literature as a hermeneutic process were similarly reflected in the growing interest of later GDR scholarly circles in the inherent malleability of textual signification. In 1973 Manfred Naumann's book titled *Gesellschaft-Literatur-Lesen: Literaturrezeption in theoretischer Sicht* (Berlin: Aufbau Verlag) began to underscore the idea of literature as dynamic relation:

> The text puts in motion stored experiences, knowledge, the mastery of reality-elements and their relationship in accordance with the laws of nature and thus allows the construction of representation in the receptive consciousness. Precisely because of that, the reconstruction is also a construction: one's own experience and the mastery of socially constructed modes of organization are drawn upon and stimulated to its own activity.[40]

The textual and hermeneutic contingency that Naumann describes resists the attempt to press thought into what Christopher Watkin elsewhere refers to as 'the mutually compounding dyad of globalisation and fundamentalism'.[41] Rather, the understanding of textual signification as event, and as the construction and reconstruction of meaning through contextual operations, begins to disable the formation of communities based on shared essence in order to gesture towards a different thinking of community, one that is based not on similarity and sameness but on finitude and singularity, or as Vivasvan Soni puts it, 'community as the finite totality of relations among singular beings'.[42]

The work of Jean-Luc Nancy is useful here because his theorization of community as relation without relation helps to articulate the paradox at the heart of the GDR as a literary community or reading-nation.[43] For Nancy, literature does not represent society nor reveal a completed reality in the way of myth or the workings of ideology. Rather, it reveals the singularity intrinsic to existence, not a singularity that is self-enclosed and absolute but one that is contingent and relative. If singularity is formed, as Attridge argues, through a nexus of structural relations that are continually being formed and reformed (or as Naumann puts it, constructed and reconstructed), then there can be sharing between singular beings but no essential being in common, precisely because singularities are formed through the complex relations of contextual operations. Ian James locates the importance of Nancy's work to the rethinking of relation in community in that it does not attempt to pass over an ethical relation of radical alterity (such as that theorized by Levinas, Blanchot and Derrida) but, rather, conceives of the ethical relation as being side-by-side.[44]

The paradox at the heart of the notion of the GDR as a literary community thus resides in the conjunction of the idea of community as a specific formation grounded within secular transcendence, with literature as an ethical singularity and recourse to a limit that cannot be transcended. As a result, the use of literature as a means of configuring the ideal community simultaneously posits the seeds of its own disfiguration. This, in turn, construes a relation with an otherness that has the potential to touch upon what Lydia Wevers posits in her recent essay on the depiction of 'full-blood' Aborigines in *Capricornia* as an 'almost invisible presence'.[45] In this sense Herbert's text can be seen to gesture towards the existence of a presence that has not been revealed, despite its removal to the edges of discourse (the Aboriginal voice) or its exclusion from the parameters of cultural imagining (acts of political resistance within the GDR).[46] In the Australian context of colonization and dispossession, as Wevers reads it, this presence continues 'despite the despoliation of its territory' and it 'revenges itself despite the dispossession of its people'.[47]

The depiction of Aboriginality in Herbert's *Capricornia* is problematized by its explicitly white, male point-of-view narration. Although narrated in the third person, the story is driven primarily by the central protagonists, the 'half-caste' Norman and the white 'blokes' who make up the population of settlers and fettlers in the world depicted in the novel. As I mentioned earlier, 'full-blooded' Aborigines are mostly located either in the camps existing on the edges of the townships or in the 'wilderness' of the bush. When Norman leaves home after a fight with Gigney on New Year's Eve and subsequently becomes lost in the wilderness, he encounters a local country man referred to as 'the savage', who is then joined by 'other savages stealing up' (342, 343). The man turns out to be a friend named 'Muttonhead', who encourages Norman to stay with the tribe: 'Proper good country dis one. Plenty kangaroo, plenty buffalo, plenty bandicoot, plenty yam […] Number-one good country' (344). In this brief interlude, the Aboriginal voice is heard only when Norman exits the world of settler society to go, seemingly, back in time to a conceivably pre-modern, primordial state of 'savage' existence.

Similarly, the troublesome figures of those referred to by Herbert as 'the half-castes', if they do not try to assimilate to white Australian society, are killed off by the brutality of colonialism, much in the same way that the steam train is consistently depicted throughout the novel as a violent means of colonizing the landscape.[48] As Wevers astutely notes, *Capricornia* alludes to an unnarrated text lying beyond the limits of the white masculinist Australian nation. The Aboriginal narrative remains ulterior to Herbert's story of white civilization. In the words of Wevers, it is 'the black line at the edge of the white gaze'.[49] This suggests that, whilst Aboriginality in the novel is constructed by white discourse, there nevertheless remains 'a thin black line of uncontainable difference, of natural violence with a suggestive edge of retribution, that suggests another, buried way of constructing nature, of characterising the land'.[50]

Whilst the issue of occlusion is not stressed in GDR readers' reports of *Capricornia*, Paul Friedländer's report nevertheless highlights the ways in which particular socio-political structures can work to oppress or discriminate against various members of society. He places an emphasis in his report not only on the fact of racial discrimination but on the way in which the 'methods used' have 'generality beyond Australia for all countries where coloured people suffer from mass persecution'.[51] The brutality and violence depicted in Herbert's novel are the result, Friedländer suggests, not necessarily of capitalism alone but of a country where people are divided into certain races and classes. 'The tragedy of the half-caste (die Tragödie der Mischlinge)' is depicted in this report as the tragedy of liminality, the figure who exists between categories.[52] Yet Friedländer's answer is not to advocate the removal of such aberrant figures but, rather, to advocate the tolerance of difference. He suggests that the mixed-heritage protagonist of *Capricornia*, Norman, is 'like all figures of the novel, a human being with his contradictions, with his good and bad aspects'.[53]

Friedländer's report would seem to confirm Wevers' later reading in her essay for *Australian Literary Studies*. By shifting his focus on the question of difference, otherness and liminality to one concerning structures of domination and control, and by suggesting that characters in Herbert's novel such as Mark Shillingsworth, Charles Ket and Frank McLash are not inherently evil but, rather, 'victims of circumstance (Opfer der Verhältnisse)', Friedländer suggests that it is the structures of state and society that are to blame for the situation depicted in the novel, rather than individual acts.[54] Indeed the report emphasizes the imbrication of certain sections of society with those of state control. He points to middle-class citizens as 'the accused ones (die Angeklagten)', noting that *Capricornia* exposes 'their hypocrisy, their brutality, and their moral debauchery'. Yet Friedländer immediately links the brutality of the middle-classes to 'the higher public officials, who are the masters of the north'.[55] This curious displacement of responsibility from the middle classes to government officials can similarly be seen to displace responsibility for the tragedy of the liminal figure from social division in general to top-down social control by a government out of touch with its people.

This alliance between Wevers' reading of *Capricornia* and Friedländer's GDR report, although situated in different geographic and temporal zones, and in different socio-political contexts, nevertheless begins to create a network of reading subjects. Wevers' essay and Friedländer's GDR reader's report together point to cracks in the structures of state power governing particular societies, thus instigating what can be seen as the sharing of a relation between those who cannot otherwise be bound by certain identity categories. For Nancy, this kind of sharing indicates the mobile circulation of singular beings within a shared space. This is a singularity that is composite rather than univocal or homogenous because singular beings are, according to Nancy, born into relations of plural encounters. They are therefore necessarily fragmented and non-identitarian. Rather than the notion of community as a collection of individuals who bind themselves together on the basis of a shared identity, exposure to the singularity of others creates a sense of 'being-with' as a plural spacing of many identities.[56] This sense of community as sharing, or being-with, has the potential to disrupt notions of community as shared essence or shared identity because the sharing of a relation that is plural, shifting and contingent cannot be reduced to or mastered by the signifying systems of mythic narrative or the structuring logos of the state.

The surplus of meaning inherent in the idea of community as being-with and as a relation of plural encounter therefore has the potential to interrupt notions of identity, nation, state and the realization of the mythic apparatus, thus opening a space into which something new might emerge as possibility. It is perhaps for this reason that, in the absence of a public sphere in the GDR as a locus of mediation between civil society and the state apparatus, claims for the space of literature as an *Ersatzöffentlichkeit* (substitute public sphere) were advanced, most memorably by Christoph Hein in his speech at the tenth Writer's Congress in 1987.[57] The idea of an *Ersatzöffentlichkeit* configures civil space through the formation of relational nexes that are engendered through reading and the circulation of texts as agents not of ideology but rather of contact and engagement.

Community as Relation

When the GDR as either *Leseland* or *Literaturgesellschaft* is understood as a literary communism of relation and plural encounter, the process of translating, transposing and adapting Australian literature into German and the GDR context thus enacts what Walter Benjamin famously refers to as stages of continued life in the work of art.[58] Benjamin's essay 'The Task of the Translator' emphasizes the way in which the process of translation configures meaning through reception and context rather than via the simple 'transmission of subject matter'.[59] Understood in this way, the literary text functions as a conductor, or what Percy Bysshe Shelley once famously referred to as 'a spark, a burning atom of inextinguishable thought'[60] that is mobilized through being taken up into a network of plural contextual relations such as that enacted by Wevers and Friedländer.

The juxtaposition of singularities that is brought about by literature therefore cannot be controlled by the workings of state and law – the structures of a society that Friedländer criticizes as responsible for the violence and oppression depicted in Herbert's novel *Capricornia*, for example. Rather, these singularities are brought into relation without being subsumed into the service of self, thus articulating a notion of community that is 'unworked', as Nancy would describe it, because it brings beings into proximity through an event-act and not through the possession of certain qualities, such as gender, race, or class, or through the adherence to certain ideologies (either communist or capitalist).

Although in this essay I have described certain similarities and alignments between the structuring logos in Australia and the GDR in order to illustrate the ways in which certain texts in translation can produce multiple meanings through their recontextualization, it has not been my intention to suggest these worlds are the same. Rather, I hope to point to the way in which the transposition of cultural artefacts can engender forms of being-with that are not predicated on the subsumption of difference or otherness. The communities created through this confrontation between seemingly disparate worlds necessarily remain incommensurate. As Sherry Simon has observed, the twentieth century has seen an increasing shift in the West towards a society that 'as a whole has turned into an immense contact zone, where intercultural relations contribute to the internal life of all national cultures'.[61] This shift articulates a notion of community figured in terms of touch, contact and exposure. It is a contact that leaves a profound disturbance, a lingering trace of otherness which cannot be elided and which leaves intact the distance and mystery intrinsic to difference and to alterity, whilst nevertheless allowing networks of community to form through the act-event of being-with side-by-side.

Notes

I wish to thank Jörg Kaufmann for his stories, memories, his persistent questioning and problematizing of this project and my involvement with it. I also wish to thank him for his invaluable assistance with translating GDR reader reports.

1 My insistence here on the binary structures of national identity formation shared by the GDR and white Australia by no means implies that the process of identity construction was complete by the period under discussion. As psychoanalysts from Freud to Lacan and Kristeva, as well as performativity theorists such as Judith Butler have shown, the process of identity construction is a process of continual renegotiation and re-inscription.
2 Fergus Hume, *The Mystery of a Hansom Cab* (Cirencester: The Echo Library, 2005), published in German as *Das Geheimnis des Fiakers*, trans. unknown (Berlin: Verlag Das Neue Berlin, 1986).
3 Xavier Herbert, *Capricornia* (London: Harper Collins, 2008), published in German as *Capricornia: die paradiesische Hölle*, trans. N. O. Scarpi (Berlin: Verlag der Morgen, 1958).
4 Sue Turnbull, writing on place and location in crime fiction, argues that the situating of a crime within a familiar location allows the reader to believe in a certain degree of reality in the events being narrated. This in turn permits the act of closure usually associated with the solving of the crime to take on a cathartic effect. 'Are We There Yet? The Place of Place in Australian Crime Fiction', *Meanjin* 58, no. 4 (1999): 50–60.
5 Quoted in Jay Rosellini, 'Poetry and Criticism in the German Democratic Republic: The 1972 Discussion in the Context of Cultural Policy', *New German Critique* 9 (Autumn 1976): 153–74 (157).
6 Ibid., 158.
7 Benedict Anderson, *Imagined Communities: Reflections on the Origin and Spread of Nationalism* (London: Verso, 2006).
8 Ibid., 6.
9 Persia Campbell, review of *Capricornia* by Xavier Herbert, *Pacific Affairs* 16, no. 4 (December 1943): 510–11 (510).
10 Ibid., 510.
11 Brian Kiernan, 'Xavier Herbert: "Capricornia"', *Australian Literary Studies* 4, no. 4 (October 1970): 360–70 (361).
12 Ibid., 364, 365.
13 Simone Barck, Martina Langermann, and Siegfried Lokatis, 'The German Democratic Republic as a "Reading Nation": Utopia, Planning, Reality, and Ideology', trans. Michael Latham and Devin Pendas, in *The Power of Intellectuals in Contemporary Germany*, ed. Michael Geyer (Chicago: University of Chicago Press, 2001), 88–112 (90).
14 David Bathrick, *The Powers of Speech: The Politics of Culture in the GDR* (Lincoln: University of Nebraska, 1995), 16.
15 Carol Anne Constabile-Heming, '"Rezensur": A Case Study of Censorship and Programmatic Reception in the GDR', in *Monatshefte* 92, no. 1 (Spring 2000): 53–67 (59).
16 Ibid., 54. Constabile-Heming also notes that in the mid-sixties the SED abandoned the prescriptive approach to the interpretation of texts in favour of one that was more 'descriptive'. This latter approach favoured dialogue between reader and writer such that literature came to be viewed as 'a dynamic communicative exchange' (56).
17 Interview with Jörg Kaufmann, Berlin, 27 December 2012. See also Barbara Korte and Christina Spittel, who discuss the dissemination of communist ideology via literature classes in the GDR school system; 'Shakespeare under Different Flags: The Bard in German Classrooms from Hitler to Honecker', *Journal of Contemporary History* 44, no. 2 (2009): 267–86.
18 Barck et al., 'Reading Nation', 94.

19 Jean-Luc Nancy, *The Inoperative Community*, trans. Peter Connor, Lisa Garbus, Michael Holland, and Simona Sawhney (Minneapolis: University of Minnesota Press, 1991), 49.
20 Elizabeth Mittman, 'Locating a Public Sphere: Some Reflections on Writers and *Öffentlichkeit* in the GDR', *Women in German Yearbook* 10 (1994): 19–37 (22).
21 Robert Hughes, *The Fatal Shore: A History of the Transportation of Convicts to Australia, 1787–1868* (London: Collins Harvill, 1996), 597.
22 L. E. Fredman, 'Follow that Cab', *Quadrant* 21, no. 4 (April 1977): 63–65 (64).
23 Vane Lindesay, 'In Print: The Mystery of a Hansom Cab', *This Australia* 2, no. 1 (Summer 1982–83): 62–64 (63).
24 Ibid., 63.
25 Edward Said, *Culture and Imperialism* (New York: Vintage Books, 1994), 52.
26 Hume, *Mystery*, 137.
27 'dieses Buch gern aufnehmen werden, zumal sein Unterhaltungswert gar night so gering ist und sich durch ihn – vielleicht nicht immer analog den vom Autor direkt verfolgten Absichten – sogar einige Einsichten über bourgeoise Moral und Unmoral herstellen', in Alice Berger, report for *Das Geheimnis des Fiakers*, undated, BArch DR1/3633/175.
28 Robert Dixon, 'Closing the Can of Worms: Enactments of Justice in *Bleak House, The Mystery of a Hansom Cab* and *The Tax Inspector*', *Westerly* 37, no. 4 (Summer 1992): 50–60 (40).
29 H. M. Greene, 'Australian Literature 1938', *Southerly* 1, no. 1 (1939): 37–41.
30 Vincent Buckley, review of *Capricornia*, *Meanjin* 19, no. 1 (1960): 13–30.
31 Kiernan, 'Capricornia', 368.
32 The depiction of the communist state as the outcome of teleological progress is most often depicted in the genre known in German as *Ankunftsliteratur*. An example of this is Dymphna Cusack's travelogue titled *Chinese Women Speak*, which clearly depicts a utopian communist state as having emerged from a prior civilization based on inequality and suffering, something noted by Erich Schreier's reader's report dated 22 June 1961 for *Auf eigenen Füßen: Frauenschicksale aus China*, BArch DR1/3960/90. More generally, David Carter discusses the idea of socialist realism as predetermined storytelling in relation to the work of Judah Waten (see 'The Story of Our Epoch, a Hero of Our Time: The Communist Novelist in Postwar Australia', in *Frank Hardy and the Literature of Commitment*, ed. Paul Adams and Christopher Lee (Melbourne: The Vulgar Press, 2003), 89–111.
33 Fiona Probyn-Rapsey, 'Some Whites are Whiter than Others: The Whitefella Skin Politics of Xavier Herbert and Cecil Cook', *Journal of the Association for the Study of Australian Literature*, special issue, *Spectres, Screens, Shadows, Mirrors* (2007): 157–73 (169).
34 Ibid., 168.
35 Sean Monahan, 'Xavier Herbert's *Capricornia*: In Praise of the Swagman Spirit', *Westerly* 30, no. 4 (1985): 15–24 (24).
36 'hier greift eins der brennenden Probleme der kapitalistischen Welt auf: die Rassenfrage', in report for *Capricornia*, 12 March 1958, BArch DR1/3998/2.
37 'eine scharfe Kritik an den kapitalistischen Verhältnissen in Australien', ibid., 2.
38 Derek Attridge, *The Singularity of Literature* (London: Routledge, 2004), 111.
39 Ibid., 19.
40 'Der Text setzt gespeicherte Erfahrungen, Kenntnisse, die Beherrschung von Realitätselementen und ihren gesetzmäßigen Beziehungen in Bewegung und gestattet so den Aufbau der Darstellung im rezeptiven Bewußtsein. Gerade dadurch ist die Rekonstruktion zugleich Konstruktion: Das eigene Erfahrungsmaterial und die Beherrschung der gesellschaftlich ausgebildeten Weisen der Organisation solchen Materials weren in Anspruch genommen und zu eigener Aktivität angeregt', in Manfred

Naumann, *Gesellschaft, Literatur, Lesen: Literaturrezeption in theoretischer Sicht* (Berlin: Aufbau Verlag, 1975), 350.
41 Christopher Watkin, 'A Different Alterity: Jean-Luc Nancy's "Singular Plural"', *Paragraph* 30, no. 2 (2007): 50–64 (52–53).
42 Vivasvan Soni, 'Communal Narcosis and Sublime Withdrawal: The Problem of Community in Kant's *Critique of Judgement*', *Cultural Critique* 64 (Autumn 2006): 1–39 (17).
43 Nancy's work in *The Inoperative Community* (translated from *La Communauté désoeuvrée*, 1983) forms part of a proliferation of scholarly rethinking of the notion of community shortly prior to and immediately after the fall of the Wall in 1989. Other texts situated in dialogue, and which aim to re-evaluate the possibilities for community after the failure of the communist experiment include Maurice Blanchot's *The Unavowable Community* (translated from *La Communauté inavouable*, 1983); Jacques Derrida's *The Politics of Friendship* (translated from *Politiques de l'amitié*, 1994); and Giorgio Agamben's *The Coming Community* (translated from *La comunita che viene*, 1990).
44 Ian James, 'On Interrupted Myth', *Journal for Cultural Research* 9, no. 4 (2005): 331–49 (343).
45 Lydia Wevers, 'Terra Australis: Landscape as Medium in *Capricornia* and *Poor Fellow My Country*', *Australian Literary Studies* 17, no. 1 (May 1995): 38–48 (39).
46 One particular act of political resistance in the early years of the GDR was the snipping of a tie worn by Communist Party officials during public ceremonies. Persons as young as 17 years old who had committed such an act were ordered to leave the country at very short notice (interview with Jörg Kaufmann, 27 December 2012).
47 Wevers, 'Terra Australis', 47.
48 As early as 1938, Furnley Maurice, in his review for *The Australian Quarterly*, pointed to the novel's depiction of the railways as monstrous. He wrote that the steam train is shown as 'a baleful dragon crawling and rushing through the country; a grotesque piece of engineering' ('The Literary Value of Human Agony', *The Australian Quarterly* 10, no. 2 (June 1938): 65–72 (67)). Indeed, throughout *Capricornia* the train scatters bodies across the land. Wevers suggests that the conflation in the novel of the railway as a sign of both technological progress and biopolitical destruction highlights the implementation of the railway as a form of 'phallic technology' ('Terra Australis', 39).
49 Wevers, 'Terra Australis', 42.
50 Ibid.
51 'die dabei angewandten Methoden haben über Australien hinaus Allgemeingültigkeit für alle Länder, wo farbige Menschen unter der Massenverfelgung zu Leiden haben', in Paul Friedländer, report for *Capricornia*, undated, BArch DR1/3998/5.
52 Ibid., 5.
53 'wie alle Figuren des Romans, ein Mensch mit seinen Widersprüchen, seinen schlechten und guten Seiten', ibid., 8.
54 The irony of this statement with relation to acts of banishment and forced exile routinely practiced by the GDR cannot be emphasized enough.
55 'ihre Heuchelei, ihre Brutalität und ihre moralische Verkommenheit […] die höheren Angestellten der Verwaltung, die maßgebenden Herren des Nordens sind', in Friedländer, report for *Capricornia*, 9.
56 See Ian James, 'On Interrupted Myth', 331–49; and Ian James, *The Fragmentary Demand: An Introduction to the Philosophy of Jean-Luc Nancy* (Stanford: Stanford University Press, 2006), 177.

57 Patricia A. Herminghouse, 'Literature as *"Ersatzöffentlichkeit"*? Censorship and the Displacement of Public Discourse in the GDR', *German Studies Review* 17, *Totalitäre Herrschaft – totalitäres Erbe* (Fall 1994): 85–99 (86).
58 Walter Benjamin, 'The Task of the Translator', trans. Harry Zohn, in *Selected Writings, Vol. 1, 1913–1926*, ed. Marcus Bullock and Michael W. Jennings (Cambridge, MA: The Belknap Press/Harvard University Press, 2004), 253–63 (254).
59 Ibid., 255.
60 Percy Bysshe Shelley, 'A Defence of Poetry', in *The Major Works* (Oxford: Oxford University Press, 2003), 674–701 (693).
61 Sherry Simon, *Gender in Translation: Cultural Identity and the Politics of Transmission* (London: Routledge, 1996), 161.

Part II

BOOKS AND WRITERS

Chapter 4

SEDITION AS REALISM: FRANK HARDY'S *POWER WITHOUT GLORY* PARTS THE IRON CURTAIN

Nicole Moore

> 'Any novel that accurately mirrors reality in Australia must read like an adventure tale.'
> Cover blurb, *Power without Glory*, Leipzig: Paul List Verlag, Panther Books, 1956.

It is the flashpoint of Australia's cultural Cold War: on 18 July 1951, in Melbourne, communist Frank Hardy emerges to cheering crowds as the victor of a trial for criminal libel brought against his novel *Power without Glory*. He had first been charged in October 1950, only five days after the federal Parliament of Australia passed a bill outlawing the Communist Party of Australia that subsequently would be overturned by the country's high court. The detailed realism of Hardy's book was at once its authority and its danger, since it was clearly based on the life of wealthy and influential Melbourne identity John West, and suggested collusion with crime on the part of both major political parties, implicating senior figures of the Catholic Church. And it seems clear that the novel was charged with criminal libel only because public opinion meant that it could not be charged with sedition successfully.[1] In East Germany, however, that notionally seditious realism was transformed, or perhaps literalized, to instead sign for Australia itself. As the cover blurb for the Panther Books English language version from 1956 suggests, for the German Democratic Republic (GDR), Australian 'reality' was rather unreal; a necessarily outlandish or hyperbolic 'adventure' that could be expected to manifest as drama and, in Hardy's novel, political drama at that.

Macht ohne Ruhm became the first piece of Australian fiction to be published in the GDR when released by the internationalist house Volk und Welt in 1952. Hardy's visit to the new nation in 1951 and his book's wide reception show him acting as at once a cultural ambassador for his home country and its political critic. He was a conduit for Australian communist writers later published in East Germany, including Katharine Susannah Prichard, Dorothy Hewett and even Walter Kaufmann, before Kaufmann's return to Germany. And, with Egon Kisch's widely read *Landung in Australien* from 1937, Hardy's work established a frame through which exotic Australia would continue to be understood by the GDR as an exemplary backward capitalist state: repressive, exploitative, materialist, sexist and racist.[2]

As a Lukácsian historical novel, invested in retrospective, 'agitational' realism and the reconstructive narrativization of identifiable place and time across late nineteenth-century and early twentieth-century Melbourne (one might say the plotting of indictable acts within place and time), *Power without Glory*'s first act was to 'produce locality', as Arjun Appadurai formulated such a process in his *Modernity at Large* in 1996.[3] Hardy's book is quintessentially local, even too close to truth, as the libel case argued, its offence seemingly particular to the reading world of Melbourne, in the ways such was riven by class rivalries and religious loyalties, and grounded on the forms of recognition available to that city as a fractious but distinctive discursive formation. Despite this powerful localism and its fiercely sustained reputation as a book about Melbourne (it is still regularly cited as *the* Melbourne book), *Power without Glory* was a worldly book from very early in its life, garnering an expanding international reception months before Hardy notoriously stood trial for it, while its distribution was still embargoed in Australia.

International communism, as this collection demonstrates, provided ready and far-reaching conduits for the book, and the scandal of its failed prosecution for criminal libel circulated in the UK, through West and East Europe and to the USA as the trial proceeded. By the time of Hardy's acquittal, at least 11 countries had contracted the book for publication and its distributor, Joe Waters, could report standing orders for 2,000 copies to the UK and 6,000 copies to the USA waiting on the verdict (although Waters also recalled that 500 copies sent to a left-wing distributor in the USA had been impounded and thrown into the sea, Pauline Armstrong's biography suggesting that 'not one copy reached the US market').[4] Hardy's papers, as well as his 17-volume Australian Security Intelligence Organisation (ASIO) file, show him in negotiations with European publishers from at least December 1950, after writing to them himself, it seems (the Polish publisher Czytelnik replied first).[5] Thanks to ASIO, we know that among the papers in his possession on the day Hardy was arrested by Victorian police was a letter from editor Stephen

Murray Smith, in 1950 still a communist and a member of the Realist Writers Group, writing from Prague to ask Hardy for candidates for a proposed Czech collection of Australian stories. Hardy's connections to the readers of the Eastern Bloc were already firmly in place.

Notably, a letter of recommendation for Hardy seems to have been separately forwarded to Eastern European publishers by the high-profile, expatriate, Australian journalist Wilfred Burchett.[6] Burchett had been reporting for the UK *Express* from East Germany since 1944 and had married Vessa Ossikovska, a Bulgarian communist, in 1949, after divorcing his German Jewish first wife, whom he had married in London in 1938. But he was in Melbourne from September 1950 until January 1951. Although he had grown up in country Victoria, Burchett was born in Melbourne's Clifton Hill, which virtually abuts Collingwood, the 'Carringbush' setting of *Power without Glory*, and he returned home for those months expressly to campaign against the Communist Party bill. Hardy's reconstruction of the events surrounding his novel's trial in *The Hard Way* suggests that Burchett took notes on the novel over a beer with him during his lecture tour.[7]

On 20 January 1951, Burchett published an article on the criminal libel case in the London-based journal of the World Federation of Trade Unions (WFTU), the *World Trade Union Movement*, in which he described Hardy's novel as the 'most powerful novel that has ever been written in this country'.[8] The *World Trade Union Movement* was published in English, French, German, Romanian, Russian, Spanish, Chinese, Japanese and Swedish, among other languages, and brought news of Hardy's predicament to significant portions of the world's organized labour movements, positioning it in a world of readers geographically very distant from those for whom and among whom it was written. If *Power without Glory* was a worldly book, the world it addressed most immediately was certainly the Second World, and it did so almost exactly as this cold war agglomeration was being brought into formal existence. While the newly established ASIO, continuing the Commonwealth Investigation Bureau's well-established surveillance of Hardy and Burchett, reported that Burchett's article 'appears to have aroused considerable interest among different readers of the WFTU Review [sic]', Hardy declared that its appearance 'launched our campaign on a world scale'.[9] A chapter of *Power without Glory* itself appeared in the journal on 5 April 1950.

The WFTU was established in October 1945, in the wake of the inaugural meeting of the United Nations that June, and given consultative status at the Economic and Social Council of the UN, which was actively supporting national liberation movements around the globe as decolonization gathered pace. By 1950 the Federation had split, however, with the British and American trade union councils withdrawing over opposition to the Marshall Plan and then

(Original cartoon, specially drawn for **World Trade Union Movement** by COUNIHAN.)

Figure 4.1 Cartoon by Noel Counihan for the *World Trade Union Movement*, no. 2 (20 January 1951): 45. (Reproduced by permission of the Counihan Estate.)

establishing the alternative International Confederation of Free Trade Unions (ICFTU), bifurcating the dream of a worldwide labour movement and marking the triumph of nation-based cold war hostilities over any utopian or non-Soviet models of international worker solidarity.[10] In 1950 the WFTU was clearly dominated by communists and communist interests, and strongly supportive of the USSR. Burchett's article on *Power without Glory* dropped Hardy's book about corrupt Melbourne into high-stake debates about the possibility and practice of planetary or global governance, then circling and informing the contemporaneous 1950 European Convention on Human Rights (ECHR), and witnessing the formal end to a post-war vision of notionally 'united' international cooperation. When the Socialist Unity Party (SED) in a National Coalition took over from Soviet control in East Berlin in October 1949, Hardy's European soon-to-be readers were experiencing the bureaucratic inauguration of the Cold War, after its pre-emptive manifestation in the Berlin Blockade and before its proxy realization in Korea. And the ECHR's purported new universalism proved divisive at its very beginning, through the exclusion of economic and social rights, which defined it as liberal and Western.[11] The question of the right to freedom of speech was prominently at stake for the convention and was also in the forefront of Burchett's formulations about Hardy's case, demonstrating the pitch of the rhetorical struggles over the ideological high ground at this time of international crisis. Burchett used the polarized discourse of the moment as the McCarthy trials unfolded in the USA, identifying 'Americanization' with new 'fascist' directions in Australia: 'The persecution of the Australian author Frank Hardy and the attempts to suppress his book *Power without Glory* [...] form part of the new pattern of Australian life to stifle freedom of speech and to rob the working class of their political parties, their leaders and their spokesmen.'[12]

International socialism is the bridge on which Burchett's article traverses the imaginative distance between Hardy's localism and his global audience, spanning their separation by way of socialist critique and solidarity under capitalism:

> To an Australian many of the characters are recognisable immediately and their connections with events described are readily acknowledged with the clues provided by Hardy's narrative. But the characters can also be recognised in any community where there are powerful men motivated by the lust for money and power, where social-democracy and clericalism walk hand-in-hand, where money can buy favours from politicians and dispensations from police and judges.[13]

Burchett's ideology of reading transposes the features of Hardy's libellous particularity onto the shared experiences of life under capitalism elsewhere. Although it certainly worked as a powerful ideological filter or censor, the Iron Curtain did not prevent the circulation of literature across borders altogether; the GDR's strong publishing apparatus furnished many well-respected translations for the West German market, for example. International socialist and communist models of aesthetics provided machines for literary translation between source cultures and target cultures, as the Introduction outlines, even as the often clandestine tactics of the cultural Cold War militated against or were in opposition to such connections. As *Power without Glory*, the pivotal text of an Australian cultural Cold War, travelled along ready-prepared routes of translation and reception into the communist world, so efforts from the FBI, the CIA and the Congress for Cultural Freedom, and British MI5 worked to forge and foster similar literary vectors, with notionally opposite politics.[14]

The antonymic receptions offered Western-authored communist texts in their source and target cultures can be modelled through David Damrosch's image of refracted mirroring, as a model for the process of textual reception that occurs in separated reading cultures, in which the translation and distinct reception of texts produces, as he describes it, a 'mutual elliptical refraction' of both cultures.[15] This transnational mirroring, as it were, refracting the role of these books in the different reading contexts, was then doubled by the fact that the Panther Books English language editions, from Paul List, later Seven Seas, were returned to Australia and circulated cheaply in that country, when Australian editions of those leftist writers (in Australia, often minor, but including Hardy) were out of print. The first encounter with *Power without Glory* recalled by influential Australian-left historian and commentator Humphrey McQueen was its two-volume East German Panther Books edition, piled in heaps in Melbourne's communist International Bookshop in the early 1960s, when no Australian publisher had it in print.[16] It is not clear, however, if Damrosch's refracted imaging is enough to describe what is a quite thorough opposition between two reading positions in this case; it is perhaps a complete inversion rather than mere refraction.

An emphasis on the material conditions through which readers come to books and books are delivered to readers is a highly productive means by which to fill out this conceptual problematic. The work of Tony Bennett and John Frow on reading formations, in its sociological detail, building on the economic frames of Pierre Bourdieu, is one site from which to take models for this, and we could look again at the localized work of Carole Ferrier and Ian Syson, arguing through the question of the existence of working-class reading formations, with *Power without Glory* as a central example.[17] In Franco Moretti's wake, contemporary work on reception and reading history is even more distinctly empirical – Katherine Bode's *Reading by Numbers* uses large volumes of publishing data, for instance, to answer similar long-standing questions for Australian literary history.[18] Did different publishing enterprises, distribution networks and reading contexts – sourced in the political structures of organized labour, for example, as Hardy's book was in Australia – make for different uses, receptions, readings, different versions of the text? How did the translation process – both as such and as a larger cultural and ideological process reconfiguring Hardy's book for a newly constituted East German readership – position *Macht ohne Ruhm*?

On 12 December 1950, Bruno Peterson, director of the GDR's internationalist publisher Volk und Welt, also Burchett's publisher, wrote to Hardy, keen to publish. Hardy replied, agreeing to a German edition on 16 February 1951.[19] Volk und Welt was the first non-Australian publisher to give Hardy a definite offer of publication, while further interest soon after translated into formal offers from Czech, Slovak, Bulgarian, Romanian, Polish, Yugoslavian, Hungarian, Russian, Chinese, French, Dutch and Belgian publishers (for both French and Dutch Belgian editions), and eventually Swedish publishers too.[20] Hardy's French publisher was Renaud de Jouvenel, director of Le Chant du Monde, which was funded by the French Communist Party; Jouvenel was an associate of Sartre's and an influential 'fellow traveller'. To him Hardy sent copies of a leaflet from the Frank Hardy Defence Fund and a letter of protest to be circulated for 'a few well-known signatures in Paris' and then forwarded to the Australian attorney general.[21] In Pascale Casanova's conception of world literature, then, Hardy's book had reached a cultural epicentre, a world literary capital – although, notably, not an English-speaking capital. Hardy's British correspondents had warned that UK publishers were unlikely to take it up, at least while the charges still stood, but the Communist Party of Great Britain ensured some circulation for the fourth Melbourne-printed edition, priced at nine shillings and sixpence for British readers. The communist bookshop in London gave it 'most-favored-author placing at the entrance […] between Stalin and Gogol,' despite the *Daily Worker's* verdict that it was 'badly written and a bore', as the Melbourne *Herald* gleefully reported.[22] It took Werner Laurie in London until 1962 to release the first British edition, with a different edition from Sphere following in 1968. No American edition was ever produced. In 1955 Coronation Press in Melbourne released another Australian edition and a year after that a further English language version was released – significantly, not in the English metropoles but by Paul List Verlag in Leipzig, where it was designed for export back to the English-speaking world.

In fact, Hardy made his first trip to the German Democratic Republic before his book had been released there, to attend the Youth Peace Festival in East Berlin in August 1951, with his wife, Rosslyn, as two of the 135 Australian delegates.[23] Hardy and Rosslyn left Australia with the delegation almost immediately after Hardy's acquittal, using money somehow sourced from the Realist Writers Groups and fundraiser meetings.[24] As a later member of the Sydney Realist Writers group, Dorothy Hewett recalled Hardy declaring that he had left for Berlin not only because of the court case but because, with the referendum on the banning of the Communist Party looming for September, 'I was likely to be one of the first victims'.[25] They arrived first in England and then set about getting permission to travel behind the Iron Curtain, knowing that they could be forced to forfeit their passports by the Australian government and knowing too that they had little money to take with them. In accounts of the trial, including one published in the Soviet *Literary Gazette* in December 1951 and forwarded to ASIO by the Department of External Affairs, Hardy declared that they hoped to pay for their return passage with royalties from foreign editions of *Power without Glory*.[26] Together, Rosslyn and Frank travelled through Holland, East Germany, Poland, Czechoslovakia and finally to the USSR, where they were guests of the Soviet Writers Union.

Plans to publish were well underway by the time they arrived in Berlin; having agreed to publish in February, Hardy signed the contract with Volk und Welt while on the spot in August 1951. The publisher had contracted translator Hermann Budzislawski in March, with copy due from him in October. Hardy himself had already prepared and forwarded to all his European publishers a set of footnotes explaining Australian usages and phrases, though there are no records as to whether Budzislawski employed them.[27] Perhaps tellingly,

Hardy's contract with Volk und Welt included an exceptional clause: 'In case of competent authorities raise [sic] the principal objections against the author resp. [sic] his creation the publishers are quite free to stop selling the book and, after written understanding, to consider the contract with the author as solved.'[28] But Hardy received a warm welcome in the GDR, on the back of the Burchett article. The reception of Hardy and *Macht ohne Ruhm* in East Germany was expansively enthusiastic, helped by Hardy's sensationalized self-promotion, ongoing press interest in the story of the trial, Budzislawski's swift work and, it seems, an approvingly expedited passage through the Ministry of Culture's permissions process. Published in late 1952 in two volumes, before the Ministry's centralized approval process for book publishing was systematized, *Macht ohne Ruhm* retains no record of its assessment by the Ministry or its publisher, but the speed with which it was translated, produced and released is testimony enough.

As Christina Spittel and I have noted in this book's Introduction, the GDR's practice in publishing foreign titles was to furnish each with a *Nachwort* (afterword), penned by a local literary figure, in order to introduce the book to East Germans. These worked as effective 'passports to the *Leseland*' or 'reading

Figure 4.2 Cover of Frank Hardy's *Macht ohne Ruhm*, volume 1 (Berlin: Volk und Welt, 1952).

nation', the conjured, utopic imaging of the GDR as a literary society or *Literaturgesellschaft* envisioned by Johannes R. Becher at the Fourth German Writers' Congress in 1956, as noted.[29] It is in *Macht ohne Ruhm*'s afterword and its press reception that we see Australia most clearly constructed as a backward capitalist product of empire, in an earlier formulation of the gulag image analyzed by Russell West-Pavlov in his discussion of Professor Anselm Schlösser's afterword to Volk und Welt's 1957 translation of Marcus Clarke's *For the Term of His Natural Life*. *Macht ohne Ruhm*'s anonymous afterword, as a German reader's introduction to the novel's contexts, steps out Australia's colonial history as a Gothic horror story of brutal capitalist self-reproduction: 'the old rotten gallows now constructed anew'.

> Sie legten Felder und Siedlungen an, erschlossen Bodenschätze – doch mit jedem dieser Werke schmiedeten sie die neuen Fesseln fester, die ihren alten ähnelten, wie ein neuer Galgen einem alten und morschen.
>
> [They constructed fields and settlements, made natural resources accessible – yet with each of these acts they forged new bonds more solidly, which were similar to the old ones – the old rotten gallows now constructed anew.][30]

This 1952 afterword can be read as the first communist attempt to construct a narrative of Australian national history for a book reading audience in the GDR: its big picture approach an indication too of the perceived (or rather constructed) distance between readers of Hardy's original or source text and the translated 'target' text. Instead of the fabled worker's paradise or a modern young nation leading the world in votes for women and the development of the welfare state, the GDR's Australia is conjured as a culture-less, corrupt, unthinkingly capitalist society, ill educated, grasping, unreflective, valuing only 'power and luxury', in a syntagm echoing Hardy's 'power without glory', as that in turn echoes Matthew 6:13. Established through penal servitude and imperial land grabbing

> Auf dem Boden einer solchen Geschichte hat die Kultur das Wachsen schwer. Die herrschende Klasse brauchte sie nicht: sich selbst mit Bildung zu schmücken, hatte sie kaum das Bedürfnis. Ihr genügten die Macht und der Luxus. Der breiten Masse warf sie die Ramschprodukte der amerikanischen Traumfabriken vor.
>
> Die Werktätigen dagegen brauchten die Kultur. Sie machten die Kunst zu einer scharfen Waffe in ihrem Kampf um Freiheit und Brot, um ein menschenwürdiges Dasein. Sie schufen eine Literatur, die ein legales Erbe der klassischen Schriften von Balzac und Charles Dickens ist. Eine junge, kämpferische Literatur, deren Reihen sich mit Frank Hardy ein vielversprechender junger Schriftsteller zugesellt hat.

[with this story as a basis, it was hard for culture to grow. The ruling class didn't need culture: they barely needed to adorn themselves with 'education'. Power and luxury were enough for them. They found fault in the mass-market, for its consumption of junk goods from factories of the American dream.

In contrast, the workers needed culture. They developed art into a sharp weapon in their fight for freedom, bread, and a humane existence. They created a literature, which was a true legacy of the classic writings of Balzac and Charles Dickens. A young, pugnacious literature, whose ranks Frank Hardy, an up-and-coming young writer, affiliated himself with.][31]

Kämpferische is translated as 'pugnacious' here, but could instead be 'belligerent', appropriately 'militant', or even just 'fighting'; the emphasis is on the literature's energetic ability to defend itself. The afterword mashes together Hardy's author's note from the final pages of the Australian edition of *Power without Glory*, Burchett's journalistic piece, Hardy's own later hyperbolic contributions, and quotations from the Frank Hardy Defence Committee including a sensationalist account of the different McCarthyite antagonisms from which, and into which, it was being launched:

In Amerika benutzte man 'Mißachtung der Obrigkeit' als Vorwand für diesen Gewaltakt, in Australien das Gesetz über die 'Veröffentlichung böswilliger Verleumdungen'. Doch was heute in Amerika und Australien geschieht, entspricht völlig den Vorgängen unmittelbar vor der Machtergreifung Hitlers in Deutschland. In Deutschland hat der Faschismus zum Kriege geführt. In Australien und Amerika strebt die Reaktion ebenfalls einem Kriege zu. Nur die vereinten Anstrengungen des ganzen Volkes können ihn verhindern.

[In America they used 'disregard for authority' under false pretences to legitimate acts of violence. In Australia, it was the law on 'publication of malicious libel'. Yet, what is happening today in America and Australia corresponds completely with the incidents that occurred directly before Hitler's takeover in Germany. In Germany, fascism led to war. In Australia and America, the reactionaries also strive for 'war'. Only the united efforts of the entire people can stop this.][32]

The rhetorical stylization of the Cold War as 'war' itself was by no means restricted to the GDR in this period, of course, and in the spirit of direct intervention, the afterword expands its reflections to encompass immediate East German conflicts with West Germany:

Dabei spielte die rechte Sozialdemokratie in Australien die gleiche Rolle, die sie in der amerikanischen Politik Adenauers in Westdeutschland übernommen hat: den Schein der Demokratie aufrechtzuerhalten und eine volksfeindliche Regierung davor zu bewahren, dass sie vom Volke hinweggefegt wird, weil sie mit offen faschistischen Methoden den Krieg vorbereitet.

[The right-wing of social democracy in Australia took over the same role in this that right-wing social democracy has played in Adenauer's American politics in West Germany: the appearance of upholding democracy, but meanwhile protecting an anti-populist government from being swept away by its people, who see that the government is preparing for 'war' with unequivocally fascist methods.][33]

Through 1950 and 1951, West German Chancellor Konrad Adenauer's government viewed a Soviet or 'East Zone' invasion as a real possibility. His ongoing refusal to recognize the GDR as a separate state was a key plank in his declared 'policy of strength', opposing what he saw as overwhelming Soviet power, but also the key point of controversy in the signing of treaties with the Western powers in the later half of 1952.[34] The GDR, meanwhile, was sending its own delegates to the West with its own proposals for reunification. A year later, the 1953 Berlin uprising, as the first outbreak of violent dissent in the Eastern Bloc, would present a different face for 'populism' in the GDR. Like Hardy's author note in the Australian editions, the afterword of *Macht ohne Ruhm* ends by listing Hardy's address in Australia and seeking readers' correspondence, since 'he is of the opinion that the best teachers for him are the rank and file of working-class readers'.[35]

Volk und Welt collected reviews of *Macht ohne Ruhm* from 23 newspapers, including Dutch, Swiss and West German papers. All of them made liberal use of Hardy's own accounts, some reproducing these in their entirety from Soviet newspapers and some publishing new quotations sourced directly while he was there. *Neues Deutschland*, the GDR-wide newspaper owned by the party, published a translation of a piece by Hardy from *Literaturnaja Gazeta*, titled 'Ein Buch vor Gericht' (A Book before Court, the same Russian *Literary Gazette* piece collected by ASIO), while the *Berliner Zeitung* ran another piece by Hardy, titled 'Dichter vor dem Fabriktor' (Poet at the Factory Gate). *Die Frau von Heute*, a women's magazine, titled its piece 'Wie er Millionär wurde' (How He Became a Millionaire); reviews appeared in the Sunday magazines as well as in the *Schulzeitung der Akademie Walter Ulbricht*.[36] *Das demokratische Dorf*, in its review of November 1952, made explicit *Macht ohne Ruhm*'s heuristic role for right-thinking East Germans, as a realist expose of the capitalist world:

Und warum erregte das Buch so großes Aufsehen? Weil an der Hauptfigur des Romans, John West, die Verhältnisse in einem Land wahrheitsgetreu dargestellt werden, das angeblich so "demokratisch" regiert wird [...] vermittelt uns [...] einen ausgezeichneten Überblick über die Zustände in all den Ländern, in denen die werktätige Bevölkerung unterdrückt und ausgebeutet wird und nur eine kleine Schicht von "Auserwählten" die Macht in ihrem eigenen Interesse ausübt.

[And why did the book cause such a stir? The main character in the novel, John West, can accurately portray the situation in a country that is supposedly 'democratic' […] Mediating for us […] an excellent overview of the situation in all countries where the working population is oppressed and exploited and only a small group of 'chosen ones' hold power in their own interests.]³⁷

The East German edition of the key German book trade journal *Börsenblatt des deutschen Buchhandels* (from the association of publishers and booksellers, with separate versions for East and West during the life of the GDR), finished its extravagant review thus: '[Hardy's] life and works present ideals for all the world's youth, on whom the enemies of life have declared war. They should heed the author, whose heart beats for the desires of peace-loving peoples.'³⁸

What is striking about many of the reviews, in their recounting (via Hardy) of the story of *Power without Glory* in Australia, is the emphasis on the process of the book's production, and not just its reception and prosecution, nor the defence campaign. This is, of course, particularly prominent in the account in the GDR edition of *Börsenblatt des deutschen Buchhandels*:

> Zunächst verbot man den Verlegern und Druckern das Buch auszubringen und zu verbreiten. Ein großer Teil der Buchhändler beugte sich aus Angst vor der Macht allen ihren Massnahmen. Trotzdem gelang es mit Hilfe der gewerkschaftlich organisierten Arbeiterschaft, das Werk erscheinen zu lassen und innerhalb eines Monats 8000 Exemplare (für australische Verhältnisse enorme Auflagenhöhe!) zu verkaufen. […] Büroangestellte, Matrosen, Werftarbeiter, Geistliche und Maurer bildeten Laienbuchbindergruppen, um 16000 Exemplare des Buches zu je 670 Seiten zu binden und für die Verbreitung zu sichern.
>
> [At first the publishers and printers were forbidden to produce and distribute the book. A large section of the booksellers buckled under the fear of the wide-reaching power of these circles. Nevertheless, with the help of the unionized workforce, the book was successfully released and within one month 8,000 copies (by Australian standards an enormous number of copies) was sold. […] Office employees and seamen, roustabouts and journalists, bricklayers and intellectuals, formed amateur book binding groups to bind the 16,000 copies of the book, each of 670 pages, and to ensure its distribution.]³⁹

Versions of this aspect of the story abound, including Hardy's own not entirely reliable account in *The Hard Way*, in which the key role of the Communist Party of Australia (CPA) executive in Victoria is downplayed. The figure of 16,000 copies is reproduced from the *Macht ohne Ruhm* afterword, but it seems impossible to determine exactly how many copies and editions were produced in the period between April 1950, when the first copies of the first edition made it into members' hands, and Hardy's acquittal in June 1951. Biographer Armstrong's detailed version recounts that 'the CPA rallied trusted party members, pensioners, trade unionists and other volunteers to collate and fold by hand each thirty-two page section of the ten thousand copies of the 672-page novel', learn the basics of hand binding and glue the covers.[40] For her, the extraordinary story 'has no parallel in the history of the Australian novel'.[41] Burchett's early article dramatized the narrative similarly: 'A group of workers volunteered to learn the art of sewing, gluing and book-binding [...] Often enough the books remained unbound for days and nights on end in trucks. Teams of amateur bookbinders worked away every hour of their spare time and the book began to circulate.'[42]

The ironies of this concern with the conditions of the book's production, as a scandal of repressive censorship under capitalism, can seem manifest, of course. As these organs of opinion in the GDR decried Australian attempts to censor Hardy, the state was building its own book censorship authority and beginning to implement full pre-publication control. Barck, Langermann and Lokatis describe how the complex and systematic work of the censors, in addition to a planned economy of book production characterized by scarcity, 'contributed to the elimination of critics of the regime and the preservation of more or less clearly defined social and political taboos'. An 'entire national literature' was subordinated to censorship.[43] But to characterize these as ironies is insufficient too: the dissonance and apparent silence about GDR control in these accounts are not unconscious, but manifestations of a cultural ideological war at its height. Hardy and Burchett were advocates of free speech but directedly: for workers and proletarian culture, for those for whom the means and products of capitalist cultural production had been out of reach. The GDR's system of centralized publishing control was not to be decried as censorship but welcomed as a concerted wresting of the means of production from capitalist interests. It was a key economic structure (or 'apparatus' in the Althusserian lexicon that Russell West-Pavlov appropriately reanimates in Chapter 2) through which to create socialist society, and Hardy and Burchett were inspired to do some wresting back of the means of cultural production at home.

Volk und Welt paid Hardy an advance, as well as his and Rosslyn's hotel bill while in Berlin. Like many other Western writers travelling in the Eastern Bloc, Hardy sought to spend that soft currency as quickly as he could and first bought a German-made typewriter, as did Christina Stead and William Blake during their visit in September 1956.[44] Then, taking this investment in East German technology further, he entrusted Bruno Peterson from Volk und Welt with the purchase, delivery and export of a book binding machine, which he selected during his time in Berlin. This could not be accomplished easily. The heightened state of cold war tensions can be seen in the extent of the surveillance exercised over Hardy's correspondence with Peterson after his return, as he worked to get the machine out of the country. ASIO was directed to this discussion in Hardy's letters from early 1952, his mention of 'those shipments arranged on my behalf in Berlin' underlined by the Department of External Affairs, which had been forwarded copies of the letters on 26 February 1952 by the Australian Military Mission in Berlin. The Department explained that, in turn,

> the letters were photographed by the US Army Intelligence in Berlin, being picked up during the course of that department's normal security checking of inwards mail. Finding the material to be of some value from their security viewpoint, they have passed the letters to this mission and I am transmitting them for your information.[45]

In June 1952 Hardy was still unable to confirm that the machine was on its way. He wrote to Peterson:

> I am still anxiously waiting for news of the book paper, newsprint and stapling machine for the purchase of which you were to make available the money. Walter [Kaufmann] knows about this; and I think the man I saw was Paul Dampmann, Zentrag, Wall street, Berlin, Tel 67 63 61. This paper and machine is now urgently needed. Please advise if these have been shipped, to whom and by which ship; and date of departure and arrival. Have shipping documents been sent?

And Burchett wanted a printer for his brother. Hardy continued, writing perhaps on his behalf while Burchett was in Australia on route to Asia:

> Regarding the machine requested by Mr Burchett. Walter Czollek and I saw this machine at a printery we inspected together. If the Mercedes high-speed printing machine at DM 18,000 is for quod crown 30 x 40 inch paper, then it sounds like the machine Mr Burchett wants. You should acquire it for him in accordance with the instructions of his brother and, I understand, of Coronation Press Ltd of Melbourne.[46]

Writing to Hardy in August from Peking, Burchett was still unclear whether the plan would work:

> Will they let you bring the machines in, in view of the latest import restrictions. Let's know how the deal works out. It seems to me our only chance to beat the publishers is to be completely independent and it seems the reading public is ready to back us up.[47]

Hardy's royalty records from Volk und Welt show evidence of payments deducted for the purchase of a book binding machine in early to mid-1952.[48] These are the months in which the newly established, CPA-backed

Australasian Book Society (ABS), its membership model touted by Hardy in his many speaking engagements after his return from the Eastern Bloc, was getting ready to print its first two books: Ralph de Boissiere's *Crown Jewel* and Hardy's apologist account of his and Ross's travels in the Stalinist USSR, *Journey into the Future*, later reviled by Hardy as 'the only dishonest book I ever wrote'.[49] This was also the second of his books translated and released for East Germans by Volk und Welt, as *Reise in die Zukunft*, contracted by Volk und Welt just after its launch in Australia.

Hardy's experience with printers in Melbourne had forcibly demonstrated the need for 'independence' from the established industry, as Burchett couched it. ABS's founding members included Burchett's father, George, and brother, Clive, and it was Clive's Coronation Press in Melbourne that released the sixth edition of *Power without Glory* in 1955.[50] Writing for the *Berliner Zeitung* in 1952, Hardy claimed that *Power without Glory*'s *Druck- und Verteilungsapparat* (print and distribution apparatus) was also used to bring out his friend Eric Lambert's privately printed *The Twenty Thousand Thieves*, and he suggests in both *The Hard Way* and a later account of the ABS that the venture was a direct furthering of that model of reader-oriented production and distribution.[51] It seems possible that, through the 1950s, as the ABS began to roll out its schedule of four books a year for its subscribed members, the East German book binder and printer became key technological devices in the creation of a self-consciously working-class, literary readership in Australia: a newly mobilized reading formation, as Syson and Ferrier identified it. By 1961 ABS was 'responsible for one third of the new fiction titles published in Australia' as Hocking reports (albeit via Hardy).[52]

For Hardy, his embrace by Eastern European publishing, then, was not merely a welcome second avenue for a book beleaguered and attacked in the English-speaking world but a manifestation of worker-controlled publishing, a wresting back of the means of cultural production from capitalism and industry, and a state-backed materialization of the mini-model of leftist DIY publishing and distribution to which he and his mates had been forced to resort. The GDR's centralized, state-controlled publishing system – it particularly, with its swift embrace of Hardy and close ties to Burchett – appeared to him not a means of controlling a dissident reading population but the opposite: a sanctioned, institutional enabling of stifled expression that was miraculously strong enough to defend itself against its enemies. And Hardy's perceived literary enemies were powerful: the Rockefeller and Ford foundations; US media and publishing conglomerates and the expansive reach of American cultural exports; the CIA-backed *Encounter* (London), *Paris Review* (Paris), *Der Monat* (Berlin) and from 1957, *Quadrant* (Sydney); the work of the British Council and the Information Research Department (IRD, a secret division of the British Foreign Office); the McCarthy trials and Menzies's Communist Party Dissolution Bill, and so on.[53] Andrew Rubin's new work on the discourses, organizations, activities and institutions of anti-communism in the early Cold War describes the fostering and development of 'an entirely new and powerful episteme' with effects that were 'multiple, vast and global'.[54] In a column for the Melbourne *Guardian* in 1952, Hardy railed against the appearance in Australia of new 'pseudo-literary journals' as a sign of the times: 'In America subsidised journals of this type are vehicles for the most reactionary propaganda, as part of the ideological campaign of the warmongers.' The 'so-called *Austrovert*' was a suspect example, supported, he suggested, by Sir Keith Murdoch.[55]

When Frank and Rosslyn returned to Australia in January 1952, their passports were confiscated, along with the passports of the entire Youth Festival delegation. Menzies had warned delegates of this possibility – writers wrote to the pair in support. In a statement to the press in Fremantle, where their ship first docked, as the CPA's *Tribune* reported it, Hardy was damning, his militancy a reflection of the authority he drew from his reception in the socialist world.

> The Temporary Government of Australia has seized my own and my wife's passport. We intend to take whatever action is necessary to recover them [...] Australian passports are quite illegally marked 'not valid for travel', listing not less than 14 countries. The first on the list is the Soviet Union. The reason is that this puppet government and the American and Australian millionaires who control it are afraid the truth about the socialist countries will get out.[56]

Here the dangers of parting the Iron Curtain are plain – famously, Burchett in his turn was denied his passport until the election of the Labor Whitlam government in 1972, for collaborating with Australia's enemies in Korea and Vietnam. Hardy's official reception in Australia upon his return was the opposite of the sanctioned feting he received in the Eastern Bloc and reminds us of the power of politico-geographic boundaries, contrary to the emphasis in contemporary globalized book histories on the porous, transnational aspects of national book industries and readerships. The free bodies of authors were at stake on both sides: belonging and citizenship neither taken for granted nor able to be transcended. Australian books were produced for an East German readership against that background of heightened tension, even profound risk.

Soon after their return to Australia, Frank 'arranged for' Ross Hardy to type the manuscript of *Voices in the Storm* by fellow Realist Writer and German Jewish refugee Walter Kaufmann (whose long East German writing career after his return to the GDR is examined by Alexandra Ludewig in Chapter 6), and then sent the typescript to Volk und Welt.[57] And through the 1950s, as Kaufmann did in his turn, Hardy continued to provide contacts for Eastern European publishers to other Australian writers. In a 1955 letter to Helen Palmer, who was looking for possible interest in an anthology of Australian historical documents edited with Jessica McLeod, and who had already received names and addresses for publishers in the USSR, Poland, Czechoslovakia, Bulgaria and Germany from Kaufmann, Hardy sent details for Dutch, French, Romanian, Hungarian, Czechoslovakian and Israeli firms. He ended: 'There is an upsurge of interest in Australian literature and history in Europe, especially in Eastern Europe. Walter Czollek [from Volk und Welt], for instance, has asked a few times for titles of Australian historical books.'[58]

Macht ohne Ruhm had an extended reception in the GDR. It was serialized in Verlag der Nation's magazine *GMBH* with a circulation of 30,000 in mid-1953 and broadcast as a radio play in 1954, with a repeat broadcast in late 1955.[59] Hardy entered into discussion with Volk und Welt about the possibility of a film in 1955, with interest from the East German film company DEFA, and that same year, *Macht ohne Ruhm* went into reprint, its 20,000 reported initial print run supplemented by a further 10,000 copies.[60] This edition began to sell well in West Germany.[61] Gertrude Gelbin's Panther Books imprint at Paul

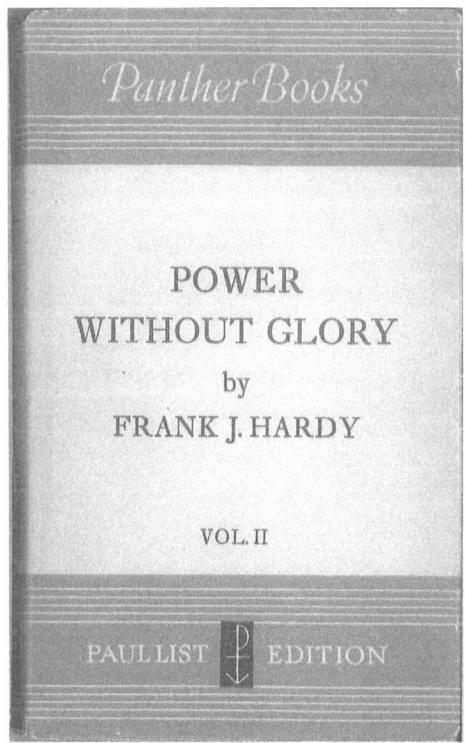

Figure 4.3 Cover of Frank Hardy's *Power without Glory*, volume 2 (Leipzig: Paul List/Panther Books, 1956).

List released its English-language edition in 1956, beginning the Australian list of Panther's successor, Seven Seas. *Die vierbeinige Lotterie* (*The Four-Legged Lottery*) was released by Volk und Welt in 1958 and by the respected cheap paperback publisher Reclam, Leipzig, on contract with Volk und Welt in 1959.[62] Through late 1960 and early 1961, Hardy's play *Black Diamonds*, set in a coal mine, was produced by Brecht's Berlin Ensemble and toured to an East German mine site for performances for miners – for Hardy, a great thrill.[63] *The Hard Way* (ABS, 1961) was revised for Volk und Welt but not released. By then a complicated royalties situation was producing extensive correspondence and required some radical solutions to allow payment in exportable hard currency to the always cash-strapped Hardy.

Table 4.1 East German Editions of Hardy Titles

Title	Translator	Publisher	Date	Print Run
Macht ohne Ruhm (*Power without Glory*) 2 vols	Hermann Budzislawski	Volk und Welt, Berlin	1952	20,000
Macht ohne Ruhm		Verlag der Nation – GMBH (serialized in magazine form)	1953	Circulation 30,000
Reise in die Zukunft (*Journey into the Future*)	Lisl Fleischhacker	Volk und Welt	1953	10,000
Macht ohne Ruhm reprint		Volk und Welt	1955	10,000
Power without Glory 2 vols		Panther Books: Paul List Verlag, Leipzig	1956	10,000
Die vierbeinige Lotterie (*The Four-Legged Lottery*)	Karl Heinrich	Volk und Welt	1958	10,000 on Hardy's contract; 12,000 on Ministry permission form
Die vierbeinige Lotterie (paperback)		Reclam, Leipzig, contracted with Volk und Welt	1959	10,000
Schwarze Diamanten (*Black Diamonds*)		Produced by Berliner Ensemble	1960–1961	
Schwarze Diamanten	Ernst Adler	Henschel, Berlin	1965	Stage script; not for sale.

Pauline Armstrong describes Hardy's treatment and reception in Eastern Europe:

> During his five known visits to the Soviet Union and Eastern Europe between 1951 and 1968, he had gained a high profile, and his work had a wide readership. His stories were used for radio and television programs. His birthdays were marked by congratulatory cables from the Union of Soviet Writers, other organisations and prominent individuals. He was treated with deference as the working-class Australian writer who had been tried for criminal libel by the capitalist courts.[64]

For the tenth anniversary of the GDR, Hardy was asked by Volk und Welt to write a public endorsement; editor Czollek acknowledged that writers do not enjoy doing such things, but Hardy duly complied and forwarded the piece soon after.[65] His East German reception was important to him, even as his faith in the Soviet Union waned through the later years of the 1960s. Party to the developing conflicts in East German cultural debates, he became 'someone who, as was said at his memorial service, knew a lot about Brecht'.[66]

John Frow's work on contemporary models of reading history and textual reception places notable emphasis on a text's 'afterlife', effectively redefining texts as their 'usage' rather than their temporally stagnant content, as précised in this book's Introduction. Frow's 1982 analysis of the reading regime implicated in the Victorian legal action against *Power without Glory* opened up its expansive definitional tensions and hermeneutic contradictions. A court room appears one of the most formalized and controlling reading contexts, but under pressure, Frow showed, its reading/text dynamic breaks down into impossible ambiguity, especially when what is at stake is the relation between text and 'truth': a book's ability to convey its generative context.[67] For *Power without Glory*, that productive dynamic looped in on itself in self-contradiction and not only text and author but their explosive political context too were caught in this process. As Hardy explained, the Wrens wanted to argue that *Power without Glory* was fictional but had to argue that it was true, to launch the charge of libel; conversely, the Hardy camp wanted to use truth as a defence but, to answer the charge, had to declare the book a fiction.

Paul Adams is critical of Frow's approach, nevertheless, because 'the processes and practices of signification, the illicit underground production of Hardy's book, the labour carried out on Hardy's texts in their creation and recreation and the reception of those texts is less important for Frow than "the forms of transmission and diffusion" of discourses'.[68] Reading its Australian reception after the trial, Adams notes that *Power without Glory* has been increasingly received as transparently thin fiction, or as a historical narrative or biography that is fundamentally factual, rather than fictive:

> The text's 'afterlife' is a matter not merely of the serial and lateral movements of its intertextuality but also of its received history as underground novel and its framing as oppositional history within the war of manoeuvre between the Wren forces and the Frank Hardy Defence Committee.[69]

The GDR was also, notionally, a highly stable reading regime, a formalized, assertively controlling regime in which the nation's reading relationship to a text was so anticipated as to be proscribed. This was even though that endorsed reading might be a highly attenuated or innovative one, pulling a text away from its lifetime of readings to assert new models of value and reference, and especially refiguring its concerns away from received readings in the West (in the censorship of modernism, for example, in rereadings of Shakespeare, and in reconstructions of many classic texts, including Australian books such as *For the Term of His Natural Life*).

The GDR offered a reception for *Power without Glory* directly opposite to that which Hardy's book received from the Victorian legal system, celebrating its threat to authority (and truth) as a bravely realist rendering of the truth about capitalist Australia. For GDR readerships, in so far as they were controlled and constructed by the Ministry of Culture (and that was very far), its portrait of corrupt capitalism was presented as a logical manifestation of the character of its country. And this can be seen as an extension of Hardy's vision inherent in his book but never fully realized. It is questionable whether *Power without Glory* has been about national character at all for Australians; it is a Melbourne book so thoroughly, and thus perhaps wholly localized for Australian readers. Appadurai's definition of 'local knowledge' draws on Clifford Geertz to insist on its 'embededdness in a non-negotiable here and now or its stubborn disinterest in things at large'.[70] The 'here and now' was certainly a key aspect of the 'locality' produced by Hardy's book, in its determined focus on Melbourne's immediate past and its contemporary, scandalized, politically riven, reading moment, but any illusion of a disregard for 'things at large' is only an obfuscatory effect of that close focus. Its wider allegorical applicability, or connotative 'afterlife', seemed apparent to regimes across the Eastern Bloc.

The critique of Melbourne/Australia/capitalism mounted by *Power without Glory* was what the GDR wanted to hear, but it was also what Hardy and his supporting network of communist authors wanted to write; they were dissident voices in what they experienced as a culture of aggressive and stifling political conservatism, and their communism was an enabling internationalist frame through which to denaturalize and indict (or libel) Australian conditions (and which brought them a large off-shore readership), even as their endeavour to build a working-class Australian culture through the 1950s was strongly nationalist. David Carter suggests that 'nationalism was a useful counter to cold war charges of importing a "foreign ideology" for Australian communists' and that 'through its identification with a popular democratic tradition, communism could be "naturalised", not as the unprecedented, transformative vision of a new world, but as the calm recognition and clarification of what had always already been there in our national history'.[71] Communist writers in Australia embraced this dual perspective through the 1950s, but it is also worth emphasizing that the 'transformative vision of a new world' was undimmed for some of them, including Hardy, whose ideas of utopia had plenty of echoes in the young GDR's aesthetic and cultural policies as they were implemented for its reading population through the 1950s. In an interview for ABC television in 1967, Hardy mused: 'The things that we thought were simple are very complicated, including the selection between national consciousness and internationalism. I want to rethink this nationalism in the context of the wider international field in creative writing of novels, stories, plays.'[72]

The paradox of *Power without Glory*'s so easily exported localism is only apparent rather than actual. Rather than transferring easily to other locations, to be readable in the GDR, Hardy's original or source text required a substantial set of material vectors for translation and distribution through the Iron Curtain, as well as discursive conduits through the combative ideological and cultural clashes of the early Cold War. And along these routes its local Melbourne scandal had to be consciously reread as representative rather than provincial, or generalizable rather than specific, and even its othered, adventurous Australianness was refigured as generic and predictable. *Macht ohne Ruhm* as produced target text had hard work to do in the Eastern Bloc. Its realist 'adventure story' would play out for more than a decade for Hardy's GDR readers in ways that were highly enabling for him and other Australian leftist writers and become a key ideological forum for the international articulation of Australia's cultural Cold War.

Notes

1 Nicole Moore, *The Censor's Library: Uncovering the Lost History of Australia's Banned Books* (St Lucia: University of Queensland Press, 2012), 71.
2 Allan Gardiner, 'Frank Hardy and Communist Cultural Institutions', in *Frank Hardy and the Literature of Commitment*, ed. Paul Adams and Christopher Lee (Melbourne: Vulgar Press, 2003), 35–52 (41–2).
3 Cf. 'Decoding Diaspora and Disjuncture: Arjun Appadurai in Dialogue with David Morley', *New Formations* 73 (2011): 43–55.

4 Pauline Armstrong, *Frank Hardy and the Making of* Power without Glory (Melbourne: Melbourne University Press, 2000), 139, 143.
5 Papers of Frank Hardy, National Library of Australia (NLA) MS 4887, series 8, box 42; Hardy ASIO file, National Archives of Australia (NAA), series A6119, 'Personal Files, Alpha-Numeric Series', Australian Security Intelligence Organisation, vols 1–15 and miscellaneous files.
6 Letter from Polish publisher Czytelnik, 6 Feb 1951, Papers of Frank Hardy, NLA, MS 4887, box 42, folder 8/2.
7 Frank Hardy, *The Hard Way* (Sydney: Australasian Book Society, 1961), 159.
8 Wilfred Burchett, 'Political Racketeers Attempt to Gag Working-Class Writer', *World Trade Union Movement* no. 2 (20 January 1951): 43–46 (44).
9 Note dated 30 May 1951, Hardy ASIO file, NAA A6119, vol. 2, item 281, 1951–56; Frank Hardy, *The Hard Way*, 159.
10 World Federation of Trade Unions website, 2007, accessed May 2013, http://www.wftucentral.org/history/.
11 Marco Duranti, 'The Human Rights Restoration Revolution', *Oxford Human Rights Hub* 3 (September 2013), accessed May 2013, http://ohrh.law.ox.ac.uk/?p=2811.
12 Burchett, 'Political Racketeers', 43.
13 Ibid., 44.
14 Cf. Andrew N. Rubin, *Archives of Authority: Empire, Culture, and the Cold War* (Princeton: Princeton University Press, 2012); James Smith, *British Writers and MI5 Surveillance, 1930–1960* (Cambridge: Cambridge University Press, 2013); Timothy Melley, *The Covert Sphere: Secrecy, Fiction and the National Security State* (Ithaca: Cornell, 2012); Joel Whitney, 'Exclusive: The *Paris Review*, the Cold War and the CIA', *Salon* (27 May 2012), accessed October 2013, http://www.salon.com/2012/05/27/exclusive_the_paris_review_the_cold_war_and_the_cia/.
15 David Damrosch, *What Is World Literature?* (Princeton: Princeton University Press, 2003), 2.
16 Conversation with Humphrey McQueen, May 2011.
17 Carole Ferrier '*Sugar Heaven* and the Reception of Working Class Texts', *Hecate* 11, no. 1 (1985): 19–25, and 'Jean Devanny, Katharine Susannah Prichard and the "Really Proletarian Novel"', in *Gender, Politics and Fiction: Twentieth Century Australian Women's Novels*, ed. Carole Ferrier, rev. ed. (St Lucia: University of Queensland Press, 1992), 101–177; Ian Syson, 'Towards a Poetics of Working Class Writing', *Southern Review* 26, no. 1 (1993): 86–100, and 'Out from the Shadows: The Realist Writers' Movement, 1944–1970, and Communist Cultural Discourse', *Australian Literary Studies* 15, no. 4 (1992): 333–51.
18 Katherine Bode, *Reading by Numbers: Recalibrating the Literary Field* (London: Anthem Press, 2012).
19 Papers of Frank Hardy, NLA MS 4887, series 8, box 42.
20 Pauline Armstrong's biography of Hardy recounts a story from a woman named only Elizabeth, who describes how a copy of *Power without Glory* had been sent to her in Budapest and she had arranged its publication with Szepriodalmi Könyvkiadó, a Hungarian publisher, and written the foreword for what was released as *John West Hatalma* (*The Power of John West*). 'It sold very well, and she said this was the first translation of Hardy's work' (Armstrong, *Frank Hardy*, 146).
21 Letter to Renaud de Jouvenal in Paris, 23 Feb 1951, NLA, Papers of Frank Hardy, MS 4887, box 42 folder 8/2.
22 *Herald*, special service 6 June 1952, clipped in Hardy's ASIO file, NAA A6119, vol. 2, item 281, 1951–56.

23 The Australia committee organizing the delegation first wrote to Hardy in April 1951 for an autographed copy of his book to take with them (NLA, Papers of Frank Hardy, 4887, box 42, folder 8/2).
24 There was some concern that they had used money from the Frank Hardy Defence Fund, particularly since their late booking on the MMS *Oronsay* meant they could only get first-class berths, but Hardy convincingly refuted this. Cf. a letter replying to Katharine Susannah Prichard, 1951 (NLA, Papers of Frank Hardy, 4887, box 42, folder 8/2); Jenny Hocking, *Frank Hardy: Politics, Literature, Life* (South Melbourne: Lothian, 2005) 131.
25 Jack Beasley, *Red Letter Days: Notes from Inside an Era* (Sydney: Australasian Book Society, 1979); cf. Carole Ferrier, '"These Girls Are on the Right Track": Hardy, Devanny and Hewett', in *Frank Hardy and the Literature of Commitment*, 71–87 (80).
26 Frank Hardy, 'Books on Trial', *Literaturnaja Gazeta* (*Literary Gazette*) (5 December 1951), translated and extracted by Joint Press Reading Service and clipped in Hardy's ASIO file, NAA A6119, vol. 2, item 281, 1951–56.
27 Cf. Letter to Bruno Peterson at Volk und Welt, 16 Feb. 1951, NLA, Papers of Frank Hardy, MS 4887, box 42, folder 8/2.
28 Signed 10 August 1951 in Berlin, Volk und Welt translation, Akademie der Künste (AdK), Volk und Welt Archive 1484, Berlin.
29 Simone Barck, Martina Langermann and Siegfried Lokatis, 'The German Democratic Republic as a "Reading Nation": Utopia, Planning, Reality and Ideology', in *The Power of Intellectuals in Contemporary Germany*, ed. Michael Geyer (Chicago: University of Chicago Press, 2001), 88–112, 89–90.
30 Anon, Afterword, trans. Hermann Budzislawski, in Frank Hardy, *Macht ohne Ruhm*, trans. Bianca Ross and the author (Berlin: Volk und Welt, 1952), 429.
31 Ibid., 430.
32 Ibid., 432.
33 Ibid.
34 Hans-Peter Schwartz, *Konrad Adenauer: The Statesman, 1952–1967* (New York: Berghahn Books, 1995), 395–96.
35 I have not yet located any letters from GDR readers in Hardy's papers or in the records of Volk und Welt.
36 Other reviews include 'Roman aus Australien: *Macht ohne Ruhm*' (*Sonntag*), 'Ein gefährliches Manuskript' (*Sonntag*), plus one further review, AdK, Volk und Welt Archive 1484.
37 'Macht ohne Ruhm', *Das demokratische Dorf*, November 1952, clipped in AdK, Volk und Welt Archive 1484, author's translation.
38 Translated by Bianca Ross, clipped in AdK, Volk und Welt Archive 1484.
39 Translated by Bianca Ross, *Börsenblatt des deutschen Buchhandels*, 11 July 1953, clipped in AdK, Volk und Welt Archive 1484.
40 Armstrong, *Frank Hardy*, 72.
41 Ibid., 73.
42 Burchett, 46.
43 Simone Barck, Martina Langermann and Siegfried Lokatis, 'The German Democratic Republic as a "Reading Nation": Utopia, Planning, Reality and Ideology', in *The Power of Intellectuals in Contemporary Germany*, ed. Michael Geyer (Chicago: University of Chicago Press, 2001), 88–112 (95).
44 Hazel Rowley, *Christina Stead: A Biography* (Melbourne: William Heinemann, 1993), 414.

45 Hardy's ASIO file, NAA A6119, vol. 2, item 281, 1951–56.
46 Ibid.
47 Papers of Frank Hardy, NLA MS 4887, box 42, folder 8/2.
48 Ibid., box 6, folder 2/24.
49 Hocking, *Frank Hardy*, 104.
50 Ibid.,102; cf. Allan Gardiner, 'Frank Hardy and Communist Cultural Institutions', about the debated beginnings of the ABS.
51 Quoted in Allan Gardiner, 'Frank Hardy and Communist Cultural Institutions', 43.
52 Hocking, *Frank Hardy*, 107.
53 Cf. Andrew N. Rubin, *Archives of Authority*, 20–21.
54 Ibid., 18.
55 Clipped in Hardy's ASIO file, NAA A6119, vol. 2, item 281, 1951–56.
56 'Menzies Afraid of Youth, says Hardy', *Tribune*, 23 January 1952, clipped in Hardy's ASIO file, NAA A6119, vol. 2, item 281, 1951–56.
57 Hardy aerogramme in ASIO file, NAA A6119, vol. 2, item 281, 1951–56; recalled by Alvie Booth, in Pauline Armstrong, *Frank Hardy*, 149.
58 Letter to Helen Palmer, 26 January 1955, NLA, Papers of Frank Hardy, MS 4887, series 3, general correspondence, box 5, folder 2/21a.
59 Letter to Volk und Welt from Staatliches Rundfunkkomitee requesting permission for broadcast 22 November 1955 and a repeat broadcast on 13 December 1955, AdK, Volk und Welt Archive 1245.
60 AdK, Volk und Welt Archive 1245.
61 Hocking, *Frank Hardy*, 126.
62 Volk und Welt specified a 10,000 print run on Hardy's contract, but 12,000 on the Ministry of Culture permission to print form; Reclam specified 10,000 to Volk und Welt. Antrag auf Druckgenehmigung (Application for permission to print) for *Die vierbeinige Lotterie*, 8 June 1957, BArch DR1/3992/276; AdK, Volk und Welt Archive 1245. This may reflect the tendency of East German publishers to inflate print runs for the Ministry, since it was these that determined their centralized funding, rather than actual sales. Siegfried Lokatis, 'Paradoxien der Zensur in der DDR', in *Der geteilte Himmel: Literatur und ihre Grenzen in der DDR*, ed. Martin Sabrow (Leipzig: Akademische Verlagsanstalt, 2004), 75–99 (79–80).
63 AdK, Volk und Welt Archive 1245; *Tribune*, 3 August 1960; Hocking, *Frank Hardy*, 130.
64 Armstrong, *Frank Hardy*, 1960.
65 Czollek to Hardy, 22 April 1959, AdK, Volk und Welt Archive 1245.
66 Cathy Greenfield and Peter Williams, 'Strangers in the Camp: The Politics of Frank Hardy's Early Writing', in *Frank Hardy and the Literature of Commitment*, 171–84 (180).
67 John Frow, 'Who Shot Frank Hardy? Intertextuality and Textual Politics', *Southern Review* 15, no. 1 (1982): 22–39, reprinted in *Frank Hardy and the Literature of Commitment*, 137–58.
68 Paul Adams, 'Intertextuality, John Frow and Frank Hardy', in *Frank Hardy and the Literature of Commitment*, 159–70 (157).
69 Ibid., 161, 165.
70 Arjun Appadurai, *Modernity at Large: Cultural Dimensions of Globalization* (Minneapolis: University of Minnesota Press, 1996), 181.
71 David Carter, 'The Story of Our Epoch, a Hero of Our Time: The Communist Novelist in Postwar Australia', in *Frank Hardy and the Literature of Commitment*, 89–111 (93).
72 Interview with Tony Morphett for ABC TV's *Spectrum*, 1967, in 'Frank Hardy on Commitment', in *Frank Hardy and the Literature of Commitment*, 23–33 (29).

Chapter 5

KATHARINE SUSANNAH PRICHARD, DYMPHNA CUSACK AND 'WOMEN ON THE PATH OF PROGRESS'

Camille Barrera

During the Cold War, rhetoric surrounding gender roles and family structure often figured prominently in the political and ideological battles between the countries of the communist (socialist) Eastern Bloc and the capitalist West. Following the Second World War, ideas about the 'proper' place of women in the home, the workplace and the world were already in a state of general upheaval in these societies in the wake of economic, political, social and demographic changes brought on by decades of war and industrialization. These ideas and realities would continue to undergo drastic changes in both the East and West throughout the Cold War, but the tendency to invoke them as evidence of the supposedly diametrically opposed values of the corresponding societies was at its height as tensions first escalated in the 1950s,[1] slowly becoming less politically relevant as second-wave feminism gained prominence in the West during the following decades and the political détente of the late seventies cooled the dichotomous East-West rhetoric to some extent.

Of course, when it came to 'women's issues', neither political ideals nor societal attitudes were ever divided cleanly by the Iron Curtain. The specific circumstances of countries on both sides heavily influenced the ways in which socialist or capitalist ideologies, and women's issues in relation to these, took hold. In East Germany, for example, the post-war population of approximately 19 million consisted of 3 million more women than men, making the mobilization of the female workforce a necessity (something that was easily compatible with socialist ideology),[2] while in Australia many women who were 'called upon to take up responsible jobs during the war […] [were]

sent back to "the home front'" as troops returned.³ Susan Sheridan asserts that in Australia

> the 25 years that followed World War Two […] were the dire years of political and social conservatism – Menzies' conservative government and Australia's Cold War against political and social radicalism; the (marriage and) baby boom, and the growth of suburbia as a way of life; dominant ideologies of unrelieved domesticity for women, and assimilation for Aboriginal people and the newly arrived immigrants.⁴

Indeed, the post-war period saw many capitalist countries embracing traditional family structures and conservative values in this way, as symbols of stability and national identity, and many government leaders seized upon the image of the happy suburban nuclear family as a political statement; this was the ideal way of life that needed protection against the threat of socialism.⁵ Yet socialist countries such as the German Democratic Republic (GDR), driven both by conservative social mores and practical concerns (a need to increase the population), were also invested in the preservation of traditional family structures and of women's value as mothers above all else.⁶ Further complicating matters was the GDR's desire to distance itself from Germany's fascist past, while trying to reconcile recent events with a new political and ideological alignment with the Soviet Union, whose occupation of East Germany after the Second World War had brought, among other brutalities, widespread rape of German women at the hands of Soviet soldiers.⁷ At the same time, Australia was struggling to distinguish itself from both its cold war enemies and its allies, to ward off the threat of communism but also to establish a national identity that was not dominated by its close cultural ties with either Britain or the United States.⁸ The embrace of 'quintessentially Australian' values such as mateship and egalitarianism helped to foster connections between socialist and nationalist sentiments, which can be seen in the leftist views of some of Australia's more prominent writers of the twentieth century,⁹ and the glorification of these characteristics in Australian society were often praised in the reception of Australian novels in the East. But these respected attributes of Australian identity were also tied up with a culture that saw them as overwhelmingly masculine virtues. In her analysis of the paucity of female literary prize candidates in Australia in 2012, Julieanne Lamond echoes Susan Sheridan's assertion that 'a set of ideas that came to define what it meant to be distinctively Australian were defined in opposition to a set of values that were identified with femininity'.¹⁰

The East German national identity was similarly tied to models of masculinity. In 'Hegemonic Masculinities in East and West Germany',

Holger Brandes asserts that 'in the GDR, a male habitude dominated, with clichés of the working-class hero [...] anchored in classic industrial work and [...] bodily engagement, discipline, and endurance'.[11] With its focus on heavy industry and its deification of the 'common man', most often represented by the physically powerful worker/manual labourer ideal, the dominant socialist aesthetic – like the Australian one – was ultimately masculine, and the feminine was expected to play a supporting but secondary role. The tendency to marry the ideals of both Australian identity and socialist ideology with masculine archetypes created an atmosphere that was not particularly receptive to women's voices. Yet many Australian women writers who explored feminist themes in their work also aligned themselves with socialist ideology, and it is clear that many held on to a belief in the power of socialist ideas to transform women's status and circumstances for the better. As leftist women writing in the capitalist West, Katharine Susannah Prichard and Dymphna Cusack explored a mix of Western feminist concerns and Marxist solutions in their work. As socialism is the implied (or directly stated) answer to many of the issues they tackle, the 'real existing socialism' of the GDR would have provided for an interpretive context very different from their native Australia. This chapter will look at those novels by Prichard and Cusack that were chosen for translation by East German publishers and approved for publication by the Ministry of Culture of the GDR. With reference to the assessor reports from the GDR print permission files on Prichard's and Cusack's work, this chapter draws out some of the ways in which an East German context may have altered the social function of these texts, highlighting interesting points of intersection and divergence in the values and priorities of these two very different societies and their views of women's roles within the life of the nation.

With the exception of Dorothy Hewett,[12] Katharine Susannah Prichard and Dymphna Cusack were the only Australian female novelists to have had their books translated and published in the GDR. But the works published by these two writers alone make up a markedly substantial portion of the total volume of Australian literature published in translation in East Germany, particularly in the earlier years of the 1950s through to roughly the mid-1970s.[13] Prichard's *The Roaring Nineties* (1946) and *Golden Miles* (1948) were published as *Goldrausch* and *Die goldene Meile* in 1954, and selected short stories chosen from the collections *Potch and Color* (1944) and *N'Goola and Other Stories* (1959) appeared as *Die Braut von Far-Away* (*The Bride of Far Away*) (1962).[14] Cusack's *Say No to Death* (1951) appeared as *Und jeden Morgen neue Hoffnung* (*And Every Morning New Hope*) in 1961 (reprinted in 1970), *Come In Spinner* (1951, co-written with Florence James) as *Jagd nach Glück* (*Pursuit of Happiness*) (1967),

The Half-Burnt Tree (1969) as *Der halbverbrannte Baum* (1972, reprinted in 1973 and 1982), and *Black Lightning* (1964) as *Wie ein schwarzer Blitz* (1973).[15] In addition, *Southern Steel* was serialized under the title 'Wolken über Newcastle' in the women's magazine *Für Dich: Illustrierte Zeitschrift für die Frau*.[16] Given that frequent disparaging comments about the quality of their writing talents can be found in the reports for both authors, one wonders what it was about these particular works that proved compelling or at least ideologically 'useful' enough to merit print runs in a country with a publishing apparatus 'characterized by persistent scarcities'.[17] While the Communist Party ties of both authors certainly played a role in their selection,[18] their work was not published as consistently in East Germany as it appears to have been in the USSR, and some of their works, including Cusack's *The Sun Is Not Enough* (1967) and Prichard's *Working Bullocks* (1921), *Coonardoo* (1929) and even *Winged Seeds* (1950), the third instalment in her goldfields trilogy (the first two parts of which *were* published), seem to have been considered by GDR publishers but ultimately deemed unsuitable for an East German audience.[19] The novels of other prominent leftist women writers such as Christina Stead were not published at all.

Figure 5.1 Dust jacket for Katharine Susannah Prichard's *Goldrausch* (Berlin: Volk und Welt, 1954).

Figure 5.2 Dust jacket for Katharine Susannah Prichard's *Die goldene Meile* (Berlin: Volk und Welt, 1954).

Figure 5.3 Dust jacket for Dymphna Cusack's *Der halbverbrannte Baum* (Berlin: Verlag der Nation, 1972).

Light Reading with Exceptional Propaganda Value

What strikes one first in the assessor reports is the dismissive tone the East German publishers and Ministry of Culture assessors frequently employed in regard to the literary merits of Prichard's and Cusack's work. While the 'literariness' of both writers' work was sometimes called into question in Australia, the specific works usually inviting such comments were not the same. In East German assessments these criticisms targeted *Coonardoo*, for example, widely regarded as one of Prichard's most important works, but dismissed by Volk und Welt editor Hans Petersen as 'shallow' (seicht), suffering from 'sentimental overtones' and therefore unsuitable.[20] On the other hand, the more commonly maligned *The Roaring Nineties* and *Golden Miles* met with relative approval, something that can only partially be ascribed to Prichard's attempts to adhere to the genre of socialist realism in those books, as *Winged Seeds*, the third volume (which Prichard claims to have written 'at the peak of [her] political development')[21] was also deemed unworthy.[22] In a series of reports on Prichard's short story collections, mined for the East German volume *Die Braut von Far-Away* (1962), Petersen notes that 'compared with the standard of a Calwell or a Crane, Katharine Susannah Prichard is "no great shakes"',[23] that many of her stories 'are nothing but badly copied life, and therefore a kind of modern Australian naturalism', adopting a 'shallow tone of reportage'.[24] Stories like 'Mrs. Grundy's Mission', 'The Mayor of Bardie Creek', and 'Bad Debts,' Petersen complains, 'are not built according to the laws of the short story, have no real climax, and are dead boring, despite the occasional note of humour'.[25] Prichard's art, finds Petersen, 'has a narrow frame, which she rarely explodes, either thematically or formally. I harbour no illusions where she is concerned, and do not want to claim her as a representative of great literature.'[26] Even when recommending publication, the assessors often qualify their support in this way, insisting that these women are popular, not 'great' writers. Petersen is particularly harsh but not alone: Paul Merker too concludes that while Prichard's stories are 'perfectly suited for publication in our magazines and in the literature pages of our newspapers', they are best understood as 'light, but politically and artistically valuable, entertainment'.[27] Likewise, while editors praise Cusack and James's *Come In Spinner* for 'its broad-ranging action and the important problems it raises', they bemoan that 'the cosmetic treatments in the beauty salon [where the novel is set] are depicted in the same level of detail as the ladies' dresses and the gossiping of the hotel staff', feeling that, as a result, 'the novel barely exceeds the level of the middlebrow.'[28]

Although many of the assessors wanted to establish that they were judging Prichard's and Cusack's work as *Unterhaltungsliteratur* (light reading), which was not up to the standards of 'real' literature, they nevertheless identified a role for these works within East German society. Since the allocation of paper was to be decided by the Ministry of Culture's *Hauptverwaltung Verlage und Buchhandel* (Main Administration for Publishing and the Book Trade) based on the 'usefulness' of the literature,[29] novels considered to be of little literary value had much to prove in regard to their ideological value. Thus the assessors' reports place special emphasis on the 'instructive' elements of the novels in relation to a readership assumed to be largely female, as evidenced by the references to female readers in the reports as well as Cusack's occasional publications in women's magazines. The lessons the assessors choose to highlight are telling, as they reveal not only the social priorities of the regime, but also the sometimes glaring disconnect between the rhetoric of the administration and the realities of life in the GDR.

The most frequently mentioned 'use' of the works in question is the opportunity they might afford their potential readers to make favourable comparisons between their own circumstances and those of people living in the capitalist West. With the constant pressures to keep up with the material living standards of cold war rivals, it is understandable that the centralized publishing regime, in its responsibility to support the goals of the ruling Socialistische Einheitspartei Deutschlands (SED), would embrace the opportunity afforded by literature such as Cusack's and Prichard's critical and socialist-sympathetic work to demonstrate that 'the grass isn't always greener' on the capitalist side. Even more valuable was the chance these works offered to critique not just the less-than-perfect realities but also the underlying values of capitalist societies. Helle Carola Gärtner-Scholle's 1961 assessment of Cusack's *Say No to Death* praises its 'remarkably high propaganda value' as an indictment of the housing and health care systems 'typical of rich imperialist countries', in which there is 'always money for weapons but no money for the needy sick'. She further surmises that GDR readers would be 'shocked' by the plight of tuberculosis patients in Australia as represented in the novel (set immediately post-war and published in 1951), and would be forced to compare this to the 'undiscriminating care every affected person would be able to receive in the worker and farmer state's battle against the illness'. She deemed this very important in light of her impression that East German citizens had become 'all too easily accustomed to' the GDR's health care system.[30] While the 'safety net' offered citizens of the GDR was certainly more extensive than that afforded the characters in *Say No to Death*, the censor's assertion that such a novel would be *astonishing* to citizens of a country where both housing and medical concerns were almost always subordinate to production goals, where sub-par housing was a perpetual problem[31] and the taking of sick days (including by TB sufferers) was attributed to 'inadequate ideological enlightenment',[32] seems a stretch. Yet she is convinced that the novel would prove 'a powerful antidote to [the] vague emigrant longings' of such misguided and ungrateful East German citizens, making them finally thankful for what their country provided them.[33]

An assessor's report for *Come In Spinner* sees that novel as proof that it is nearly impossible to live a happy, fulfilling life in a capitalist country,[34] praising its deft illustration of the 'inhumane effect the capitalist way of life has on people'.[35] In another report, the depiction of the everyday difficulties of working women in *Come In Spinner* is declared a good means by which to destroy any stubbornly held illusions about life in Australia: 'It offers an unvarnished picture of the every-day life in a big Australian city and the difficulties with which working women are struggling, and can assist in destroying any lingering illusions about life on the Fifth Continent.'[36] Cusack and James are praised for their elucidation of the oppressive effect capitalism has on the working class but at the same time faulted for the deficiencies of their 'bürgerlich-demokratisch' viewpoint, which makes them, according to one assessor, unable to offer a clear vision of a way out of the mess they have described: '[A] real way out is not shown, but at best implied […] [T]he authors focus more on the effects of the capitalist system than on their root causes, and as a result their critique is also more of a moral than a political one'.[37]

Given the economic realities of life for many in East Germany, and especially for many women, the expressions of cultural and ideological superiority found in these reports indicate problematic assumptions regarding women's supposedly improved status in the socialist state. Since women, regardless of their employment status, were almost invariably left to take care of meals, housework and childcare, they were the ones to directly suffer assaults on their time and energy as a result of shortages of food, household goods, and childcare places, meaning that for many women in the GDR, the much-vaunted high employment rates amongst women are now widely acknowledged to have created not emancipation but, rather, a 'double burden' of almost sole responsibility for running a household in addition to paid employment outside the home.[38] Wage disparities, factory-based social services that tended to favour men's interests and recreation over housewife-helping amenities such as laundries and day-cares, and a low glass ceiling in the political and professional realms (largely due to discriminatory attitudes from male counterparts, as well as the fact that many women simply did not have time to train for higher positions in the face of all of their unpaid domestic duties), made things difficult for female heads-of-household.

In Praise of Love and Motherhood

In light of the fact that the GDR simply did not have the resources or infrastructure to function without the unpaid domestic labour of women and thus had a vested interest in maintaining certain domestic arrangements,[39] it is interesting to note which characters' personal circumstances the GDR assessors choose (or choose not) to highlight in their assessments of the novels' usefulness. Depictions of traditional family values are often praised, while unconventional lifestyles or non-traditional choices are lamented, albeit not from a moral perspective, but as products of the problems inherent in capitalist societies – characters' actions, desires and circumstances are almost always attributed to economic forces, not to personal agency nor any combination of other societal factors. Endorsements for depictions of stable nuclear families, women as mothers and carers, 'true love,' and other traditional values can be found throughout the reports. For example, assessors appreciate *Come In Spinner*'s hardworking, honest, and happy farmers Helen and her war-injured husband Alec,[40] Deb's sister Nelly, 'who lives a frugal life off the land, devoted only to her husband and children',[41] and Guinea's eventual return to her Kim. In one report, the assessor points to the love story as the second main source of *Say No to Death*'s 'exceptional propaganda value', citing the 'ethical process' through which even those who have been 'corrupted' by their experiences can be refined and matured through love, and emphasizing how important it is that East German youth realize that love is more than sex and comradeship:

> Here love is depicted again, at long last, the love of today, among people who are no angels, people who are partly corrupted by circumstance, but who atone and mature in an ethical process through their love relationship. Empathy with the young couple at the centre of the action will lead the readers to absorb the social situation characterized above in a captivating way, will lead them to indignation, but also to the insight that love is more than sexual camaraderie. A highly necessary insight for our youth![42]

Fritz Raddatz's report for *Golden Miles* identifies the artful rendering of the mother figure as the greatest strength in Prichard's work, praising the way in which all of the threads of the story are brought together through the central figure of wife and mother Sally Gough. He commends both the portrayal of a mother's concern for her children 'in factory and field' and the 'loving' and 'truthful' depiction of the common socialist realist trope of the politically naive Sally's gradual journey to comprehension of wider political and societal concerns, under the influence and guidance of her communist son Tom.[43]

Come In Spinner's depiction of the fatal abortion undertaken by Mary Parker, mistress to a married American serviceman (one of the elements contributing to concerns of indecency in Australia at the time of its original publication, albeit over a decade earlier)[44] is in the GDR assessments couched in exclusively economic-political terms. One 1966 report declares the problem to be a result of the invasion of the American (read: capitalist) way of life into Australia, coupled with the 'double standards' of the upper classes and inadequacy of prevailing 'bourgeois' regulations in Australia.[45] Another points to the life of poverty and destitution a mother and her 'illegitimate' child would face in Australia as the real source of tragedy.[46] Both of these attitudes, but especially the latter, implying as it does that such financial ruin would not befall a single mother within a socialist society, are notable in light of the fact that although abortions were not illegal in the GDR (as they were in Australia and West Germany), they were still severely restricted. The confident diagnosis of the capitalist origins of such problems fails to acknowledge the high number of deaths from illegal abortions that were occurring in the GDR too, where – even after a reform in 1965 that expanded legitimate reasons for an abortion to include indications such as rape, incest, or having more than five children – legal abortions were tightly controlled and still required approval from a 'termination board' that would decide whether or not a woman's reasons were valid.[47] In principle, any woman who truly needed an abortion would be able to get one, provided they went through the correct channels. But in practice the bureaucratic decision makers' assessment of the level of a woman's 'need' was often very different from that of the woman herself. Evidence suggests that the underlying reason for many of the abortions undertaken in the GDR was in fact social and economic hardship and that by the mid-1960s some GDR officials were starting to admit this but were still prevented from legitimizing such a 'social indication' for abortion in the face of demographic concerns and a need to keep the birth rate up.[48] The assessors' statements about Mary Parker's death, then, seem particularly paternalistic, given that even under the new, more liberal abortion laws, women who had an unauthorized abortion were to be not prosecuted but 'condemned or castigated by public shame'.[49] East German women's own sense of economic desperation was still not considered a legitimate reason by the state for granting a legal abortion, leading some East German women to an end similar to Mary's. While the lack of moral and especially religious outrage of the kind that tended to dominate abortion debates in the West would seem to indicate more progressive attitudes toward abortion in the GDR, in the assessors' identification of illegal abortion as an issue of simple economics, they not only expose the hypocritical and illogical character of their own abortion policies but also deflect attention away from related assumptions about a woman's responsibility and natural desire for motherhood (at least in the absence of extreme economic hardship) that still dominated the culture and the prevailing expressions of communist ideology. These sorts of ideological blind spots highlight the kind of difficulties faced by women working within or in support of a socialist paradigm who also wished to question women's roles in society.

Misguided Bourgeois Feminism

As committed socialists, Prichard and Cusack, as with all writers within the GDR, were discouraged from addressing feminism and women's rights in a way that recognized these as issues distinguishable from the overarching class struggle. As Lorna Martens notes in *The Promised Land? Feminist Writing in the German Democratic Republic*, communist ideology had long been tied to feminism, albeit a feminism that had a very different tone from the 'radical' second-wave feminism that eventually became prominent in the West. She cites August Bebel's 1879 publication *Woman and Socialism*, which 'called for full legal, social, and erotic emancipation of women' while also claiming that 'there could be no genuine emancipation of women outside of socialism […] [T]he "bourgeois" notion of an independent "feminism" was misguided […] [W]omen were encouraged to fight for socialism side by side with men as comrades. Class was of paramount importance. Sex was not considered class'.[50] This is not to say that socialist ideology did not recognize the oppression of women as real. Pavla Vesela asserts that although socialist literature frequently mentioned the emancipation of women, early socialist documents critical of patriarchal family structure and gender relations tended to be so vague about what emancipation and ideal, non-exploitative gender relations would entail that in the wake of the Bolshevik revolution the reigning ideology easily morphed into a form that was not as 'confusing' and 'overwhelming' to populations 'anxious about the breakdown of familiar personal relations'.[51] As a result, the revolutionary message of the transformation of gender relations under socialism came to be understood as mainly an economic imperative: 'gradually, women's liberation came to mean women's participation in the public sphere, and later came to include motherhood closely supervised by the state.'[52] In addition, the indictment of separate feminist concerns as ideologically unenlightened would become a standard defence used to quell discontent voiced by women about their status in actual socialist societies.

At its founding in 1949, the GDR included in its constitution several items explicitly declaring men and women to be equal and nullifying all laws that would undermine this equality. (The constitution furthermore stated that births occurring out of wedlock should not hinder either the child or its parents in any way, and decreed that women would be entitled to particular care and protection by the state during motherhood.[53]) However, at an SED party conference in 1948, Walter Ulbricht's future wife, Lotte, was already criticizing the feminist stance of other women in the party, citing Lenin's warning to Soviet party members about the dangers of allowing feminist concerns to become a separate entity independent from the party.[54] The castigation continued in the party paper *Neues Deutschland* that same year, where she wrote 'since when are there men's and women's interests in the party? [...] [W]e want to develop the class consciousness of the female workforce'.[55] Feminist elements would continue to be frustrated in this way, leaving the fundamental gender hierarchy basically untouched for the life of the GDR. As the 'Father State' had already ostensibly assumed responsibility for women's equality with its 'paternalistic-patriarchal "Fürsorgepolitik"',[56] to question its policies and intentions would be to undermine socialist solidarity and the principal objective of class emancipation in the name of 'individualistic' concerns, ultimately hurting women and society as a whole. So East German women continued to shoulder the 'double burden' resulting from the GDR's state-building 'Muttipolitik'[57] and 'Familialismus',[58] while being treated, paradoxically, in the workplace as 'simultaneously adequate and yet deficient'.[59]

Similar relations between women and the 'needs' of their nation were echoing in Australia during this time, although the rhetoric took on different guises in the absence of state socialism. In her master's thesis *Representations of the Mother Figure in the Novels of Katharine Susannah Prichard and Eleanor Dark*, Jenny Noble points to a comparable natalist phenomenon in Australia, 'a young nation preoccupied with its birth rate'.[60] While Noble sees challenges to dominant masculine discourses in Prichard's early novels *Working Bullocks* and *Coonardoo* (both of which were deemed unsuitable by Verlag der Nation), she views the goldfields trilogy as works in which

> representations of the mother-figure are completely aligned with contemporary nationalist ideologies, reinforced through popular forms of culture such as advertising, film and women's magazines which identify women and femininity with the maternal body and domesticity. These ideologies claim that women are 'born' to be mothers, are 'naturally' domestic and conserving of virtuous, ordered lives. This culturally constructed mother-figure is the embodiment of health and wholesomeness, fulfilling her reproductive role in a young nation preoccupied with white women bearing children.[61]

Australian women were being encouraged to stay at home as housewives during the 1950s, while East German women were being encouraged to work. Both, however, were constantly reminded of their responsibilities to create the citizens of the future, which would ensure the continued health of their respective societies and the preservation of the society's values. The GDR's ideal citizen would demonstrate adequate political 'enlightenment' and thus the political participation of the mother was of concern in creating the 'right' kind of people. In Australia, the focus was on the white mother, who would preferably be married and a housewife, in order to best maintain the status quo. Although the range of acceptable and desirable behaviours in regard to the rest of women's lives varied greatly between the two countries, both managed to communicate the idea that a woman's most valuable contribution to society was in her role as mother, not only to her own children but to the nation.

Likewise, women in both countries faced a certain amount of diminishment of their value as people and as citizens beyond their roles as mothers and 'helpers', as the prevailing images of the ideal socialist and the ideal Australian had both become so unabashedly masculine. The concept of mateship, in its celebration of egalitarianism and brotherhood, has been equated many times with both Australian national identity and socialism.[62] The exclusion and denigration of women that can occur in the face of such a celebration of male camaraderie has also been frequently explored, though mostly since the mid-1970s. In her 1975 book *Damned Whores and God's Police*, Anne Summers lamented the marginalization in Australian society of women who do not conform to their prescribed roles as wife and mother, claiming that

> women in Australia are forced to eke out a precarious psychic and physical existence within a society which has denied them cultural potency and economic independence and hence has prevented women from being able to construct their own identities or from having more than a very restricted choice about what they can do with their lives.[63]

While the expectations dictated by the GDR included such seemingly progressive elements as near-universal women's workforce participation and the resulting possibility for economic independence that Summers called for, at the same time it has been claimed that this served to obscure greater underlying disparities between men and women.[64] Women in any case were still not accorded 'the crucial issue for Women's Liberation' – that is, 'self-determination'.[65] In a way, women in both East Germany and Australia faced similar pressures to conform to the expectations laid out for them by their paternalistic cultures, as the bonds of brotherhood evoked by workers' movements and concepts of mateship were seen as so central to the national identities of both cultures that to question them would be to challenge the heart of the nation's identity and thus the nation itself. Yet in Australia's more outwardly repressive and antagonistic attitude toward women, the stage was set for the more aggressive feminism that would develop there and in other Western countries, while East German women seem to have internalized the socialist idea of independent feminist movements as misguided, an attitude that would create friction in their relations with West German feminists after reunification.[66] This does not mean, of course, that feminist reforms did not happen in the socialist state; while much remained unquestioned, East

German women did have a much higher rate of economic participation and independence than those in Western countries, and whether East or West German women were 'better off' at the time of reunification is a point of contention and perpetual debate. But, as Pavla Vesela states, the difference in attitudes about 'feminism' as a movement came from the fact that 'in the West, feminists arose in opposition to the state, while in the East, the state took responsibility for women's liberation', with this 'history of state feminism [making it] hard for opposition to patriarchy to re-establish itself in the East.'[67] The way the feminist elements of Cusack and Prichard's social critiques were neutralized by officials in the context of the GDR's 'real existing socialism' would seem to support this claim.

As independent, opinionated and unconventional women who often faced barriers as a result of their gender, Prichard and Cusack both expressed discontentment with the status quo of gender relations in Australia and the world, and evidence of their feminist leanings can be found in both their work and their lives. Cusack had a 'reputation as a rebel who spoke out at every opportunity about social injustice' and was not afraid to broach sensitive subjects that she saw as important, particularly as concerned women's rights.[68] Her first novel, *Jungfrau*, 'shocked the world' (or rather Australia, the only place it was published in 1936), with its frank treatment of the topic of abortion.[69] Delys Bird paints Prichard as a 'thoroughly modern woman' who maintained an interest in women's movements and led an independent lifestyle rare for women of her time, travelling abroad and to the Outback alone, speaking on behalf of and being involved in various political movements, especially communism, focusing on her career before marrying late and keeping her name, among other things.[70] Prichard's novels feature strong women protagonists, but in keeping with her commitment to socialist ideology, these women are shown heroically fulfilling their ordained domestic roles more often than challenging the patriarchal structures behind them. As Prichard's commitment to socialist realism and to socialism in general grew, her willingness to explore issues such as gender equality and female subjectivity in her work appears to have diminished, and particularly in her goldfields trilogy, these roles seem to remain uncontested. Likewise, the social struggles of the women in Cusack's GDR-published novels are all easily traced back to the economic imperatives of the socialist class struggle by the GDR assessors. In this way, the real socialist context of these books within the GDR would seem to diminish the critical potency they may have contained, pressing them into a purely propagandistic function. But it is under these conditions that perhaps the strongest possibility of textual resistance lies within elements of the texts generally regarded as flaws.

Clashes of Genre and Context

In her doctoral dissertation on Dymphna Cusack, Tania Peitzker theorizes that the hybrid genre of romantic realism employed by Cusack serves to destabilize gender within her texts, in that the competing demands of the 'opposite genres of popular romance and social realism' require men and women to 'perform' incompatible versions of their genders as dictated by each genre, thus serving a deconstructive purpose in the exposure of those gender performances as just that: performances.[71] Interestingly, the oft-bemoaned 'sentimentality' of Australian literature was apparently 'toned down' in both *The Half-Burnt Tree* and *Come In Spinner* at the behest of East German editors. In the cover letter to the print permission file for *Jagd nach Glück*, editors Hofé, Feudel and Schütze wrote:

> In the love scenes a sentimental note always sneaks its way in. Here a shot of irony would often be more suitable. The translators have moderated these parts at the advice of the editors; however they couldn't be completely eliminated.[72]

Similarly, in the cover letter for *Der halbverbrannte Baum*, the editorial team wrote:

> Assessor Prof. Dr. Georg Seehase (Karl-Marx Universität Leipzig) regards with reason the aesthetic construction of Brenda as not very successful. In her endeavors to put petit bourgeois women on the path of progress, Cusack happily employs melodramatic means that are sometimes at the expense of the believability of the intended conversion. This is particularly striking in the main character of the novel *Black Lightning*, serialized in *Für Dich*. To minimize this weakness we have eliminated or reduced the more pretentiously naturalistic elements.[73]

Though presented as purely aesthetic concerns, these editorial decisions give some credence to Peitzker's claims about the deconstructive function of the competing genres in Cusack's work and make one wonder whether the assessors did in fact get a sense of the danger of this 'flaw'. Was this alteration by the publishers an attempt to lessen the dissonance, and therefore the deconstructive capacities, within the hybrid genre Cusack employed?

From a Western standpoint, resisting the label of pure propaganda has been difficult for *The Roaring Nineties* and *Golden Miles*. While Prichard took great interest in the place of women in society, most Western criticism holds that her attempts to adhere to the socialist realist genre of literature weakened her later writing and compromised her feminist leanings. But, as Bird has noted, Prichard's hopes for a transformation of women's circumstances had always been inextricably tied up in her belief in the transformative powers of socialism and never in competition with it, even before her adoption of socialist realism as a genre.[74] Prichard was not immune to the great amounts of sexist discrimination women faced from male members within the Communist Party of Australia, a sexism that positioned these men's attitudes toward women as perhaps no worse, but more notably, no better than Australian society as a whole at the time, but this did not seem to dissuade her from her belief in this ideology, and it seems that she thought their working toward a common goal would be 'worth it' in the end. In this light, perhaps the context of real existing (that is, post-revolutionary) socialism in the GDR would have allowed Prichard's work to take on a more dialogic function for women as readers. Cath Ellis declares Sally Gough to be 'the strongest central female character of Prichard's novel canon', while her husband Morris is 'surely the most inadequate and incompetent'.[75] But although their marriage resembles those of Prichard's earlier novels ('an adoring, strong wife and an indifferent, incompetent husband'), Sally is presented, as Jane Sunderland puts it, as a woman 'less critical of [her] role as wife, mother, grandmother, lover, provider of men's meals and nurse', than some of Prichard's earlier female protagonists, who 'are oppressed and shown to be so', as 'the problematic of matrimony [is] displaced by politics' within the goldfields trilogy.[76] But as Ellis observes, Prichard, in her attempts to adhere to the genre of socialist realism, 'could not simply present enthusiastic workers in industrial settings as her Soviet colleagues could [...] [as] in an Australian context this would suggest compliant workers content with their exploitation'.[77] Instead, the ever-present 'progressive political motivation'[78] that underpins the novels also compels the reader to call into question every element of the pre-revolutionary society depicted, entrenched as it is shown to be in an exploitative and corrupt system that at times seems almost inescapable.

Sally's daily domestic servitude is firmly entrenched in this specific context of the late nineteenth-century Australian goldfields, a time and place in which many characters suffer oppressions that they do not manage to overcome. Although her seemingly unquestioning acceptance of her role could be taken as an indication that she is a 'compliant worker content with [her] exploitation', there is room in the text as well for questioning this assertion. Brenton Doecke notes the shifting narrative perspectives Prichard employs in the goldfields trilogy. As a large portion of the novel's events are related second-hand through the various characters' storytelling, 'yarning and reminiscing', Prichard 'suggests a play of perspectives that makes mateship and the other values celebrated seem relativized' and indicates to the reader that 'this is something more than an objective account of events [...] [opening] up a space for conflicting interpretations of what went on'.[79] In this way Sally's own internal voice censoring her thoughts and telling her what she should and should not do would seem to suggest internal as well as external forces at work in sustaining these oppressions, rather than an endorsement of the situation on Prichard's part. Sally's confinement to and seeming acceptance of her prescribed role in the domestic realm need not seem any more 'natural' or necessary than the oppressions faced by other characters in the novels, all of whom have yet to attain their goal of liberation from the various oppressive forces at work in their capitalist society, even if the struggles and political imperatives of 'the workers' are foregrounded and put into more definite terms. But as the novels offer up socialism as the solution that yet remains unachieved for the characters, East German women who were already living that 'dream' in the most general sense may have experienced their own cognitive dissonance in the clash of the romance of the socialist 'realist' text with the decidedly un-romantic socialist reality, and perhaps would have been able to see Sally's condition from a more critically nuanced position than those who would criticize the work on the grounds of the naiveté of the single political answer it seems to offer. As this political 'answer' was the backdrop for everything in their lives, they would have been able to pay attention to the more specific workings of the novel and see what else was wrong with the picture, and thus what still needed to be done.

Prichard and Cusack's writing explored women's struggles within a wider framework of a capitalist society that they saw as corrupt, exploitative and damaging to all of its members, advocating for socialist ideas as the path to more equitable power structures and healthy life circumstances for all people. In the works that were chosen for publication in the GDR, publishing officials found it easy to write off the multiple social criticisms they contained with a simplistic economic framework that interpreted every potentially troubling element as inherent to the capitalist system and therefore of no concern to East German citizens in their own lives. They assumed that, when read within a country where the dream of a socialist state had been achieved, the works would merely offer the potential reader an entertaining (if sometimes overly 'sentimental' or 'melodramatic') chance to appreciate how far they had come as a society in comparison to the capitalist countries, and how much better off they were than the characters in the books and the real people who faced similar circumstances within these capitalist societies. Prichard and Cusack both clearly pinned many of their hopes for women's progress and 'self determination' on the dream of a socialist transformation of societal values as a whole. But despite increased workforce participation, the position of women in East German society remained in many ways unchanged under the socialist regime. In addition, while ostensibly promoting women's equality as comrades in the class struggle, in the GDR and elsewhere, the socialist world was rife with masculinist policy and imagery that continued to place women and the feminine in supporting roles at best. Read within this context, the answers to the questions raised in Prichard and Cusack's work would have appeared much less simple than the GDR assessors and perhaps even the authors themselves seem to have believed, and the dissonance caused by both the clashing genres employed in the works and the disconnect between the dream and the reality of a socialist state would have given the works more progressive and dissentient potential than the publishers allowed.

Notes

1 The 1959 'Kitchen Debate' between American president Richard Nixon and Soviet premier Nikita Krushchev is one of the most famous examples. Speaking from within a model kitchen for a 'typical American house', Nixon pointed out the many modern conveniences that he claimed the average American could afford, meant to 'make life more easy for our housewives', while Krushchev held that the Eastern Bloc countries '[did] not have the capitalist attitude toward women'. Quoted in William Safire, 'The Cold War's Hot Kitchen', *New York Times*, 23 July 2009, accessed 10 December 2010, www.nytimes.com/2009/07/24/opinion/24safire.html?_r=0.
2 Donna Harsch, *Revenge of the Domestic: Women, the Family, and Communism in the German Democratic Republic* (Princeton: Princeton University Press, 2007), 20.
3 Susan Sheridan, 'Cold War, Home Front: Australian Women Writers and Artists in the 1950s', *Australian Literary Studies* 20, no. 3 (May 2002): 155–66 (156).
4 Ibid., 158.
5 John Murphy, 'Shaping the Cold War Family: Politics, Domesticity and Policy Interventions in the 1950s', *Australian Historical Studies* 26, no. 105 (October 1995): 544–67.
6 See Harsch, *Revenge of the Domestic*.
7 Donna Harsch, 'Society, the State, and Abortion in East Germany, 1950–1972', *The American Historical Review* 102, no. 1 (February 1997): 53–84 (56).
8 See Murphy, 'Shaping the Cold War Family'.
9 Martha Bruton Macintyre, 'Recent Australian Feminist Historiography', *History Works* 5 (Spring 1978): 98–110 (100).
10 Julieanne Lamond, 'Stella vs Miles: Women Writers and Literary Value in Australia', *Meanjin* 70, no. 3 (2011): 32–39.
11 Holger Brandes, 'Hegemonic Masculinities in East and West Germany (German Democratic Republic and Federal Republic of Germany)', *Men and Masculinities* 10, no. 2 (2007): 178–96 (188).
12 Hewett's 1959 novel *Bobbin' Up* was published in English by Seven Seas Publishers in 1961 and in German translation as *Die Mädchen von Sydney* in 1965 by Volk und Welt.
13 From the mid-1970s on, the majority of Australian literature published in German in the GDR was in the form of collections of short stories by a variety of Australian authors or, sometimes, a reprint of a previously published edition. See Russell West-Pavlov and Jens Elze-Volland, *Australian Literature in German Translation: A Catalogue of Titles, Translators, and Trends 1789–2010* (Berlin: Freie Universität Berlin, 2010).

14 Although many Australian writers' short stories were published in collections, this book is notable as a rare single-author collection.
15 Katharine Susannah Prichard, *The Roaring Nineties: A Story of the Goldfields of Western Australia* (London/Sydney: Australasian Publishing Company in association with Jonathan Cape, 1946); *Golden Miles* (London: Cape, 1948); *Goldrausch*, trans. Karl Heinrich (Berlin: Volk und Welt, 1954); *Die goldene Meile*, trans. Karl Heinrich (Berlin: Volk und Welt, 1954); *Potch and Colour* (Sydney: Angus and Robertson, 1944); *N'Goola and Other Stories* (Melbourne: Australasian Book Society, 1959); *Die Braut von Far-Away*, trans. Gisela Petersen (Berlin: Volk und Welt, 1962); Dymphna Cusack, *Say No to Death* (London: Heinemann, 1951); *Und jeden Morgen neue Hoffnung*, trans. Olga and Erich Fetter (Berlin: Verlag der Nation, 1961); Dymphna Cusack and Florence James, *Come In Spinner* (London: Heinemann, 1951); *Jagd nach Glück*, trans. Olga and Erich Fetter (Berlin: Verlag der Nation, 1967); Cusack, *The Half-Burnt Tree* (London: Heinemann, 1969); *Der halbverbrannte Baum*, trans. Olga and Erich Fetter (Berlin: Verlag der Nation, 1972); *Black Lightning* (London: Heinemann, 1964); *Wie ein schwarzer Blitz*, trans. Olga and Erich Fetter (Berlin: Volk und Welt, 1973).
16 Also published but not considered in this chapter was Dymphna Cusack's book of reportage *Chinese Women Speak* (Sydney: Angus and Robertson, 1958); *Auf eigenen Füßen: Frauenschicksale aus China* (Berlin: Volk und Welt, 1961).
17 Simone Barck, Martina Langermann and Siegfried Lokatis, 'The German Democratic Republic as a "Reading Nation": Utopia, Planning, Reality and Ideology', trans. Michael Latham and Devan Pendas, in *The Power of Intellectuals in Contemporary Germany*, ed. Michael Geyer (Chicago: University of Chicago Press, 2001), 88–112 (94).
18 Prichard was a founding member of the Communist Party of Australia. While Cusack was never an official member of the CPA, her husband and agent, Norman Freehill, was heavily involved, and Cusack herself is generally acknowledged to have had socialist sympathies.
19 See Petersen, for example, report for *N'Goola and Other Stories*, April 1960, in 'Katharine Susannah Prichard: *Die Braut von Far-Away*', BArch DR1/5057/127–152 (143–45), and 'Cusack, Dymphna, *The Sun Is not Enough*', BArch DY17/4963.
20 Petersen, report for *N'Goola and Other Stories*, 143.
21 Quoted in Cath Ellis, 'The Triumph of Ideology', in *Frank Hardy and the Literature of Commitment*, ed. Paul Adams and Christopher Lee (Melbourne: The Vulgar Press, 2003), 199–219 (202).
22 Nevertheless extracts from *Coonardoo* appeared in *On Strenuous Wings: A Half-Century of Selected Writings from the Works of Katharine Susannah Prichard*, a collection of Prichard's writing published by English-language publisher Seven Seas in 1965.
23 Petersen, report for *N'Goola and Other Stories*, 143.
24 Ibid., 144, 145.
25 Petersen, report for *Potch and Colour* and two story MSS, October 1960, in 'Katharine Susannah Prichard: *Die Braut von Far-Away*', BArch DR1/5057/127–152 (150).
26 Ibid.,149.
27 Paul Merker, report for *N'Goola and Other Stories*, 143.
28 Hofé, Feudel and Schütze, publisher's report for *Jagd nach Glück*, 25 October 1966, BArch DR1/2399/62–86 (81).
29 Barck et al., 'The German Democratic Republic as a "Reading Nation"', 98.
30 Helle Carola Gärtner-Scholle, report for *Und jeden Morgen neue Hoffnung*, 20 June 1961, BArch DR1/3960/111–133 (116).

31 Harsch notes that 'in 1971, more than 60 percent of […] housing […] was over a century old. Ninety-two percent of [homes] had no central heating, sixty percent no bathroom, twenty-nine percent no running water,' causing constant petitions to the authorities to improve living conditions, in *Revenge of the Domestic*, 277.
32 Ibid., 109.
33 Gärtner-Scholle, report for *Und jeden Morgen neue Hoffnung*, 120.
34 In the original: 'Dabei zeigt sich, daß ein erfülltes Glücklichsein in einer kapitalistischen Gesellschaft gar nicht oder nur in sehr engen Grenzen möglich ist' – Wilfriede Eichler, report for *Come In Spinner*, BArch DR1/2399/62–86 (82).
35 In the original: 'In der Darstellung der inhumanen Auswirkung kapitalistischer Lebensformen auf die Menschen, verschärft noch durch den Kriegszustand, sind die Autoren sicher und überzeugend', ibid., 84.
36 In the original: 'Es vermittelt ein ungeschminktes Bild des Alltags in einer australischen Großstadt und der Schwierigkeiten, mit denen die berufstätigen Frauen dort zu kämpfen haben, und kann deshalb dazu beitragen, noch bestehende Illusionen über das Leben in fünften Erdteil zu zerstören' – Hofé et al., report for *Jagd nach Glück*, ibid., 81.
37 In the original: 'doch wird ein realer Ausweg nicht gewiesen, allenfals nur angedeutet […] Die Autoren gehen also mehr auf die Auswirkungen des kapitalistischen Systems als auf deren Ursachen ein, und ihre Fragestellung ist demzufolge auch mehr eine moralische als eine politische' – Hofé et al., report for *Jagd nach Glück*, ibid., 80.
38 Katja M. Guenther, *Making Their Place: Feminism after Socialism in Eastern Germany* (Stanford: Stanford University Press, 2010), 28.
39 Harsch, *Revenge of the Domestic*, 28–43.
40 In the original: 'Aus dem Rahmen ihrer Gesellschaftsklasse heraus fällt die saubere, schwer auf der großen Farm ihres Vaters arbeitende Helen McFarland, die Nichte Angus McFarlands. Sie wird mit ihrem Alec, dessen Hand im Krieg verstümmelt wurde, ein glückliches, arbeitsames Leben führen' – Gerhard Schie, report for *Jagd nach Glück*, 68.
41 In the original: 'Kontrastfiguren zu Deborah und McFarland sind Debs Schwester Nelly, die auf dem Lande ein genügsames, nur ihren Kindern und ihrem Mann gewidmetes Leben führt' – Hofé et al., report for *Jagd nach Glück*, 78; and 'Neben der oft harten Sprache bei den Gesellschaftsschilderungen steht die Poesie von Gedanken über die Liebe, stehen die von fraulicher Wärme zeugenden Schilderungen des gesunden Familienlebens im Hause von Deborahs Schwester, stehen einprägsame Darstellungen der Natur Australiens am Meer und auf dem Lande' – Schie, report for *Jagd nach Glück*, 69.
42 In the original: 'Hier ist endlich einmal wieder Liebe geschildert, Liebe von heute, von Menschen, die keine Engel, die z.T. durch die Verhältnisse verdorben sind, aber durch ihre Liebesbeziehung in einem ethischen Prozeß geläutert werden und reifen. Die Anteilnahme an dem im Mittelpunkt der Handlung stehenden jungen Paar führt die Leser auch in fesselnder Weise zur Aufnahme der oben ausgeführten gesellschaftlichen Bedingungen, zur Empörung dagegen sowie zur Erkenntnis, dass Liebe mehr ist als geschlechtliche Karaderie. Eine für unsere Jugend höchst notwendige Erkenntnis!' – Gärtner-Scholle, report for *Und jeden Morgen neue Hoffnung*, BArch DR1/3960/111–133 (116).
43 Fritz Raddatz, Report for *Die goldene Meile*, DR1/5057/153–158 (157).
44 Nicole Moore, 'Obscene and Over Here: National Sex and the *Love Me Sailor* Obscenity Trial', *Australian Literary Studies* 2, no. 4 (October 2002): 316–29 (320).
45 Hofé et al., report for *Come In Spinner*, BArch DR1/2399/62–86 (80–81).
46 Eichler, report for *Come in Spinner*, BArch DR1/2399/62–86 (84–85).
47 Harsch, 'Abortion', 62.

48 Ibid., 63–65.
49 Ibid., 63.
50 Lorna Martens, *The Promised Land? Feminist Writing in the German Democratic Republic* (New York: State University of New York Press, 2001), 4.
51 In addition to Bebel's text, Vesela considers Friedrich Engels' *The Origin of the Family, Private Property and the State* and Aleksandra Kollontai's *The Social Basis of the Woman Question*, among others; Pavla Vesela, 'The Hardening of Cement: Russian Women and Modernization', *NWSA Journal* 15, no. 3 (Fall 2003): 104–123 (109).
52 Pavla Vesela, 'The Hardening of Cement', 109.
53 Renate Ullrich, 'Frauen in DEFA-Dokumentarfilmen', in *Patriarchat in der DDR*, ed. Rainer Ferchland, Ursula Schröter and Renate Ullrich (Berlin: Karl Dietz Verlag, 2009), 64–119 (85).
54 Ursula Schröter, 'Die Frauenorganisation im Rückblick', in *Patriarchat in der DDR*, 11–63 (11).
55 'Seit wann gibt es in der Partei Männer- und Fraueninteressen? […] Wir wollen das Klassenbewusstsein der Arbeiterinnen und Angestellten entwickeln', quoted in Schröter, 'Die Frauenorganisation im Rückblick', 11.
56 Irene Dölling, 'Zum Verhältnis von modernen und traditionalen Aspekten im Lebenszusammenhang von Frauen in der DDR,' in *Unter Hammer und Zirkel, Frauenbiographien vor dem Hintergrund ostdeutscher Sozialisationserfahrungen*, ed. Zentrum für interdisciplinäre Frauenforschung der Humboldt-Universität Berlin (Berlin: Centaurus, 1995), 23–34 (30).
57 Guenther, *Making Their Place*, 27.
58 Dölling, 'Lebenszusammenhang', 29.
59 Ibid., 27.
60 Jenny Noble, 'Representations of the Mother-Figure in the Novels of Katharine Susannah Prichard and Eleanor Dark', MA thesis, University of New South Wales, 2005, 10.
61 Noble, 'Mother Figure', 1.
62 Martha Bruton Macintyre, 'Recent Australian Feminist Historiography'.
63 Anne Summers, *Damned Whores and God's Police: The Colonization of Women in Australia* (Ringwood: Penguin, 1975), 16.
64 Dölling, 'Lebenszusammenhang', 30.
65 Barbara Burris quoted in Summers, *Damned Whores*, 19.
66 Guenther, *Making Their Place*, 43.
67 Vesela, 'Hardening of Cement', 120.
68 Cusack, 'A Sense of Worth', in *Coming Out!*, ed. Julie Copeland and Julie Rigg (Canberra: ABC, 1985), 60.
69 *Coming Out!*, 59; Dymphna Cusack, *Jungfrau* (Sydney: Penguin Books, 1936).
70 Delys Bird, 'Katharine Susannah Prichard: A Thoroughly Modern Woman', *Southerly* 58, no. 1 (Autumn 1998): 98–115.
71 Tania Peitzker, 'Dymphna Cusack (1902–1981): A Feminist Analysis of Gender in Her Romantic Realist Texts', PhD dissertation, University of Potsdam, 2000.
72 In the original: 'In den Liebesszenen schleicht sich immer wieder eine sentimentale Note ein. Hier wäre oft ein Schuß Ironie am Platze gewesen. Die Übersetzter haben diese Züge auf Anraten des Lektorats gemildert; ganz konnten sie jedoch nicht beseitigt werden' – Hofé et al., report for *Jagd nach Glück*, BArch DR1/2399/62–86 (81).
73 In the original: 'Zu recht schätzt der Gutachter Prof. Dr. George Seehase (Karl-Marx Universität Leipzig) die Gestalt der Brenda als ästhetisch wenig gelungen ein. In ihrem

Bemühen, kleinbürgerliche Frauen auf den Weg des Fortschritts zu bringen, bedient Dymphna Cusack sich gern melodramatischer Mittel, die mitunter auf Kosten der Glaubwürdigkeit der beabsichtigten Wandlung gehen. Besonders eklatant wird das bei der Hauptfigur des Romans "Black Lightnings" den "Für Dich" in Fortsetzungen abdruckt. Um diese Schwäche zu mildern, haben wir in der Vergangenheitsgeschichte der Brenda naturalistisch Hochgestochenes gestrichen bzw. gekürzt' – Hofé, Menard, Schütze, report for *Der halbverbrannte Baum*, 17 August 1971, BArch DR1/2404/113–124 (106).

74 Bird, 'A Thoroughly Modern Woman'.
75 Ellis, 'Triumph of Ideology', 206.
76 Ibid.
77 Ibid., 205.
78 Ibid.
79 Brenton Doecke, 'Australian Historical Fiction and the Popular Front: Katharine Susannah Prichard's Goldfields Trilogy', *Westerly* 3 (Spring 1994): 25–36 (30–31).

Chapter 6

WALTER KAUFMANN: WALKING THE TIGHTROPE

Alexandra Ludewig

Walking along the Märkisches Ufer one wintry and icy cold Sunday morning in Berlin, Walter Kaufmann notices a bundle. Coming closer he realizes it is a homeless person:

> A guilty feeling came over me – the poor guy – in this cold. It seemed to me to be a sign of the times, a harbinger of 2009 – banking crisis, financial crisis, world economic crisis, increasing poverty […] Seventy years ago, almost exactly to the day, I lay curled up – though not out in the open, […] on a pallet in a dormitory for the homeless in the East End of London.[1]

These are the opening lines of a 2009 reflective piece by Kaufmann published in the former East German party organ *Neues Deutschland*. For this surviving newspaper relic of the communist era, Kaufmann reminisces and retraces his life from his teenage years in Britain and Australia, a topic that he has returned to over and over again during a career that has spanned almost seven decades. Notably, it is really only in work produced since the fall of the Berlin Wall that he touches on the crucial period during which he lived in the German Democratic Republic (GDR), though even then he is rarely very critical – his criticism seems limited to the pinpointing of moments of doubt. For the bulk of his career and throughout most of his oeuvre, he has chosen instead to transport the reader elsewhere.

The London dormitory passage and the following detailed recollections of his experiences as a 15-year-old Jewish refugee in England are programmatic for his entire literary work: a fusion of autobiography, social critique and adventure. Now more than 90 years old and still living on the banks of the River Spree in central Berlin, Kaufmann is in a position to look back proudly and to feel that he has been lucky in life. Having escaped the Holocaust, he returned to the – by then divided – land of his birth holding Australian citizenship. He worked as a foreign correspondent for several East German newspapers and magazines and led a very privileged life in the GDR, remaining free to travel outside the tightly controlled borders of his adopted homeland. His travelogues made for popular reading in East Germany and their high print runs allowed him to maintain a comfortable existence as a professional author. Kaufmann has published well over 100 books, stories and newspaper articles in both German and English, many of which have been translated into several other languages – a testament to his success. However, closer analysis of his work demonstrates that the short-hand description of him, as 'Jewish', 'German' and 'Australian', is quite inadequate, as his writing allows glimpses of the author as a nonreligious, *heimatlos* and footloose figure who occupies a third space. He is curiously detached from, dreamily above, and only tangentially connected to German-Australian literary traditions (such as the Anglo-Australian short story tradition or socialist realism) or cultural debates (including Aboriginal deaths in custody, native-title, and German unification, to name a few). Until the 1980s, he wrote mostly in English and being published in translations made by GDR-commissioned professionals, his literary voice was mediated, and any stylistic deficiencies or even the removal of controversial concepts and expressions could thus be blamed on the translators, editors and censors.[2] In many ways, his life and writings bear witness to an escapist mindset, evident from his travels, which finds expression in his widely disparate – and dispersed – protagonists, who face ever-changing topical issues in a variety of countries around the world. His work brought the world to the GDR and an exotically flavoured socialist perspective to Australia in a fitting way that meshed with the GDR's official narrative of communist highlights and capitalist lowlights.

The episode inspiring the literary piece quoted at the beginning of this chapter predates his years in Australia. As a 15-year-old, Kaufmann was one of around 10,000 unaccompanied Jewish children brought from the European mainland and resettled in Britain between December 1938 and the outbreak of war in 1939, as part of a large-scale rescue by the Refugee Children's Movement Ltd., now considered one of the great evacuation stories of the Second World War. However, Britain proved to be only an interim place of refuge for some of the older male teenagers, who found themselves declared 'enemy aliens' in June 1940 and, on Churchill's orders, not only interned but subsequently deported by ship to Canada or, as in Kaufmann's case, Australia.

Beginnings

Walter Kaufmann was born [Sally] Jizchak Schmeidler on 19 January 1924, the illegitimate son of a 17-year-old, Polish-Jewish, working-class girl. Until he was three, he lived with his mother Rachela in the Scheunenviertel in central Berlin, then virtually a Jewish ghetto. He was adopted by Dr Salim and Johanna Kaufmann, a wealthy couple from Duisburg on the Rhine, where his adoptive father was a well-regarded solicitor running a successful practice and chairman of the Jewish Community. Kaufmann has speculated that this man was his biological father, as the adoption files show that Salim Kaufmann was specifically interested in Jizchak. From that time on the child was known as Walter Kaufmann. For the next 10 years he lived in Duisburg in the prosperous suburb of Duissern, attending the local primary school and later the Steinbart-Realgymnasium, where he and his Jewish classmates were excluded from *Rassenkunde* (teachings on race) and bullied by teachers and students.[3] As it did for all Jews in Germany, life grew increasingly difficult for this liberal Jewish family after the Nazis came to power in 1933. The Nuremberg Laws of 1935 spelled doom for Dr Kaufmann's professional activities, and discrimination and fear increasingly became part of the family's daily existence.[4] The realization soon dawned on Walter Kaufmann that, as a Jew, he was not considered to be German and therefore did not belong, and he has continually reflected on the implications of living as a Jew in Nazi Germany in his writing.[5] In 1938, when Jewish children were banned from attending public schools in Germany, Walter was transferred to the Jewish Senior School in Düsseldorf, but soon, and even prior to Kristallnacht, when their home was raided and vandalized, and his father arrested and sent to Auschwitz for three weeks, the Kaufmanns realized that Germany was no place for their son and decided to get him out of the country.[6]

Walter was registered with the Refugee Children's Movement in Stuttgart in October 1938 and on his 15th birthday (19 January 1939) he reached the relative safety of England. However, he was not met, as expected, by his London-based uncle, Hugo Daniels, who was supposed to act as his legal guardian. Subsequently, as he relates in the story quoted above, Walter spent his first night in the country in a shelter for the homeless. Daniels, who owned a shipping company, did meet him the next day and saw to it that Walter was taken on at New Herrlingen School, a private boarding school relocated in 1933 from Baden-Württemberg to Otterden in Kent, where around 75 per cent of the pupils were Jewish refugee children.[7] Although he enjoyed his time at the school, Kaufmann could never forgive his uncle's indifference and rejection, not only for failing to greet him on his arrival in London, but also for not intervening, despite his wealth, to rescue Walter's parents from Germany, or to prevent him from being interned and deported from Britain.

His time at Bunce Court, as the New Herrlingen school was known to its staff and students, was cut short when France fell to Germany in June 1940, and the consequent wholesale internment of foreign passport holders aged 16 and over meant that Jewish refugees, too, were sent to hastily set-up camps. The British Government then made the decision to deport some of the foreigners and Kaufmann left war-torn Europe less than a month later as one of the *Dunera* boys bound for Australia.[8] Together with around 2,500 mostly Jewish refugees who had fled the German Reich for England, Kaufmann found himself aboard the severely overcrowded HMT *Dunera* sailing from Liverpool to Australia in July 1940.

Becoming a Writer

By writing about his traumatic experiences years later, Kaufmann continues to process his departure from Nazi Germany, desolation and sense of loss on arrival in London, misery on the *Dunera*, arrival in Australia, and the subsequent period spent in internment camps in New South Wales. He also uses other events as material for his short stories, reinterpreting, for example, his journey to Australia aboard the *Dunera* in a thinly veiled, autobiographical short story titled 'Exile' (1954) and presenting it as an example of ongoing persecution and victimization.[9] In other accounts, Kaufmann's semi-fictionalized memories change from a gritty grey to a soft rosy glow as he begins to recall his landing in Sydney in 1940 and the subsequent train ride to yet another internment camp, in Hay, New South Wales:

> The flavour of Australia hit us when we came here through the Australian soldiers that guarded us. There was one guy that was supposed to guard us but after a while he realized that we were no enemies but were friends and he put his gun down on the rack in the train and started rolling himself a cigarette and handed the tobacco round to us, and we started rolling a cigarette, which was difficult because we were not used to rolling cigarettes, but he taught us and then he said: 'Jesus, I thought all of you guys were enemies but you are friends. Jesus, Christ Almighty,' he was really upset about it. And then he said: 'Look at these teeth I have in my mouth. They are made by a Jew in Sydney – he was a clever guy – and all you guys are all like him, I can't believe it. You are being interned, why the hell do they intern you?' And he never took that gun out of the rack again for the rest of the journey. He sat down and talked to us all the way.[10]

All Kaufmann wanted to do was follow in this Australian soldier's footsteps. Joining the war effort against Germany was a logical consequence of his ideological convictions and he viewed it as a *moralische Pflicht* (moral duty).[11] As recorded in the files of the Australian Military Forces, Kaufmann was released from internment on 20 March 1942 and was accepted into the Pioneer Unit, 8th Employment Company, Broadmeadows, on 7 April 1942.[12] Working for this youthful group, which was also known as 'Enjoyment Company', proved to be a resoundingly positive experience for all involved, despite the menial work that included 'unloading ships and trains'.[13] As part of a tight-knit group, many of the young men made up for their lost youth and forged strong bonds. For Kaufmann, this period signified his initiation into the Australian working class, where he found lasting connections.

When Kaufmann heard of his parents' deaths in Auschwitz in 1943, he decided to remain in Australia.[14] In a gesture of reconciliation, residency was granted to him and 913 other *Dunera* boys. As a soldier of the 8th Employment Company and further encouraged by an Act of Parliament from March 1944 granting refugee aliens eligibility 'for Australian citizenship',[15] Kaufmann applied for permanent residency on 26 July 1944, stating: 'If permitted to remain in Australia I intend to work in the book trade or a publishing firm.'[16] After the Commonwealth Investigations Bureau had conducted checks and written several intelligence reports about him, his wish was granted on 13 November 1944:

> It is his intention to seek employment in the publishing or books trades, or in a clerical capacity. He has £20 in the Commonwealth Saving Bank, Melbourne, and his accrued deferred pay to date totals approximately £76. He is a good type, and has not come under adverse notice during his residence in Australia.[17]

By then Kaufmann had married Tasmanian-born Barbara Jessie Frances Dyer (nee Boyd) in 1944, having met her in Tocumwal, NSW, where their military companies were stationed. She was a woman 14 years his senior, a non-commissioned officer who was employed in an army intelligence unit doing encryption work but had been forced to leave her job when it became known that she was in a relationship with a German alien. The couple settled in Melbourne's inner-city suburb of Parkville, where Kaufmann embarked on a literary career, with his experiences as a Jewish child in Nazi Germany and the subsequent periods of internment in Britain and Australia inspiring his fictional work. While Kaufmann's sympathies lay with many of the refugee academics he had met during internment, his failure to pass the school leaving examination and to enrol through the Army Educational Service for an Arts Degree (as he did not pass his maths examinations even after three attempts) meant that he initially had to opt for a labourer's life and found work 'unloading ships and trains'.[18]

For Kaufmann, the male bonding he encountered as one of the *Dunera* boys, which was further reinforced by his time in the military under the charismatic Captain E. R. Broughton, amounted to a seminal experience of belonging that he was keen to rekindle and maintain as a husband and budding writer, and also to laud in his writings. Upon his transition into civilian life, he came across this sense of camaraderie in the Eureka Youth League and in his unionized places of work. Harbours formed the setting for his introduction to socialist ideas and the working class, as he proudly states: 'My "universities": life, wharfs'.[19] It was here that he found his literary subjects and the courage to share his drafts and stories. In 1944 Kaufmann's short story 'The Simple Things' won him a prize in a Melbourne literary competition, albeit on a very local level. Kaufmann's remark, 'I would have become a writer anyhow, either you have it in you or not',[20] expresses a stoic attitude that was keenly supported by the Melbourne Realist Writers Group, founded in 1944 and which he joined in the same year.[21]

> More from curiosity than any will to create I joined the Melbourne Realist Writers Group where in time the stimula [sic] of literary discussions, reading, contact with other writers such as Morrison and Hardy and later Martin and de Boissiere rekindled a will to try again.[22]

John Morrison, Frank Hardy, Ralph de Boissiere, A. A. Phillips (who coined the term 'cultural cringe'), Alan Marshall of *I Can Jump Puddles* fame and David Martin were some of the group's members,[23] all of them united by the wish to belong to a 'left-wing' organization supporting literary ambitions among the workers; a 'training ground for young writers from the working class and for those whose political convictions make them allies'.[24] The journal produced by this communist-dominated group published Kaufmann's early story 'Against Hitler and the Boss' (1952), the title of which married the ideologies of the Realist Writers Group: anti-fascism and Marxism.[25] Ralph de Boissiere recalled:

> Because of the nature of the times [...] we had the idea that we would make a great impact [...], would change the world. This was part of the belief that had sprung up with the successful conclusion of the war, the years of the spread of the cult of Stalin. We believed that change was around the corner.[26]

Kaufmann's contacts with left-wing groups, his membership of the Australian Communist Party, and the fact that a poster of Stalin adorned a wall in his home meant that his movements were carefully watched by secret intelligence informants.[27] His anti-fascist stance was noted, with his secret service files from the 1940s revealing: 'It is believed that he is thoroughly anti-Nazi and wishes to abandon all connections with Germany.'[28] Nevertheless, this rejection of his birthplace was soon to change.

In 1953 the Australasian Book Society, a left-wing publishing association connected to the Realist Writers (as Nicole Moore's chapter on Frank Hardy details), published Kaufmann's first novel, *Voices in the Storm*, a strongly autobiographical work that expressed criticism of totalitarian systems. Sales were insufficient to recoup even the printing costs, although Kaufmann had invested considerable time in marketing and selling the book as a travelling salesman. It was on one of these tours that he realized that 'the workers are hungry for progressive literature. They were particularly interested in the current German situation'.[29] However, this 'German situation', the beginning of the Cold War with the Berlin blockade, the foundation of the two states and the emergence of a socialist Germany were issues about which Kaufmann had no first-hand knowledge. His 'current' issues were quickly becoming out of date, as he would have realized when sales of his book remained disappointing. Most hurtful, however, must have been several negative reviews of his work by fellow union members published in the communist weekly *Tribune*.[30]

Kaufmann continued to find it hard to live from the proceeds of his book sales and when he was nominated in May 1955 as one of 50 working-class delegates for the Fifth World Youth Conference in Warsaw, he decided he needed to move on and to continue his literary career by responding to new issues and debates in a fresh environment: 'I have seen fascism and I have seen war. Of both I have written and told. I want to write and speak of life and peace and the youth of the world singing songs of peace. That is why I am going to Warsaw to the Vth Festival of Youth.'[31]

Billed as the most literate representative of the Realist Writers, Walter Kaufmann went to Europe not just as the author of *Voices in the Storm* but of the work-in-progress *Where Men Belong*.[32] He was definitely preoccupied by questions of belonging, as he also used the opportunity to revisit the West German Ruhr region, where he had spent 10 years of his childhood. However, he did not find what he had hoped for; instead of a denazified society, he discovered his parents' house occupied by opportunists from the Nazi period, was met with insults from people his father had worked with and appallingly insensitive remarks from others he had known as a child. Kaufmann was greatly disappointed and depressed by the old Nazis he came across, and it was in this mood in January 1956, by which time he had travelled on to Berlin, that he took up an invitation from the Ostberliner Schriftstellerverband (East Berlin writers' union) to visit the 'better' Germany, the GDR.[33] There Kaufmann met anti-fascist communist writers and other renowned authors who, upon their return from exile after 1945, had made the East German state their philosophical and physical home. These writers included Willi Bredel, Anna Seghers, Ludwig Renn, Eduard Claudius, and Stefan Heym. In turn, Kaufmann left an impression on them:

> It was a man in his early thirties, an athletic, strong figure with a clever face beneath dark wavy hair who climbed onto the stage, stepped up to the lectern

and began to speak in an impassioned voice. He spoke German and his pronunciation was clear and comprehensible, but he articulated his words in an unmistakable English accent. […] Until that point only a few had known of his existence, let alone of his fate.[34]

At this point, his decision to stay had been made and Walter Kaufmann used his speech to justify it.[35] An offer had been made to him that was simply irresistible: he would settle in the GDR and continue to write and work as a travel correspondent for several state-owned newspapers; that is, effectively live as a *Berufsschriftsteller* (professional writer), who would no longer need to carry out menial jobs to keep himself and his wife afloat but would earn a steady income and not have to pay for the printing costs of his books. Memories of having to work as a 'waterside worker, butcher's labourer, deck hand, etc' in Australia were still fresh when he decided to take up the GDR's offer.[36]

Kaufmann reflected on his move as a fact-finding mission of sorts, and maintained that the GDR made for great literary material: 'Just the conflict between the East and the West in Berlin is worth a story, is enough for a novel, constitutes enough material for many years. And then there's the rest of the GDR.'[37] It is telling, however, that he chose not to concentrate on writing about life in the GDR. The advertisement for one of his recent publications tries to present him as a dissident voice, highlighting the fact that he wrote a novel and a short story that encountered censorship:

> His novel *S* was dropped by the publishing house, as it thematized the building of the Wall, 'Getaway', a story about an escape from East to West Germany, kept under wraps. And the Stasi had him in its sights. In his files there are informants' reports made by prominent colleagues.[38]

Instead Kaufmann focussed his attention on Australia and other exotic destinations. In October 1956, he acted as an assistant attaché for the GDR sports team when it competed in the Olympic Games in Melbourne and travelled from there to Japan before returning to a life as a correspondent and writer in the GDR. He seemed to acclimatize well to the regime of censorship and state approval, submitting his manuscripts in English, getting them professionally translated at the expense of the publishing houses, and responding mostly agreeably to criticism and suggestions for corrections. Touted as a recently returned exile, weaknesses in his literary style were easily forgiven, especially since Kaufmann was politically on song: highlighting international socialism and unmasking the brutality of fascism, capitalism and imperialism.[39]

Travelling the World

Kaufmann's short story collection *The Curse of Maralinga* was released in 1959 by the East German English-language publisher Seven Seas, after it had been published in translation by Neues Leben in 1958. Including the title story, which deals with the nuclear experiments (mainly carried out in 1956 and 1957) by British and Australian military personnel on Aboriginal land, the collection contains many unflattering tales about life in Australia. For his novel *Kreuzwege* (literally: *At the Crossroads*, though it was never translated into English), 'in which he portrays the struggle of the Australian working class for its liberation from the corrupt capitalist system and where he demonstrates proletarian internationalism as a decisive economic, political and moral force assisting the Australian worker,'[40] he received the city of Potsdam's Fontane-Preis in 1961, the year the Berlin Wall was built.[41] He did not comment on this seminal point in history, explaining years later in an interview: 'In August 1961, I was in Cuba. I was far off the beaten track [...]. I was that far away.'[42] By then he was in a new relationship with the actress Angela Brunner and had become a father for the first time.[43] Nevertheless, his newly assumed fatherhood did not prevent him from having numerous brief romantic encounters abroad, and he took his personal and professional freedom for granted. He continued with his journalistic contributions to the Australian *Tribune*, praising GDR society and pointing his finger at social problems on the other side of the Iron Curtain, while continuing to travel happily to a variety of countries, both socialist and non-socialist, outside the 'protective wall against saboteurs, spies and aggressors'.[44] Many of his literary works are compilations of articles commissioned for the GDR's party-newspaper *Neues Deutschland*, its publication for young people, *Junge Welt*, and the daily *Berliner Zeitung*, which fiercely endorsed socialist values, displaying a consistently strong Marxist standpoint and exposing 'the meanest means' of the capitalist ruling class in Australia, America, and West Germany, or, ironically, the brutal acts of the secret police in Australia.[45]

In the following years Kaufmann's overseas travels increasingly came to resemble escapes from the GDR. After tangling with one of his publishers (the Hinstorff Verlag),[46] Kaufmann approached the magazine *Berliner Illustrierte* and asked to be sent out into the world as a foreign correspondent: 'Schickt mich in die Welt.'[47] Although in doing so he increasingly turned his back on his adopted country, he stayed politically loyal by calling attention to mistakes made elsewhere in the world. For this freedom, Walter Kaufmann found many admirers amongst his East German writing colleagues but also a number of false friends. Due to his lively contacts with people from class enemy states and his extended journeys abroad, Kaufmann was regarded critically and also with envy. He continued to submit many of his short stories and reports in English, leaving the translations to his publishing houses, and was marketed as an international writer, although many assessors commented that he was not quite at home in the English language and that his literary talent was not of world-class standard.[48] His socialist convictions were beyond doubt, with the reader reports from the publisher praising the fact that in international settings such as Australia Kaufmann demonstrated the 'strength and solidarity of the working class' (Kraft und Solidarität der Arbeiterklasse), as well as 'the leading role played by the communists in the unions' (die führende Rolle der Kommunisten in der Gewerkschaft).[49] Seven Seas Publishers in Berlin marketed his English language text *American Encounter* as 'the story of a man's impression', who moves about '[f]oot-loose and fancy-free' following 'his insatiable curiosity' thereby 'taking the armchair traveller' – the fate of most other GDR citizens – to faraway destinations.[50] With his Australian passport Kaufmann could travel easily even to the capitalist enemy states, as publishing house Mitteldeutscher Verlag in Halle and Leipzig explained to the readers of Kaufmann's novel *Flucht* (*Flight*), while also lauding Kaufmann's ability to fuse the dialectics of *Weltoffenheit und Heimatliebe* (cosmopolitanism and patriotism).[51]

The GDR tried to make use of Kaufmann's cosmopolitanism and charisma. In April 1963 the Stasi attempted to recruit him as an IM, a so-called *Inoffizieller Mitarbeiter* (unofficial collaborator or agent), but he ruled out any cooperation. On this occasion he also rejected any interference in his work as a writer.[52] He evidently cherished his view of himself as an independent spirit: 'I write about conditions in the capitalist world and manage alright. I have neither the time nor the patience to allow myself to be press-ganged.'[53] Both sides were aware that his case was a special one. As a foreign national he could temporarily step out of the system, but as he produced literature that toed the line, he was an important representative for the state.

Some of his colleagues and, most importantly, the officials remained suspicious of Kaufmann and his exuberant self-confidence in dealing with them. Where could he possibly get this strength from? Was he backed by powerful forces? In 1963 the Ministerium für Staatssicherheit started an investigation, an *Operativer Vorgang* (operative procedure) into his activities, as Kaufmann was by then suspected of spying for the British Secret Service:

> The person Walter Kaufmann […] is being investigated for the following reasons: K. presents himself to the outside world as a committed Communist. Upon scrutiny the comrades from the HVA [Hauptverwaltung Ausland/Head Office for Foreign Intelligence] have come to the view that K. is probably an agent working for the English Secret Service. […] 1.6.1963.[54]

As Kaufmann had no inkling of these suspicions, his everyday life continued undisturbed. In the USA in 1963 he tried out a new writing technique influenced by newspaper and television, which featured snippets and short passages of writing rather than longer, more descriptive paragraphs. Instead of subscribing to one genre, he fused several styles and conventions (*Bildungsroman* and travelogue; reportage and short story; realism and drama; adult and young fiction material), which censors noted repeatedly.[55] Using this method the narrator takes on more of the role of listener and chronicler, depicting seemingly unmediated slices of life that endorse the socialist world-view without labouring the political point explicitly. This new technique found recognition, and in 1964 Kaufmann was awarded the Fontane-Prize for the second time, this time for *Begegnungen mit Amerika heute* (*American Encounter*).[56] Although no records of the jury's deliberations or their final justification for the award survive, it is to be expected that he was rewarded as much for his anti-capitalist and conformist stance as for the way he represented exotic and out-of-reach locations to the citizens of the GDR.[57] Upon reading about American society and its woes, which ranged from racism and poverty to unemployment and child abuse, East Germans would presumably no longer feel inclined to travel there anyway. His depictions of evil Western societies also found new readers among the younger population when Kaufmann turned to writing politically tendentious children's literature between 1966 and 1988.

Whether it was a matter of losing touch or of living in a dream world, Kaufmann's professional and personal choices were a matter of concern to his one-time friends in Australia. As the prominent writer David Martin recalled:

> We [David Martin and his wife Richenda] met Walter Kaufmann again in East-Germany in 1967. I went there as a guest of the German writers' union though I had ceased to be a member of the Communist Party after I went to Vietnam [...] I and Richenda met Walter and Barbara in East-Berlin. Walter was already living with a blonde German woman, an actress, near Pankow. He had a child, a girl, with the German woman but Barbara looked after the child (and after Walter Kaufmann) when we were there.[58]

In his biography, Martin also recalls his meeting with Kaufmann with mixed emotions. 'I knew him as cheerful, flirtatious and personable, but when we met again in Berlin politics of writing was beginning to come between us.'[59] Kaufmann retained his fondness for Martin, describing him as 'a dear, warm-hearted person to whom I have much to be grateful for'.[60] Where Martin turned his back on communist ideology, in view of the real-existing deficiencies of socialism and communism, Kaufmann remained a preacher, if not a believer, and his loyalty to the state was rewarded with high print runs (mostly between 10,000 and 20,000), second editions, a special 50th birthday edition, and more literary prizes.[61] In 1967 he received the Heinrich-Mann-Prize from the Academy of the Arts (Preis der Akademie der Künste), which awarded 18,000 Ostmark to a writer who 'promoted the democratic and socialist education of our people by means of socially relevant works'.[62] Accordingly, he made no mention in his writing of the crushing of the Prague Spring in 1968, an omission that he defended as follows: 'It almost sounds as if I'm avoiding answering the questions you are asking me […] again, I was so far away. I was in Yugoslavia at that time.'[63]

His silence was also noted with concern by his dissident, ex-communist friends abroad. David Martin spoke of a lack of courage and publicly distanced himself from Kaufmann.[64] Having been in Prague in 1968, Martin was personally disappointed, as he recalled that Kaufmann had confessed to misgivings in private, but did not use his public platform to express these:

> He told me once I would not like all the things done in the DSR [sic] to 'build socialism'. – We didn't hear from Walter Kaufmann the next year, when we were in Prague as the Russians marched in (and the East-Germans!). We lost contact with him until the fall of the GDR.[65]

The events in Prague did indeed affect Kaufmann, as they brought him into contact with the source material for *Death in Fremantle*, a story about a young Australian Aboriginal boy who, with his foster mother, fled Prague for East Berlin. Again his story, although championing egalitarianism and socialist ideals, is concerned with an exotic individual; so many of Kaufmann's protagonists are less exemplary types than specific and special cases who are at the same time strange and extraordinary, but who represent the universal desire for the pursuit of freedom and happiness. The answer, in contrast to the American motto, lies in working-class solidarity and a humane socialism. For this reason, Kaufmann felt that he was on the right side of history and affirmed his belief when the Biermann affair rocked the GDR in 1976: 'all in all Socialism can provide constructive answers to all the complicated questions of our modern world today', maintaining that 'he feels comfortable living in the GDR and knows that he can work here productively and meaningfully'.[66] Amid a flurry of censorship activity and punishment of disloyal voices, Kaufmann's then current manuscript, which had already been approved for publication in early 1976, received an increased print run in November of that year, in recognition of his continued public support for the GDR's cause.[67]

His extensive travels, however, speak of his restlessness in both private and political matters, mirroring perhaps his increasing difficulties in facing reality.

He made at least one international trip per year to Western enemy nations and to socialist brother states alike: the USA, Ireland, Denmark, Hungary, Belgium, Poland, Czechoslovakia, and Yugoslavia were favourite destinations. These journeys and his personal experiences from childhood onwards served as a quarry for his writing. Increasingly hiding behind the persona of a youthful narrator, Kaufmann's literary work becomes a sounding box for minors and victims, as well as innocent and victimized figures, as if he is disappearing behind literary individuals who – due to their age or circumstances – cannot express a political opinion, nor act in self-determination, and perhaps form a cover for an author who cannot face the music. Until 1990 any social criticism expressed in his works is directed westward.

Avoiding Free Fall

On 23 March 1970 his second daughter, Deborah, was born. However, not even his children could move Kaufmann to stay with his second wife, Angela. In the same year he moved in with Elisabeth (Lissy) Kemter, a radiography assistant employed at the Charité hospital, with whom he has spent much of the following decades. She also organized for him to be able to move into a spacious old apartment on a bend of the Spree River in Berlin-Mitte, not

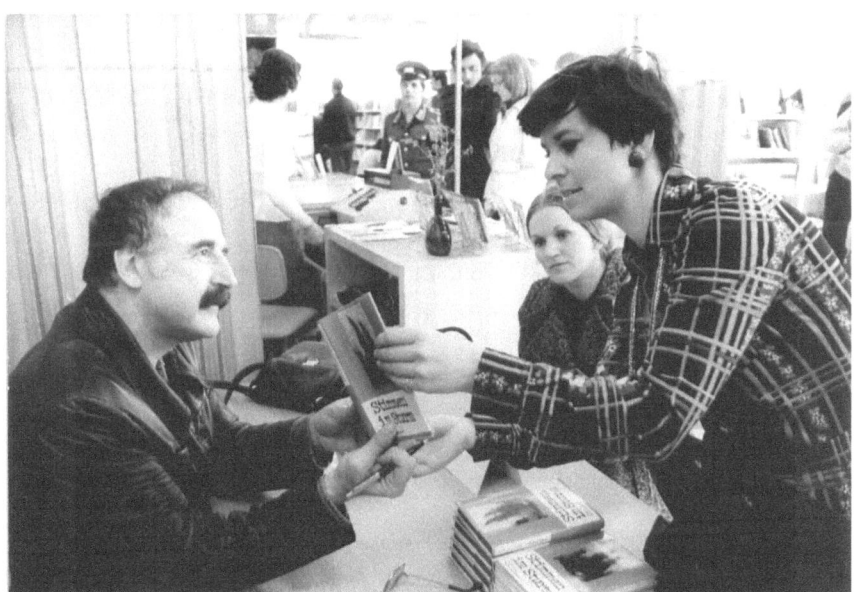

Figure 6.1 Walter Kaufmann signing books in a GDR bookshop; photograph by Klaus Franke, 28 April 1977 (BArch Berlin, Digital Picture Archives 183-S0428-0043).

far from the former Palast der Republik, or for that matter, the site where the Schloss is being rebuilt. Other women came into his life again and again, inspiring his literary oeuvre, with many of them transformed into characters in his short stories and novels. If we are to believe his fellow GDR author Christa Wolf's personal and somewhat insulting comment in the IM report she made to the Stasi about him, this obsession with conquering women in all parts of the globe became a fetish, to such an extent that his work was considerably impaired: 'Although Kaufmann promises to become a great talent, he is hindered not inconsiderably by his frequently changing relationships with women.'[68] The freedoms he afforded himself had the potential to make him appear non-committal to any cause, something other colleagues have also pointed out.

In 1982 the Trinidad-born Australian communist and novelist Ralph de Boissiere received Walter Kaufmann's address from a friend and resumed contact with him. They exchanged several letters in the lead up to Kaufmann's visit to Melbourne in 1983. Kaufmann 'was on assignment […] to research and write three stories that, through the characters, connected Germany and Australia'.[69] However, when Kaufmann and de Boissiere met again, the reunion was disappointing. Kaufmann remembers the de Boissiere couple as decadent and snobby.[70] Likewise, his friend regretted the change in Walter Kaufmann:

> Yes, he had changed when we met in '83. I did not see enough of him to figure out in what way he had changed and why. I had the impression of an aloofness in him that had not been there before, that it had to do with his new life over there. I don't know.[71]

Another of Kaufmann's friends was more familiar with this new life. The younger writer and academic Manfred Jurgensen who, along with his wife, visited him and Elisabeth Kemter in January 1988, wrote about their encounter:

> Our author drives a West German car and watches West German television on his 'Philips'-TV. There can be no doubt about his privileged status […] When our author drove us to Checkpoint Charlie early in the morning and explained to the East German soldiers on duty that we are his 'special guests' I attempted to clown around.[72]

Walter Kaufmann's position of privilege at this time was a result of his prominent public role. Between September 1985 and January 1993 he represented the East German PEN-Centre as its secretary general, retaining his title and role despite the massive changes brought about by the fall of the Wall in November 1989 and Germany's unification in October 1990, which resulted in the demise of many of the old guard.[73] This official role meant that he was once again regularly pursued by Stasi collaborators and personnel, though he refused to report to the Stasi official who attended the PEN meetings, earning him the wrath of Ursula Ragwitz, a senior cultural functionary and member of the Central Committee of the ruling Sozialistische Einheitspartei Deutschlands (SED).[74] And it was in the dying days of the regime that Kaufmann himself offered to become an unofficial collaborator, or IM, in order to enable his second wife, Angela, to travel outside the GDR to visit her seriously ill sister in hospital in West Berlin. Only the unexpected breakup of the GDR stopped Kaufmann from becoming further entangled with the Stasi. Although the fall of the Wall prevented him from potentially making a mistake, as a committed socialist, Kaufmann had been mostly satisfied with life in the GDR and was shocked to lose his adopted homeland, whilst simultaneously feeling relieved that its people would now have the freedom to go beyond its borders. Furthermore, in contrast to the ideological control with which he was able to live for decades on end, Kaufmann felt his literary world to be under threat due to the competition of the free market.[75]

Ironically, although he would always have liked to refer to himself as a *freier Schriftsteller* (independent writer), this has only been true since 1989, as Kaufmann was only free of political interference and censorship threats from that point on.[76] Despite his fears that he would lose his readership after the Wall came down, his writing continues to be published by a variety of (West) German publishing houses. He was awarded the (West) German *Literaturpreis Ruhrgebiet* in 1993, and in 1994 he received funding to attend the Australian conference, 'German-Australian Cultural Relations since 1945' (with a stipend from the Deutsche Forschungsgemeinschaft). It was on the occasion of this conference that he was able to meet up again with many of his old friends, together with his partner, Elisabeth. He was delighted to rekindle friendships with some of the attendees whom he knew from Sydney, Brisbane, Mooloolaba, Darwin, and Fiji. Nevertheless, after nearly 40 years' absence (except for short trips to Australia in 1956, 1983, 1986, 1990 and 1994) his rediscovery of Australia was defined by disappointments and readjustments. His partner, Lissy, was unable to recognize the Australia depicted in Kaufmann's narratives. He may have realized only at that point that he was no longer at home in Australia and stopped writing and publishing in English. His publications since Germany's unification, mainly reprinted and newly edited collections of short stories interspersed with snippets of GDR life, are of a different literary quality. Kaufmann seems to have found a new voice and has begun to deal with some of the GDR's shortcomings, particularly issues concerning censorship,

Figure 6.2 Walter Kaufmann and Lissy Kaufmann in Brisbane in 1994, personal photograph provided to Alexandra Ludewig.

freedom of movement, the harsh treatment of dissenting individuals, groups and nations, and the activities of the Stasi and its sister organizations in other socialist countries. The recent crisis of capitalism alluded to in the passage quoted at the beginning of this essay might have given him some sense of satisfaction that he always knew that the West's way of doing things was not the right one. However, Kaufmann must also re-evaluate the path taken by the East – along with some of the choices he made himself during his long and eventful life.

In a barely disguised autobiographical short story titled 'On the Tightrope', the Jewish-German child protagonist Stefan encounters several members of the Hitler Youth. Stefan denies his identity out of fear of being beaten up and claims that he is Catholic. Feeling guilty for lying about who he is and thus also betraying his family, Stefan flees to the roof of his parents' house and balances on the parapet, only coming down after repeatedly demanding from his mother that she swear she loves him unconditionally. He does not have the courage to tell her afterwards what had happened, saying only, 'No, Mother, I can't tell you why I did it!'[77] However, the reader knows – because all humans are fallible – that we all do many questionable things in moments of fear and uncertainty, and that just by living our lives we all make mistakes.

Notes

1 In the original: 'Ein Schuldgefühl hatte mich erfasst – der arme Kerl – in dieser Kälte. Ein Bote der Zeit, wie mir schien, Vorbote des Jahres 2009 – Bankenkrise, Finanzkrise, Weltwirtschaftskrise, zunehmende Armut […] Fast auf den Tag genau, siebzig Jahre zurück lag auch ich eingeigelt – nicht im Freien zwar […] auf der Pritsche eines Schlafsaals fuer Obdachlose im Osten von London.' Walter Kaufmann, 'Ich war fünfzehn', *Neues Deutschland*, 17 January 2009, accessed January 2011, www.neues-deutschland.de/artikel/142290.walter-kaufmann-ich-war-fuenfzehn.html. See Walter Kaufmann, *Im Fluss der Zeit* (Berlin: Dittrich Verlag, 2010), 62.

2 Indeed, many assessments of his work speculated about the quality of the translations: 'His style (in this case you are really talking about the translator's style, even if the translation has been authorized!) […] is strikingly simple.' [In the original: 'Der Stil (in diesem Fall muss man wohl in erster Linie von dem Stil der Übersetzerin reden, wenn auch die Übersetzung autorisiert ist!) […] ist bestechend einfach', in Anne Martens, report on Walter Kaufmann, *Stefan: Mosaik einer Kindheit* (1966), undated, BArch DR1/2253/85. Assessing *Jenseits der Kindheit* (1984), one reader observed: 'Kaufmann's convoluted sentences are not always easy to read. Sometimes a detail could be expressed more precisely. Some things could be said more simply. *Stefan* seemed to me to speak in a more mature fashion. Could it have something to do with the translation?' [In the original: 'Kaufmanns Schachtelsätze lesen sich nicht immer einfach. Manchmal ließe sich ein Detail präziser darstellen. Einiges ginge einfacher zu sagen. Mir erschien *Stefan* sprachlich gereifter. Es mag an der Übersetzung liegen?')] H. Hilzheimer, report on Walter Kaufmann, *Jenseits der Kindheit*, 19 March 1984, BArch DR1/2301/390.When he was asked to revise his manuscript *Tod in Fremantle* for artistic and aesthetic reasons in 1986, the censors were told by Mitteldeutscher Verlag's editor-in-chief that Kaufmann was unwilling to do so, as he was 'not prepared to make further changes'. [In the original: 'zu keinen weiteren Überarbeitungen bereit'] Helga Duty, report on Walter Kaufmann, *Tod in Fremantle*, 27 May 1986, BArch DR1/2192/412.

3 Kaufmann has repeatedly returned to his traumatic childhood memories in his writing, most recently in his autobiographical collage *Im Fluss der Zeit*, 145, and the semi-autobiographical collection of short stories based around his literary alter ego, Markus Epstein; Walter Kaufmann, *Die Welt des Markus Epstein* (Dresden: ddp goldenbogen, 2004), 80–82.

4 See *Im Fluss der Zeit*, 274–88.

5 His experiences as a 9-year-old inspired the story 'The Simple Things', which has been reprinted in translation numerous times since its publication in *The Curse of Maralinga* in 1958. See *Markus Epstein*, 12–15. As a 13-year-old, his childish love of the Karneval parade is spoilt forever when he sees anti-Semitic propaganda on a Karneval float ridiculing Jews and is reminded once and for all that he does not belong in this society; see the autobiographical story 'Weiberfastnacht', in Walter Kaufmann, *Gelebtes Leben: Ein Geschichten-Kaleidoskop* (Berlin: Karl Dietz Verlag, 2000), 21–23.

6 See *Im Fluss der Zeit*, 146–47; See *Die Welt des Markus Epstein*, 15 and 98–99.

7 The school insisted that the children only communicate in English in order that they learn the language as quickly as possible, and Kaufmann (who floundered initially) was told, 'German is for the Germans […] and we are outcasts and don't belong'. Walter Kaufmann, 'Bunce Court, England 1939', in *Die Zeit berühren: Mosaik eines Lebens auf drei*

Kontinenten (Berlin: edition q, 1992), 97–99 (98). See also 'Englisch, Markus Epstein', in *Die Welt des Markus Epstein*, 113–15, and 'Die Abreise', 104–108.

8 In one of his recent publications Kaufmann queries whether he volunteered to board the *Dunera* and encouraged others to do so, as several other *Dunera* boys have claimed: 'Wurde ich […] über die Meere nach Australien abgeschoben oder meldete ich mich freiwillig, wie es fünfzig Jahre später Kurt Henle […] behaupten sollte?' (Was I deported […] across the seas to Australia or did I volunteer to go, as Kurt Henle […] supposedly claimed 50 years later?) Walter Kaufmann, *Im Fluss der Zeit*, 148. Without the support of or intervention by his uncle, Kaufmann had little chance of being rescued from internment and deportation, and on other occasions when he writes about this episode, recalls his distress and powerlessness, using the words 'abgeschoben' (deported), 'verschleppt' (displaced) and 'Verbannung' (exile and ostracization); see *Markus Epstein*, 129–36.

9 Walter Kaufmann, 'Exile', *Meanjin* 13, no. 4 (1954): 537–42.

10 Walter Kaufmann in the SBS documentary *When Friends Were Enemies* (Australia, TV), 1990. See also his recollection of this train ride in *Im Fluss der Zeit*, 71–73, as well as *Markus Epstein*, 138–40.

11 Walter Kaufmann, in an unpublished interview with A. Ludewig, 14 December 1994.

12 'Kaufmann Walter', Commonwealth Investigation Branch, NAA, series A367, C58483.

13 Walter Kaufmann, in an interview with the Australian Nine News Network, *East Meets West*, 30 September 1990 (Australia, TV).

14 Kaufmann found out in 1943 that they had died in Auschwitz: 'Im Dezember 1943 erhält Walter Kaufmann über das Rote Kreuz doch noch eine Nachricht von seinen Eltern. Es ist ein Abschiedsgruß im doppelten Wortsinn, verfasst am 24. Juni 1943, einen Tag vor ihrer Deportation nach Theresienstadt. Der Brief wird dem Sohn mit sechsmonatiger Verspätung zugestellt. Er bedarf keines Kommentars: "Liebster Walter! Wir reisen heute nach Theresienstadt und senden Dir innige Abschiedsgrüße und Küsse. Hoffen auf ein Wiedersehen. Vati; Mutti".' (In December 1943 Walter Kaufmann actually did receive news from his parents via the Red Cross. It was a farewell letter in both senses of the expression, written on 24 June 1943, one day before they were deported to Theresienstadt. It was delivered to their son six months later and requires no comment: 'Dearest Walter! We are travelling to Theresienstadt today and send you our heartfelt goodbyes and kisses. We do hope to see you again. Dad; Mum.') *Jüdische Zeitung*, accessed 25 June 2013, http://www.j-zeit.de/archiv/artikel.1556.html. See Walter Kaufmann, 'Albury: Australien 1943', in Walter Kaufmann, *Die Zeit berühren: Mosaik eines Lebens auf drei Kontinenten*, 22–23.

15 Fred Gruen, 'Of Economics and Other Things', in *From Strauss to Matilda: Viennese in Australia: 1938–1988*, ed. Karl Bittman (Leichhardt: Wenkart Foundation, 1988) 169. Before 1948, it was actually 'naturalization,' as the status of Australian citizenship was only created by the Nationality and Citizenship Act, 1948.

16 Walter Kaufmann, ASIO file, NAA, series A6119, C515, item 8334494.

17 Report by Acting Inspector E. Hattam to the director of the Commonwealth Investigation Branch in Canberra, 13 November 1944, NAA, A367, C58483, item 780776.

18 Walter Kaufmann in an interview with Nine News Network, *East Meets West*, 30 September 1990.

19 Ibid.

20 Ibid.
21 Jack Beasley, *Red Letter Days: Notes from inside an Era* (Sydney: Australasian Book Society, 1979), 173; Frank Hardy, *The Hard Way* (Sydney: Australasian Book Society, 1961), 42.
22 Walter Kaufmann, 'How I Write', *The Realist Writer* 4 (December 1952): 5.
23 Closest to Kaufmann was the Hungarian Jew David Martin, a man of the world and a veteran of the Spanish Civil War. Of all Kaufmann's friends he stayed in touch for the longest period and visited him in the GDR. Kaufmann also mentions them in recent works: Hardy in *Im Fluss der Zeit*, 9–10, *Die Zeit berühren*, 121–124; *Gelebtes Leben*, 101–103; Marshall in *Im Fluss der Zeit*, 8; and Martin in *Im Fluss der Zeit*, 11.
24 In the original: 'Sie ist das Übungsfeld für junge Schriftsteller aus der Arbeiterklasse und für diejenigen, deren politische Überzeugung sie zu Verbündeten der Arbeiterklasse macht.' Walter Kaufmann, 'Literaturbrief aus Australien', *neuere deutsche literatur* 1 (1956): 152.
25 Kaufmann was briefly affiliated with modernist writers when he was first published: 'It is Then That You Love Most' (poem), in *Barjai* 9 (Sydney, 1945): 18; and 'The Manhunt' (short story), in *Angry Penguins* 8 (1945): 18. His first pieces to be edited by the Realist Writers Group were 'How I Write' (letter to the editor), in *The Realist Writer* 4 (December 1952): 3–4, and 'Against Hitler and the Boss' (excerpt from the novel *Voices in the Storm*), in *The Realist Writer* 4 (December 1952): 7–9.
26 Ralph de Boissiere, in an interview with Allan Gardiner, quoted from his dissertation: *Ralph de Boissiere and Communist Cultural Discourse in Cold War Australia* (St Lucia: University of Queensland, 1993), 83.
27 Since 1989, Kaufmann has reflected critically on his naïve allegiance to the figure of Stalin. See *Im Fluss der Zeit*, 224 and 233; *Gelebtes Leben*, 20.
28 Confidential file note on Walter Kaufmann, made by the deputy director of security, 13 April 1945. NAA, Walter Kaufmann, ASIO file, series A6119, C515, item 8334494.
29 'We had to go out and sell the book to pay the printer', Ralph de Boissiere in an interview with Allan Gardiner, from his dissertation *Ralph de Boissiere and Communist Cultural Discourse in Cold War Australia*, 92; 'Author Tours Newcastle', *Tribune* (Sydney), 30 September 1953.
30 His short narrative 'Midnight Sailing', published in *Tribune*, 10 March 1954: 7, received mostly damning reviews and criticism in a letter to the editor signed by six seamen, 'Seamen's View on "Midnight Sailing"', *Tribune*, 24 March 1954, 7. This was followed by more letters to the editor, 'More Letters on Kaufmann's Story', *Tribune*, 7 April 1954, 8; and by a conciliatory piece by Len Fox, 'Short Stories; Problems and the Way Forward', *Tribune*, 13 April 1954, 7.
31 *The Challenge*, Sydney, 18 May 1955.
32 *West Australian*, Perth, 29 June 1955.
33 East German writer Eduard Claudius asked him 'Wo kannst du am meisten für das Neue tun?' thereby urging him to stay in the GDR. Quoted in Klaus-Dieter Schöneweck, 'Blick für Geschichten und Sinn für Geschichte', *Neues Deutschland* 21, no. 22 (January 1989): 4.
34 In the original: 'Ein Mann Anfang Dreißig war das, der, sportlich, kräftig, gescheites Gesicht unter dunklem welligem Haar, die Tribüne hinaufstieg, ans Rednerpult trat und mit erregter Stimme zu sprechen begann. Er sprach deutsch, und seine Aussprache war klar und verständlich, aber seine Worte artikulierte er mit unverwechselbar englischem Akzent [...] nur ganz wenige Menschen [...] hatten zuvor von seiner Existenz oder gar von seinem Schicksal gewußt.' Joachim Schreck, from the epilogue in Walter

Kaufmann, *Am Kai der Hoffnung*, trans. Elga Abramowitz (Berlin: Verlag der Nation, 1974), 391.
35 Walter Kaufmann in his speech to the delegates of the 4th East Berlin Writers' Conference, January 1956, in *Beiträge zur Gegenwartsliteratur*, Protokoll, part 2, ed. Deutscher Schriftstellerverband (Halle: Märkische Volksstimme, 1956), 28–29.
36 File Note from 1953, NAA, series A6119, C515, item 8334494. During that year Kaufmann had worked in a slaughterhouse, but when he took part in a strike, he was sacked and remained unemployed for a while.
37 Walter Kaufmann, in his speech to the delegates of the 4th East Berlin Writers' Conference, January 1956, in *Beiträge zur Gegenwartsliteratur*, 29.
38 In the original: 'Sein Roman *S* wird vom Verlag fallen gelassen, da er den Mauerbau thematisiert, "Flucht", eine Geschichte über eine Flucht von Deutschland Ost nach Deutschland West, öffentlich totgeschwiegen. Und auch die Stasi hat ihn im Visier. In seiner Akte finden sich Spitzelberichte prominenter Kollegen.' Advertisement for the book *Im Fluss der Zeit: Ein Leben auf drei Kontinenten*, 2010, accessed January 2011, http://www.dittrich-verlag.de/buecher/im-fluss-der-zeit/.
39 Many of the GDR readers' reports lament a lack of artistic quality in Walter Kaufmann's work. See Hinstorff Verlag's report on *Hoffnung unter Glass* (1966), 7 April 1966, BArch DR1/2146/133. Here, the publisher argues that Kaufmann's book would be even more effective if it had been crafted better. In the margins of the report, a censor commented: 'Why wasn't it possible to achieve a better literary quality, in collaboration with the author?' As if anticipating this question, the publisher explains on the following page: 'As before, collaboration between the publishing house and the author is made more difficult by the fact that Kaufmann plans and writes in English, and the manuscripts reach the publishing house via the translator, some time after' (134). One report even laments the author's lack of literary competence ('Unvermögen'). Joachim Schreck, report on Walter Kaufmann, *Stimmen im Sturm* (1976), ca. August/September 1975, BArch DR1/2408/133.
40 'Literary Prize for Walter Kaufmann', *Tribune*, 4 April 1962, 7.
41 Walter Kaufmann, *Kreuzwege* (novel) (Berlin: Verlag Neues Leben, 1961); *Tribune* (Sydney), 2 February 1962.
42 In the original: 'Im August 1961 war ich in Kuba. Ich war weit weg vom Schuss und in einem dermaßen aufregenden Fluidum von Guantanamo, die Schweinebucht. [sic] Ich war dort zu der Zeit, als die Invasion stattfand und bin danach auch noch dort geblieben. Ich habe damals von dem Mauerbau überhaupt nichts mitbekommen. Ich war weit weg.' Walter Kaufmann, in an unpublished interview with A. Ludewig, 9 October 1994.
43 Barbara, Kaufmann's Australian wife, had followed him to East Germany in 1956. She had been unable to have more children after suffering a miscarriage earlier in their marriage and, after putting up with Kaufmann's philandering for a few years, eventually confronted him about one of his affairs. They divorced in the late 1950s. With his second wife, Angela Brunner, Walter had two daughters: Rebecca (1961), a photographer, and Deborah (1970), an actor. Walter and Barbara remained close friends until she died in 2007. She looked after his daughters when they were young and continued to show a great interest in Kaufmann's work, editing his English in the process. See also *Im Fluss der Zeit*, 98.
44 Walter Kaufmann, 'Socialism in an East Berlin Taxi', *Tribune*, 19 December 1962: 7; Walter Kaufmann, 'Lopsided Justice in West Germany', *Tribune*, 4 September 1963: 7;

Walter Kaufmann, 'Berlin's Nazi Murder Wave', *Tribune*, 2 October 1963: 7; Unnamed Berlin Correspondent (possibly Kaufmann), '13th Anniversary of the Only Peaceful German State in History', *Tribune*, 10 October 1962, 7.

45 In his assessment of *Hoffnung unter Glass* (1966), East German writer Klaus Schlesinger reminds assessors of the successful publication of the book's predecessor, *Begegnung mit Amerika heute*, in *Neues Deutschland*. Report on Walter Kaufmann, *Amerika-Amerika* (working title), 2 April 1966, BArch DR1/2146/125. Assessor Peter Lübbe found *Gerücht vom Ende der Welt* 'enriching our socialist literature about the United States'; Report on Walter Kaufmann, *Gerücht vom Ende der Welt*, 17 December 1968, BArch DR1/2149/158). See also the detailed plot summaries provided in the unsigned publisher's report on Walter Kaufmann, *Kreuzwege* (1961), undated, BArch DR1/5011/139 and the external assessor's report for the same title, undated, BArch DR1/5011/145.

46 Kaufmann, in an unpublished interview with A. Ludewig, 9 October 1994. Here, Walter Kaufmann is referring to his story 'Verlagshaus: Rostock 1964', which was published in 1992, well after the fall of the Wall, in *Die Zeit berühren*, 64–65.

47 Walter Kaufmann, 'Verlagshaus' in *Die Welt des Markus Epstein*, 237–39 (239).

48 Seven Seas' assessors, reviewing *Beyond the Green World of Childhood* (1971) for publication in English, observed that 'the author is not entirely at home in the English language and the manuscript needs correcting', that 'as far as style is concerned, Kaufmann's writing is stilted and clearly affected by his German'. In the original: 'Der Autor ist nicht völlig zuhause in der englischen Sprache und das Manuskript müsste redigiert werden.'; 'was den Stil betrifft, so schreibt Kaufmann manchmal gestelzt, mit starkem deutschen Einschlag'; Florence Knepler of Seven Seas Publishers, report on Walter Kaufmann, *Beyond the Green World of Childhood* (1971), undated, BArch DR1/2349/63. Rosemary Dawson, report on Walter Kaufmann, *Beyond the Green World of Childhood* (1971), undated, BArch DR1/2349/63.

49 Unsigned publisher's report on Walter Kaufmann, *Kreuzwege* (1961), undated, BArch DR1/5011/138 and publisher's report on Walter Kaufmann, *Gerücht vom Ende der Welt* (1969), 30 December 1968, BArch DR1/2149/156.

50 From the preface, 'Briefly, about the Book' (of Walter Kaufmann), in *American Encounter* (Berlin: Seven Seas Publishers, 1966), 1.

51 Afterword ('Auskünfte'), in Walter Kaufmann, *Flucht: Roman* (Halle/Leipzig: Mitteldeutscher Verlag, 1984) 219–23 (222–23).

52 It is clear from his work written after 1990, as well as files released by GDR publishing houses and the former Ministry of Culture, that Kaufmann was not immune to this intervention: translators made suggestions that he accepted; assessors suggested cutting passages and 'Entdeckung' ('Discovery'), one of the stories from *Stefan*, did not receive permission for publication because the assessor considered it unsuitable for 10-year olds, the recommended minimum age for the collection. Anne Martens, report on Walter Kaufmann, *Stefan: Mosaik einer Kindheit* (1966), undated, BArch DR1/2253/86. See also, for example, Konrad Reich, Hinstorff Verlag, to Meta Borst, Ministerium für Kultur, HV Verlage und Buchhandel Abt. Belletristik, Kunst- und Musikliteratur, 5 July 1966, BArch DR1/2146/118, Peter Lorf to Meta Borst, 7 January 1964, BArch DR1/5011/125 and 126.

53 Report of Major Zörner, 26 April 1963, Die Behörde des Bundesbeauftragten für die Unterlagen des Staatssicherheitsdienstes der ehemaligen Deutschen Demokratischen Republik (BstU), ZA, MfS, AOP 2642/64 T,I; Bl.134f.

54 In the original: 'Die Person W. K. [...] wird aus folgenden Gründen operativ bearbeitet: K. gibt sich nach außen hin als überzeugten [sic] Kommunisten. Bei der Überprüfung sind die Genossen der HVA [Hauptverwaltung Ausland] zu der Ansicht gelangt, daß es sich bei K. vermutlich um einen Agenten des englischen Geheimdienstes handelt. [...] 1.6.1963.', BStU, ZA, MfS; AOP 2642/64, T, I; Bl.137.

55 External assessor's report on Walter Kaufmann's *Kreuzwege* (1961), undated, BArch DR1/5011/146 and 147.

56 Walter Kaufmann, *Begegnungen mit Amerika heute* (Reiseliteratur); trans. Helga Zimnik (Rostock: VEB Hinstorff, 1965).

57 'Presumably the files exist no longer.' In the original: 'Vermutlich existieren die Akten nicht mehr.' Dr Manfred Horlitz, head of the Theodor-Fontane-Archive, in a letter to A. Ludewig from 15 August 1994. In this context, Kaufmann points out that prizes in West Germany were likewise used for political purposes, such as the honours heaped on Wolf Biermann in the West after his expatriation from the GDR in 1976. Unpublished interview with A. Ludewig, 9 October 1994.

58 David Martin, in a letter to A. Ludewig, 22 May 1994.

59 David Martin, *My Strange Friend* (Sydney: Pan Macmillan, 1991), 234f.

60 In the original: 'lieben und warmherzigen Menschen, dem ich viel zu verdanken habe'. Unpublished interview with A. Ludewig, 14 December 1994.

61 Reader Anne Martens was not alone in attesting to in Kaufmann's work a 'strong political message' ('starke politische Aussage'); report on Walter Kaufmann, *Stefan – Mosaik einer Kindheit* (1966), undated, BArch DR1/2253/82. This view was shared within the Ministry of Culture, where Meta Borst, of the Hauptverwaltung Verlage und Buchhandel, noted that Kaufmann had 'no politically questionable convictions' ('keine politisch falschen Auffassungen'); Meta Borst to Hinstorff Verlag, 2 May 1966, about *Hoffnung unter Glas*, BArch DR1/2146/119.

62 In the original: 'durch Werke gesellschaftlichen Charakters die demokratische und sozialistische Erziehung unseres Volkes gefördert'; Nachtrag zum Statut vom 30.11.55 durch Dr. Abusch am 18.2.1966, quoted from a copy of the 'Statut', held in the Stiftungsarchiv, AdK, Berlin.

63 Unpublished interview with A. Ludewig, 9 October 1994.

64 Irmtraud Petersson, *German Images in Australian Literature from the 1940s to the 1980s* (Frankfurt: Peter Lang, 1990), 45.

65 David Martin, in a letter to A. Ludewig, 22 May 1994.

66 In the original: 'daß der Sozialismus insgesamt konstruktive Antworten geben könne auf die komplizierten Fragen unserer heutigen modernen Welt, [...] er fühle sich in der DDR wohl und wisse, daß er hier produktiv und sinnvoll arbeiten könne.' GI 'Köhler', BStU, ZA, MfS, AP 9886, T, II; Bl.29.

67 Walter Kaufmann's *Stimmen im Sturm* was to be released in a print run of 10,000 (as agreed in April 1976), but an additional 3,500 was granted in November 1976 'within the limits of our quota for paper'. In the original: 'im Rahmen unseres Papierkontingents'; Hahn of Verlag der Nation to Ministerium für Kultur, HV Verlage und Buchhandel, 10 November 2011, BArch DR1/2408/129.

68 In the original: 'Obwohl Kaufmann ein großes Talent zu werden verspricht, hindern ihn jedoch daran nicht unwesentlich seine oftmals wechselnden Frauenbekanntschaften'; Christa Wolf, as IM 'Margarete', *Stasi-Akten zu Walter Kaufmann*, BStU, ZA, MfS; AOP 2642/64, T, I; Bl.76. In his autobiography Kaufmann details many of his romantic

encounters that show him to have been a serial philanderer. See Walter Kaufmann, *Im Fluss der Zeit* (Berlin: Dittrich Verlag, 2010).
69 Ralph de Boissiere, in a letter to A. Ludewig, 4 June 1994.
70 Unpublished interview with A. Ludewig, 14 December 1994.
71 Ralph de Boissiere, in a letter to A. Ludewig, 4 June 1994.
72 In the original: 'Unser Autor fährt ein westdeutsches Auto und sieht westdeutsches Fernsehen auf seinem "Philips"-Gerät. Über seinen Privilegierten-Status kann es keinen Zweifel geben [...] Als unser Autor uns frühmorgens zum Checkpoint Charlie zurückfährt und dem wachhabenden Volksarmisten erklärt, wir seien seine "Spezialgäste", versuche ich zu clownen.' Manfred Jurgensen, *Deutsche Reise* (Bern: Peter Lang, 1990), 57.
73 Wolf Biermann wrote about the questionable independence of the East German PEN: 'Erinnern Sie sich noch an den letzten PEN-Kongress in Hamburg 1986? [...] Aber der Spitzel Kannitzer sah alles. Hagers und Mielkes Apparatschiks waren noch an der Macht und hatten ihre Aufpasser im Hamburger Kongreßzentrum plaziert.' Wolf Biermann, *Über das Geld und andere Herzensdinge: Prosaische Versuche über Deutschland* (Köln: Kiepenheuer & Witsch 1991), 66–67.
74 See Dorothée Bores, *Das ostdeutsche P.E.N.-Zentrum 1951–1998: Ein Werkzeug der Diktatur?* (Berlin: de Gruyter, 2010), 783.
75 See *Im Fluss der Zeit*, 7–8, as well as *Markus Epstein*, 298.
76 Walter Kaufmann, in a letter to A. Ludewig, 7 April 1994.
77 Walter Kaufmann, 'On the Tightrope', in *Beyond the Green World of Childhood* (Berlin: Seven Seas Books, 1972), 67–69.

Chapter 7

FICTIONALIZING AUSTRALIA FOR THE GDR: ADVENTURE WRITER JOACHIM SPECHT*

Patricia F. Blume

Readings with Joachim Specht must have been impressive: archival photos show him gesticulating wildly, holding his books in the air for all to see, pointing to a place on a map of Australia, passing around large photographs, and showing off a boomerang and his trapper hat. Whether he was addressing childcare workers, men in overalls, school groups or teenage apprentices, Specht never grew tired of talking about his experiences: 'Readers wanted to know how I came to live in Australia and why I came back. And who taught me to write. And by the time I had told them, the hour was already up.'[1]

Like his captive listeners, the author lived in the GDR. The big difference between them was that he had seen the world, and they had not. Thanks to his rich travel experiences on the Fifth Continent and the support he received from the GDR's cultural policy, Joachim Specht became one of the country's best-selling authors. Specht's career began in the early 1960s and collapsed only with the fall of the Berlin Wall in 1989. His books were written in German and set, with few exceptions, in Australia. Much of his life centred on his role as an intermediary between these two worlds. Characterized by circumstantial realism and narrated from an assuredly socialist, 'partisan' viewpoint that clearly recognized social inequality and racial discrimination, his narratives pleased East German publishers and censors alike. While his titles promised to take readers away from the GDR to the exotic Great Barrier Reef and mangrove swamps, they assured censors that life under the Southern Cross was as distant as it was undesirable – indeed, Specht's publishers were quick to couch his own experiences there as reformatory. Yet, his audience in the socialist country, without freedom to travel, was mesmerized: 'Because I am so drawn to this continent – Australia – I would like to learn even more about

Figure 7.1 Joachim Specht at an outdoor reading with teenage apprentices in the late 1970s; photographer unknown (Stadtarchiv Dessau-Roßlau, N 3.13 – Specht – 9, 18).

Figure 7.2 A group of pupils listening to tales of Australia in a school library; photographer unknown (Stadtarchiv Dessau-Roßlau, N 3.13 – Specht – 10, 62).

it'[2], wrote one young lady in a fan letter to the author, after she had listed the 14 books of his that she owned. How did Specht succeed in directing the East German reader's diffuse wanderlust to a specific yearned-for place, and why did Australia become more and more an abstract projection for Specht himself?

From Dessau to Darwin and Back Again

Joachim Specht was born in 1931 and grew up in the Dresden region and in Dessau, where he trained as a locksmith. After failing to get into university, he left East Germany for Hamburg. From there, at the age of 21, he set course for Australia, having signed a two-year contract with a railway company. From May 1952, he lived there for almost four years, at first in a migrant camp in South Australia, helping to build the railway. Later, he explored the country, working as a casual labourer on farms, at an Aboriginal mission and for a uranium mine. He returned to Hamburg in late 1955 to find a wife who would live with him in Australia. But when it transpired that he was needed in Dessau, in the family's locksmith business, he decided to stay in the GDR permanently.

Specht's sister, a librarian, told him about a group of *schreibende Arbeiter*, 'writing workers', meeting in Dessau, which he joined in 1960. This decision would have a crucial, transformative influence on the locksmith, and ultimately help him forge a career as an author. Creative circles similar to the Dessau group had been set up across the GDR. They formed a substantial part of the *Bitterfelder Weg*, a cultural-political experiment that existed on a large scale only in the GDR. In 1959 the motto of the eponymous author conference in the industrial town of Bitterfeld had been: 'Greif' zur Feder, Kumpel! Die sozialistische Nationalkultur braucht Dich!' ('Buddy, seize your pen! Socialist national culture needs you!'). Intended to bridge the gap between artists and the general population, this movement, on the one hand, encouraged workers to derive artistic ideas from their everyday experience. On the other hand, artists were supposed to mingle with industry workers so they could share their reality and more authentically portray what it was like to be part of a socialist society. Many artists also supported the numerous amateur groups created throughout the country to help popularize artistic activity among the masses. These groups saw workers perform ballet and theatre, paint, shoot films and write. By early 1960 there were 2,500 *schreibende Arbeiter*, organized in 220 circles.[3] The workers composed shorter texts, such as for *Wandzeitungen*, bulletin boards that informed colleagues of political and production-related goings-on, but they also wrote fictional prose, verse and drama. With widespread cultural-political support, their writing attempts were published in numerous anthologies, individual publications and in the separate monthly magazine *ich schreibe* (I Write).

It was due entirely to the Bitterfeld movement that Specht's life took the course it did, as he acknowledges even today: '*Schreibender Arbeiter* – now that was something, in the otherwise often boring GDR. Who knew how long the trend would last? I definitely got on board at the right time and above all had the right advocate.'[4] This is a reference to his mentor, Werner Steinberg (1913–1992), instructor of the Dessau writing circle in its first decade.[5] Steinberg was a busy author who took his mentoring work seriously. He has been quoted as declaring that most of the workers' circles were created to generate propaganda for the GDR.[6] Notwithstanding this, Steinberg taught the workers how to open a novel, introduce characters or expedite conflicts by drawing on selected works of world literature, such as Graham Greene's *The Quiet American*, first published in the GDR in 1957.[7] Beyond these influences, Joachim Specht unsurprisingly mentions Egon Kisch's *Australian Landfall* (1937): 'I read that first.'[8] His other literary idols included Jack London, Joseph Conrad and Friedrich Gerstäcker, a popular German author of nineteenth-century adventure novels and travelogues. Among Gerstäcker's many works are various stories about Australia, written after his extensive trip to the continent in the early 1850s.

A First Success

Steinberg saw Specht's potential and in 1961 recommended one of his stories to Verlag der Nation, where his talent was immediately recognized.[9] In early 1962, the publisher signed him for a collection of stories, based on material from the diary Specht had kept in Australia. The 13 stories were compiled in a book called *Peterborough Story*. They follow European migrants whose diverse destinies converge in the scant, rough, migrant camps, uranium mines, railway companies and building sites of Australia. They labour in the heat, buckle under exploitation at the hands of profit-oriented bosses and learn that as 'new Australians' they are now effectively stateless and disenfranchised. Simultaneously, the history of post-war Germany unfolds in the everyday life of the camp. Here war trauma resurfaces—for example, when Jewish Holocaust survivors encounter Nazis in hiding. This range of themes fell unmistakably within the duties of Verlag der Nation, specializing as it did in *Wandlungsliteratur* (transformative literature), which was intended to re-educate former members of the Nazi Party. And this explains why Specht was taken on by this publisher and not Mitteldeutscher Verlag, usually the first point of contact for contemporary socialist literature from writing workers.

Political commentary takes the foreground in the story 'Freunde' ('Friends'), which reflects on the workers' attempts at solidarity: 'A few days ago, when we wanted to strike due to abysmal sanitary conditions in the lavatories, the police were at the camp before the call to strike had even reached the mine.'[10] In this story, Specht reproduces the mid-1950s Soviet communist line portraying established labour organisations as traitors to the workers' cause. The reader learns that the Australian Workers Union promotes 'the worst suppressors and enemies of the workers'[11] to control its top ranks, the type of person whom Jürgen, the protagonist, hoped to escape by leaving Europe. Instead, Jürgen becomes involved in the illegal peace movement and receives its straightforward support as he helps an outlaw leave the country.

A central theme in his debut – which set the standard for Specht's future work – is the depiction of discrimination against Australia's indigenous population. In 'Nordwind' ('Northwind') Specht links the contemptuous treatment of Aborigines at the hands of white Australians with a criticism of nuclear weapons testing, carried out by the British Government in Australia between 1952 and 1963. He has workers find a dead, partly burnt Aboriginal man. As the circumstances surrounding the death slowly come to light, the reader learns how Aboriginal people in isolated areas of South Australia were knowingly exposed to radiation.

In 'Der Buschbrand' ('The Bushfire'), Tom, a new Australian, works for money-hungry McNamara, the owner of a sheep station. Tom's assistant is Jonas, an Aborigine, who has been mute since

> his tongue was torn apart in a tribal feud. White people picked him up and brought him to the mission station, where he grew up and learnt technical skills. Jonas likes to laugh and, when he does so, reveals teeth as white as snow, which exude vitality and good health. Despite all attempts by pious men to turn him into a devote subject of the crown, he remains an unspoilt man of the Stone Age. His sense of direction has no equal.[12]

In the character, Specht creates a typical 'noble savage', clearly resorting to primitivism. However, Jonas is not limited to this, and Specht adds depth by describing the friendship between Tom and Jonas, who drink from the same water canteen. Disaster strikes when the owner of the sheep station sets fire to its buildings in a bid to defraud the insurance company. When Tom searches the scene, he finds the burnt corpse of Jonas and is outraged at McNamara: 'He could at least have taken the native away beforehand. But no, he was just a black, no one minds if he kicks the bucket!'[13] Tom presents this point of view to the boss himself in front of a group of people in the pub, and accuses him of murdering Jonas. When Tom dies in an accident at the end of the story, it is implied that McNamara is behind it.

Often the Aborigines in Specht's earlier stories, such as 'Der Buschbrand', only live amongst white people if they grew up on a mission or are of mixed heritage. In contrast, he depicts indigenous Australians as communities living beyond the reaches of white settlement, as for example in 'Die Kinder von Broom Tank' ('The Children from Broom Tank'). In this story from the period of assimilationist policies and the stolen generations, the protagonist Nick and his mate are supposed to deliver two Aboriginal children to a mission station at Koonibba in South Australia, near Ceduna. But instead of travelling to the station, Nick drives to the 'reservation' where the children's community lives: 'Suddenly bearded, wild-looking faces were looking through our car windows […] and the next second we were busy supplying greedily outstretched hands with cigarettes.' Nick behaves in a manner similar to many of Specht's heroes: against agreed arrangements, convention or even against the law, because his sense of justice for the helpless prevails:

> The children were meant to go to the mission, and they would have to stay there forever. Forever. Do you understand? Their parents and the clan would never see them again. And when they got older and wanted to live like white people, then they would never have been able to adapt […] and for that reason, I think it is better that they stay with their own kind, and live like savages and be happy.[14]

This depiction of Aborigines as wild, uncivilized, yet good-natured people is a common feature of Specht's early writing. Through the lens of Aboriginal protests and later post-colonial theory, this is clearly a discriminatory attribution of characteristics from preconceived Western notions. Nevertheless, Specht's texts are ambiguous: while he keenly and repeatedly relies on the noble savage and its inherent dichotomies (civilized/wild, us/them), he also denounces the disenfranchisement of the indigenous population. Although his narration indirectly advocates for civil rights for Aborigines, the perspective of the (similarly marginalized) new Australians on the indigenous population does not protect Specht's stories from a stereotypical characterization of non-whites prevailing during the era before the Australian civil rights movement. At the same time, Specht's work implicitly argued that the class conflict required a solidarity that transcended ethnic differences, and such a political bias was unlikely to displease the GDR party officials.

Socialist Labelling

Today, Specht is convinced: 'The GDR citizens read over the political background of my stories, for them it was purely about the adventure.'[15] Yet, in its reports the publisher praised Specht for his partisan point of view.[16] It was intended that the author's turn towards socialism, as evidenced in his books, shape the GDR audience's image of Australia:

> Without a doubt, vague ideas about the Fifth Continent haunt the minds of many of our readers. The author, who allowed himself to be recruited to Australia out of a sense of adventure (and because of difficulties finding suitable employment in West Germany), shows our readers some of the real (and extraordinarily immoral) sides of the 'golden' overseas.[17]

The publishing house quoted him multiple times in blurbs and suchlike with the words: 'I had to hitchhike to the end of the world to understand the theory of Marxism-Leninism and class conflict in practice.'[18] One afterword explained: far away from the GDR, Specht had understood the distance between Australia and West Germany was merely geographical and that their political systems were similar.[19]

Specht's return to the GDR thus constituted extremely important evidence of the problems of capitalism. From his debut on, the author was presented to the Ministry of Culture as well as to the readers as a repatriate having undergone an ideological catharsis. This image helped to overcome the difficulties which arose from the anti-working class setting in a foreign country, on the one hand, and the middle-of-the-road depictions of everyday life in the GDR as prescribed by the *Bitterfelder Weg*, on the other hand. In the words of one external reader: 'We must be clear that these stories are exotic to us, which means that they have no direct link to our everyday lives in the GDR.'[20]

Moreover, the example of Joachim Specht shows that promising *schreibende Arbeiter* received support at every level. The publisher not only contracted a respected illustrator for *Peterborough Story*, but *neue deutsche literatur* (New German Literature) even featured a review. Published by the East German writers' union, this magazine was a literary institution in the GDR. The reviewer introduced Specht, 'reformed' by his emigration to Australia, and then discussed a few of his stories, drawing an interesting comparison with prominent Australian communist writer Katharine Susannah Prichard about the portrayal of Christian missions, 'which often have a highly unchristian impact and above all serve the monetary interests of the whites. These problems have been depicted here much more harshly than in the volume *Die Braut von Far-Away* (The Bride from Far Away) by Australian author K. S. Prichard.'[21] Obviously, the reviewer seems to imply here that the GDR author was able to view the conditions in the country more clearly than Australian authors. Volk und Welt had published ten of Prichard's stories in German translation in 1962 as *Die Braut von Far-Away* – with a heavy heart, it would appear. Editor Hans Petersen explained in his moody reports to the censors that he had excluded many stories because 'they are nothing but badly copied life and therefore a kind of modern Australian naturalism'.[22]

After having completed *Peterborough Story*, Specht immediately began to work on his first novel, *Die Gejagten* (The Hunted), published in 1966. It has as its heart the love story of Marcus, a white lieutenant in the navy, and Sadi, an Aborigine of mixed heritage who works as a nurse on an island for leprosy patients. This island, where Marcus is also being treated, forms a remote, parallel society. The sick are divided along the colour line, co-existing in a form of segregation, which is, however, 'not as strict as onshore'.[23] Specht includes a sympathetically drawn minor Aboriginal character, O'Koola. As the 'small lady', gravely sick, looks at her rugged face in the mirror, she is swayed with terror:

> Nobody would recognize her ever again. She isn't O'Koola anymore, she has become N'Gomo, a jumping ghost, half animal, half human, who is at one with the souls of dead children and slain warriors, spreading fear among her tribe's people. Only one small step to take. And she will go the predestined way of all tired souls: the way into the endless desert. There the gods will dance with her and her body will be absorbed into the great crowd, and will be brought to rest in the rhythm of the stamping dances of the dead up to the high tree trunks.[24]

Shortly after this O'Koola throws herself from the rocky cliffs into the surf and is eaten by the sharks.

Still on the island, Marcus and Sadi fall in love, get married, and in spite of great reservations and warnings from those around them, have a son. When they return to the mainland together, their odyssey as 'the hunted' begins. They face blackmail, discrimination and separation. Marcus undertakes a long journey to meet Sadi on the east coast, punctuated by difficulty and trials, including allusions to British nuclear testing in the desert. In a twist typical of Specht's work, Marcus joins a group of nomadic Aborigines, while Sadi is forced to give their son to a mission in order to continue work as a cleaner. A pastor brings her into contact with the world peace movement. Marcus and Sadi meet again coincidentally at a peace congress in Melbourne, where he is one of the speakers. Together, they attempt a new beginning, but again, racial discrimination takes effect and prevents them from securing an apartment. The novel ends with Marcus accepting an offer from trade union officials to work in a mine in the north, with the plan that, after a year, Sadi will follow with their son. According to the publisher's report, this open ending was a necessity: 'In fact, the living conditions of the Aboriginal people have changed considerably in the years between when the events in the book take place [1953–54] and the present. Nevertheless, the author had to avoid an all-too optimistic tone so as not to rouse misconceptions.'[25]

Figure 7.3 Dust jacket of Joachim Specht's *Die Gejagten*, designed by well-respected illustrator Hans Baltzer (Berlin: Verlag der Nation, 1966).

'Pristine and Authentic'?

The majority of his assessors commended Specht as a storyteller with a remarkably captivating style: his narration was regarded as 'pristine and authentic', illustrating Australian realities knowledgeably, as Wolfgang Joho put it. Joho was editor-in-chief of *neue deutsche literatur* and an author himself, but absolutely no expert on Australian matters. Nevertheless he asserted *Die Gejagten* to be 'full to the brim with life. It is adventure fiction in the best and truest sense.'[26] Indeed, there is a high degree of clarity and atmospheric density in Specht's prose. The continent is animated for the GDR reader through well-observed specifics of everyday life and the natural environment. Writing from Australia, Germanist Manfred Jurgensen shares this impression: 'It is this transmission of facts and information about Australia which gives Specht's books their special significance. In the light of continued widespread ignorance about this country in Europe such precisely observed, if fictionalized reports serve a cultural purpose which should not be underestimated.'[27] Small details contribute to the overall impression, such as short colloquial expressions in

English interspersed in direct speech: Specht's characters yell 'Good luck to you!', 'Cheerio!' or 'Bloody bastard!'. Rather uncommon in written and spoken language in the GDR, English words abound – 'high speed', 'story', 'sheep station', 'squatter', 'supper' and 'bullets' – alongside impromptu German-English composites, such as *Chefclerk* (head clerk), *Abrechnungsoffice* (accounting office) and *Maschinenshop* (machinery shop). Then, there are the diverse geographic names and the depictions of native flora and fauna: the obligatory emus, kangaroos and eucalyptus trees, but also cockatoos, goannas, black snakes, and sleepy lizards (shinglebacks), brigalow trees and mallee scrub. Specht's protagonists drive Chryslers, Bedfords and Holdens – brands unfamiliar to GDR readers – and they travel for miles instead of kilometres, fill up at Shell petrol stations and drink West End beer.

Eventually, Specht's renderings received confirmation from a reliable source. At one of his readings in 1964 he met Australian sculptor Renee Heisler, who had become a citizen of Great Britain and recently relocated to the GDR.[28] Specht had been reading from his story 'Die Begegnung' ('The Encounter') when a member of the audience doubted the realism of his depictions. In this story, a German-speaking Australian is travelling through a remote area and witnesses a procession of emaciated Aborigines appearing out of nowhere, chained together, completely naked and accompanied by two riders. Renee Heisler chimed in and told her fellow listeners that having returned from Australia only six months ago, she could assure them that Specht understated, rather than exaggerated the truth. In fact, she was overwhelmed by the realistic description of racial discrimination in *Peterborough Story*, and affirmed Specht's point of view at the reading.

Heisler not only credited Specht with authenticity, she also encouraged him to enlarge his area of influence:

> Mrs. Heisler *implored* me to let her translate my collection of stories into English. Her colleague, Joan Smith, with whom she fled, is of mixed race and lives in Karl-Marx-Stadt. Together they would see to it that my stories were translated into genuine Australian slang. Mrs. Heisler introduced her request very passionately. I never would have dreamt that my stories would meet with such resonance.[29]

Steinberg, Specht's mentor, suggested export of the collection via Great Britain or India. For this reason, Specht pressured his publisher Verlag der Nation to offer his book in markets further afield: 'The stories would have to be smuggled into Australia by any means *so that they could have an effect there.*'[30] Although well meaning, the Berlin publishing house had no connections with Australian publishing houses, and Australia did not have a booth at the GDR book fair in Leipzig, where companies generally initiated export or licensing

Figure 7.4 Illustration by Hans Baltzer for the story 'The Encounter' from Joachim Specht's fiction collection *Peterborough Story* (Berlin: Verlag der Nation, 1963), which was judged one of the 'most beautiful books of the GDR' in 1964.

negotiations.[31] Nevertheless, Renee Heisler translated 'Die Begegnung', which she then sent on to her university friend, expatriate Australian author Jack Lindsay. He was writing for the *Daily Worker*, the newspaper of the Communist Party in Great Britain, but any hopes that he might recommend publishers were soon shattered. An intervention from Dymphna Cusack also amounted to nothing. It was only in 1984 that expatriate Germanist Manfred Jurgensen published an English extract from *Peterborough Story* in the first issue of his journal of multicultural literature in Australia, *Outrider*.[32]

Even though Renee Heisler could not help Specht reach the Australian book market, his contact with her proved useful. For example, Heisler sent Specht a speech by Kath Walker on audiotape. Walker, who later took on the name Oodgeroo Noonuccal from the language of her country on Queensland's Stradbroke Island, is often credited as the first Aboriginal poet to publish in English and her work remains iconic in indigenous Australian literature. She joined the Communist Party of Australia (CPA) for a short period, when it was the only party to oppose racial discrimination, and campaigned for full civil rights for Aborigines, playing a definitive role in the 1967 referendum on Aboriginal recognition in the constitution. Specht was thrilled by the live audio recording and used it for *Die Gejagten*. 'I'll never get material like this again!', he wrote to his editor.[33] Hence, the beginning of the second part of the novel features an excerpt from Walker's speech, in which she points to the fact that she is not blaming the general Australian population but, rather, 'the entire legal system.'[34]

The Remarkable Rise of 'Australia Specht'

Notably, Specht did not become a full-time writer until as late as 1972. Before that, he worked during the day as a locksmith and only devoted himself to composition, at night, after work. In any case, GDR readers loved Specht's prose: *Die Gejagten* and *Peterborough Story* did not gather dust on the shelves of bookstores as did other titles by writing workers. One reader reported: 'Often when a book of his was in store, it was almost immediately sold out again. My search was often in vain.'[35] Specht's acceptance into the writers' union in the mid-1960s marked an atypical jump of a writing worker into the ranks of professional authors, into which only those with already published works and corresponding recommendations were invited.

Paradoxically, what worked for Specht had failed on a larger scale. The mass cultural movement, as a mixture of ideology and a creative free-time activity, was considered at a dead end even before the beginning of the 1970s, not least because it was too strongly connected with the era of Walter Ulbricht.[36] Although the *Bitterfelder Weg* is recognized by researchers as having contributed to an extensive amateur art movement and the writing circles continued to exist until the end of the GDR, even in the 1960s consensus not to treat *schreibende Arbeiter* as budding authors gained acceptance.[37] Indeed, the fact that their books were being produced in great numbers but met with no demand almost caused the entire GDR book distribution system to collapse. However, it can be established that these economic forces ultimately promoted certain literary standards for professional authors and thus indirectly advanced the development of a critical contemporary East German literature.[38]

Indisputably, Specht contributed enormously to GDR *Literaturpropaganda*, understood as a strategy of systematic advertising and distribution of books. When he introduced his debut work at numerous readings, he could feel the impact of his texts: 'Adventure writers were popular', he recalled later. 'They did not bore readers with production activities, the smell of the big wide world wafted through their texts.'[39] In the following years his networks included state-owned companies, regional libraries, book stores and club houses that regularly invited him to speak. By the late 1980s Specht attended 150 to 200 literary

Figure 7.5 Joachim Specht in a reading, his books in front of him on the table. The poster on the wall translates as 'The GDR my state'; photographer unknown (Stadtarchiv Dessau-Roßlau, N 3.13 – Specht – 10, 179).

events a year throughout the GDR, covering around 31,000 miles: 'At "Book Week" I felt like a travelling preacher. And with time I developed the image of "Australia Specht"'.[40] Aside from the intensive contact with his audience, these readings granted him additional financial independence and helped him cope with the material scarcities of daily life in the socialist country.[41]

Refining Skills

Specht admits in retrospect that 'work with the written word did not always come naturally to me.'[42] He experienced a literary education and formation on two levels. Apart from Steinberg's mentoring, his editors too looked after Specht extensively, offering encouragement and praise, for example, during his work on *Peterborough Story*.[43] Specht remembers the publisher Verlag der Nation as open and supporting:

> I was lucky enough to meet Irmgard Schütze there, who as editor took me by the hand and patiently let me babble when I began to rhapsodize about Australia.

> She recognised that the well-travelled young man, who struggled with spelling, was full of experiences which needed channelling. Through friendly letters she encouraged me to transform my adventurous experiences into written sentences.[44]

The files at the federal archives show how much time, effort and diligence the editors put into Specht's drafts in order to mould his talent for fabulation into readable texts. This insistent care was, without question, part of the editors' political mandate, by which they had to abide – supporting working writers, especially those like Specht who showed a 'capacity for development'.

Soon Verlag der Nation pressured Specht to devote himself to contemporary socialism, a 'change of topic: From Australia to the GDR'.[45] The publisher persuaded the author to turn his short story, 'Der Fünfer' ('The Fiver'), into a novel, which depicts how a win in the lottery affects a brigade of locksmiths. The reasons for the change towards a GDR setting were clear to the publisher: 'Australia was exotic for the reader and thus ungovernable; every person needs repair mechanics'[46]. But certainly this shift was not easy for Specht. Two years of hard work went into the manuscript and not only for stylistic reasons. Although the topic picked up on ideas typical of the Bitterfeld movement, the publisher found Specht overly criticized incidents of everyday life.[47] In the end, as the Party identified, authors depicting the situation in the factories too realistically became one of the reasons the *Bitterfelder Weg* failed. For Specht, his torture finally came to an end and the book could be promoted as his departure for the 'great quest for discovery along the lines of socialist latitudes'.[48]

All in all, the engagement with contemporary life in the GDR was extremely unsatisfying and exhausting for Specht because so many 'know-it-alls' kept interfering. After one more project, he turned back to his beloved Australia, so he could maintain his expertise. For the time being, he left his first publishing house, proposing new manuscripts to the publisher Das Neue Berlin, the first and only place in the GDR for genre fiction. It was from there the novel *Blütenhölle in Banusta* (Floral Hell in Banusta, 1971), set in Papua New Guinea, was published. In this story, the reader witnesses the gradual disillusionment of a doctor who wants to bring the dealings of an American excavation company to light. Tolerated by the Australian Government, the enterprise destroys a region, thereby displacing the indigenous people. Critics reviewed the book positively, which reconciled Specht with his job again.[49] When Neues Berlin held a contest in 1974 to promote socialist adventure literature, Specht came second together with Harry Thürk, a well-known GDR author whose books were mostly set in Southeast Asia.[50] In all, Specht published seven titles, among them *Leuchtfeuer Eastern Reef* (Lights of Eastern Reef, 1976) through Neues Berlin.

In the mid-1970s, his first publisher, Verlag der Nation, rejected his novels on the basis that his experience in Australia 'has been used up in a literary sense'[51], and Specht turned to Neues Leben, a publisher for young people. It accepted not only Specht's *Korallen-Joe* (Coral Joe) and *Paraipagold* (Paraipa Gold) but also published six further collections and novels between 1978 and 1990. They bore titles like *Tippet, In den Mangrovensümpfen* (In the Mangrove Swamps), or *Segelflug unterm Kreuz des Südens* (Gliding under the Southern Cross). These books were published in popular series with initial print runs of more than 150,000 copies.[52] Specht, now addressing a younger audience, stayed within the same paradigm but toned down the 'horny farmer', Susann's 'full bosom' and the 'gasping breaths' coming from the bordello caravan of his Peterborough collection.[53] Although Verlag der Nation complained that Specht only provided variations on his one central theme, Neues Leben enabled him to maintain just that. In this way, the GDR publication system supported his outdated image of Australia.

Secondary Sources versus First-Hand Experiences

The persistence of Specht's particular version of Australia can be traced back to the strength of his original experience, but also to his increasing problems getting access to up-to-date information. In the 1970s he attempted to visit Australia once more. For the writers' union, he drew a comparison with a famous German adventure writer from the turn of the century who created the better part of his successful stories about Native Americans without having travelled to North America. Specht

> did not want to sit within the confines of four walls like Karl May and use secondary sources [...] Aside from Walter Kaufmann and Prof. Frederick Rose, I am probably the only author [in the GDR] who has provided information about the Australian indigenous people in his texts [...] I am not interested in Africa, America, Western and Eastern Europe, I somehow want to travel to Australia, that is my subject and I want to stick with that![54]

Unlike other authors from the adventure and suspenseful light fiction genres, such as highly circulated Wolfgang Schreyer who was allowed to travel to the Caribbean, Harry Thürk to Vietnam, or Lieselotte Welskopf-Henrich to Canada,[55] all Specht's attempts to return to his yearned-for place failed. This was a painful experience for him. It made little difference that Verlag der Nation also campaigned for his trip, citing the stagnation of Specht's artistic construction.[56] The author made more attempts, securing support from the writers' union and the Main Administration for Publishing and the

Book Trade. The latter even sent him a travel report that Hans Petersen, the important proponent of Australian literature in the publishing house Volk und Welt, had written about his trip to the continent in late 1986.[57] Specht's last, unsuccessful attempt to obtain permission to travel was just a few months before the fall of the Berlin Wall.

Another way to overcome the distance between himself and his subject had to be found. Specht discovered an influential advisor in Frederick Rose (1915–1991), professor of anthropology at the Humboldt University in Berlin. Rose was born in London and, after finishing his university study in Cambridge in the late 1930s, had emigrated to Australia with his German wife Edith. There he worked as a meteorologist, wharfie, anthropologist and government advisor, and was a high-profile member of the CPA. His pioneering field work with remote northern Aboriginal communities won him some recognition, but suggestions that he was working for Soviet intelligence saw him brought before the 1954 Petrov Royal Commission on Espionage, after which, residence in Australia became very difficult. Fred followed Edith to East Berlin in 1956.[58] In 1960, with an academic publisher in the GDR, Rose released his now 'classic' ethnological study of kinship structures in the Groote Eylandt Aboriginal community, where he had lived in the 1930s. Through the 1960s, he returned to Australia twice to study the indigenous Anangu community at Angas Downs in central Australia and continued to publish books and articles in English and German.

A later volume, which was semi-autobiographical and intended for the general public, *Ureinwohner, Känguruhs und Düsenclipper* (Indigenous People, Kangaroos and Jet Planes) was published in 1966 by Brockhaus in Leipzig. An English edition appeared in 1968, also in East Germany, with Seven Seas, as *Australia Revisited: The Aborigine Story from Stone Age to Space Age*. In this book, Rose shows his fierce political commitment and does not hold back when it comes to developments in Australia in the mid-1960s. He also calls to attention the political climate prior to his immigration to the GDR, condemning the everyday vilification of the indigenous population in the 1930s and 1940s and the repressive atmosphere of the Menzies era in the early 1950s. His highly accessible ethnographic research, his multi-faceted anecdotes from the tropics and the desert, his experiences with indigenous people and their behaviour make up the better part of the book. The English edition ends optimistically:

> In the short historical period of thirty years the Aborigines have burst their tribal bonds and are today on the Fifth Continent, part of the world-wide movement against colonialism, racial discrimination and exploitation. They are on their way to becoming a small but nonetheless esteemed and equal member of the world-wide family of peoples.[59]

The German edition further concludes that the Aborigines know that they 'can rely on the working class as active allies'.[60]

Specht's contact with Rose came about through Verlag der Nation, which asked him to assess *Die Gejagten*. 'Above all', the publisher appealed to Rose's insider knowledge, 'we would like your report to assess all facts that we can only partly, or not at all, verify from here: the situation of the indigenous peoples, the organisation of trade unions, the living conditions of Australian citizens, special geographical details and such like.'[61] Because the professor was busy, his wife, Edith, assessed the manuscript. She was East German, had studied in Melbourne and, having accompanied her husband to northern and western Australia, proved to be a wealth of knowledge. For example, she advised the publisher that it is beetle larvae (witchetty grubs), not worms, that are eaten and that 'to speak of Stone Age people, who run around stark naked in the bush would be an exaggeration.'[62] Specht's final text lets a trade unionist character express these ideas, in an ironic polemic to propose that most of the officials in the trade unions believed the indigenous people to be uncivilized.[63] In all, Fred Rose not only furnished appraisals of the ethnological, geographical and political facts in Specht's texts as an external reader, he also advised the author as he developed his manuscripts. Soon, the material provided by Rose's institute constituted the most important source of information for Specht.

The Australian Microcosm in the GDR

Rose and his departmental library came into play when Specht worked on Albert Namatjira. In 1962 the author had already proposed to make the life of the high-profile indigenous watercolourist the subject of his next novel, but he feared potential rivalries. He wrote to his editor, asking 'if he would listen out to see if my big competitor Walther [sic] Kaufmann had already written on this topic, and how he had written and so on. He would be the only one who could thwart my plans from an expert position'.[64] Indeed, a comparison with Kaufmann seems to impose itself. Alexandra Ludewig describes this author's extensive East German literary career in her chapter. The two GDR-based writers' biographies reveal numerous surprising parallels, with one decisive difference: Kaufmann was always allowed to travel, because he had retained his Australian citizenship. Ultimately, Specht warned his editor about mentioning his Namatjira idea to his rival at all: 'The great man could get the notion to do something with it himself'.[65] Interestingly, Kaufmann had mentioned one of Namatjira's pictures in passing in his novel *Kreuzwege* (Crossroads), published by Verlag Neues Leben the previous year.

Several people had advised against writing about Namatjira because of his perceived ambiguous status. The West German artist HAP Grieshaber, a friend of Steinberg, wrote to Specht:

> Albert Namatjira is a tragic figure. You guys in East Germany probably thought the tragedy lay in the question of civil rights, because Namatjira is black. The first thing that comes to everybody's mind is the oppression by white people. But this savage was an honorary member of the Society of Arts and has made more than £80,000 with his worthless little paintings.[66]

In the end, only a few remnants of the painter's destiny remained when Specht finally used this material in his novel *Daniels Weg in die Steinzeit* (Daniel's Path to the Stone Age), published in 1985 by Verlag der Nation. The novel is above all about Daniel, a young teacher, through whom the readers learn of the living conditions of indigenous Australians. In spite of all the civil rights they had been awarded, the novel suggests that many of them continue to live on the fringes of society, with no regular work and an addiction to alcohol.

Specht had done extensive research for the novel, and on the final page he thanks not only Rose and HAP Grieshaber, but also 'Mrs Dymphna Cusack, Melbourne' for their 'expert knowledge and support in the preparatory work for the book'. Verlag der Nation had published the German translation of Cusack's *Say No to Death* in 1961. The publisher knew her personally through her visits to Berlin and had asked her for a copy of C. P. Mountford's *The Art of Albert Namatjira* to help Specht. Cusack posted a copy to Berlin, confirming the editor's impression that 'Mrs Cusack is a very cooperative woman'.[67]

In *Daniels Weg in die Steinzeit*, Specht combines an adventure plot with a love story. An older colleague of Daniel's, Jeannette, is involved in the peace movement and shows Daniel 'the contradictory conditions that the integration of indigenous people into civilization has created'.[68] Daniel teaches at a mission in Hermannsburg in the Northern Territory. Here, 'pagan' customs of the Aboriginal people, like corroborees, have been prohibited, one aspect of missionary reality he strongly disapproves of. Again, criticism of 'religion as an illusory resort' is a prominent feature.[69] Daniel's understanding that the Aboriginal people cannot be effectively helped in Hermannsburg steadily grows:[70]

> Always preaching reconciliation, practicing leniency, exercising meekness, but never being allowed to bang one's fist on the table in anger because of the injustice and discrimination faced by indigenous people? No [...] that's not going to work anymore. The world is changing, the younger generation can be silenced no longer [...] they want freedom and equality, and they want it now.[71]

With the novel *Daniel*, the microcosm of fictionalized Australia was animated once again and its protagonists were set in motion: Bernhard Scheller, a lecturer in English who promoted the study of Australian literature at the University of Leipzig, reviewed the new release in the local newspaper.[72] He immediately drew on Australian journalist Rupert Lockwood's book *Der Kontinent des Känguruhs* (The Continent of the Kangaroo), which had appeared in 1961 with GDR publisher Rütten & Loening. Lockwood also explicated Namajitra's story on almost six pages that Specht had actually absorbed. Overall, Scheller did not have much praise for *Daniel*: Specht's style was better suited to reporting and his attempts at a work of fiction had failed.[73]

Following Namatjira, Specht took up anthropologist Daisy Bates as fodder for his next novel. Bates studied Aboriginal culture at the beginning of the twentieth century and advocated the state care of indigenous people. Specht portrayed Bates's life through the eyes of a contemporary journalist who visits the places where she worked, while simultaneously relating which of the social problems faced by Aborigines remained unsolved. Verlag der Nation was quickly persuaded by this topic: 'This woman's active humanism and selfless

Figure 7.6 Specht in 2011, at his house, in front of hunting boomerangs and spears; photograph by Patricia F. Blume.

commitment to a minority, whose very existence was threatened, justify the author's attempt to preserve her life's work in literary form and to familiarize our country's readers with her.'[74] Evidently, Specht made quick work of it. Almost a year before his deadline, at the beginning of 1988, he sent the manuscript to the publisher. As a title he chose *Kabbarli* – a grandmotherly person, as one indigenous community had called Bates, formally inducting her into kinship structures. Specht's editor appealed to his patience, as he saw no possibility of bringing the manuscript forward. The draft of the publisher's report is dated 6 October 1989, three days before 70,000 people demonstrated in Leipzig for democratic reforms in the GDR.[75] In January 1991, when, after the monetary, economic and social union between the GDR and the Federal Republic, no-one showed interest in books from East Germany, the director of the publishing house informed Specht, with reference to 'current societal developments' and the 'abundant offerings in the book store', that the print run of *Kabbarli* would be reduced. The author complained immediately: 'If the text had been edited quickly by your editors, we wouldn't need to worry about the book's sales today. But as it is, I see that my work and I have been lost in the capitalist rat race.'[76]

'The Most Important Subject Matter Is Your Own Life'

When Verlag der Nation cancelled *Kabbarli* four months later and returned the rights to Specht, he could nonetheless look back on a total of seven successful first editions with them, and abundant reprints and licenses – first and foremost in the GDR, but also in Eastern Europe. Over the course of 25 years, Joachim Specht published over 20 titles, most of which were about Australia. And this figure does not even take into account the numerous new editions, paperback versions, licensed editions, and the titles he brought out after the fall of the GDR. For this reason, fittingly, the *Bibliography of Australian Literature* lists his works.[77] Specht's books reached a total circulation of more than 1.6 million copies in the GDR. Despite the fact he is little known today, he was one of the most successful authors in the GDR, which he explains as follows: 'The people read my books because they couldn't get away. [...] That sounds cynical, but it's true: the wall in Berlin was my friend and helper. It was because of the wall that my wares sold so well.'[78]

He always remembered the motto of his mentor, Werner Steinberg: 'The most important subject matter is your own life'.[79] Specht's experiences as a young man served him throughout his writing career, and provided a seemingly never-ending source for his artistic production, for his literary interpretation of Australia. For him, writing about the continent had a therapeutic function initially; it was his way of finding a place in East German society. Later it allowed him to revisit Australia in his mind time and time again, something he couldn't do in reality. After having been far removed from the country that had most influenced him, his yearning equalled that of his readers, who never had the chance to go there.

Australia eventually became Specht's niche in the GDR's literary market, in which different authors in the light fiction and adventure genres occupied certain regions of the world.[80] Publishers dispersed Specht's version of Australia to different target groups in accordance with their profiles, and as a result, his books had a decisive influence on the perception of the continent in the GDR.

Joachim Specht is a noteworthy author for many reasons. His example now stands for authors of popular mass literature who, in terms of recognition in the GDR, were ranked below their more 'serious' colleagues and who are neglected by researchers today. Aside from this, Specht is paradoxically both an exemplary and an exceptional product of the *Bitterfelder Weg*. On the one hand, he profited from the cultural-political movement, turning himself into a prototypical writing worker, as the shaping influences of both the writing circle and Verlag der Nation show. On the other hand, he stands out because of his chosen topic, his persistent career and because he was one of the few who actually reached a wide audience.

As a literary subject, Australia actually did not conform at all to the themes of the *Bitterfelder Weg*, which centred on everyday life in factories between brown coal dust, screw wrenches and soldering irons. But with skill, Specht overcame the geographical distance and the genre discrepancies at play in his works, so that they succeeded both for the Ministry of Culture and for his readers. In his East German adaption of Australia he combined arresting adventure literature, set in an exotic, capitalist location, with contemporary themes that he handled with a decreed, hefty dose of social critique. Even if his texts could easily be shaped towards party doctrine, the vivid detail from his own experiences more than eclipses the propaganda. Acquainted with both worlds, Joachim Specht inimitably bridged the two hemispheres and brought GDR readers closer to distant Australia.

Notes

* This chapter was translated by Christina Spittel, Niels Holger Blume and the author.

1 Unpublished interview with P. F. Blume, 5 September 2011, 00:37:59. In possession of the author. Except for English sources, all quotes are translated from the German originals by Christina Spittel and the author.
2 Reader's letter to Specht, approx. January 1989, Stadtarchiv Dessau-Roßlau, N 3.13 – Specht – 67.

3 Simone Barck, '"Ein ganzes Heer von schreibenden Arbeitern?"' in *Bitterfelder Nachlese: ein Kulturpalast, seine Konferenzen und Wirkungen*, ed. Simone Barck and Stefanie Wahl (Berlin: Karl Dietz Verlag, 2007), 141–61 (148).
4 Joachim Specht, *Zwischen Dessau und Australien* (Emsdetten: First-Minute-Taschenbuchverlag, 2010), 164.
5 Steinberg was born in Silesia and settled in West Germany after World War II. In 1956 he came to the GDR. See various notes by Heinz Dieter Tschörtner, such as 'Der Erzähler Werner Steinberg: mit Bibliographie', *Aus dem Antiquariat* 10 (February 2006): 31–36.
6 Steinberg to Jan Philipp Reemtsma, 8 June 1992, quoted in *Biographische Stationen eines Grenzgängers: Der Schriftsteller Werner Steinberg 1913–1992*, ed. Jan-Christoph Hauschild (Darmstadt: Häusser, 1993), 57.
7 See Werner Steinberg, 'Die richtige Methode finden', *ich schreibe* 3 (1961): 6–7; Specht, *Zwischen Dessau und Australien*, 165.
8 Unpublished interview with P. F. Blume, 5 September 2011, 01:15:16. In possession of the author.
9 Steinberg to Schütze, 29 May 1961, SAPMO-BArch DY17/4911.
10 Joachim Specht, *Peterborough Story* (Berlin: Verlag der Nation, 1963), 91.
11 Ibid., 96.
12 Ibid., 136.
13 Ibid., 149.
14 Ibid., 166.
15 Joachim Specht, *Kreuz und quer aus meinem Leben* (Halle: Förderkreis der Schriftsteller in Sachsen-Anhalt, 1997), 23.
16 Application for permission to print for *Australisches Abenteuer*, 27 August 1965, BArch DR1/2398/292.
17 Grünewald (Verlag Kultur und Fortschritt), report on *Die Muschelfalle*, approx. 1964, BArch DR1/5080/33.
18 See, for example, Günter Creutzburg, 'Final Remarks', in Joachim Specht, *Australisches Abenteuer* (Berlin: Verlag der Nation, 1966), 153–59 (154).
19 See Richard Christ, Afterword, in Joachim Specht, *Stippvisite* (Berlin: Verlag der Nation, 1968), 185–89 (186).
20 Gert Hillesheim (Berlin), report on *Peterborough Story*, 13 February 1963, BArch DR1/5080.
21 H. D. Tschörtner, 'Im Kontinent der Känguruhs', *neue deutsche literatur* 5 (1964), 146–48 (147).
22 Hans Petersen, April 1960, BArch DR1/5057/144. On the publication and reception of Prichard's work in the GDR, see Camille Barrera's chapter in this volume.
23 Joachim Specht, *Die Gejagten* (Berlin: Verlag der Nation, 1966), 67.
24 Ibid., 80.
25 Publisher's report on *Insel der schmerzlosen Ewigkeit* (working title) (Hofé, Menard, Schütze, Christ), 5 April 1966, BArch DR1/2398/276.
26 Report from Wolfgang Joho on *Die Gejagten*, 25 March 1966, BArch DR 1/2398/270.
27 Manfred Jurgensen, *Eagle and Emu: German-Australian Writing 1930–1990* (St Lucia: University of Queensland Press, 1992), 293.
28 'Appeals over "Hostage" Girl', *The Canberra Times*, 14 January 1971, 8.
29 Specht to Creutzburg, 24 November 1964, SAPMO-BArch DY17/4911, emphasis in original.

30 Ibid.
31 Creutzburg to Specht, 25 November 1964, SAPMO-BArch DY17/4911. See Patricia F. Zeckert, 'Die Internationale Leipziger Buchmesse', *Aus Politik und Zeitgeschichte* 11 (2009), accessed 5 February 2014, http://www.bpb.de/apuz/32148/die-internationale-leipziger-buchmesse?p=all.
32 Jurgensen to Specht, 25 May 1987, SAPMO-BArch DY17/4659.
33 Specht to Creutzburg, 30 November 1964, SAPMO-BArch DY17/4912.
34 Specht, *Die Gejagten*, 153.
35 Reader's letter to Specht, approx. January 1989, Stadtarchiv Dessau-Roßlau, N 3.13 – Specht – 67.
36 Matthias Braun, 'Walter Ulbrichts Traum vom neuen Menschen', in *Bitterfelder Nachlese*, 53–78 (75).
37 Barck, '"Ein ganzes Heer von schreibenden Arbeitern?"', 145.
38 Siegfried Lokatis, 'Der Mitteldeutsche Verlag in Halle', in *Bitterfelder Nachlese*, 113–30 (127, 130).
39 Specht, *Kreuz und quer*, 23.
40 Ibid., 24.
41 Specht to Brandl, 25 May 1975, SAPMO-BArch DY17/4915. Also see the compilation of readings in the Dessau-Roßlau Stadtarchiv, N 3.13 – Specht – 1.
42 Specht, *Kreuz und quer*, 18.
43 Specht to Schütze, 18 August 1962, SAPMO-BArch DY17/4911.
44 Specht, *Kreuz und quer*, 19.
45 Christ to Specht, 3 June 1966, SAPMO-BArch DY17/4912.
46 Publisher's report (Menard, Schütze, Christ) on *Der Fünfer*, 23 September 1970, BArch DR1/2403a/381.
47 Ibid., 379.
48 Christ, afterword to *Stippvisite*, 188.
49 Specht, *Kreuz und quer*, 21.
50 Specht to Brandl, 17 January 1975, SAPMO-BArch DY17/4914.
51 Brandl to Specht, 8 March 1979, SAPMO-BArch DY17/4912.
52 See also Anita M. Mallinckrodt, *Das Kleine Massenmedium: Soziale Funktion und politische Rolle der Heftreihen-Literatur in der DDR* (Köln: Verlag Wissenschaft und Politik, 1984).
53 Specht, *Peterborough Story*, 101, 169, 64.
54 Specht to Sommer (writers' union, Halle region), 21 December 1974, SAPMO-BArch DY17/4914.
55 Gerd Labroisse, 'Interview Erich Loest', in *German Monitor: DDR-Schriftsteller sprechen in der Zeit*, ed. Gerd Labroisse and Ian Wallace (Atlanta and Amsterdam: Rodopi, 1991), 27–38 (30).
56 Brandl to Beuchel, 8 August 1979, SAPMO-BArch DY17/4915.
57 Goldschmit (Ministry of Culture) to Dyk (Secretary of the writers' union), 6 February 1987, N 3.13 – Specht – 68. See also Siegfried Lokatis's and Christina Spittel's chapters in this volume.
58 See Kenneth Maddock, 'Frederick Rose, 1915–1991: An Appreciation', *Oceania* 62 (1 September 1991): 66–69. See also Peter Monteath and Valerie Munt, *Red Professor: The Cold War Life of Frederick Rose* (Adelaide: Wakefield Press, 2015).
59 Frederick Rose, *Australia Revisited* (Berlin: Seven Seas, 1968), 260–61.
60 Frederick Rose, *Känguruhs, Ureinwohner und Düsenclipper: Fünfundzwanzig Jahre unter Australiern* (Leipzig: Brockhaus, 1966), 274.
61 Schütze to Rose, 1 March 1966, SAPMO-BArch DY 17/4912. About the contact between Rose and Specht, see also Stadtarchiv Dessau-Roßlau, N 3.13 – Specht – 25.

62 Attachment to Edith Rose's report on *Die Gejagten*, 26 March 1966, BArch DR1/2398/281.
63 Specht, *Die Gejagten*, 125.
64 Specht to Schütze, 18 August 1962, SAPMO-BArch DY17/4911.
65 Specht to Schütze, 11 September 1962, SAPMO-BArch DY17/4911.
66 Some of Grieshaber's letters to Specht have been published – HAP Grieshaber, *Botschaften – Zeitzeichen: Bildbriefe, Holzschnitte, Texte, Notate* (Leipzig: Reclam, 1983), 99. See also Reclam Archive, University of Leipzig, Box 473.
67 Schütze to Specht, 17 September 1962, BArch DY30/4911.
68 Assessor's report (Günter Ebert) on *Daniels Weg in die Steinzeit*, 1 March 1984, BArch DR1/2413a/585.
69 Ibid., 586–87.
70 See notice of publication in *Vorankündigungsdienst/Nova* 4 (1985).
71 Joachim Specht, *Daniels Weg in die Steinzeit* (Berlin: Verlag der Nation, 1986), 199.
72 See his interview with Christina Spittel in Chapter 11 of this volume.
73 Bernhard Scheller, 'Bumerang für einen Helden', *Leipziger Volkszeitung*, 3–4 May 1986, 13.
74 VDN Lektorat II, Vorlage für die Verlagsleitung, 6 May 1987, SAPMO-BArch DY17/4659.
75 Lektorat II, draft for the report on *Daisy Bates*, 6 October 1989, SAPMO-BArch DY17/4659.
76 Specht to Lecht, 23 January 1991, SAPMO-BArch DY17/4659.
77 See *Bibliography of Australian Literature: P–Z*, ed. John Arnold and John Hay (Kew: Australian Scholarly Publishing, 2008), 403–404.
78 Unpublished interview with P. F. Blume, 5 September 2011, 00:10:15.
79 'Das wichtigste am Material aber ist das eigene Leben [...] Hagen Bartusch befragte Werner Steinberg', in *Positionen 4: Wortmeldungen zur DDR-Literatur*, ed. Eberhard Günther and Hinnerk Einhorn (Halle and Leipzig: Mitteldeutscher Verlag, 1988), 53–78.
80 Thomas Kramer, 'Abenteurliteratur', in *Metzler-Lexikon DDR-Literatur: Autoren – Institutionen – Debatten*, ed. Michael Opitz and Michael Hofmann (Stuttgart and Weimar: Metzler, 2009), 1–2.

Chapter 8

'TO DO SOMETHING FOR AUSTRALIAN LITERATURE': ANTHOLOGIZING AUSTRALIA FOR THE GERMAN DEMOCRATIC REPUBLIC OF THE 1970S

Christina Spittel

'As you see, it is an uphill struggle trying to do something for Australian literature, and as yet I am not sure of the outcome.'
GDR editor Hans Petersen to Australian writer Dal Stivens, 4 September 1975.[1]

Half way through 1973, Dr Hans Petersen, who was head of the English department of Volk und Welt, the lead publisher for contemporary international writing in the German Democratic Republic (GDR), set to work on an anthology of Australian short stories in German translation. In the same year, former East German head of state Walter Ulbricht died a lonely old man, the Australian embassy opened in East Berlin and Patrick White became the first Australian writer to win the Nobel Prize for Literature. In the three years following Volk und Welt's last foray into Australian literature, Xavier Herbert's *Der vertauschte Traumstein* (1970, orig. *Seven Emus*, 1959), the political climates in both countries had changed, shrinking distances in world literary space and transforming local scenes of reading – that is, the various concrete institutional, cultural, geopolitical and other frames through which a text is read at a particular moment in time.[2] For the first time in 23 years, Australia had elected a Labor government. In East Berlin Erich Honecker's new leadership was ushering in a similarly brief yet significant period of liberalization.

Conceived as an act of public diplomacy at a key moment of political détente, an attempt to 'do something for Australian literature', as Petersen put it in a letter to Australian writer Dal Stivens, the anthology features 31 writers previously unpublished in the GDR, many of them translated into German for the first time. These include Frank Moorhouse, Peter Carey, Murray Bail, Vicki Viidikas and black Australian author Mudrooroo, then still working under his birth name Colin Johnson. Writing in November 1975, Petersen concluded his afterword by boldly casting his fellow citizens as custodians and sponsors of a literature still undervalued by the world at large: 'It is time to realize that Australia is no longer a literary backwater. Its literature has long had relevance, even though it does not yet enjoy the international recognition it deserves.'[3]

Erkundungen: 31 australische Erzähler first appeared in 1976 as a slim volume of just over 300 pages and achieved an overall print run of 80,000 copies, becoming the most frequently reprinted volume in Volk und Welt's popular paperback series of international short fiction, beating the also popular Irish, Czech and even West German volumes.[4] The title of the series, *Erkundungen*, translates as 'explorations' and conveys hints of reconnaissance, surveying and prospecting. To Volk und Welt's editors, the series posed an invitation to test and broaden existing routes of literary import into the GDR.[5] This essay shows how Petersen astutely used the discursive frames of the popular series and the more liberal political climate of the early 1970s to significantly reorient the existing East German narrative of Australian literature for a new generation of readers.

Honecker's Germany: 'No Taboos'

Honecker's accession to power in May 1971 promised a thawing in East German cultural policy. His predecessor, Ulbricht, had frequently intervened in cultural matters, insisting that formalist, modernist or decadent art was not conducive to socialist thinking and feeling. Ulbricht's final years had seen heavy-handed attempts to claw back interpretive authority over East German life from writers and artists perceived as unruly and uncooperative: some, like Christa Wolf, had their readership restricted by reduced print runs; others, like Wolf Biermann and Stefan Heym, were banned outright.[6] Heym's provocation lay in passionately committing to socialism while drawing attention to the fraught relationship between power and the truth within it:

> I have always tried to fight for an order of things in which no finger is raised before my lens when I want to snap the truth; and I believe socialism is such an order. But […] at present we have quite a few socialist fingers raised before our socialist lenses, and we have quite an assortment of socialist taboos.[7]

Figure 8.1 Bright orange cover for *Erkundungen: 31 australische Erzähler* (Berlin: Volk und Welt, 1976).

Published in Yugoslavia, France, Italy, West Germany and Australia, Heym's 1965 essay, 'Die Langeweile von Minsk' ('The Boredom of Minsk') did not appear in the GDR, where Ulbricht denounced as 'an American writer with a GDR passport' the author who had resettled in East Germany in 1952 after returning from exile in the USA.[8]

In 1971 it seemed that Heym had been heard: Honecker proclaimed that 'if one starts from the firm position of socialism, there can be in my eyes no taboos in the realm of art and literature'. And this concerned 'all aspects of artistic mastery': content *and* style.[9] Indeed, the Party was fully 'aware of the difficulties, the complexity of the processes of artistic creation' and therefore 'fully sympathetic towards the creative artists' search for new forms'.[10] Honecker's words rightly met with some suspicion but, together with efforts of East German literary scholars to rethink as complex and dialogic the relationships between literature, history and society, they helped make legitimate work previously deemed unpublishable. 'It is necessary and, from the established position of socialist realism also possible,' argued Helmut Findeisen of Karl-Marx Universität Leipzig, 'to draw attention to writers and works who give voice to many ambivalent elements, but who had significant effect on the course of literary history, and the methods and possibilities of artistic creation.'[11] This 1976 reader's report (on *Mrs Dalloway*) helped Virginia Woolf into print in East Germany for the first time, alongside fellow modernists Marcel Proust, Erich Maria Remarque and James Joyce, and a range of East German writers, including (albeit briefly) Heym himself.

This new hospitality on the part of East German print culture made it easier for Petersen to keep shut his address book of Australian writers then well known to East Germans; even to relegate them to literary history. Their way of writing, he argued in the afterword to his anthology, assigns 'K. S. Prichard, Judah Waten, Alan Marshall, Xavier Herbert and others [...] to a rather different period'.[12] In the GDR's early decades, these Australians' embrace of realism had signalled that the new German literary nation's foundational aesthetic was also being embraced in the wider world. Through their visits and correspondence, writers like Frank Hardy, Alan Marshall and, most notably, Dymphna Cusack, effectively served as the stubborn, unaccredited ambassadors of a country that recognized the Federal Republic of Germany from 1950 but adopted a rigorous policy of non-recognition for the GDR.[13] In 1961, Katharine Susannah Prichard informed Volk und Welt how pleased she was to 'interpret the life of the Australian people to the brave people of the German Democratic Republic'.[14] To name the new country as she did was a highly political gesture. In 1965 Australian Minister for Foreign Affairs Paul Hasluck still dismissed it as a 'zone under Soviet military occupation not possessing national sovereignty or independence'.[15] During the 1950s and '60s, the Federal Republic insisted that it alone represented the German nation and threatened to sever diplomatic relationships with any state (except the Soviet Union) that recognized the East Germans. Only 20 countries had accepted East Berlin diplomatically by 1969; Australia was not among them.[16]

Whitlam's Australia: 'Progress in All Areas'

The stories Petersen was garnering for his volume, however, hailed from a very different Australia, a young nation that was making 'progress in all areas', as he argued to the Ministry. The 1972 election win of the Australian Labor party had edged Canberra much closer to East Berlin than ever before, and not only because the result was quickly interpreted as a vote against the Americans (given Whitlam's explicit anti-Vietnam stance).[17] To dismiss, as W. H. Auden had done, the dominions as profoundly provincial, was snobbish and ignorant, Petersen insisted, casting himself as a discerning citizen of the world and an 'attentive observer' in his afterword.[18] Here was a newly relevant, vibrant, progressive Australia, emerging from two decades of conservative politics, he reported to the Ministry in mid-November 1975:

> Gough Whitlam's Labor government, in office since December 1972, has been making efforts (not least under the pressure of the strong left wing of the party and the trade unions) to reduce social injustice and abolish old privileges, to further relax traditional ties with the 'Mother Country', and to work towards a humanistic resolution of the problem of the Aborigines. In 1972 the government handed out 150 grants to talented writers.[19]

One of Prime Minister Gough Whitlam's first foreign policy moves was to normalize relationships with East Berlin.[20] Whitlam's foray occurred on the back of a general wave of détente, ushered in by Willy Brandt, former mayor of West Berlin and chancellor of the Federal Republic from 1969. Working towards what he envisaged as the peaceful co-existence of 'two states in one nation',[21] Brandt signed several treaties that recognized European borders as set after the Second World War. One day after the two German states had signed the *Grundlagenvertrag (Basic Treaty)*, agreeing to pursue 'normal good-neighbourly relations',[22] Australia afforded official recognition to the GDR – before the UK and the USA did so in 1973 and 1974 respectively. On 2 April 1973 the GDR opened its embassy in Canberra; in June that year, Australia became the first non-socialist country to host an East German consulate; in October, Australia set up an embassy in the East Berlin suburb of Pankow.[23]

Hans Petersen recalled the instant effect of these developments: 'All in all, the international recognition of the GDR from 1971/72 made our work noticeably easier. Many things became more relaxed.'[24] Eventually, Petersen would even fly to Australia: first, in 1979 to visit writers like Dal Stivens and marvel at his collection of Aboriginal art ('Really haunting!') and again in 1986, to renew connections and forge further contacts.[25] Meanwhile, East

Berlin, newly alive with diplomats and foreign correspondents, was keen to demonstrate its openness to the world that had just recognized its borders. In 1965 preparations for the International Writers' Congress in Weimar had included moves to appear receptive to 'difficult' writers such as Franz Kafka and Jean-Paul Sartre.[26] Now, in the mid-1970s, Petersen's Australian *Erkundungen* volume was part of a spate of international anthologies produced to satisfy the state's worldly aspirations, adding a significant number of names to the Ministry of Culture's list of foreign authors published in the GDR.[27] And there was much to add: the Australian literary landscape, Petersen observed in his afterword, 'has become animated – as far as the short story is concerned, especially since the 1970s'. The 'dry spells, and the momentary stagnation of the 1950s and '60s have been overcome'.[28]

A New Diversity

Petersen's work on the anthology did indeed coincide with a period of vibrant growth in Australian letters, registered in accounts of Australian literary history as a new wave, a new dynamic and a new diversity.[29] The short story was one particularly prominent genre manifesting this diversity: the realists of the Left continued writing alongside new migrant authors, and established authors Peter Cowan and Hal Porter alongside the representatives of a new urban counter-culture. The short story became a site where the boundaries of literary expression could be challenged – through the postmodern experiments of Murray Bail and Peter Carey but also through advances in printing and experiments in publishing that created new outlets for creative work. Moreover, the short story was also where many of the period's memorable debates occurred, as the cold war polarizations between Left and Right, realists and modernists gave way to a more complicated landscape of social movements agitating for change on a wide range of issues.[30]

The series within which Petersen was working could easily accommodate such a plethora. According to editor-in-chief Georgina Baum, '[t]he *Erkundungen* series offers many possibilities. To use them smartly is an attractive task for an editor.'[31] Indeed, 'explorations' is a usefully elastic term for paperbacks of international short fiction: it allowed anthologists to build the necessary connections between a society and its literature via the privileged paths of realism, and to treat literary texts as 'seismographs', as the editor of the very first volume, issued in 1964, put it, recording in this case the motions of 'West German every-day life'.[32] But the series could also be conceived as encouraging 'a broad foray into literary terrain that is new to us',[33] as a reader's report pointed out in 1966, yielding new names and forms. Each volume would claim its place between these two readings and thus also explore what was possible in the tightly controlled regime of East German publishing. The striking, colourful covers of the series are telling in this context: they clearly promise contemporary fare but their bold abstraction – colorful patterns of abstract shapes rather than recognizable landscapes or national characters – is also a cheeky comment on the nexus between art and reality.

The mosaic-like patterns point towards the anthologist's role in combining diverse elements. Petersen read his material as forming the most recent chapter in a narrative of literary growth and emancipation – a shedding of the 'parochial Australian timbre'.[34] The history of Australian literature elaborated in his report for the Ministry begins with a long period of isolation – geographical *and* cultural – gradually overcome through metropolitan influences: Russian and French models in the 1920s and 1930s, the contributions of migrants who arrived with the Second World War, and the literary magazine *Meanjin*, which he posited as playing a significant role in helping maintain 'an outward-looking view'.[35] With his insistence on Australian literary ties with Europe, Petersen's account seems to echo Anselm Schlösser's attempt, described in Russell West-Pavlov's chapter, to insert nineteenth-century Australian writer Marcus Clarke into a European tradition.[36] Yet, if in 1957 Schlösser suggested that Clarke's *For the Term of his Natural Life* could advance the cause of socialist realism, Petersen, on the other hand, tried to depart from this tried and tested route of literary import. Instead, he insisted that Australian literature, and surely by implication East German publishing of it, needed to abandon certain 'antiquated modes of representation' if it was to 'catch up' with the literatures of Europe ('will sie den Anschluss an die europäischen Literaturen gewinnen').[37]

'I made an effort to include fresh texts wherever possible', Petersen reported to the Ministry. 'Most contributions appeared in the past 10 years, a pleasingly high percentage even between 1970 and 1975.'[38] In line with the policy of the series to keep expenditure of licensing fees to a minimum, Petersen printed only two stories that had previously been translated into German, contracted from Horst Erdmann Verlag in Tübingen in West Germany.[39] The remainder came from a wide range of sources: anthologies and authors' collections from new and established publishers in Australia and the UK, as well as *Meanjin* (available to East German literary professionals).[40] In the hope of selling translation rights, independent Melbourne publisher Dennis Wren airmailed proofs of an anthology titled *Festival and Other Stories* (1974), edited by Brian Buckley and Jim Hamilton, from which Petersen took two winning entries to short story competitions run by the Melbourne-based newspaper *The Sun*.[41] Even an issue of *Tabloid Story*, the experimental, even radical 'travelling exhibit' of short fiction inserted into Australian magazines or newspapers, made it to

East Berlin. Some authors sent work directly, following calls for submissions in the newsletters of the Australian Society of Authors, like this one:

> Mr. Jurgen Gruner of West Germany [...] is planning [...] an anthology of Australian short stories published within the last 10 to 15 years. The volume will be one of a series featuring young or unknown writers of unusual talent. Sorry we have no further details except the address: Jurgen Gruner, c/o Verlag Volk und Welt, 108 Berlin, Glinkastrasse 13–15, West Germany.[42]

As news of Volk und Welt's plans travelled, director Jürgen Gruner not only lost his umlaut but also the most crucial part of his address: *East* Berlin. This omission was perhaps a useful indicator of the work that lay ahead of Petersen as he sought to extend his list beyond the dozen Australian authors for whom Volk und Welt was a household name.

Petersen's selection mingles writers of recognized achievement with names that have left barely a trace in accounts of Australian literary history. C. B. Christesen, co-founder and long-time editor of *Meanjin*, was the only writer with an East German 'connection', having been a delegate to the 1965 Writers' Congress in Weimar. Other well-known names include older, established writers such as Judith Wright, Peter Cowan, T. A. G. Hungerford, Hal Porter and Dal Stivens, and members of the newly emerging generation who were demonstrating their promise with well-received collections: Frank Moorhouse, Peter Carey, Murray Bail and Vicki Viidikas. (But not Michael Wilding, whom Petersen found refreshing but obscene.[43]) They sit alongside obscure figures such as Victor Venn, John Box, Judy Hiener and Russell Beedles, as well as O. E. Middleton, whose letter clarifying his New Zealand identity arrived when the collection was already at the printers: 'From a far-away place like Europe, our small islands may seem to be mere appendages of Australia, but nothing could be further from the truth.'[44]

Petersen was well aware of the diversity he had collected: the blurb announces 'established authors and barely proven talents, professionals and amateurs' whose varied accomplishments are detailed in the painstakingly researched biographical sketches at the volume's back. To the Ministry, Petersen presented his anthology as a democratic sweep across Australian print culture: 'Thirty-two authors, ranging from a Nobel Prize winner to a hotel manager, give an impression in their prose texts of the problems and conflicts which have emerged as the country developed into an imperialist industrial power.'[45] The hotel manager was Maxwell Wilcox of Glen Iris in Victoria, who submitted a story told from the point of view of an artist whose latest exhibition is opened by his wife's pretentious and expensive psychiatrist.[46] Offering rather striking evidence for the paradoxical role of translations that Russell West-

Pavlov analyses in chapter 2, constitutive of a national literary culture, yet so often invisible to it, Petersen's volume is the only record of Wilcox's work as a producer of Australian literature.[47] Not even the English-language title of his short story is included in Petersen's bibliographical apparatus; nor is an English-language version held at the publisher's archives in Berlin. But, finally, the Nobel Prize winner was the only author to refuse permission to print.

A few weeks after Petersen had submitted his collection to the Ministry, Patrick White's definite refusal, communicated via his UK agent, reached Volk und Welt. Petersen had in fact planned two projects with White for 1976 – the *Erkundungen* volume and a small, separate collection of White's stories – and White disliked both, as Molly Waters of Curtis Brown explained on the author's behalf.

> [H]e makes it quite clear that while he has no objection, of course, to being published by you, he does feel that the work you have selected is insufficiently representative of his writing to appear in the anthology and neither does he like the idea of taking small skimmings from two of his complete volumes to make up a German translation of four short stories.[48]

Volk und Welt had been following White's career through the West German press, and fought hard to sway him, pleading with him not to withhold himself from a potentially large readership in the GDR, and pointing to Volk und Welt's impressive list of authors and to the sheer embarrassment White's absence would cause: 'It would be a bit awkward to publish an anthology of contemporary Australian short stories (in a series called "Erkundungen") without including the Australian Nobel laureate.'[49]

Petersen had chosen one of White's shorter, satirical stories about a suburban Australian dinner party, 'Willy-Wagtails by the Moonlight', often considered one of the weaker pieces from his first volume of short prose, *The Burnt Ones* (1964).[50] (Karl-Heinz Berger, in his reader's report, was surprised to see the Nobel Prize winner content himself with a 'middlebrow magazine-style'.[51]) But Petersen was adamant and wrote to White directly, in English:

> As far as I can see, 'Willy-Wagtails by Moonlight' has not been anthologized so far, but that does not prove anything except that our editorial policies seem to differ from those of other publishers. By way of explanation why we chose this story, I may add that I (as the editor of this particular collection) think it fairly characteristic of your description of a specific class of Australian society, that I enjoy its grim humour, and also that it was chosen because of its length. Any anthologist will try to squeeze in as many writers as possible in a selection of about 320 pages.[52]

Promises of increased royalties, agitated meetings at the Frankfurt Book Fair, a complex correspondence with agents in Hamburg and London – the experience with White showed that leaving the paths of international communism along which Australian literature had previously travelled into the GDR could incur some steep challenges.[53]

Youth Culture

Volk und Welt's last foray into Australian short fiction, Prichard's *Die Braut von Far-Away* (1962, *The Bride of Far-Away*), had promised readers 'a foreign world – the continent of the kangaroo, with its deserts, fertile fields and the barren bush' (jacket). Petersen's anthology opens with a truck ride to a big metropolitan centre: Maree Teychenné, the collection's youngest author, barely a few months older than the GDR itself, has her sixteen-year old protagonist hitch-hike to Melbourne.[54] Such an opening affords a new generation of East German readers with an entry point into Australian writing, not least because Teychenné's is one of a number of stories interested in a youthful urban counter-culture:

> Candles in green wine bottles lined the floor, and at the far end, the girl caught glimpses of colourful kaftans that swirled to the music, and tattered jeans and bare feet, and she heard the silvery din of tiny bells that were tied to ankles and wrists. The music pushed itself over the chatter, until someone fell against the record player.[55]

Significantly, here and elsewhere in the volume, student bohemia is experienced at one remove, by outsider characters – Teychenné's young Queenslander has travelled 'long and hard' only to feel 'strangely illegal […] in the dimly lit passage' of the Carlton shared house. Colin Johnson's nameless protagonist feels on 'foreign territory' in a student café with its 'sneaky, classic-type music'.[56] And the parents in Laurel Cunningham's 'The Good Mother' observe their son's transformation into a long-haired, jeans-wearing university student from the vantage point of their farm.

East Germans were also looking on in 1968, wedged as they were between a rebellious Czechoslovakia brutally defeated by Soviet tanks and a Federal Republic firmly in the grip of student revolt. While opportunities for protest in the GDR were limited, some East Germans, as Timothy Brown has argued, still considered themselves part of the generation of '68, 'a "discourse community" connecting people across national and bloc boundaries'.[57] Opportunities to participate in this wider, global network of affinities came via books, radio and television, while clothing could signal belonging. Jeans, for example, as Ina

Merkel has pointed out, offered a 'way of symbolising border transgression'.[58] In 1973 Edgar Wibeau, the drop-out protagonist of Ulrich Plenzdorf's East German cult novel, *Die neuen Leiden des jungen W.* (*The New Sorrows of Young W.*), proclaimed denim a matter of faith: 'Jeans are the noblest pants in the world [...] I mean, jeans are an attitude, not a pair of pants.'[59] Helen Hunt's 'Leila' participates openly in this transnational genre of blue jeans fiction:

> Everyone has it in for us because we like lounging around the streets and the coffee bars [...] They all have a go at our tight jeans and our long hair and seem to reckon that if we look like that we must be delinquent or something. We don't mind the delinquent part but they might give us credit for doing our hair and choosing our tight jeans. But they never do. They reckon we are no hopers.[60]

The jeans-clad students in the stories by Teychenné, Cunningham and Johnson, on the other hand, appear less 'sociable' and more distant. They form groups that the stories' outsider protagonists find hard to penetrate, highlighting perhaps the difficulty of transgressing the boundaries that did separate East Germans from the '68ers' in the West.

Realisms

Praised by the judges of a Melbourne short story competition for its 'vivid description of the Carlton scene and a finely thought-out ending',[61] Teychenné's is one of several stories to unfold within a more conventional format, although it restricts itself to the limited perspective of her young protagonist, foregrounding reality as a subjective experience. Other texts are more radically engaged in expanding, even challenging notions of realism. Bouncing off socialist realist writer Alan Marshall's concerns that with the disappearance of critical realism Australian literature was beginning to lose its distinctive features, Petersen's afterword argues that the complexities of bourgeois Australian mass society require an expanded creative repertoire.

The limits of a narrowly didactic realist aesthetic were also preoccupying East German writers, perhaps most notably Christa Wolf, whose 1969 essay 'Lesen und Schreiben' ('Reading and Writing') posits that prose fiction needs to tackle the 'truth aside from the important world of the facts', that it can and must 'stretch the boundaries of what we know about ourselves'.[62] In words that very much echo Wolf's, Petersen commends in his afterword Judith Wright's (frequently anthologized) story 'The Fig Tree' for its 'deeper, poetical penetration of reality' and points to a range of more experimental writers who stretch the boundaries of the classical short story in an 'attempt to expand their understanding of the world'.[63] He singles out Helen Pavlin's and Vicki

Viidikas's innovative renderings of difficult heterosexual love relationships and mentions almost in passing Peter Carey's indebtedness to Jorge Louis Borges.

Carey's 'A Windmill in the West' (1972), about an American soldier who guards an arbitrary, mysterious border dividing east from west in the Australian desert, is one of the volume's most politically charged stories. Dropped into the desert without much guidance or orientation, Carey's American spends his days trapping and killing scorpions – symbols of his own helplessness – until he shoots down a pilot. In his profound isolation, the soldier buries the wreck, weeping, wondering whether the windmill overlooking the scene 'could possibly hear him'.[64] Despite Carey's claims that the story is grounded in actual experience, his Australian readers have often highlighted its fabulist, surreal quality, considering it one of several 'fables of human powerlessness' that endow 'everything with a quality of frightening remoteness and alienation.'[65] In the early 2000s, German critic Cornelia Schulze interpreted the story as a parable for the accidental firing of nuclear warheads.[66] But when Petersen's anthology was first published in late 1976, the government of the GDR had just prohibited singer Wolf Biermann from returning from his West German tour to his East German home. In the context of the Biermann affair, and the exodus of disenchanted East German intellectuals that followed, Carey's scenario would have been just as absurd and frightening, but also terribly close and concrete – hyper-real, rather than surreal. Indeed, Petersen insists in his afterword, as he still must, of course, that his volume's authors are all realists: 'they often have an almost aggressive sense for this-worldliness […] they do not block access to reality with ludicrous fantasies'.[67]

Reflections on Reading

Carey's is one of numerous stories to invite reflections on reading – the soldier has brought *Playboy* and the Bible. Barbara M. Benedict has pointed to the close connection between anthologies and modern reading, dating the emergence of the early modern anthology to the point when readers became 'dissociated from direct literary interplay, engaged [via the anthology] in the solitary and imaginative recreation of culture through critical reading'.[68] Anthologies are at once liberating and restrictive, 'sample-bags of the actual and potential joys of reading', as Australian poet Chris Wallace Crabbe puts it, enabling readers to make their own connections within disparity, while also reminding them, as Leah Price argues, 'that the parts have been chosen for their difference from those left out.'[69] Petersen's anthology heightens this awareness in several ways: his afterword abounds with names of authors then unpublished in the GDR, such as Henry Lawson and Christina Stead.[70] The bio-bibliographical notes at the volume's back are like shop windows displaying wares out of stock, especially because the titles of untranslated work are only given in English. And reader characters in several stories further remind readers of the sharp limits of East German scenes of reading.

In the anthology's opening story, partying students greet a Queensland schoolgirl as hailing from a police state, and begin 'imitating the sound and walk of pigs',[71] a gesture that clandestine readers of Orwell could have interpreted as a reference to *Animal Farm*, banned in the GDR.[72] The migrant protagonist of the anthology's final story, Austrian-born Heinz Nonveiller's 'That Part of the World', spends his days proofreading the manufactured news of *The Daily Truth*, and feeds another migrant character books about Austria that increase her sense of belonging there.[73] Potentially the most subversive story in this context is Johnson's 'Bohemian Party', really chapter eight of *Wild Cat Falling* (1965), for some time considered the first novel by a writer who identified as Aboriginal. Petersen's volume was long out of print when Johnson's/Mudrooroo's belief in his Aboriginal (Nyoongah) ancestry was refuted amidst much media clamour in the mid-1990s. His place in Australian literary history is perhaps less easily challenged: Maureen Clark has argued that 'the author has made a very significant contribution to Australian literature'[74] and for Jeanine Leane, one of Mudrooroo's Wiradjuri readers, *Wild Cat Falling* does important work, 'introduc[ing] an Aboriginal speaking subject at least to the edges of mainstream consciousness'.[75]

Just out of jail, Mudrooroo's nameless, mixed-heritage protagonist is acutely aware of his place on the edges of the mainstream: 'I suppose I'm not what they call Australian. I'm just an odd species of native fauna cross-bred with the migrant flotsam of a goldfield.'[76] He feels out of place among the hip middle-class crowds on the university campus where Petersen's readers find him. In an effort to create himself a 'front' behind which to wait for the girl he has agreed to meet, he makes his way to the university bookshop.[77] Between the well-stocked shelves, his own marginalization is briefly suspended, while the East German reader's becomes apparent: the well-read young man is momentarily at ease, recognizing familiar Russian classics (having read *Crime and Punishment* in jail), relishing the pull of the psychology section and rejoicing over Samuel Beckett's *Waiting for Godot*.

This classic of the theatre of the absurd was hardly a sensational find in a 1960s Australian bookshop, but for East German readers, the small snatches quoted from it in Petersen's *Erkundungen* volume were all they would see of it until its premiere performance in Dresden in 1987 and subsequent publication with Volk und Welt in December 1988.[78] As well as explanations for 'Waltzing Mathilda', zucchini and coq au vin, Petersen's glossary at the back of the volume reminded readers of what else they may not know: '*Waiting for Godot*: Theatre play (1952) by Irish dramatist and Nobel Prize winner Samuel Beckett (born 1906).'[79] And the story's central character too does not let the matter rest: seated amongst the chattering students in the café, he wonders about all the lectures, music recitals, plays and books he has missed out on.

Frames of Interpretation

Not all the stories are challenging in this way. Some portray Australia and Australians using generic conventions similar to those of the communist writers previously published in the GDR, and return their readers to these older contracts of reading. Victor Venn's story 'Deep Well' (1965), for example, is reminiscent of Prichard's short fiction in its portrayal and condemnation of Aboriginal dispossession. It culminates, in true socialist realist fashion, with a moral victory, a demonstration of *Parteilichkeit* (a partisan attitude), when Venn's protagonist Dan Jeffreys, himself of mixed heritage, finally decides to defend the last remaining well from being poisoned:

> Suddenly he realised he had made a stand and won. Perhaps the nomads had never believed he would take sides – but now? [...] He told the refugees: 'Deep Well is clean. It's yours.'[80]
>
> [Plötzlich wurde ihm bewußt, daß er seinen Standpunkt vertreten und gesiegt hatte. Vielleicht hatten die Nomaden niemals geglaubt, daß er Partei ergreifen würde, aber jetzt? [...] Er sagte den Flüchtlingen: 'Deep Well ist sauber und gehört euch.'][81]

But in many other stories, the frames of interpretation can be seen to have altered. The only red flag in the entire collection 'hangs, stirless and sodden, from the lowest branch of a senile elm', signalling an auction in Hal Porter's 'The Sale'.[82] Some stories are not as 'localized', but unfold in nameless towns and suburbs rather than a clearly identifiable, capitalist Australia. Removed as it is from the discontinuous narrative of *The Americans, Baby* that establishes its broader (Sydney) settings, even Frank Moorhouse's 'A Person of Accomplishment' forms part of this significant group. Other stories, like Thelma Forshaw's 'The Grand Passion', do recall previous certainties, only to mock them:

> 'I was married at a miserable registry office,' her aunt flung at her. Zelda felt like a capitalist reproved by a Communist [...] 'I had no bridesmaids', Mrs Nesbitt went on communistically.[83]

Forshaw's story was one of two stories contracted from Horst Erdmann Verlag in the Federal Republic, and her West German translator heightened its satirical dimension, translating the adverb 'communistically' as a 'communist battle speech' ('*kommunistische Kampfrede*').[84]

The manuscript for the anthology was submitted to the Ministry together with Petersen's own report on it, and an assessment by an external reader, freelancer Karl-Heinz Berger. Berger rejoiced at the volume's freshness, commending the absence of outdated problems or modes of writing.[85] Not one of the authors could be found in the recent edition of the GDR's dictionary of foreign writers, Berger pointed out: 'Someone has literally been exploring here, and has collected unknown material.'[86] As a result, Berger, who had been concerned by a certain 'chubby-faced wholesomeness' in Australian letters now felt 'much more at home in a world that, as distant as it may be, bears astonishing resemblance to the world we know from other Western literatures closer to us'.[87] Berger was not alone in finding the project a success: the Ministry granted approval in just over three weeks, plans for a reprint were underway even before the first edition had been distributed in late 1976,[88] and three further reprints followed.

From West Germany, observing the scene for his PhD thesis on the German reception of Australian literature, Volker Wolf considered Petersen's anthology a pioneering achievement, significantly broadening the narrow East German canon of Australian literature and gathering material that could easily counter any ideological packaging.[89] In East Germany, Petersen's Australian collection appeared alongside a Cuban *Erkundungen* volume, and one review is revealing in its praise for the Cubans' focus on one event (the revolution), while finding Petersen's Australians lacking such a central point of reference. This, of course, as well as a certain 'longing for an undetermined freedom', which the same reviewer identified across the volume,[90] might well have constituted its attraction for East German readers, reading as they were in the increasingly icy cultural climate that took hold of Honecker's GDR in the late 1970s. In an effort to seize back control, the East German government banned the Klaus Renft rock band, expatriated singer Wolf Biermann and had a significant number of writers expelled from the writers' union, including Stefan Heym. Heym remained in East Berlin but countless East German writers and artists left in protest, and the population increasingly retreated from identifying with the state. During that time, the slender orange volume of Australian short stories remained available, pushing the boundaries of East German reading with its glimpses of Western youth culture, its experiments with realism and its subversive gestures to Orwell and Beckett. As it reconnected the inhabitants of the closed republic of letters with the 'world' in world literature, the volume both reminded readers of their own entrapments and, as Bernhard Scheller pointed out in his review for *Neues Deutschland*, showed them that 'the threat to the humane can be overcome, circumstances can […] be changed'.[91]

In May 1990, several months before reunification, plans for a second volume of Australian *Erkundungen*, originally scheduled for 1989, were put

Table 8.1 Contents of *Erkundungen: 31 australische Erzähler*

Author (year of birth)	English title (date of first publication)	Petersen's source	German title (year, translator)
G. Maree Teychenné (1949)	'The Wisdom of Getting …' (1972)	Brian Buckley, Jim Hamilton, eds., *Festival and Other Stories* (1974)	'Der Weisheit Anfang' (1976, Gisela Petersen)
Thelma Forshaw (1923)	'The Grand Passion' (1966)	Frank Auerbach, ed., *Eine Frau im Busch* (1970)	'Die große Leidenschaft' (1970, Frank Auerbach)
Judith Wright (1915)	'The Weeping Fig' (1953)	Judith Wright, *The Nature of Love* (1966)	'Der Banyanbaum' (1976, Gisela Petersen)
C. B. Christesen (1911)	'As the Time Is' (1970)	C. B. Christesen, *The Hand of Memory* (1970)	'Der Mensch ist wie die Zeit' (1976, Gerhard Böttcher)
Laurel Cunningham (1932)	'The Good Mother' (1973)	Frank Moorhouse, ed., *Coast to Coast, 1973* (1973)	'Die gute Mutter' (1976, Klaus Schultz)
Peter Carey (1943)	'A Windmill in the West' (1972)	*Meanjin* 4 (1972)	'Im Westen ein Windrad' (1976, Reinhild Böhnke)
Laurence Collinson (1925)	'Preliminaries' (1966)	Clement Semmler, ed., *Coast to Coast, 1965–1966* (1966)	'Vor einem langen Tag' (1976, Christiane Agricola)
Victor Venn (1920)	'Deep Well' (1965)	Kylie Tennant, ed., *Summer's Tales 2* (1965)	'Vergiftete Brunnen (1976, Gunther Böhnke)
Peter Cowan (1914)	'The Tins' (1965)	Peter Cowan, *The Tins and Other Stories* (1973)	'Leere Konservendosen' (1976, Christiane Agricola)
Douglas Terry (1926)	'On the Road' (1963)	Mary Lord, ed., *Modern Australian Short Stories* (1971)	'Auf der Straße' (1976, Reinhild Böhnke)
Helen M. Hunt (1932)	'Leila'	Kylie Tennant, ed., *Summer's Tales 1* (1964)	'Leila' (1976, Hans Petersen)
Helen Pavlin (1940)	'Spring Visit' (1973)	*Tabloid Story 3 Part 1* (1973)	'Ein Wiedersehen im Frühling' (1976, Gisela Petersen)
Hal Porter (1911)	'The Sale' (1971)	Frank Moorhouse, ed., *Coast to Coast, 1973* (1973)	'Die andere Welt der Miss Marly' (1976, Christiane Agricola)
T. A. G. Hungerford (1915)	'Final Round' (1969)	Thea Astley, ed., *Coast to Coast, 1969–1970* (1970)	'Endrunde' (1976, Gisela Petersen)

Author	Story	Source	German translation
Ethel Webb (1925)	'Towers of Darkness' (1973)	Author's submission	'Türme der Finsternis' (1976, Gerhard Böttcher)
Frank Moorhouse (1938)	'A Person of Accomplishment' (1972)	Frank Moorhouse, *The Americans, Baby* (1972)	'Ein vollkommener Mann' (1976, Gisela Petersen)
Murray Bail (1941)	'The Dog Show' (1966)	*Meanjin* 2 (1966)	'Die Hundeschau' (1976, Gunther Böhnke)
Russell Beedles (1940)	'Zoom Out' (1973)	Author's submission	'Abschied' (1976, Gisela Petersen)
Joan M. Bean (1931)	'A Slipper for Adriana' (1973)	Oscar Mendelsohn/Harry Marks, eds., *Australian New Writing* (1973)	'Ein Pantoffel für Adriana' (1976, Gisela Petersen)
Judy Hiener (1931)	'The Strawberry Picker' (1970)	Thea Astley, ed., *Coast to Coast, 1969–1970* (1970)	'Die Erdbeerpflückerin' (1976, Gunther Böhnke)
John Box (1943)	'Artistic Licence' (1974)	Brian Buckley, Jim Hamilton, eds., *Festival and Other Stories* (1974)	'Die blaue Periode des Jesaulenko' (1976, Gunther Böhnke)
Osman E. Middleton (1925)	'Drift' (ca. 1966)	Clement Semmler, ed., *Coast to Coast, 1965–1966* (1966)	'Drift' (1976, Klaus Schultz)
Don Diespecker (1929)	'Dragonfly' (1969)	Frank Moorhouse, ed., *Coast to Coast, 1973* (1973)	'Die Libelle' (1976, Hans Petersen)
Colin Johnson (Mudrooroo) (1938)	'Bohemian Party' (1965)	Geoffrey Dutton, ed., *Modern Australian Writing* (1966)	'Unter Künstlern' (1976, Christiane Agricola)
Esme A. Gollschewsky (1917)	'Ultimate Summer' (1967)	*Meanjin* 4 (1967)	'Der letzte Sommer' (1976, Christiane Agricola)
Maxwell Wilcox (1934)	- (1975)	Author's submission	'Wir laden Sie herzlich ein …' (1976, Christiane Agricola)
Gwen Kelly (1922)	'Mini Skirts' (1968)	Author's submission	'Miniröcke' (1976, Gunther Böhnke)
Vicki Viidikas (1948)	'The Treadmill' (1974)	Vicki Viidikas, *Wrappings* (1974)	'Das Getriebe' (1976, Hans Petersen)
Gerald Marcus Glaskin (1923)	'It's Often Delayed' (1967)	G. M. Glaskin, *The Road to Nowhere* (1967)	'Beinahe zu spät' (1976, Gerhard Böttcher)
Dal Stivens (1911)	'Warrigal' (1969)	Dal Stivens, *Selected Stories, 1936–1968* (1969)	'Der Dingo' (1976, Klaus Schultz)
Heinz Nonveiller (1938)	'That Part of the World' (1967)	Frank Auerbach, ed., *Eine Frau im Busch* (1970)	'Jener Teil der Welt' (1970, Frank Auerbach)

on hold.[92] In September that year, Petersen was still hopeful. 'Lots of things have happened,' he wrote to Elizabeth Jolley, whom he had met in Australia in 1986,

> and Volk und Welt has changed, too. In fact the whole publishing scene in East and West Germany [...] has seen changes that deeply affect our programme [...] There are a couple of books that I will have to return now – by separate mail – *Milk and Honey* and *Stories*. As you know I was planning to do another collection of Australian short stories. However, the project has been shelved for the moment. I hope, though, that in a couple of years Volk und Welt will be in a position to go ahead with the collection in which I have invested quite a lot of work up to now. One of your stories will be definitely in, I xeroxed those that I like most [...] At the moment all is very difficult and many East German companies go out of business. Let's hope for the best. I hope that you and Leonard are well. With affection, Hans Petersen.[93]

Work never resumed. Petersen took his research notes with him, leaving a gap in the publisher's records; the names and titles that dot the report of his trip to Australia in 1986 are a shadowy archive of what might have been. The 1990s still saw nine new additions to the *Erkundungen* series, but its heyday was over. Its success and importance had relied on the very walls it helped to bring down.

Notes

1. Akademie der Künste, Berlin (AdK), Volk und Welt Archive, 1351. Unless otherwise indicated, all translations from the German are mine.
2. On the usefulness of the term 'scene of reading', see Robert Dixon and Brigid Rooney, 'Introduction: Australian Literature, Globalisation and the Literary Province', in *Scenes of Reading: Is Australian Literature a World Literature?* ed. Robert Dixon and Brigid Rooney (Sydney: Australian Scholarly Publishing, 2013), ix–xxxvi (ix).
3. Hans Petersen, 'Nachwort', in *Erkundungen: 31 australische Erzähler*, ed. Hans Petersen (Berlin: Volk und Welt, 1976), 296–303 (303).
4. Siegfried Lokatis, 'Das Volk und Welt-Lektorat V für englischsprachige Literatur', in *Britische Literatur in der DDR*, ed. Barbara Korte, Sandra Schaur and Stefan Welz (Würzburg: Königshausen und Neumann, 2008), 13–22 (21). See also Siegfried Lokatis's essay in chapter 1.
5. This chapter significantly expands on Gabriele Pisarz-Ramirez's rich survey of the *Erkundungen* series, written without access to the archives available to me. Pisarz argued that the series progressed from (merely) thematic preoccupations to genuinely literary ones. Gabriele Pisarz-Ramirez, 'Internationale Kurzprosa in Anthologien der Deutschen Demokratischen Republik: Die Reihe "Erkundungen"', in *International Anthologies of Literature in Translation*, ed. Harald Kittel (Berlin: Erich Schmidt, 1995), 199–238.

6 Wolfgang Emmerich, *Kleine Literaturgeschichte der DDR* (Leipzig: Kiepenheuer, 1997), 56 and 230.
7 Stefan Heym, 'The Boredom of Minsk', *Meanjin* 25, no. 2 (1966): 196–99 (198).
8 Conversation with writers, November 1965, quoted in Michael Westdieckenberg, *Die 'Diktatur des anständigen Buches': Das Zensursystem der DDR für belletristische Prosaliteratur in den sechziger Jahren* (Wiesbaden: Harrassowitz, 2004), 152.
9 Fourth meeting of the Central Committee, December 1971, quoted in Pisarz-Ramirez, 'Internationale Kurzprosa in Anthologien der Deutschen Demokratischen Republik', 207.
10 Eighth Party Congress, July 1971, quoted in Sara Jones, *Complicity, Censorship and Criticism: Negotiating Space in the GDR Literary Sphere* (Berlin: Walter de Gruyter, 2011), 97.
11 Helmut Findeisen, report on Virginia Woolf, *Mrs Dalloway*, 14 June 1976, BArch DR1/3481/318–320 (318). The 1970s mark the heyday of German reception theory, developed in East and West Germany. For Manfred Naumann, one of the figureheads of GDR 'Rezeptionstheorie', these works offered a way out of the cul de sac created by the binaries of Lukáscian theory and the even more restrictive official discourse. See Mandy Funke, *Rezeptionstheorie Rezeptionsästhetik: Betrachtung eines deutsch-deutschen Diskurses* (Bielefeld: Aisthesis, 2004), 41.
12 Petersen, 'Nachwort', 301.
13 Cusack, for example, had visited eight times by 1972. See Charlotte Heitzenröther, 'Beeindruckt vom Land und seinen Menschen', *Neues Deutschland*, 5 January 1972, 4. At the 1965 Writers' Conference held in Weimar, the Australian delegation was the second largest, beaten only by the group from the Soviet Union – *Internationales Schriftstellertreffen in Berlin und Weimar 1965: Protokoll* (Berlin: Aufbau, 1965).
14 Katharine Susannah Prichard to W. Neumann of Volk und Welt, 5 May 1961, AdK, Volk und Welt Archive, 1259.
15 Quoted in Peter Monteath, 'The German Democratic Republic and Australia', *Debatte: Journal of Contemporary Central and Eastern Europe* 16, no. 2 (2008): 213–35 (220).
16 Ibid., 220.
17 'Australier wählten gegen Washington', *Neues Deutschland*, 5 December 1972, 7.
18 Petersen, publisher's report on *Erkundungen: 32 australische Erzähler*, November 1975, BArch DR1/2360a/449–455 (450); Hans Petersen, 'Nachwort', 300.
19 Petersen, publisher's report on *Erkundungen*, 450.
20 See Monteath, 'The German Democratic Republic and Australia'.
21 Ibid., 223.
22 Terms of the treaty, quoted in Inge Christopher, 'The Written Constitution: The Basic Law of a Socialist State?', in *Honecker's Germany*, ed. David Childs (London: Allen & Unwin, 1985), 15–31 (26).
23 'Australien: DDR-Botschaft nimmt ihre Tätigkeit auf', *Neues Deutschland*, 2 April 1973, 2. Monteath, 'The German Democratic Republic and Australia', 230.
24 Hans Petersen, 'Über Faulkner und die Erschließung der amerikanischen Literatur', in *Fenster zur Welt: Eine Geschichte des DDR-Verlags Volk und Welt*, ed. Siegfried Lokatis and Simone Barck (Berlin: Christoph Links, 2004), 175–78 (178).
25 Petersen to Dal Stivens, 16 October 1980, Papers of Dal Stivens, NLA MS 4713, box 4, folder 25. See also copy of Petersen's travel report dated 6 February 1987, Stadtarchiv Dessau N3.13 – Specht – 68.
26 Westdieckenberg, *Die 'Diktatur des anständigen Buches'*, 129.
27 Roland Links, 'Der Umgang mit deutschprachiger Literatur von 1954 bis in die siebziger Jahre', in *Fenster zur Welt: Eine Geschichte des DDR-Verlags Volk und Welt*, 97–102 (100).

28 Petersen, 'Nachwort', 300.
29 See, for example, Bruce Bennett, 'Literary Culture since Vietnam: A New Dynamic', in *The Oxford Literary History of Australia*, ed. Bruce Bennett, Jennifer Strauss and Chris Wallace Crabbe (Melbourne: Oxford University Press, 1998), 239–64 (239), and Ken Gelder, 'Representing Short Stories', in Paul Salzman and Ken Gelder, *The New Diversity: Australian Fiction: 1970–88* (Melbourne: McPhee Gribble, 1989), 11–25 (15).
30 See Bruce Bennett, *Australian Short Fiction: A History* (St Lucia: University of Queensland Press, 2002), 145–224.
31 Georgina Baum, publisher's report on *Erkundungen: 35 Schweizer Erzähler*, BArch DR1/2354a/368–372 (367), undated, ca. January 1974.
32 Werner Liersch, 'Nachwort', in *Erkundungen: 19 Westdeutsche Erzähler*, ed, Werner Liersch (Berlin: Volk und Welt, 1964), 273–78 (277). On this volume, see my chapter, 'Reading the Enemy: East German Censorship across the Wall', in *Censorship and the Limits of the Literary: A Global View*, ed. Nicole Moore (New York: Bloomsbury, 2015), 147–160.
33 W. Friedrich, reader's report on *Erkundungen: Schwedische Erzähler*, undated, ca. November 1966, BArch DR1/2331a/436–443 (436).
34 Hans Petersen, publisher's report on *Erkundungen*, 449.
35 Ibid., 450.
36 Ibid., 452.
37 Ibid., 452.
38 Ibid., 453.
39 Thelma Forshaw's 'The Great Passion' and Heinz Nonveiller's 'That Part of the World' had appeared in Frank Auerbach's anthology, *Eine Frau im Busch und andere australische Erzählungen* (*The Drover's Wife and Other Australian Stories*) (Stuttgart: Horst Erdmann Verlag, 1970).
40 See my interview with Bernhard Scheller in chapter 11 of this volume.
41 Dennis Wren to Jürgen Gruner, Volk und Welt, 9 October 1973, AdK, Volk und Welt Archive, 1355.
42 Australian Writers' Professional Service, 'They seek stories', *Writers' World: A Newssheet and 'Meeting Place' for Australasian Writers and Journalists* 126 (October 1973): 2.
43 Petersen, publisher's report on *Erkundungen*, 449.
44 O. E. Middleton to Petersen, 10 February 1976, AdK, Volk und Welt Archive, 1348. Middleton's story 'Drift' remained in the volume, but from the second reprint onwards, his biographical note would identify him as a New Zealander.
45 Petersen, publisher's report on *Erkundungen*, 454.
46 Maxwell Wilcox to Jürgen Gruner, 27 April 1975, AdK, Volk und Welt Archive, 1355.
47 *AustLit*, the authoritative database about Australian literature and storytelling, has no entry for him.
48 Molly Waters of Curtis Brown London to Petersen, 19 November 1975, AdK, Volk und Welt Archive, 1344. The stories selected for the separate collection were 'Dead Roses', 'A Cheery Soul', and 'Down at the Dump' from *The Burnt Ones* (1964), and 'A Woman's Hand' from *The Cockatoos: Shorter Stories and Novels* (1974).
49 See clippings held at AdK, Volk und Welt Archive – ZA 3955, Petersen to Patrick White, via Molly Waters, 27 October 1975.
50 Bruce Clunies Ross, 'Some Developments in Short Fiction, 1969–1980', *Australian Literary Studies* vol. 10, no. 2 (1981): 165–80 (168); Elizabeth Webby, 'Australian Short Fiction from *While the Billy Boils* to *The Everlasting Secret Family*', *Australian Literary Studies* 10, no. 2 (1981): 147–64 (153).

51 Karl-Heinz Berger, report on *Erkundungen: 32 australische Erzähler*, November 1975, BArch DR1/2360a/456–459 (456).
52 Petersen to White, c/o Molly Waters, 27 October 1975, AdK, Volk und Welt Archive, 1344.
53 See the correspondence held at AdK, Volk und Welt Archive, 1344.
54 Teychenné is another of the collection's more obscure authors, 'The Wisdom of Getting …' was her first published story and is the only publication listed under her name on the *AustLit* database.
55 Maree Teychenné, 'The Wisdom of Getting …' in *Festival and Other Stories*, ed. Brian Buckley and Jim Hamilton (Melbourne: Wren, 1974), 139–46 (141).
56 Teychenné, 'The Wisdom of Getting …', 141 and 139. The German translation softens the girl's feeling of illegality by making her feel 'strangely out of place', 'merkwürdig fehl am Platze'; Maree Teychenné, 'Der Weisheit Anfang', in *Erkundungen: 31 australische Erzähler*, 5–12 (7); Colin Johnson, 'Bohemian Party', in *Modern Australian Writing*, ed. Geoffrey Dutton (Manchester: Collins, 1966), 76–84 (77).
57 Timothy S. Brown, 'East Germany', in *1968 in Europe: A History of Protest and Activism, 1956–1977*, ed. Martin Klimke and Joachim Scharloth (Houndmills: Basingstoke, 2008), 189–97 (191).
58 Ina Merkel, 'The GDR: A Normal Country in the Centre of Europe', in *Power and Society in the GDR, 1961–1979: The Normalisation of Rule?*, ed. Mary Fulbrook (Oxford: Berghahn, 2009), 194–203 (199).
59 Ulrich Plenzdorf, *Die neuen Leiden des jungen W.* (Rostock: Hinstorff, 1973), 20.
60 J. M. Hunt, 'Leila', in *Summer's Tales*, ed. Kylie Tennant (Melbourne: Macmillan, 1965), 66–72 (66). On blue jeans fiction, see Rado Pribic, 'Blue Jeans Fiction of Yugoslavia', *Journal of Reading* 26, no. 5 (1983): 430–34. Indeed, the impulse to imagine young Australians in denim is so strong that Christiane Agricola, who translated Colin Johnson's 'Bohemian Party', pictures even the female students who sport 'casual slacks' as wearing jeans.
61 E-mail from Maree Teychenné to the author, 21 January 2014.
62 Christa Wolf, 'Lesen und Schreiben', in Christa Wolf, *Fortgesetzter Versuch: Aufsätze Gespräche, Essays* (Leipzig: Reclam, 1982), 7–41 (31 and 41).
63 Petersen, 'Nachwort', 300, 301.
64 Peter Carey, 'A Windmill in the West', *Meanjin* 31, no. 4 (1972): 385–92 (392).
65 'Peter Carey' (excerpt from an interview with Craig Munro), *Australian Literary Studies* 8, no. 2 (1977): 4–9 (8); Bruce Bennett, *Australian Short Fiction*, 198; Clunies Ross, 'Some Developments in Short Fiction, 1969–1980', 179.
66 Cornelia Schulze, 'Peter Carey's Short Stories: Trapped in a Narrative Labyrinth', in *Fabulating Beauty: Perspectives on the Fiction of Peter Carey*, ed. Andreas Gaile (Amsterdam: Rodopi, 2005), 117–36 (126).
67 Petersen, 'Nachwort', 301.
68 Barbara M. Benedict, *Making the Modern Reader: Cultural Mediation in Early Modern Anthologies* (Princeton: Princeton University Press, 1996), 220.
69 Chris Wallace-Crabbe, 'Spaces, Cargoes, Documents, Values and Principles: Some Recent Poetry Anthologies', *Australian Literary Studies* 15, no. 4 (1992): 323–27 (324); Leah Price, *The Anthology and the Rise of the Novel: From Richardson to George Eliot* (Cambridge: Cambridge University Press, 2000), 6.
70 On Stead, see Susan Lever's essay in Chapter 9 of this volume.
71 Teychenné, 'The Wisdom of Getting …', 141.

72 On clandestine reading in the GDR, see *Heimliche Leser in der DDR: Kontrolle und Verbreitung unerlaubter Literatur*, ed. Siegfried Lokatis and Ingrid Sonntag (Berlin: Links, 2008). 'Pig' is Australian slang for 'police', but this, and the allusion to Brisbane as a 'pig city', would have been lost to Petersen's readers.
73 Heinz Nonveiller, 'That Part of the World', in *Coast to Coast: Australian Stories 1967–1968*, ed. A. A. Phillips (Sydney: Angus & Robertson, 1968), 36–46 (46).
74 Maureen Clark, 'Mudrooroo, Crafty Impostor or Rebel with a Cause?' *Australian Literary Studies* 21, no. 4 (2004): 101–110 (109).
75 Jeanine Leane, *The Whiteman's Aborigine* (thesis submitted to the University of Technology, Sydney, in fulfilment of the requirements for the doctor of philosophy degree, 2010), 154, accessed 14 January 2014, https://opus.lib.uts.edu.au/bitstream/10453/20379/2/02Whole.pdf?
76 Johnson, 'Bohemian Party', 77.
77 Ibid., 78.
78 In the 1950s, Brecht briefly considered *Waiting for Godot* for the Berliner Ensemble, but East German theatres in the 1960s and '70s stayed clear of Beckett, unpublished in the GDR until 1979, when one of his stories featured in Petersen's Irish *Erkundungen* volume. Plans to publish Beckett's plays in 1980 or 1981 did not come to fruition until 1988; Jochanan Trilse-Finkelstein, 'Samuel Beckett in der DDR', in *Britische Literatur in der DDR*, ed. Barbara Korte, Sandra Schauer and Stefan Welz (Würzburg: Königshausen & Neumann, 2008), 101–107; Gaby Hartel, Klaus Völker and Thomas Irmer, 'The Reception of Beckett's Theatre and Television Pieces in West and East Germany', in *The International Reception of Samuel Beckett*, ed. Mark Nixon and Matthew Feldman (London: Continuum, 2009), 75–96.
79 Hans Petersen, 'Anmerkungen', in *Erkundungen: 31 australische Erzähler*, 313–16 (315).
80 Victor Venn, 'Deep Well', in *Summer Tales 2*, ed. Kylie Tennant (Melbourne: Macmillan, 1965), 78–84 (84).
81 Victor Venn, 'Vergiftete Brunnen', trans. Gunter Böhnke, in *Erkundungen: 31 australische Erzähler*, 70–75 (75).
82 Hal Porter, 'The Sale', in *Coast to Coast: Australian Short Stories 1973*, chosen by Frank Moorhouse (Sydney: Angus & Robertson, 1973), 79–86 (82).
83 Thelma Forshaw, 'The Grand Passion', in *Goodbye to Romance: Stories by New Zealand and Australian Women Writers 1930–1988*, ed. Elizabeth Webby and Lydia Wevers (Sydney: Allen and Unwin, 1989), 148–54 (152).
84 Thelma Forshaw, 'Die große Leidenschaft', trans. Frank Auerbach, in *Erkundungen: 31 australische Erzähler*, 13–20 (18).
85 Karl-Heinz Berger, report on *Erkundungen: 32 australische Erzähler*, 457.
86 Ibid., 459.
87 Ibid., 456.
88 Jürgen Gruner to O. E. Middleton, 7 September 1976, AdK, Volk und Welt Archive, 1348.
89 Volker Wolf, *Die Rezeption australischer Literatur im deutschen Sprachraum, 1845–1979* (Tübingen: Stauffenburg, 1982), 31–32.
90 Ch. Funke, 'Kuba und Australien', *Der Morgen*, 29 April 1977.
91 Bernhard Scheller, '31 Erzähler aus dem "unbekannten Südland"', *Neues Deutschland*, 3 October 1976.
92 Jürgen Gruner to Hans Petersen, 18 May 1990, AdK, Volk und Welt Archive, 1357.
93 Hans Petersen to Elizabeth Jolley, 6 September 1990, AdK, Volk und Welt Archive, 3325.

Part III
LITERARY EXCHANGE

Chapter 9

'THERE I'M A NOBODY; HERE I'M A MARXIAN WRITER': AUSTRALIAN WRITERS IN THE EAST

Susan Lever

In March 1950 Australia's now-celebrated novelist Christina Stead waited in London while her partner, William Blake, visited the newly established German Democratic Republic (GDR) in hope of an appointment to the University of Leipzig as a lecturer in American Literature. Stead had left Australia in 1928, aged 25, leading a wandering life until her eventual return in 1974. Blake went to the GDR in February 1950 to give some lectures, and he had good reason to expect a tenured post at the urging of his friend Henryk Grossmann, professor of politics at the university. Another communist friend from New York, a German who had spent the war there, Max Schroeder, was literary editor at Aufbau Verlag in East Berlin and was arranging for the translation and editing of Blake's novel about German immigrants in the American Civil War, *The Copperheads* (published in German as *Maria Meinhardt* in 1952).

Blake wrote to Stead that he 'was a nobody in America relatively, but here I am a Marxian writer'. He was 'enchanted' by Leipzig and felt at home in a city with a picture of Stalin on every wall, where only the 'stupid, sorry lot' of conservative Germans criticized the new regime, and he admired the 'magnificent physical specimens of Russian troops (beautifully clothed) omnipresent, Russian the alternate language and where I am instantly at home'.[1] Leipzig was a country town compared to Berlin, with its stark division between the capitalist West and socialist East: 'On one side of the street is a socialist society, everything rational and "poor", on the other a mass of vendors of luxury articles in a "free" economy where at fantastic prices everything can be bought'.[2]

Though he was full of hope for the appointment, Blake expressed some concern about Stead's future as a novelist in the East. He assured her that 'I truly believe that for you it would be an occasion worth much more than the community of language in Britain. True, one could not stay here forever: an English writer must return to her sources'.[3] He proposed two or three years. Though Blake went through all the interviews and checks necessary for the appointment, it was never offered to him. His friend Grossmann was seriously ill throughout his visit and died shortly after, and suspicions from the Soviet Occupation Authorities meant that there was unwillingness to appoint another American academic. But it was a near thing – Christina Stead may have become a GDR novelist. Would she too have become a 'somebody' in the GDR?

The evidence is all against this prospect. By 1950 she had published the major novels that established her reputation, *Seven Poor Men of Sydney* (1934), *The Man Who Loved Children* (1940) and *For Love Alone* (1944). She had already written *The People with the Dogs* (1952) and *Cotters' England* (1966) and she was halfway through a first draft of *I'm Dying Laughing*.[4] Though these novels were published years later – after her death in the case of *I'm Dying Laughing* – Stead's most productive period of writing was almost over.

At the same time, GDR publishers were not eager to translate any of her published work. Even though Max Schroeder and his wife, Edith Anderson, had been among her close circle of communist friends in New York during the war, Aufbau Verlag showed no enthusiasm about Stead's novels. In 1950, when Aufbau was preparing Blake's novel *The Copperheads* for publication, they did not propose publishing any of Stead's work. In August 1957 Stead visited East Germany for the first time with Blake; by then, he had a second novel ready for publication by Aufbau, *Späte Liebe* (*Evergreen*, 1957). By this time, Max Schroeder was dying of lung cancer, but it is apparent that Aufbau did consider Stead's work sometime after that: in the publisher's archive, now held at the Staatsbibliothek Berlin, Christina Spittel has found an undated reader's report for *The Salzburg Tales*. Only parts of the lengthy report survive, but they clearly convey the reader's rejection of this collection of stories. Its perceived acceptance of the capitalist status quo, Sigrid Bachmann observed, rendered the book a missed opportunity for Stead and unpublishable for Aufbau. In the fictional setting of upper-class Salzburg, 'there can be no misunderstandings or tensions, and indeed such were not intended by this author who never takes a stand against this world', was Bachmann's damning verdict.[5]

We can presume that the German-speaking setting is the reason for considering the *Tales* over, say, *The Man Who Loved Children* or *For Love Alone*, or perhaps, a collection of short stories seemed more manageable than one of Stead's long novels, though it is easy to see that *Letty Fox* or *Cotters' England* might baffle German readers as much as they do readers in English. Of these, only *For Love Alone* has a clear Australian setting, so unlike Frank Hardy's or Katharine Susannah Prichard's work, Stead's novels did not offer any of the more exotic settings of the South. The reader for Aufbau thought the *Tales* had insufficient critical perspective on the pleasure-seeking storytellers gathered in Salzburg. Bachmann found the stories cruel and full of horrors, enough to drive the reader to coffee and alcohol ('Welch grausame Geschichte! Man muß sogleich Kaffee und Likör bestellen, um sie zu vergessen').[6] Individual stories, such as 'The Gold Bride', 'The Triskelion' or 'To the Mountain' seemed to seek out sexual perversion and exhibit a certain ghoulish infatuation with the dead. The report noted some apparent criticism of the way young women were disposed of in marriage and that one story was set immediately before the French Revolution ('Gaspard') but otherwise could not see that Stead adopted a sufficiently critical approach to the capitalist world of her stories: on the rare occasions where such criticism became manifest, for example in 'Lost Causes', whose farmers protest against high workloads and unbearable leases, it was 'papered over […] by the mysterious', Bachmann regretted.[7]

They are, of course, a mixture of the fantastic and the real; some are modern fairy stories, others whimsical jokes or extended gossip, all without any clear moral purpose. Stead was interested in sexual taboos, and many of the stories explore adultery, even incest, ending in horrific deaths. We know that in life Stead was a committed Marxist, even a Stalinist, but her fiction refuses to be didactic. It is a naturalist art of character observation and projection that resists simple ideological messages. Even her novels about politics, such as *Cotters' England* and *I'm Dying Laughing*, continue to defy readers trying to pin her down. *The Salzburg Tales*, like *Letty Fox: Her Luck* (1946) or even *For Love Alone*, reveals Stead's interest in sexual behaviour and the violation of sexual convention. 'The Schoolboy's Tale' refers to Sydney as an 'honest city, where the "Decameron" is forbidden and England's colonial history is expurgated for the school books'.[8] This suggests a link between sexual repression and political hypocrisy. But the GDR was another 'honest' society repressing the sexual. At a time when *Letty Fox* appeared on the banned list in Australia, Stead's work was also too sexually perverse for the GDR.[9] By the mid-1950s, Stead had an ASIO security file in Australia, partly because her brother Gilbert was a public member of the Communist Party of Australia, but it is difficult to see her fitting in to the new communist society of the East. She was an outsider on both sides of the political divide: while her books were rejected by Aufbau and Blake denied a GDR position because of his American citizenship, in the USA their communist friends were enduring the extremes of McCarthyism. Nevertheless, she remained a faithful Stalinist throughout the Cold War and continued to correspond with Edith Schroeder until 1965, so maintaining a personal contact within the GDR.

As this volume has shown, this enthusiasm for the GDR in the early 1950s was not exceptional among left-leaning writers and intellectuals in the English-speaking world. A more dramatic story is that of Doris Lessing's second husband, Gottfried Lessing. After the war, the communist Lessings moved to Britain from Southern Rhodesia (Zimbabwe), where Gottfried, a German of Jewish heritage, had spent the war. Unable to find work in a post-war Britain suspicious of Germans and communists, he returned to East Germany in 1947 and, within two years, gave up all contact with his wife and son across the political divide. He rose through the ranks of the GDR foreign ministry and was later killed during the Idi Amin riots in Uganda, where he was ambassador (the Soviet Union and the GDR were supporters of Amin's regime). Doris Lessing's autobiography speculates about his membership of the KGB and the peculiar circumstances of his death.[10] Stead and Lessing are now regarded as major writers of English-speaking culture, but as a result of their partners' commitment, both came close to living in the new GDR, a society that was seen in the 1950s, even more than the Soviet Union, as the culmination of the socialist dream by those critical of their own conservative and rigid post-war governments.

An acquaintance of Stead's, the novelist Dymphna Cusack, provides another example of personal Australian links with the Eastern Bloc. Camille Barrera's chapter in this volume explains how Cusack's novels set in Australia – *Black Lightning*, *Say No to Death* and *The Half Burnt Tree* – were more to the GDR publishers' taste than anything by Stead (who thought Cusack's novels were weak and full of 'valueless clichés'[11]). Royalties from Eastern Bloc publishers enabled Cusack to spend months in China, North Korea, the USSR, the GDR, Czechoslovakia and Romania, writing some of her novels while travelling. She and her husband, the communist Norman Freehill, were among the few Australians to have direct access to these nations. By and large, her novels are blameless arguments for humanist values such as racial tolerance and sexual equality, rather than politically explicit. Clearly, in the GDR's early decades, East German publishers were interested in the presentation of social problems in capitalist Australia, together with relatively exotic settings, rather than literary sophistication. (In chapter 5, Barrera quotes a reader's report on *Come In Spinner*: 'the novel barely exceeds the level of the middlebrow'.)

Freehill's account of his travels with Cusack insists that they found communist societies to be beacons of egalitarianism. Cusack found East Germany a miracle not only of material progress but in the 'mental and spiritual change that had been wrought by a generation of anti-Nazi education'.[12]

Cusack wrote most of *Heatwave in Berlin* (1961) while staying at a castle in Roztez, then in Czechoslovakia. Based on observations of Berlin in 1956 and 1959, including Cusack's accidental witnessing of an SS officers' reunion, according to Marilla North,[13] the novel proposes the existence of a continuing Nazi political movement in West Berlin, supported by elements of the

American military. Cusack's naive Australian protagonist finds herself married into a Berlin Nazi family who are plotting to take political power. As the novel progresses, the young woman discovers more sinister aspects to the family, including their friendship with a monstrous doctor from the concentration camps and their part in the continuing persecution of returning Jews, such as her old music teacher. There is little discussion of the East in the novel, except for a reference to a superior dramatic performance of *The Diary of Anne Frank* in East Berlin, and an American journalist's comment that 'all they want over there is to be left alone to build more factories, more houses and eat more butter than anyone in Europe'.[14] *Heatwave in Berlin* was published in the Soviet Union, Hungary, Estonia, Albania, Romania and Bulgaria, as well as many western European nations but not, it seems, in the GDR, though Freehill reports that Soviet soldiers performed a dramatized version of it in East Germany in 1967.[15] One wonders about the political sensitivities behind this. Perhaps GDR editors found its revival of the Nazi threat unhelpful or unconvincing for a German audience; perhaps the Soviet soldiers enjoyed reminding the Germans of their Nazi past.

Cusack's Australian reputation provides an interesting comparison with that of Stead. The novel she wrote with Florence James about the social effects of the American troops in Sydney during the war, *Come In Spinner*, won a newspaper literary competition in 1947 but publication was stymied by concern that it might offend Americans and draw prosecutions for obscenity.[16] Cusack took the manuscript to London where it was published by Heinemann in 1951. It became a best-seller in Australia and was picked up by Angus & Robertson as one of its Australian classics. It has remained in print for long periods, boosted by a successful television adaptation in 1990. Though her later novels sold well in Australia, her work has never been critically acclaimed; it is the kind of fiction that Patrick White derided as 'the dreary, dun-coloured offspring of journalistic realism' in his famous 1958 attack on Australian philistinism.[17]

In the late 1980s and early 1990s, republication of some of her titles and work by feminist scholars such as Debra Adelaide and Marilla North revived interest in Cusack's work, along with the work of writers such as Kylie Tennant and Ruth Park, who wrote about Australian 'battlers' and called on a national spirit of egalitarian values. Yet, Cusack is probably best remembered for her plays, *Morning Sacrifice* and *Pacific Paradise*, still performed in amateur, and occasionally professional, productions. Most were produced on ABC radio in Australia, and several were also performed in the Soviet Bloc countries. Cusack was not formally a member of the Communist Party of Australia and was never regarded as a 'socialist realist' writer by Australian communist critics, who placed her work within traditional left nationalism but without the clear socialist program they advocated. She was neither the kind of 'literary' writer admired by academic critics, nor the ideological socialist promoted by the communists. She did, however, have a popular readership.

Of Australian writers, Stead was probably the most complex in her engagement with communism – and she was certainly one of the most faithful Stalinists, remaining loyal to the Soviet Union until her death. While *The Man Who Loved Children* established her critical reputation, especially in the United States, she could never be a popular writer, and had difficulty finding publication for her post-1950 novels. Her current high reputation as a literary writer has followed strong feminist interest in her work, but few critics have come to terms with the nature of her communist commitment.[18] The difficulty of her fiction, even without the problem of translation, makes it little surprise that GDR publishers rejected it. Clearly, they were not looking to publish ground-breaking or difficult Marxist fiction. They were choosing material for wide dissemination among East German readers, and they were promoting a particular view of Australian society, preferring Australian settings and Australian social problems such as those presented in Cusack's Australian novels. These pressures on East German publishing lessened considerably, as Christina Spittel's chapter shows, in the early 1970s. In 1984 Stead was included in *Australische Erzähler von Marcus Clarke bis Patrick White*, a substantial anthology of Australian short stories of more than 500 pages, again edited by Hans Petersen, who chose Stead's novella 'The Rightangled Creek: A Sort of Ghost Story', from her collection, *The Puzzle-Headed Girl: Four Novellas* (1967). By then, Stead's Marxism was irrelevant (and might even have worked against her) so that the biographical sketch Petersen provides of her does not mention it.

As a result of publication in the East, several Australian writers visited the GDR and other Soviet states during the Cold War years in order to spend their royalties. For some poverty-stricken Australian writers, this meant they could travel and live in Eastern Europe – but it also meant that they were among the few Australians with first-hand experience of these societies. No doubt, they also felt they were 'nobodies' in Australia, but Marxian writers in the East. Among the Australian communist writers who travelled in the Soviet Bloc were Frank Hardy, Dorothy Hewett, Judah Waten and David Martin. Some of them published accounts of their journeys, to the extent that David Carter considers the Australian author's memoir of a journey to the East might constitute a genre of its own.[19] They were all enthusiastic about what they saw there, with Hardy publishing his paean to the Soviet republics, *Journey into the Future*, on his return from a visit to the GDR, Poland, Czechoslovakia and the USSR in 1952.

Hardy's correspondence with other writers in the 1950s and 1960s provides an account of shifts in understanding of the socialist writers' role.[20] Dorothy

Hewett had doubts about the socialist realist enterprise as early as 1961 when she wrote to Hardy that she found much Australian communist writing mechanical and clichéd, and distorting of Marxist theory.[21] Hewett later emerged as a playwright and poet, with a distinctively personal, rather than social, approach to writing. David Martin, a German writer of Hungarian background who shifted to writing in English when he settled in Britain and then Australia, lost confidence in communism after Soviet troops moved into Hungary in 1956 and was forced to resign from the Party in 1959 over his interview with Ho Chi Minh in Hanoi for an Indian newspaper.[22] In 1967 he was visiting Prague (again, on the royalties from books published in the East) when the tanks moved in and he saw that East German troops supported the Soviet intervention – hence, as Alexandra Ludewig has noted in chapter 6, his final falling out with Walter Kaufmann. For Martin, the evidence of Soviet suppression of any protest was too much to ignore any longer.

Communist party members and supporters represented one of the strongest intellectual forces in Australia in the 1940s and 1950s – not only in literature but in all aspects of culture. During this time they faced intimidation from powerful institutions and attempts at legal suppression. They were sometimes excluded from employment opportunities. For a long time, they also were apologists for regimes that we now know to have been cruelly repressive. They were, no doubt, allowed to see only the most positive elements of the new socialist republics on their journeys. Nevertheless, they appear to have been naively (even vainly) uncritical of their hosts, perhaps overjoyed at the sales of their work and the experience of being 'somebodies'. Publishing in the GDR was a closed market, with the authorities determining which books could be published and stocked in bookshops.

It appears that GDR publishers favoured Australian writing with a left nationalist viewpoint – writing that was distinctively Australian, concerned about social issues and written in a straightforward realist style. By the 1970s, this kind of writing had become the basis for many Australian television adaptations, and some left novelists had renewed careers as a result of television success – *Power without Glory* was both a critical and popular success on television, but so were series based on the novels of Alan Marshall, David Martin, Ruth Park, Kylie Tennant and, later, Dymphna Cusack.[23]

In Australia the cold war deformed cultural and critical discussion, with writers often categorized into one of two camps – communist or anti-communist. On one side, Kylie Tennant and others were denounced in Parliament as communists with attempts to prevent them from receiving public support, but, on the other, a writer like Patrick White could be read as reactionary by the Left. In the 1960s, publication in *Overland* or *Quadrant* marked a writer as communist-left sympathiser or anti-communist respectively. As late as 1974 the Liberal

Party could campaign featuring 'the little old lady from Eastern Europe' as a warning against the likely communist consequences of a Labor vote.[24] In this way, the terrible history of communism in Europe was used to counter even the mildest social reform in Australia. Even today, the word 'socialism' can be used by politicians to conjure up visions of repression and class warfare. There is a right-wing rhetoric that depicts any idea that might benefit the general population at the expense of the wealthy as creeping socialism/communism. Just as Orwell's novel *1984* was recruited for the propaganda interests of the right during the cold war, for decades it was almost impossible in Australia for anyone to criticize the communist societies of Eastern Europe without being classified with the *Quadrant* group, or allied with the Democratic Labor Party and then the right wing of the Liberal party.

In this context, Anna Funder's *Stasiland* (2002) indicates the change in possibilities over the last few decades, in that it has not been categorized as the work of a right-wing intellectual even though it investigates the effect of the surveillance system of the GDR on individuals, particularly women. Funder's nationality matters to her book: her Australianness seems to arm her with a kind of innocence as she contacts former Stasi agents and interviews them about their pasts. Some of her interviewees treat her as a naïf, distant from history and untainted by Cold War politics. It is unlikely that a German, or even an American or British writer would be accepted as so free of prejudice. Funder's book has been criticized (as by Leah Gerber in chapter 10) for some inaccuracies or too vague an understanding of the politics of the GDR, and even on the grounds that an Australian outsider has no right to comment – but its author has not been attacked as a member of some conservative political group within Australia. At last, an Australian writer is able to criticize a communist regime without the automatic assumption that this is propaganda for capitalism.

To read about Australian writers' enthusiasms for the Soviet Bloc countries is to understand something of the state of post-war Australia and the devastation of Europe in the wake of the Second World War. The information we now have about the publication of their books in the GDR alerts us to the complex nature of history, where Australian communist writers, resisting the authoritarian aspects of their own society, enjoyed the prospect of a utopian communist society in Eastern Europe that would celebrate their work. For most of them, this dream lasted only until the 1960s, as a series of violent responses to rebellion awakened them to the repressive nature of the Soviet regime. Despite their anti-authority stance in Australia, through the publication of their books they found themselves in the curious position of enjoying some of the benefits of the authoritarian nature of GDR society.

As Ludewig tells us, Walter Kaufmann found that in the GDR, writing to please authority brought considerable rewards. In the capitalist world, writing to please the public can bring immense financial returns. In both societies, sophisticated writing that does not conform to expectations is likely to be neglected. One of the many paradoxes of a situation where Australian writers were published and welcomed in the communist Eastern Bloc is that in the decades in which East German engagement with Australian letters was strongest, the GDR's publishers promoted a fairly straightforward, realist kind of writing, while rejecting the more challenging work of Christina Stead or Patrick White. It can seem as if the writer, Marxian or not, ready to push the boundaries of literary style, or to criticize society too satirically was unlikely to find acclaim in either East or West. Yet, when White's short fiction became publishable in East Germany at last, White initially refused, as Christina Spittel's chapter in this volume shows. When Stead and White finally did make it into East German print in 1984, the days of this heavily protected literary culture with its large, state-approved print runs were already numbered. And Stead's death at the age of 80 in March 1983 meant that, finally, she never saw herself in print in the GDR.

Notes

1 Christina Stead and William Blake, *Dearest Munx: The Letters of Christina Stead and William Blake*, ed. Margaret Harris (Melbourne: Miegunyah Press, 2005), 486.
2 Ibid., 503.
3 Ibid., 497.
4 Letter to Nettie Palmer, 5 December 1950, in Christina Stead, *Web of Friendship: Selected Letters 1928–1973*, ed. R. G. Geering (Pymble, NSW: Angus & Robertson, 1992),121.
5 Publisher's report on *The Salzburg Tales*, signed Sigrid Bachmann, undated, incomplete, Archiv des Aufbau-Verlags, Lektorat Ausland/Titelakten Anglistik, Staatsbibliothek Berlin, SBBIIIA Dep38/3091/42r–46r, 43r. My thanks to Christina Spittel for locating and translating this report.
6 Ibid., SBBIIIA Dep38/3091/43r.
7 Ibid., SBBIIIA Dep38/3091/46r.
8 Christina Stead, *The Salzburg Tales*, first published in 1934 (London: Virago, 1986), 465.
9 Nicole Moore, 'The Totally Incredible Obscenity of *Letty Fox*', *Journal of the Association for the Study of Australian Literature (JASAL)* 2 (2003): 67–79.
10 Doris Lessing, *Under My Skin: Volume One of My Autobiography to 1949* (London: Harper Collins, 1994), 404–19.
11 Hazel Rowley, *Christina Stead: A Biography* (Melbourne: Miegunyah Press, 2007), 360.
12 Norman Freehill with Dymphna Cusack, *Dymphna Cusack* (Melbourne: Thomas Nelson, 1975), 132.
13 Marilla North, 'Dymphna Cusack', in *Dictionary of Literary Biography, vol. 260 Australian Writers, 1915–1960* (Farmington Hills, MI: Gale, 2002), 59.
14 Dymphna Cusack, *Heatwave in Berlin* (London: Heinemann, 1961), 118.

15 Freehill, *Dymphna Cusack*, 140.
16 Bridget Griffen-Foley, 'Revisiting the "Mystery of a Novel Contest"': The *Daily Telegraph* and *Come In Spinner*', *Australian Literary Studies* 19, no. 4 (2000): 413–24.
17 Patrick White, 'The Prodigal Son', in *Australian Letters* (1958), reprinted in *The Oxford Anthology of Australian Literature* (Melbourne: Oxford University Press, 1985), 337.
18 Cf. Michael Ackland, 'Dreaming of the Middle Ages: The Place of the "mittelalterlich" and Socialist Awareness in Christina Stead's Early Fiction', *Australian Literary Studies* 26, nos. 3–4 (2012): 54–68; Michael Ackland, '"Socialists of a New Socialism"? Christina Stead's Critique of 1930s America in *The Man Who Loved Children*', *English Literary History (ELH)* 78, no. 2 (2011): 387–408.
19 David Carter, 'Journeys in Genre: Australian Literary Travellers to the Soviet Union', in *'And What Books Do You Read?' New Studies in Australian Literature*, ed. Irmtraud Petersson and Martin Duwell (St Lucia: Queensland University Press, 1996), 164–79.
20 Papers of Frank Hardy, NLA, MS 4887, series 23, box 1.
21 For further discussion see Susan McKernan, *A Question of Commitment: Australian Literature in the Twenty Years after the War* (North Sydney: Allen & Unwin, 1989), chapter 1.
22 David Martin, *My Strange Friend* (Chippendale, NSW: Pan Macmillan, 1991).
23 I argue this with reference to the work of Cliff Green in 'The Social Realist Tradition and Australian Television Drama', paper delivered to ASAL conference, Toowoomba, 1998, https://www.academia.edu/7006385/The_Social_Realist_Tradition_and_Australian_Television_Drama.
24 John Singleton and Gordon Alexander, 'These Elections Were Genuine', *Quadrant* 19, no. 1 (1975): 36–94 (54).

Chapter 10

BEHIND THE WALL, THROUGH AUSTRALIAN EYES: ANNA FUNDER'S *STASILAND*

Leah Gerber

In an Australian radio interview in May 2006 about her best-selling book *Stasiland* (2002),[1] a non-fiction, personal account of the GDR's aftermath, Anna Funder was asked by commentator Terry Lane: 'What was a nice Australian girl doing poking around in Germany's dirty linen?'[2] When Funder first started writing the book, only seven years after the fall of the Berlin Wall, information regarding the activities of the East German secret police was still emerging in the media. Although she grew up in Melbourne, Funder lived and worked in Germany over several years and speaks fluent German. After studying in West Berlin in the late 1980s, where she heard stories from behind the Wall, Funder returned to Berlin in 1997 with the intention of writing a text that would delve into a very specific part of Germany's recent past, uncovering the untold stories of various victims of the Stasi. She wanted to explore the lives of those who had stood up to the regime, thus revealing significant acts of courage.[3] Readers of *Stasiland* are progressively introduced to these figures as the protagonist 'Anna' encounters them: Miriam, whose husband, Charlie, died in a Stasi prison; Julia, who sublets her apartment in the former eastern part of Berlin to Anna, and whose education and career chances were cut off by the Stasi, and Frau Sigrid Paul, whose sickly baby was stuck on the western side of the Wall, prompting Frau Paul and her husband to undertake an escape attempt through a tunnel into West Berlin.

On her journey through this so-called Stasiland, Anna also meets the state cartographer responsible for painting the line of the Berlin Wall through the city, while her friend, the late East German rock star Klaus Renft, divulges to her his experiences of living behind the Wall. Funder presents these 'real stories' – mediating them as they have been conveyed to Anna – as a means of validating her creative non-fiction text.

In terms of *Stasiland*'s reception, the question of genre is extremely relevant. Frequently, non-fiction is read as truth; Funder argues that, by its very nature, non-fiction holds 'the cachet of being true. This means that things which are literally stranger than fiction can have a place there'.[4] Nevertheless, readers are usually aware that subjective opinions and factual inaccuracies can easily penetrate a work that pertains to be correct (both are certainly true of *Stasiland*). Kate Mitchell remarks on the generic complexities of *Stasiland*, claiming that Funder's text, overtly marketed as non-fiction, 'embellishes testimony with literary techniques that create a memorable engagement with the past'; in doing so, Funder creates a text better affiliated with 'investigative journalism rather than with history'[5]. Indeed, in 'creative non-fiction', a somewhat sketchy term, this is precisely the point and would appear to best describe Funder's text – its hybrid aims are rationalized by Gutkind as the process whereby 'writers turn to the creative non-fiction genre because they feel passionately about a person, place, subject, or issue and have no interest in or intention of maintaining a balanced or objective tone or viewpoint'.[6] Funder's text has often been likened to a novel (she also mentions this). It is written in a light, often-humorous, first-person narrative that is at the same time unmistakably didactic and moralistic in tone and told through the actions of a distanced protagonist rather than a direct authorial voice. Such an approach to non-fiction writing is common in Australia, adopted by other Australian authors who have embraced the style of creative non-fiction including Helen Garner, Chloe Hooper and David Marr.[7] Reviewers of the English text have commented repeatedly on *Stasiland*'s hybridity: Vanessa Thorpe, writing for *The Observer*, notes how *Stasiland* 'is leaving bookshops at a rate rarely seen with serious factual work [...] At times it reads more like a thriller than a historical survey'.[8] *HQ Magazine* calls it 'a compelling hybrid of journalism, biography and personal history', while the *Irish Times* deems it 'stylishly-written'. The *Leeds Guide* refers to its 'compelling narrative' and the *Sunday Times*, its 'literary flair'.[9]

In Germany, the genre of creative non-fiction is less common, with Josephi and Müller claiming that in Germany 'literary journalism has to be an eyewitness report'.[10] Despite this key difference, Funder is referred to at one point as 'Die australische Antwort auf Jana Hensel und Claudia Rusch' (the Australian answer to Jana Hensel and Claudia Rusch) (*Deutschland Archiv*).[11] Both Hensel and Rusch are young authors who grew up in the GDR and used this as the premise for their biographical texts; Leipzig author Jana Hensel published the highly popular *Zonenkinder* in 2002 (translated into English in 2004 as *After the Wall: Confessions from an East German Childhood and the Life That Came Next*), while Claudia Rusch's *Meinefreie Deutsche Jugend* (*My Free German Youth*) (2003) explored similar issues. It is clear that Funder's intention in writing *Stasiland* was to present a suite of 'real' stories about those who suffered under the Stasi – via the Australian protagonist Anna – and, in doing so, to present a veritable truth about this period of German history. Furthermore, she has always argued that her ability to gain access to people's histories and to provide them with an authentic voice in her narrative was made easier by the fact that she was *not* German. She claims:

> I think that it was a great advantage for me to be foreign, because I don't think that East Germans would have spoken nearly as openly to a West German asking them these questions, and I think in some ways, West Germans wouldn't have noticed some of the things I noticed from the outside. So in the end I thought it was an advantage.[12]

Unsurprisingly, many German readers viewed the situation differently. When the German translation by Harald Riemann was published in 2004, as she recounts it, Funder was instructed by her Hamburg-based publicist to '[w]ear a flak jacket. The booksellers, especially in the former East Germany, are livid'.[13] Despite the unquestionable significance of the subject matter for Germans and notwithstanding its success in many other major markets, 23 German publishers refused to purchase the rights to the book. One of the explanations Funder received was that, while it was by far the best book 'by a foreigner' on the issue, there was no way of publishing it in the 'current political climate'.[14] Finally, a German translation was commissioned by Europäische Verlagsanstalt (EVA) in Hamburg, a small publishing house that publishes mainly non-fiction titles. When the translation was launched at the 2004 Leipzig Book Fair in the 'Runde Ecke' building (the former Stasi Headquarters), Funder was met with a shout from the back of the room from a woman yelling, 'Who gave you the right to write about us?' Funder recalled her response was: 'Where I come from, writers can write about almost anything they choose', and 'from what authority should I have sought permission?' Variations of this question pervaded the interviews she undertook with the German media during her publicity tour. One East German journalist asked, 'But what will they think about us abroad now?' Funder was asked why she had not written about 'normal life' in the GDR; why did she search for extreme stories? Again, her answer was clear: 'I didn't make up the Stasi and their extreme methods. I also didn't have to look very far at all to find stories of resistance and its terrible consequences. And I didn't find the world that the East German state created in any way "normal"'.[15]

Funder's attempt to normalize the Stasi experience – as something so commonplace that the GDR becomes, as a whole, a 'Stasiland' – permeates the narrative, in which the young Australian former lawyer and documentary filmmaker Anna, whilst living in the former eastern part of Berlin, repeatedly chances upon those who have a story to tell. As observed by Eva Behrendt in *Die Tageszeitung*, she thereby becomes a kind of self-styled journalist, whose *Gespräche und Beobachtungen* (conversations and observations) created 'ein spannendes, journalistisch genaues Buch in bester angelsächsischer Tradition' (an exciting, journalistically-accurate book in the best Anglo-Saxon tradition).[16] Yet, as many Germans will argue, this focus overlooks a central element of what it was like to be a GDR citizen: East Germany was much more than just the Stasi, a point brought home by one of Funder's key 'characters', singer Klaus Renft, when he tells Anna: 'You know, for us the GDR wasn't just Stasi, Stasi, Stasi'.[17] This is the opinion of various other 'eye-witnesses', including academic Gert Reifarth who wrote: 'I had never lived in Stasiland [...] So I'm worried about the possible misimpression [sic] that Funder's book describes the whole GDR, when it doesn't.'[18] In a similar vein, Matthias Gretzschel, writing for *Die Welt*, critiqued Funder's presentation of the truth in *Stasiland*, recounting his impression of the GDR as follows:

> Für solche Art Kritik ist die Autorin taub [...] Sollte ich in Anna Funders 'Stasiland' gelebt haben? Die Bilder meiner Erinnerung, auch die dunklen, ergeben ein anderes Puzzlebild – eines, das sehr viel mehr Farben und Nuancen hat als das der engagierten australischen Journalistin, der ich bei unserem Gespräch gern ins Gesicht geschaut hätte.
>
> [For the author, such criticisms fall on deaf ears [...] Should I have lived in Anna Funder's 'Stasiland'? The images in my memory, including the dark ones, provide a different puzzle-picture – one that has many more colours and nuances than those of the committed Australian journalist, whom I would have liked to be able to look in the face during our conversation.][19]

In the UK's *The Socialist Review*, fellow outsider Alasdair Smith attempted to problematize this issue further, stating:

> (Funder) is good at getting people to talk about their harrowing experiences. Occasionally she probes them to see how they interpret the destruction of the wall. It is this aspect that is perhaps the book's greatest weakness. Funder herself appears to have little understanding of the collapse of the Eastern Bloc beyond the conventional account of the 'fall of Communism' [...] She also fails to probe how people evaluate the new, united Germany and the 'free market' that promised so much. Ultimately this helps to reinforce the stereotype – West was good, East was bad.[20]

Funder often cites the forcible omission of a significant passage of *Stasiland* in the German translation as proof of the continued existence of some kind of Stasiland, whereby German society still represses the atrocities carried out by the Stasi. Her German publisher was sued by a group of ex-Stasi men due to the inclusion of a paragraph that made certain claims about their post-1989 activities.[21] In translation studies, this kind of omission falls under the broader notion of 're-writing', which Belgian translation theorist André Lefevere describes as actions undertaken by figures within the literary system who rewrite or alter texts with the aim of making them fit within the dominant (or one of many) ideological or 'poetological' (aesthetic) currents of their time. It serves to describe how certain 'patrons' – societal forces, generally driven by ideological concerns – can have a profound influence on the nature of the translation produced.[22] In her text, Funder recounts how she comes across the so-called *Insiderkomitee* or the 'Society for the Protection of Civil Rights and the Dignity of Man', which she admits to having already 'heard of' (84). She proceeds to describe in detail the kind of threats made by members of this group to various members of the public whom they feared may uncover them as former Stasi agents, including such things as delivering porn to unsuspecting wives, car brakes being cut and other acts (84). When EVA was sued by the 'Society for the Protection of Civil Rights and the Dignity of Man', which took offence at the passage, two rather sizeable paragraphs were removed from the German translation (page 90 of the Fischer version, see Table 10.1 below).[23]

The reaction from the German publisher – to bend to the demands of this group – highlights the very real sensitivity of this particular target audience to Funder's account, as well as perhaps its ongoing power in German society, despite the unrepresentative numbers. It also serves to underscore Funder's belief that 'the reworking of this history is incredibly difficult. The former Stasi men are very keen not to be portrayed as latter-day Nazi heirs, as thorough [sic]. Obviously the regime wasn't on a catastrophic scale so awful, but the level of detail was much, much greater'.[24] She claims that she was simply reporting things that had already appeared in *Der Spiegel* or had been publicly released, or that she had known those involved.[25] The effect of this omission in the German translation is not only to gloss over Funder's attempt to reveal this important 'level of detail', but also to illustrate the continued difficulties involved in the question of Germany's coming to terms with its recent past, particularly when communicated by an outsider. It also highlights how patronage of this kind still exists, more than two decades after the fall of the Wall.

Regarding the presentation of the GDR in literature and elsewhere, debate continues to rage over the use and validity of fact versus fiction. Professor of German literature at Oxford University Katrin Kohl distinguishes between the very diverse conceptualizations of the GDR that exist today, as history, fiction, museum, memory, ideal and threat. She regards works of fiction about the GDR as 'pressed into service to provide historical evidence'; these 'awaken'

Table 10.1 Material Omitted from the Second German Edition of *Stasiland*

Source text	Target text

The *Insiderkomitee*. Civil Rights and the Dignity of Man? I have heard of this group. It is a more or less secret society of former Stasi men who write papers putting their side of history, lobby for entitlements for former Stasi officers, and support one another if facing trial.
  They have close links to the successor party to the SED, the Party of Democratic Socialism, and it is alleged that together they may have access to the tens of millions of marks which belonged to the SED and remain unaccounted for.
  It is widely suspected, however, that these men also harass people who they fear may uncover them. A former border guard who appeared on a television talk show was threatened with an acid attack and had to be placed under police protection. Home-delivered to his doorstep; wives have had to sign for porn not ordered by their husbands. The strangest incident I heard of was when a man was delivered a truckload of puppies, yelping outside his door and the driver demanding a signature. Car brake-leads have been cut, accidents and deaths reverse-engineered. The child of an outspoken writer was picked up from school by a person or persons unknown and taken to drink hot chocolate, just for an hour or so. Detaining people clearly has its own pleasures; a habit hard to break. (84)
	Das Insiderkomitee. Ich habe von dieser Gruppe gehört. Es ist eine mehr oder weniger geheime Gesellschaft früherer Stasi-Männer, die Artikel schreiben, in denen sie ihre Seite der Geschichte darstellen, eine Lobby für die Ansprüche früherer Stasi-Offiziere, die sich gegenseitig unterstützen, wenn ihnen ein Gerichtsverfahren droht. (90) *Omitted*

the memories of former GDR citizens. For other readers, they become 'a "Zeugnis" (testimony) that goes beyond what an account of historical facts can provide'.[26] One could suggest that a work such as *Stasiland* does the same. In fact, *Stasiland* was initially conceived as a novel and submitted as part of Funder's master's thesis in creative writing at the University of Melbourne. This would feasibly account for its discernible likeness to fiction, an impression aided in part by the kind of peritextual material employed in the original edition. On the cover of the Australian edition (Fig. 10.1) a promotional by-line is provided by fellow Australian non-fiction writer Helen Garner, who declared it 'the kind of book that makes us love non-fiction'. In Australia, Garner is one of the pioneers of this genre, with the successful yet controversial *The First Stone* (1995) followed by *Joe Cinque's Consolation* (2004). The cover art (still used in subsequent Text Publishing editions in Australia), with its image of a striking young woman posed as if ready for a dance party, gazes directly at the viewer, subverting traditional covers of non-fiction and moving into the kind of conceptual territory usually reserved for the marketing of novels. Conversely, the interculturally 'translated' UK (Granta Books) and US editions (Harper Collins) use cover images that position the text more securely within traditional estimations of non-fiction. They are representative of a rather conventional approach to the marketing of a historical text, using instantly recognizable cultural markers of the GDR, including an image of Stasi files and a photo of guards atop the Berlin Wall. The original EVA edition used the same image as Text, while the first German Fischer version used popular

Figure 10.1 Cover of the Australian edition of *Stasiland* (Melbourne: Text, 2002).

Figure 10.2 Cover of the second German edition of *Stasiland* (Frankfurt/Main: Fischer Verlag, 2006).

GDR symbols images similar to the UK and US editions; the ubiquitous *Ampelmännchen* (figures from pedestrian signal lights) that were visible in the GDR and now have been implemented throughout the German capital. A more recent Fischer version (Fig. 10.2) employs the similarly recognizable image of the 'Trabi' or Trabant car sold in the GDR. It could be argued that the use of these images positions the text even more solidly within the realm of *Ostalgie* (indicating a glorification of or longing for the former East). Both the *Ampelmännchen* and Trabant cars are now extremely popular markers of East German culture, adorning T-shirts, stickers, fridge magnets and the like in tourist hubs throughout Berlin. The Granta and Harper editions also carry the longer title: *Stasiland: Stories from behind the Berlin Wall*.

Contextualizing *Stasiland*

Funder's text was published in the early 2000s when accounts – fictional or otherwise – about East Germany were relatively limited. Timothy Garton Ash's

The File (1997), an autobiographical account of life as a British student in Berlin in the 1970s and '80s (and a subject of Stasi investigation), is perhaps the best-known English-language forerunner to Funder's *Stasiland*, although it never reached the same level of popularity. Berlin author Thomas Brussig's 1999 novel *Am kürzeren Ende der Sonnenalle* (*At the Shorter End of Sonnenallee*) was hugely popular in Germany and made into a successful film by Leander Hausmann in the same year but was never widely released in other markets. Hensel's *Zonenkinder* (2002) and Rusch's *Meine freie Deutsche Jugend* (2003) also fall into this category, although the latter did not experience any success in Anglophone markets. Wolfgang Becker's film *Good Bye, Lenin!* (2003), on the other hand, had vast international appeal, reaching large audiences in the Anglophone world. *Good Bye, Lenin!* is essentially a comedic text, which provided many audiences with their first real taste of life behind the Wall and adopted an upbeat perspective on life in the former GDR – the focus is often on everyday aspects of GDR life such as foodstuffs and cultural activities, many of which disappeared after the fall of the Wall – while simultaneously grappling with the gravity of its deficiencies. These texts are often assigned the label *Ostalgie*. Yet as Gareth Dale contends, while *Good Bye, Lenin!* thematizes *Ostalgie* (as does *Sonnenallee*), it is in fact an antithesis of a typical *Ostalgie* film, as 'it does critically engage with the past, and with the *Ostalgie* phenomenon itself'.[27] Katharina Gerstenberger argues that 'writers trying to present truthful accounts of East Berlin and East Germany must confront nostalgic idealization of East Germany'[28] and Anna comments briefly and perhaps necessarily on *Ostalgie* in *Stasiland* (123, 252).

But it is Funder's staunchly factual presentation of the GDR as a Stasiland that is raised again and again in German reviews of the book; this is often traced back to her foreignness, her Australianness. In 'Die Lady, die Opfer und die Täter: Mit australischem Blick – Anna Funders Stasiland beschreibt deutsche Lebenslügen' ('The Lady, the Victims and the Perpetrators: From an Australian Perspective – Anna Funder's *Stasiland* Depicts German Myths'), journalist Marko Martin attempted to problematize Funder's perspective on the GDR by referring to Australia as a distant land that had never had to struggle with questions about ideology.

> Ist so etwas dem Glück der größeren Distanz von Down Under geschuldet, der Abwesenheit von Ideologien auf dem fünften Kontinent? Kommt Anna Funder also aus einer Art gelobtem Land, wo Pragmatismus kein Euphemismus für Mitläufertum, sondern eher ein Synonym für Fairness ist?
>
> [Does this happen because those Down Under have the benefit of being so far away; is there an absence of ideologies on the fifth continent? Does Anna Funder come from such a promised land, where pragmatism is not a euphemism for merely following, but rather a synonym for fairness?][29]

Predictably, much is made of Funder's Australianness in these reviews and interviews, including Terry Lane's question cited at the beginning of this chapter. All of these comments seem to reinforce Martin's problem with Funder's approach to the topic: that the distance between the perhaps inconceivable goings-on in one of the strongest regimes of socialism in the Western world, and a relatively detached, democratic nation all the way 'Down Under' is in some way insurmountable. Funder has of course claimed that her 'distance' or 'outsider status' was crucial to her ability to elicit the stories that form her text. Yet to what extent was her outsider status aided by the fact that Australia is often still regarded as – in historian Geoffrey Blainey's words – a land 'on the opposite side of the globe [… where its] people seemed to walk upside down'?[30] Even the use of the phrase 'Down Under', as well as the reference to Funder's 'geographical distance' in the review from *Die Welt*, aptly perpetuates the still-common European perception of Australia as a remote and even inferior land.

In the *Hamburger Abendblatt*, attention was again drawn to Funder's outsider status, with the cautionary heading: 'Der kühle Blick von außen. *Stasiland*: Das Buch einer Australierin über den Stasi-Terror und Erinnerungen daran. Kann sie als Außenstehende gerechter urteilen?' ('The Cool Perspective from Outside. *Stasiland*: An Australian's Book about the Stasi Terror and Its Memories. Can She, as an Outsider, Judge Fairly?'). Matthias Gretzschel wrote: 'Schon als ich die Druckfahnen las, hatte ich den Eindruck, dass das meiste zwar stimmt, gut recherchiert und vorzüglich geschrieben ist, am Ende für mich aber unbefriedigend bleibt' (After reading the proofs I already had the impression that although most of it was probably true, well-researched and excellently written, in the end it was disappointing). Gretzschel, who stated in his review that he hailed from the former East, found it difficult to accept the world Funder presents:

> Funder sagt, sie wolle zeigen, wie das DDR-Regime funktioniert und was dieses Funktionieren an Opfern gekostet habe. Damit hat sie ja Recht, und ich ärgere mich, weil es mir nicht gelingt, ihr begreiflich zu machen, dass ich die DDR nicht nur so, sondern eben oft auch ganz anders erlebt habe.
>
> [Funder says that she wants to show how the GDR regime functioned, and what this functioning cost in terms of victims. In that sense, she is right, and it makes me angry, because I haven't succeeded in making clear to her that the GDR wasn't only like that, but that I often experienced it in a totally different way.][31]

In a way, Funder's text aims to counteract such 'positive' impressions of East German life; she has been openly critical of *Good Bye, Lenin!* and other *Ostalgie* films as presenting 'romanticised, completely fictitious, fun versions of a dictatorship',[32] taking issue with the portrayal of the Stasi as anything beyond the compliant men she interviewed when researching *Stasiland*. In an article written for *The Guardian* in 2007, in which she discusses West German filmmaker Florian Henckel von Donnersmarck's Oscar award-winning film *Das Leben der Anderen* (*The Lives of Others*), Funder is particularly uncomfortable with the film's 'fantasy narrative that could not have taken place (and never did) under the GDR dictatorship'. Moreover, she claims: 'the film has, then, an odd relation to historical truth, a truth that is being bitterly fought for now'.[33] Again, Funder appears fiercely defensive of the way in which so-called historical truth is presented in relation to the GDR. Garton Ash also reviewed *The Lives of Others* for the *New York Review of Books*. He is equally critical of several 'factual inaccuracies' but ultimately contends:

> The point is that this is a movie. It uses the syntax and conventions of Hollywood to convey to the widest possible audience some part of the truth about life under the Stasi, and the larger truths that experience revealed about human nature. It mixes historical fact (several of the Stasi locations are real and most of the terminology and tradecraft is accurate) with the ingredients of a fast-paced thriller and love story.[34]

With so much emphasis in the epitextual material placed on Funder's Australianness and her passage from Australia to Germany – via the character of Anna but also via the translation from English into German – the interculturality of the text itself also comes into question, as well as *Stasiland*'s transition from its (source) English-speaking context into its (target) German-speaking one. Although the original text is set in post-1989 Germany, it is narrated by a young Australian woman who is culturally and linguistically 'fluent', the figures she speaks to are mainly East German and therefore it is the source text that contains inherently foreign material. This means that the translation (the target text) contains material largely familiar to German readers – the opposite of the usual translation equation, whereby 'through the foreign works, features [...] are introduced into the home literature which did not exist there before'.[35] Whilst the reader is aware of Anna's Australianness at the outset, Funder rarely stresses this aspect in the text, conducting her interviews and conversations in German (she also imports a lot of German words and expressions), the content of which is mediated by Anna; somehow, the source text becomes an act of translation in itself. Seldom does she use Australian expressions or references. Her mention of 'a map of Tasmania' (169), which is a colloquial expression denoting a woman's pubic hair, is one rare instance, but this is omitted from the target text (it is unclear why). A reference (146) to 'our Dawnie' (the Olympic swimmer, Dawn Fraser) is translated as 'unsere Dawnie' (153) in an amusing scene where Anna dodges wayward German swimmers at the local pool – although in no way an expert swimmer, in contrast to the Germans she feels as strong and fast as Dawn Fraser. Here it could be said that the idea of Anna's outsider status, to which she frequently refers in epitextual material about the text, trickles through somewhat; despite her bilingual and bicultural competence, she still feels in some way different or detached from the Germans and, arguably, their history. References to the vastly different political contexts of Australia and East Germany are highlighted on occasions – for example when Anna comments: 'If easterners thought about Australia at all, it was an imaginary place to go in the event of a nuclear catastrophe' (80), or later, 'I think he hopes, through me, to sow the seeds of socialism in an untainted corner of the world' (84). There are echoes here of comments made in some of the German reviews about *Stasiland*. Finally, despite Anna's ability to penetrate German culture via her ability to speak German, Julia tells her that she doesn't look German: her hair, her eyes are not the 'right' colour (90). All of these references, albeit minor, serve to reinforce Anna's outsider status to readers of the text, who may understandably lose themselves in the factual and German-centric world Anna creates.

In the German translation, however, the Germanic aspects that are so foreign to source text readers have no alienating effect on target readers – the setting, the language, much of the content is familiar – thus the necessary concessions Funder applies in order to account for the uninformed 'implied' English-speaking reader are also omitted. For example, when Funder explains terminology specific to the GDR, she usually includes the German term and provides an English translation, such as: 'Leipzig was the hub of what everyone now calls *die Wende* – the Turning Point' (5). Naturally, in the German translation, these explanations are not needed and as such, the foreignness of the source text is somewhat (necessarily) reduced. But what becomes most obvious when reading the target against the source text is the number of factual inaccuracies found in Funder's original – a text that flaunts itself as non-fiction – that are then corrected in the translation. These are detailed in Table 10.2.

In 2010 Funder published her second book, *All That I Am*, about a group of anti-Hitler activists, which is her first novel. In an interview titled 'Facts and Fiction Tricky for Funder', she reports: 'This novel has been fact-checked out of its mind […] There's a tea-drinking scene, and the London editor told me such people would not have put the milk in first, so I had to change it'.[36] The errors present in *Stasiland* are not necessarily ones that source text readers would pick up on – they may not even be regarded as important by some. But the thorny question remains: in a non-fiction text, where the author is

Table 10.2 Corrections Made from the English to German Editions of *Stasiland*

Source text	Target text
The death of a Communist in a skirmish in Berlin prompted the Party to order revenge. On **8 August**, at a demonstration at Bülowplatz, Mielke and another man killed the local police chief and his off-sider by shooting them in the back at point-blank range. (58)	Der Tod eines Kommunisten 1931 bei einem Geplänkel in Berlin bewegte die Partei zu unverzüglicher Rache. Bei einer Demonstration auf dem Bülowplatz **am 9. August** ermordete Mielke, zusammen mit einem anderen Mann, den örtlichen Polizeichef und seinen Fahrer durch Schüsse in den Rücken aus nächster Nähe. (65)
In **1937** he was arrested by the Gestapo and sentenced to ten years. (59)	**1939** wurde er von der Gestapo verhaftet und zu zehn Jahren Gefängnis verurteilt. (66)
When Mikhail Gorbachev came to power in the Soviet Union in 1985 he implemented the policies of *perestroika* (economic reform) and *glasnost* ('openness' of speech). In **June 1988** he declared a principle of freedom of choice for governments within the Eastern Bloc and renounced the use of Soviet military force to prop them up. (61)	Als 1985 Michail Gorbatschow in der Sowjetunion an die Macht kam, leitete er eine Politik der *Perestroika* und *Glasnost* ein. **1989** hob er die Breschnew Doktrin auf und ließ später freie Wahlen in den sozialistischen Ländern zu, ohne das Militär einzusetzen. (68)
On **17 October** Honecker was ousted by his deputy Egon Krenz, who, although younger, was just as disliked. (65)	Am **18 Oktober** wurde Honecker von seinem Stellvertreter Egon Krenz aus dem Amt verdrängt, der, obwohl viel jünger, nicht weniger unbeliebt war. (72)
In August 1961, a fresh Stasi recruit named Hagen Koch walked the streets of Berlin with a tin of paint and a brush, and painted the line where the Wall would go. He was twenty-one years old, and he was **Secretary-General Honecker's personal cartographer**. (155)	Im August 1961 ging der frish rekruierte Stasi-Mann Hagen Koch mit einer Dose Farbe und einem Pinsel durch die Straßen von Berlin und zog die Linie, auf der die Mauer entlanggehen sollte. Er war einundzwanzig und **persönlicher Kartenzeichner von Walter Ulbricht**. (163)
In **1948** they handed over these institutions to the newly created Federal Republic of Germany (West Germany) together with massive injections of funds from the Americans' Marshall Plan. (160)	**1949** wurde die Bundesrepublik Deutschland gegründet, die durch den Marshallplan große finanzielle Unterstützung erhielt. (168)
By **February 1946** Heinz Koch [...] **In October of that year**, the first 'free democratic' elections were held in East Germany. (162)	**Im Februar 1946** wurde Heinz Koch [...] **Im Oktober 1949** wurden die ersten freien demokratischen' Wahlen in Ostdeutschland abgehalten. (169)

clearly comfortable with her material and openly fastidious about presenting her stories as historically accurate, why do these errors exist in the first place? Here, there are obvious parallels between the critical assessment of *Stasiland* and texts such as *The Lives of Others*. The question of historical accuracy, which Funder herself has drawn attention to, arises in the evaluation of both texts, despite their different genres. Daniela Berghahn, who has written extensively on the topic of cinema in East Germany, argues that historical films (she names *Downfall, Sophie Scholl – The Final Days, Schindler's List*, among others) are essentially about entertainment and are not meant as 'historical documentaries or history lessons'.[37] However, there will always be those who argue that such texts do play a part in education, particularly for audiences who may have little to no knowledge about the precise historical context of such periods or events.

What is perhaps most troubling about Funder's presentation of the GDR in *Stasiland* is the way in which Funder positions herself in regard to the East German past, not only in discussing the text but also in the many interviews and commentaries she provides on things related to East Germany. She displays an almost brutal rigidity when it comes to 'remembering' or 'recollecting' the past. For example, in her review of *The Lives of Others*, she writes:

> [T]he terrible truth is that the Stasi provide no material for an expression of belief in humanity. For demonstrations of conscience or courage, one would need to look at the resisters. And it is this choice – to make a film about the change of heart of a Stasi man – that turns *The Lives of Others*, for some, into an inappropriate plea for the absolution of the perpetrators.[38]

Garton Ash, reviewing the same film for *The New York Review of Books*, contends:

> Now I have heard of Stasi informers who ended up protecting those they were informing on. I know of full-time Stasi operatives who became disillusioned, especially during the 1980s. And in many hours of talking to former Stasi officers, I never met a single one who I felt to be, simply and plainly, an evil man. Weak, blinkered, opportunistic, self-deceiving, yes; men who did evil things, most certainly; but always I glimpsed in them the remnants of what might have been, the good that could have grown in other circumstances.[39]

Moreover, Garton Ash believes that 'the net effect of *The Lives of Others* will not, after all, be to unleash a wave of worldwide sympathy for former Stasi officers' (as Funder implies). Instead, he claims 'it will be to bring home the horrors of that system, in a stylized fashion, to viewers who would have known little or nothing about them before'.⁴⁰ Perhaps this is in a similar way to which *Ostalgie* films such as *Good Bye, Lenin!* do not solely romanticize a particular 'version' of East Germany, but highlight, via this precise trope, the sadness of life in a land where politics tore families and individuals apart.

With *Stasiland* continuing to be an international best-seller, translated into 16 languages, published in 20 countries and appearing on numerous text lists in Australia, the UK and America, such questions are no doubt important ones. Through her Australian eyes, Funder has managed to not only construct a text about a so-called reality of the GDR but to prompt worldwide discussions on the advantages or disadvantages of observing a sensitive past from outside. In a sense, she has created a well-oiled marketing machine, not only providing countless interviews to promote her books but also writing regular commentaries for publications around the world, specifically *The Monthly* in Australia and, with the late Anna Politkovskaya, for the Norwegian magazine *Ny Tid*. In her writing, Funder continues to knit together issues related to Germany's complicated history, fusing together ideas about political insurgency and courage – themes central to both *Stasiland* and her Miles Franklin award-winning novel *All That I Am*. In this, her latest book, published in Germany in 2014 as *Alles was ich bin*, she tackles another true story, but claims to take a strictly fictionalized route. Again, she juxtaposes Australia (the protagonist and émigré Ruth lives in modern-day Sydney) with Germany (in the lead up to the Second World War). In reviews, however, the novel seems to invite similar questions to those posed about *Stasiland*. Joanna Kavenna, reviewing *All That I Am* in *The Observer*, finds Funder's 'claims of authenticity, of "reconstruction"[…] risky and complicating'.⁴¹ And, according to Rachel Cusk in *The Guardian*, '[w]hat is truth and what is fiction remains frustratingly unclear in this novel based on a real-life tale of wartime resistance'.⁴² While Funder this time deals with Nazism and removes herself from the narrative – she must be aware that she is on safer ground here – there still appear to be problems with her presentation of history. Yet in her introduction to *All That I Am*, she writes: 'I have made connections and suppositions, for that I take full responsibility.' Perhaps, despite the safer ground, Funder has realized that writing from afar is not without its risks.

Notes

1 Anna Funder, *Stasiland* (Melbourne: Text, 2002).
2 Terry Lane, 'Big Ideas: Terry Lane Interviews Anna Funder', *Australian Broadcasting Corporation*, 14 May 2006.
3 Ibid.
4 Anna Funder, '*Stasiland*: Writing a World Gone Wrong', *The Sydney Papers* (Autumn 2002).

5 Kate Mitchell, 'The Migratory Imagination: Anna Funder's *Stasiland* as Prosthetic Memory', *Crossings: Journal of Migration and Culture* 4, no. 1 (2013): 91–110 (96–99).
6 Lee Gutkind, *The Art of Creative Nonfiction: Writing and Selling the Literature of Reality* (New York: Wiley, 1997), 12.
7 Sue Joseph, 'Australian Creative Non-Fiction: Perspectives and Opinions', Ejournalist.com, 40, accessed 6 January 2012, http://ejournalist.com.au/v11n2/Joseph.pdf.
8 Vanessa Thorpe, 'Story of the Stasi Holds Secret of a Bestseller', *The Observer*, 27 June 2004.
9 Quoted in http://annafunder.com/stasiland/media-stasiland/, accessed 6 January 2014.
10 Beata Josephi and Christine Müller, 'Differently Drawn Boundaries of the Permissible in German and Australian Literary Journalism', *Literary Journalism Studies* 1, no. 1 (2009): 67–78 (74).
11 Quoted in http://www.fischerverlage.de/buch/stasiland/9783596167463, accessed 6 January 2014.
12 Terry Lane, 'Big Ideas'.
13 'A Stranger in the East', *The Daily Telegraph*, 7 June 2004.
14 Ibid.
15 Ibid.
16 Eva Behrendt, 'Gehorsame graue Männer' ('Obedient Grey Men'), *Die Tageszeitung*, 5 May 2004.
17 *Stasiland*, 187.
18 Gert Reifarth, 'Born in the GDR', *Meanjin* 66, no. 2 (2007): 164–71 (165).
19 Matthias Gretzschel, 'Der Kühle Blick von außen. Stasiland: Das Buch einer Australierin über den Stasi-Terror und Erinnerungen daran. Kann sie als Außenstehende gerechter urteilen?' ('The Cool Perspective from Outside. *Stasiland*: An Australian's Book about the Stasi Terror and Its Past'), *Hamburger Abendblatt*, 26 March 2004.
20 Alasdair Smith, 'Really Existing Big Brother', *The Socialist Review*, July 2004.
21 Terry Lane, 'Big Ideas'.
22 André Lefevere, *Translation, Rewriting and the Manipulation of Literary Fame* (New York: Routledge, 1992).
23 Anna Funder, *Stasiland*, trans. Harald Rieman (Frankfurt/Main: Fischer Taschenbuch Verlag, 2006).
24 Terry Lane, 'Big Ideas'.
25 Ibid.
26 Katrin Kohl, 'Conceptualizing the GDR: 20 Years After', *Oxford German Studies* 38, no. 3 (2009): 265–77 (269).
27 Gareth Dale, 'Heimat, "Ostalgie" and the Stasi: The GDR in German Cinema, 1999–2006', *Debatte: Journal of Contemporary Central and Eastern Europe* 15, no. 2 (2007): 155–75 (166).
28 Katharina Gerstenberger, *Writing the New Berlin: The German Capital in Post-Wall Literature* (Rochester, NY: Camden House, 2008), 134.
29 Marko Martin, 'Die Lady, die Opfer und die Täter: Mit australischem Blick – Anna Funders Stasiland beschreibt deutsche Lebenslügen' ('The Lady, the Victims and the Perpetrators: From an Australian Perspective – Anna Funder's *Stasiland* Depicts German Myths'), *Die Welt*, 27 March 2004.
30 Geoffrey Blainey, *The Tyranny of Distance: How Distance Shaped Australia's History*, 21st century ed. (Sydney: Pan Macmillan, 2001), 320.

31 Matthias Gretzschel, 'Der kühle Blick von außen'.
32 Terry Lane, 'Big Ideas'.
33 Anna Funder, 'Tyranny of Terror', *The Guardian*, 5 May 2007.
34 Timothy Garton Ash, 'The Stasi on Our Minds', *The New York Review of Books*, 31 May 2007.
35 Itamar Evan-Zohar, 'The Position of Translated Literature within the Literary Polysystem', in *The Translation Studies Reader*, ed. Lawrence Venuti (New York: Routledge, 2012, 3rd edition), 162–67 (163).
36 Stephan Romei, 'Facts and Fiction Tricky for Funder', *The Australian*, 26 August 2011.
37 Daniela Berghahn, 'Remembering the Stasi in a Fairy Tale of Redemption: Florian Henckel von Donnersmarck's *Das Leben der Anderen*', *Oxford German Studies* 38, no. 3 (2009): 321–33 (323).
38 Anna Funder, 'Eyes without a Face', *Sight and Sound* 17, no. 5 (2007): 16–20 (18).
39 Timothy Garton Ash, 'The Stasi on Our Minds'.
40 Ibid.
41 Joanna Kavenna, '"All That I Am" by Anna Funder', review in *The Observer*, 4 September 2011.
42 Rachel Cusk, '"All That I Am" by Anna Funder', review in *The Guardian*, 16 September 2011.

Chapter 11

'BECAUSE IT WAS EXOTIC, BECAUSE IT WAS SO FAR AWAY': BERNHARD SCHELLER IN CONVERSATION WITH CHRISTINA SPITTEL

Dr Bernhard Scheller studied English and German at Karl-Marx Universität Leipzig in the 1960s and then taught English and some Australian literature until his retirement in 1993. His 1986 professorial thesis (*Habilitationsschrift*) on Australian drama is one of three substantial theses of research on Australian literature to emerge from the GDR, alongside Erich Gronke's dissertation on Henry Handel Richardson (Humboldt Universität Berlin, 1952) and Helmut Findeisen's on James Aldridge (Karl-Marx Universität Leipzig, ca. 1958).[1] In his bibliography Scheller lists a number of smaller theses (*Diplomarbeiten*) on Australian literature produced by Leipzig undergraduates under his supervision in the 1970s and 1980s.

Scheller agreed to meet me in his favourite café in Windmühlenstraße, Leipzig, just a couple of tram stops from the city centre, to talk about his experiences researching and teaching Australian literature in the GDR as well as his involvement in editing work.

He arrives, under his arm one of the slim, light-brown editions of Reclam Leipzig's *Voss*, to which he wrote the afterword. He quickly spots me: next to my coffee lies Hans Petersen's bright orange *Erkundungen: 31 australische Erzähler*. The café is alive with students who are chatting, reading, typing on their laptops, and Scheller clearly feels at home in this vibrant atmosphere, although he is also a little bemused that these young men and women should be just a few clicks away from the rest of the world. (The café has wireless Internet.) A few minutes into our conversation, he relaxes and orders a beer. What follows is a transcript of my recording, translated and slightly edited for readability and augmented by details Scheller has since provided over the phone.

You studied English in the German Democratic Republic?
Yes, and that came a bit out of the blue, really. I completed my *Abitur* in Altenburg, a small town in Thuringia in 1962. At that time we all had to learn a trade before going on to university, to gain an appreciation for the world of work. So I went to a printer's and trained to become a typesetter, with good old metal type. That doesn't even exist anymore. But at the same time, I applied to go to university to become a teacher of English and German. You could study English in Jena, Greifswald, Berlin, Leipzig, Rostock, and the Pädagogische Hochschule, Potsdam, and I sent off several applications. When Leipzig University accepted me, this also meant that the two-year apprenticeship only lasted for a year. My study at Leipzig got extended when the departing head of our institute, Professor Martin, came to watch me teach a class at school during my teaching prac. I was doing a Shakespeare play with my year-twelves. I wasn't much older than them, really, and some teachers found it hard to tell us apart. Professor Martin liked what I was doing so much that he told his colleagues in the department, 'You've got to take him.' And then I stayed at Leipzig University, and taught there for thirty years until 1993.

Can you still remember which play it was?
I have been thinking about that. It might have been *Macbeth*. That was usually on the school curriculum; we had a national curriculum. But I'm not sure now. My favourite Shakespeare play is *Hamlet*.

Mine too. Shakespeare was published well in the GDR, of course. But can you tell me how you got hold of other reading?
Well, we read a lot in German, including things we weren't meant to read, even as students of English – Orwell, for example, who wasn't published in the GDR. We had a couple of West German editions of *1984* and *Animal Farm* and swapped those between us. Some of us also stole books from the Leipzig Book Fair. West German publishers were well aware of that and stocked their stalls accordingly. Sometimes the person minding the books would look away, just at the right moment, and then a book would be snatched up. But I didn't dare to do that, really. It was hard to get hold of English-language texts, apart from the Seven Seas books, which were sold in the international bookshop. [Australian/British writer and journalist] James Aldridge, for example, was available that way. Other than that, you just had to use what was available in German, really, so when I taught a later-year subject on the Australian short story in the 1980s, I mainly used Hans Petersen's *Australische Erzähler: Von Marcus Clarke bis Patrick White*, a beautiful anthology.[2] Lawson is in there too, of course. The short story is the genre of the pioneer society, really; and those Australian short stories are good. And full of suspense. Teaching that was a lot of fun and the students enjoyed it too. Stefan Welz, one of my former students, is now professor of English literature at Leipzig University.

Can you remember the most popular short stories in your Australian literature classes?
'Cheery Soul', Patrick White's long novella, wasn't a hit, but Marcus Clarke was popular, as was 'The Funerals of Malachi Mooney'.[3] Quite funny. They're so drunk that they forget to take the dead body with them to the cemetery. And so they have to repeat the entire funeral. That story was really popular. But I'd always been a theatre enthusiast, so I really threw myself at drama. I've always preferred reading plays or lyrical poetry over long, long novels.

And you wrote your PhD thesis on drama too…
Yes, but that started much earlier, with my *Diplomarbeit*, the thesis with which I concluded my undergraduate degree. I wrote about Edward Albee. I had to do my compulsory military service straight after finishing my degree, and when I went to the army, I coped with the stupidity of it all by translating *Cymbeline*, one of Shakespeare's more obscure plays. When I got back from the army, we put that on with Leipzig University's student theatre group in a massive effort involving a team of 30. I shortened the play's text, of course. Our twenty performances were all sold out. And my PhD thesis was about contemporary English and American drama on the GDR stage, from 1961, when the wall was built, until 1973, when I was writing.

And then in the 1980s, for your next research project, your Habilitation, the qualification required for professorship in German academia, you tackled Australian theatre.
Yes, exactly. I wanted to do something out of the ordinary. And my boss, Eberhard Brüning, who was very interested in theatre himself, put me onto Australian drama. He said that that was an unstudied field, and I could break some new ground. I had a great time, collecting my materials, and interviewing directors across the GDR – Joachim Tenschert, for example, who put on Brecht's *Mutter Courage* in Melbourne.[4]

Australian drama was barely published in the GDR…
There were three plays. Two by Mona Brand, *Stranger in the Land* and *Here under Heaven*, and then a Proletarian play by Frank Hardy, *Black Diamonds*. And they were being performed, at least in the 1950s. And the *Schauspielführer* (*Drama Guide*) initially lists them under Australia, and later under England/Ireland, and then they drop out altogether. The 1980s *Schauspielführer* (*Drama Guide*) includes none of these plays.

You write about Brand and Hardy's work but also about so much else: early twentieth-century playwright Louis Esson, and then mid-century writers Ray Lawler, Jack Hibberd, Alan Seymour, David Williamson, Alexander Buzo, Barry Oakley, Patrick White, Hal Porter […] How did you get hold of the materials that make up your thesis?
Through interlibrary loans from Australia, from libraries around the world […] and everything that had been translated into German in the Federal Republic

came from there. It was possible to request international interlibrary loans if you could demonstrate that you needed them for academic purposes. I read all of that here in Leipzig in the *Deutsche Bücherei*, which is now the *Deutsche Nationalbibliothek*. And then the Australian Embassy helped us out. When they closed up in Friedrichstraße in East Berlin, and moved to Warsaw, they donated their entire library to our institute, just in time for me to finish the thesis.[5] Those books are now in the university library. I also wrote letters with Bahumir Wongar. Wongar's not a real Aborigine, but a Yugoslav who's lived with the 'blacks'. But I also discovered two real Aborigines – I can't think of their names now – who also wrote plays.[6] And then I just explored everything, and interviewed every Australian I could catch.

Were there any?
We had two at our university, Robert Spence and Philip Gould. They taught English language classes in the 1980s for five or six years, in what was then the Department of Theoretical and Applied Linguistics. We were friends […] Australia is so close now. Back then it was a little exotic. There's a wonderful travel book [about Australia] by the Russian writer Daniil Granin, *Vier Wochen mit den Beinen nach oben* (*Four Weeks with Your Legs Up*). It came out in the GDR too. It's such a charming book. You should read that if you have time.[7]

I think you also thank Hans Petersen from Volk und Welt in your acknowledgements. Did you have much contact with him when you were writing your thesis?
Not much. He could often get hold of books more easily than I could, but we didn't have very close contact. We wrote letters and spoke on the phone. I don't have a clear recollection of him as a person. I know that he was working on an edition of Australian plays in the 1980s. I would have liked to help him with that. But then that didn't come out, I don't know why. There was quite a lot of drama published in the GDR, but then it was all over. These days this has virtually died off, as a genre. The theatres are all in a crisis. And people just want novels, novels, and more novels. Even my students, whom I had to torment with drama, they'd much rather read novels.

You've mentioned teaching Australian short stories to your students who disliked Patrick White but loved nineteenth-century writers Edward Dyson and Marcus Clarke. Did you get to teach much Australian literature?
Not that much, apart from the short stories. My guiding star was Shakespeare, of course. I was *Oberassistent* at Professor Seehase's Chair for English Literature and just had to follow the curriculum; we didn't have that much freedom. So I started off teaching Shakespeare, until Seehase found out that he could get onto the board of the *Shakespeare-Gesellschaft* (*Shakespeare Society*) and then he took over Shakespeare himself.[8] I always taught an introduction to drama, a course

that I really enjoyed teaching, a unit on contemporary British literature after 1945, and from the 1980s, a really popular later-year course on Australian short stories. It took a long time to collect material about Australia, for me to order all the books via interlibrary loans, and for them to finally arrive. My dear Lord. But I supervised a number of final theses on Australian topics. I had a whole catalogue of topics in mind, and while students didn't have to stick with a topic I suggested, they were generally enthusiastic. Juliane Lochner wrote on Jack Hibberd, for example, and there were a few other students working mainly on Australian drama, on socialist realist plays, say, but also on Patrick White as a dramatist. I also recall supervising a thesis about novels, Cusack, Prichard and so on. I actually wanted to expand this work on Australian literature a little bit; it really interested me, and I had Professor Brüning's support.

And the students were keen?
Yes, I could motivate them. Because it was exotic, because it was so far away, because that's where the GDR citizens' longing to be far away, their travel trauma, came into play. News about Australia was scarce in the mediocre newspapers. Once, *Neues Deutschland* reported briefly that Marlene Dietrich had broken a leg in Sydney. That was a sensation. Not least because she had such beautiful legs. Well insured, probably.

And then you were involved in the publication of Voss *by Reclam Leipzig. The afterword bears your name.*
This type of work almost came with the job. When you were working in an English department in the GDR, you'd find yourself reviewing books, and involved in their publication. I really enjoyed that, quite apart from the fact that it provided additional income and of course, you received a copy of the book as well! I had a very good relationship with Reclam Leipzig, although I did some work with Insel Verlag too. I was on first-name terms with Gabriele Bock, Reclam's literary editor, and we met often. I did a lot of work for her. Gabriele gave me lots of authors; sometimes I produced an entire edition of a work; sometimes I just wrote an afterword. I did William Golding, who then went on to win the Nobel Prize. We were there first, before that happened, with our edition of *Pincher Martin*, and that immediately went into a reprint when he won the prize. Then I did Dylan Thomas, *Brave New World* by Huxley and some Americans – Jack Kerouac, Alan Sillitoe, James Baldwin – and Nobel laureate Patrick White was really overdue. He'd been published in West Germany in the fifties, but not here, funnily enough. Australian literature was always a bit 'down under'; the Mother Country didn't really take note of it. But why he came out so late here I really don't know. They could have published him much earlier. Gabi Bock asked me: 'So what shall we publish of Patrick White?' And I said, '*Voss*, of course.' Because of that German fox, Leichhardt.

An explorer whom the GDR adored …
Yes, that's right. There was a *Leichhardt Komittee*, and then a conference, where I spoke about *Voss*. So really, the time was ripe for *Voss*. That was towards the end of the GDR, in the mid-eighties, when everything was collapsing ideologically, and things were very open. And there was nothing to indicate that White was an undesirable author. But we still needed several reader's reports.

Do you still remember what you liked about Voss*?*
I once forced myself to read several long novels of Thomas Mann's. And I just discovered parallels in the complexity of their writing. My boss, Brüning, had to write a reader's report for *Voss* and he was bitterly disappointed that this should be such a psychologically complex novel, subtly reflecting on classes and social strata. He wanted a proper adventure novel about Leichhardt.

À la Marcus Clarke.
Yes, exactly. That was what he was expecting. But he did write a very good, glowing report.[9] Only that I do think he was a little bored with the book. I wasn't. I didn't much enjoy writing the afterword, though; it seemed so unnecessary. When I wrote these, I always tried to include lots of biographical information about the author and keep my own interpretations of a text, my own readings, to a minimum.

Apart from Voss, *did you have your eyes on other Australian texts that you would have liked to see published?*
Yes, I would have liked to assist Hans Petersen with his selection of plays, to support him. But we weren't that close. I actually don't know whether he read my thesis.

Your thesis makes recommendations for the theatre, for plays to put on. Do you know whether any of your recommendations were taken up?
No, I don't. Here in Leipzig we had our own theatre, a student theatre, the Ballhaus. And there we played whatever I wanted: my translation of *Cymbeline*, but before that, we played Edward Albee, who had been the subject of my *Diplomarbeit*. We did *Bethy Smith*, then *Zoo Story* a little later – we performed that over 100 times – and then *Sandbox*. I wanted to do a production of *Who's Afraid of Virginia Woolf* too, but that was just too big a challenge for our amateur actors.

And what about Australian authors?
None. I don't like Mona Brand's plays. They were a bit tendentious, blunt. They are psychological chamber plays, really, and they just don't have enough psychological depth. That's where I just prefer Eugene O'Neil and Tennessee Williams and Edward Albee. And all our performances were in German. English would have been too elitist.

Were you allowed to travel?
Yes, to a point. I went with the student theatre to the Federal Republic in 1968 for the 150th birthday of Karl Marx. And we found ourselves in all the unrest. That was very exciting. From then on I could always travel. A small study trip to Leeds, Yorkshire, in 1974. Short trips to London and Edinburgh. My time in the army interrupted all this. The student theatre group kept travelling to the West. And I was at the base and suffered.

While your translation of Shakespeare's Cymbeline *was keeping you company.*
Yes, that was my comfort, my counsel, my support, my psychological assistance amongst all this stupidity. I had always had invitations, but in the 1980s they didn't let me travel anymore. I didn't want to collaborate with the Stasi. After the fall of the Wall I travelled like crazy! I designed a little workshop where I produced Edward Albee's *Sandbox*, first with Stanislawsky's method, then with Brecht's. And that workshop was so popular I ran it from Liverpool to Innsbruck. I really can't remember all the places I went. Hence the burn-out. I was very sick, and so the doctors recommended early retirement. That was fine with me, really. I could improve my pension with translations and reviews; afterwords were no longer required. I didn't make it to Australia in the end, although I always wanted to. I did plan a world trip, on ship, but I can't do that for health reasons. I can't be away from the doctors for that long.

Do you still remember the first Australian book you read?
Marcus Clarke, in German, *Lebenslänglich* (*For the Term of His Natural Life*). That was a cracker. We read that when we were children. This is such a creepy, exciting read. It had an enormous print run. It was *the* adventure novel, really, alongside Jack London, of course. And I read that as a child. I was scared to death.

And do you remember the first Australian book you read in English?
If only I knew […] That's a difficult question. James Aldridge, perhaps. In a Seven Seas edition, probably. You could buy them. There was an international bookshop that sold them. But Seven Seas did mostly novels. And I wanted to read plays, or poetry.

Do you still read Australian books today?
If it's poetry.

Petersen published a volume of Judith Wright's poetry, right at the very end.
Yes, in the Weiße Reihe.[10] I'm really not much of a reader anymore; I can't concentrate as well as I used to. I did read *Meanjn Quarterly* for a while. Brüning got that sent to him and passed it on to me. That was possible.

[They're playing Louis Armstrong in the small café where we sit. Scheller hums along.]
The first American to visit the GDR, I think.

Did Australian writers ever come to Leipzig or did they just come to Berlin?
James Aldridge was here a few times. But I never saw him. Is Jack Lindsay, with his proletarian novels, from Australia?

Yes, he is, but he left Australia in the 1920s and lived and worked in England.
He must have been here. Can't think of any more, really. That someone should be interested in those old stories. You're making my emotions run high.

Scheller gives me his edition of Voss *as a farewell present. On the train home, I discover tucked in the book's covers a yellowed newspaper review cut out from* Neues Deutschland. *Prof Dr Wolfang Wicht (the GDR's expert on literary modernism) calls Patrick White's novel 'compulsory reading for every lover of world literature' and highlights White's interest in his characters' inner lives: 'As White switches from his own neutral standpoint to the subjective perspective of his characters he combines a distancing representation with the immediate reproduction of interior monologues, dreams and hallucinations. The "dramatic dialogue" is paired with daring towers of poetic imagery which produce a frequently startling effect.'*

———————

Theses Completed on Australian Literature at the University of Leipzig

Findeisen, Helmut. *James Aldridge: Schriftsteller und Kämpfer* (*James Aldridge: Author and Fighter*) (based on his 1959 Leipzig PhD thesis of the same title). Halle (Saale): VEB Max Niemeyer Verlag, 1960.

Herzog, Juliane. *Jack Hibberd und einige Entwicklungstendenzen der australischen Gegenwartsdramatik* (*Jack Hibberd and Recent Developments in Contemporary Australian Drama*), Diplomarbeit, Karl-Marx-Universität Leipzig, no date.

Röhlig, Martina. *Australische Dramatik der Gegenwart, deren Traditionslinien und nationale Eigenständigkeit* (*Contemporary Australian Drama, Its Lines of Tradition and National Independence*), Diplomarbeit, Karl-Marx-Universität Leipzig, 1977.

Winkler, Karl-Heinz. *Die Herausbildung des sozialistischen Realismus in der australischen Dramatik* (*The Emergence of Socialist Realism in Australian Drama*), Diplomarbeit, Karl-Marx-Universität Leipzig, 1977.

Reschke, Renate. *Aspekte der Entwicklung des zeitgenössischen australischen Dramas.* (*Aspects of the Development of Contemporary Australian Drama*), Diplomarbeit, Karl-Marx-Universität Leipzig, 1979.

Seidel, Barbara. *Frauengestalten in Werken von D. Cusack und K. S. Prichard* (*Women Characters in the Works of D. Cusack and K. S. Prichard*), Diplomarbeit, Karl-Marx-Universität Leipzig, 1983.

Timm, Christian. *Four Plays: Das Menschenbild im dramatischen Schaffen des australischen Romanciers Patrick White* (*Four Plays: The Concept of Man in the Dramatic Work of Australian Novelist Patrick White*), Diplomarbeit, Karl-Marx-Universität Leipzig, 1984.

Scheller, Bernhard. *Nationaler Anspruch und internationale Einflüsse: Studien zur australischen Dramatik* (*National Ambitions and International Influences: Studies in Australian Drama*), Dissertation zur Erlangung des akademischen Grades Dr sc. phil. Eingereicht dem Wissenschaftlichen Rat der Karl-Marx Universität Leipzig, angenommen 24 March 1987. (Dissertation in fulfilment of the requirements for the degree of Doctor of Philosophy, submitted to the Academic Board of Karl-Marx Universität Leipzig, awarded 24 March 1987.)

Notes

1 Erich Gronke, *Entwicklung und Eigenart der Romankunst der anglo-australischen Schriftstellerin Henry Handel Richardson (1870–1946)* (*The Development and Uniqueness of the Novelistic Art of Anglo-Australian Writer Henry Handel Richardson (1870–1946)*), Inaugural-Dissertation zur Erlangung der Doktorwürde einer Hohen Philosophischen Fakultät der Humboldt-Universität zu Berlin 1952. (Dissertation in fulfilment of the requirements for the degree of Doctor of Phiolosophy, at the Faculty of Philosophy, Humboldt University Berlin, 1952).
2 Published in 1984, this anthology contains the first piece by Patrick White to appear in the GDR.
3 A much-anthologized story by Edward Dyson, published first in *The Bulletin Story Book* in 1901, ed. A. G. Stephens (Sydney: *The Bulletin*), 131–38.
4 Tenschert's ensemble performed at the Princess Theatre, Melbourne, on 20 June 1973. 'Joachim Tenschert', *Ausstage Database*, accessed 30 January 2013, http://www.ausstage.edu.au/pages/contributor/231100.
5 The Australian embassy in East Berlin closed in late 1986 out of disappointment over the lack of growth in trade, and the ambassador, resident in Warsaw, continued representation; Peter Monteath, 'The German Democratic Republic and Australia', in *Debatte: Journal of Contemporary Central and Eastern Europe* 16, no. 2 (2008): 213–35 (231).
6 The two Aboriginal dramatists discussed in Scheller's thesis are Jack Davis and Robert James Meritt. Meritt's *The Cake Man* (1974) was the first black Australian play to be published, televised and to tour overseas. 'The Cake Man', *AustLit* Database, accessed 4 February 2014, http://www.austlit.edu.au/austlit/page/C16106.
7 Distinguished writer Daniil Granin was chairman of the Soviet writers' union. *Vier Wochen mit den Beinen nach oben* is the German translation of his lively, humorous account of his trip to Australia, undertaken with Oksana Krugerskaya (who had translated Marshall's *I Can Jump Puddles* into Russian) in the early 1960s. It was first published in German by Volk und Welt in 1968 and charts numerous encounters with Australian writers, including Alan Marshall, John Morrison and Frank Hardy.
8 Founded in Weimar in 1864, on the occasion of Shakespeare's 300th birthday, the German Shakespeare Association is one of the oldest literary associations in Germany. In 1946 the Association received permission from the Soviet military authorities to resume its activities in Weimar but split in two in 1963: the Deutsche Shakespeare-Gesellschaft West e.V. (Bochum), and the Deutsche Shakespeare-Gesellschaft. The two were reunited in Weimar in 1993; Ruth Freifrau von Ledebur, 'Die Geschichte der Deutschen Shakespeare-Gesellschaft', accessed 30 January 2014, http://shakespeare-gesellschaft.de/gesellschaft/ueber/geschichte.html.
9 About *Voss*, Eberhard Brüning wrote: 'Published in 1957, the novel *Voss* is without doubt an excellent example of White's narrative art and at the same time a milestone in contemporary Australian literature, and it is recognised as such nationally and internationally. Voss, the novel's eponymous hero, is none other than the legendary German researcher and explorer Ludwig Leichhardt (1813–1848), whose disappearance with his companions in 1848, while attempting to cross the Australian continent from East to West, remains a mystery. White does not take up this interesting phenomenon from Australia's pioneer era to tell an adventurous, suspenseful expedition story, but instead uses the authentic historical character of this deeply ambivalent, eccentric German, possessed by the urge for scientific research, to realise two principal artistic

aims. Firstly, this special human case offers a possibility to think about human nature and behaviour, especially by drawing on the author's experiences of more recent times, and secondly, White "regionalizes" or "nationalizes" Voss' individual tragedy and his failed enterprise by locating it in Australian society, with all its social strata, its cultural and economic manifestations, problems and contradictions. This is by no means achieved in a historicizing fashion; rather Australian reality is made transparent here – predominantly in family and group portraits – whose key traits can be traced right into the present, which renders the critical undertones really palpable', undated report on Patrick White, *Voss* (early 1986), BArch DR1/2200a/438–439, translated by Christina Spittel.

10 See Siegfried Lokatis's essay in chapter 1.

CONTRIBUTORS

Camille Barrera holds an MA degree in English Studies from the Freie Universität Berlin, where her research interests include intermediality, adaptation, performativity and postmodernism. She has studied in the USA and in theatre at the University of Tasmania and has worked extensively in educational, professional and fringe theatre as a director, performer and dramaturge.

Patricia F. Blume holds an MA degree in English and Media and Communication Studies from the University of Leipzig; during her studies she spent one year in Brittany, France. She is currently completing a doctoral thesis on the International Leipzig Book Fair in East Germany. She works for the Department of Book Studies at the University of Leipzig and coordinates a Polish-German research project. She has published on the Leipzig Book Fair, the unread book phenomenon, and is editor of *Flachware: Footnotes on Leipzig Book Studies*.

Leah Gerber works as a Lecturer in Translation and Interpreting Studies at Monash University in Melbourne and is the author of *Tracing a Tradition: The Translation of Australian Children's Fiction into German from 1945* (2014). She is co-editor with Rita Wilson of *Creative Constraints: Translation and Authorship* (2012) and has co-authored a number of research projects in the area of translating and interpreting service provision.

Susan Lever taught Australian literature at various universities in Australia for three decades. She is the author of *A Question of Commitment: Australian Literature in the Twenty Years after the War*, an influential study of cold war cultural contexts, and her subsequent books include *Real Relations: The Feminist Politics of Form in Australian Fiction*, *The Oxford Book of Australian Women's Verse* and *David Foster: The Satirist of Australia*. She is an editor of the *Journal of the Association for the Study of Australian Literature (JASAL)* and is currently working on the history of Australian television drama.

Siegfried Lokatis is Professor of Book History and Head of the Department of Book Studies at the University of Leipzig. He has been researching the history of publishing in the GDR since the collapse of the East German state. His major publications in the field include *Jedes Buch ein Abenteuer: Zensursystem und literarische Öffentlichkeit in der DDR bis Ende der sechziger Jahre* (*Each Book an Adventure: The Censorship System and the Literary Public in the GDR until the End of the 1960s*) with Simone Barck and Martina Langermann; *Der rote Faden: Kommunistische Parteigeschichte und Zensur unter Walter Ulbricht* (*The Red Thread: Communist Party History and Censorship under Walter Ulbricht*); *Zensurspiele: Heimliche Literaturgeschichten der DDR* (*Censorship Games: Secret Literary Histories of the GDR*) with Simone Barck, and *Fenster zur Welt: Eine Geschichte des DDR-Verlags Volk und Welt* (*Windows on the World: A History of GDR Publisher Volk und Welt*) with Simone Barck.

Alexandra Ludewig is Professor of German Studies and Head of the German Department at the University of Western Australia. Walter Kaufmann's life and writings were the topic of her PhD thesis at the University of Queensland. Her publications include a biographical study of Thomas Bernhard and, most recently, her *Habilitationsschrift*, published as *Screening Nostalgia: 100 Years of German Heimat Film* (2011). Currently, she is engrossed in researching the World War One internment camps at Ruhleben near Berlin and on Western Australia's Rottnest Island.

Nicole Moore is author of the prize-winning study *The Censor's Library: Uncovering the Lost History of Australia's Banned Books* (2012) and co-author of *Banned in Australia*, an annotated bibliography of Australian titles banned by federal censorship (2008). She is a co-editor of *The Literature of Australia* (2009) and with Nicholas Birns and Sarah Shieff of *Teaching Australian and New Zealand Literature* (forthcoming). Another edited volume, *Censorship and the Limits of Literary: A Global View* was published in 2015. She is Professor and Australian Research Council Future Fellow in English at the University of New South Wales, Canberra.

Bernhard Scheller studied English and German at Karl-Marx Universität Leipzig, and was awarded his PhD for a thesis on the reception of contemporary British and American drama in the GDR (1974) and his *Habilitation* on Australian drama (1987). He taught at Leipzig until 1993, and collaborated with Reclam Leipzig on numerous book projects, including the East German edition of Patrick White's *Voss* (1987). He regularly included Australian material in his classes and supervised several *Diplomarbeiten* on Australian authors, effectively turning his university into a small centre for Australian literary studies in the East.

Christina Spittel is a Lecturer in English at the University of New South Wales, Canberra. Her research into the literary legacy of the First World War in Australia and the publishing history of the Cold War has appeared in several collections, and in journals such as *Book History*, *Australian Literary Studies*, *The Australian Journal of Politics and History* and *The Journal of Contemporary History*. She is currently completing a book on the First World War in Australian novels.

Jennifer Wawrzinek is Professor of English at the Free University, Berlin. She is the author of *Ambiguous Subjects: Dissolution and Metamorphosis in the Postmodern Sublime* (2008) and co-editor of the collections *Frontier Skirmishes: Literary and Cultural Debates in Australia after 1992* (2010) and *Border-Crossings: Narrative and Demarcation in Postcolonial Literatures and Media* (2012). In 2010 she was British Academy Visiting Research Fellow at the University of London and in 2014 she was Australian Research Council HoE Visiting Research Fellow at the University of Melbourne.

Russell West-Pavlov is Professor and Chair of English at Eberhard-Karls Universität Tübingen. His recent book publications are *Temporalities* (2013), *Imaginary Antipodes: Essays on Contemporary Australian Literature and Culture* (2011) and *Spaces of Fiction/Fictions of Space: Postcolonial Place and Literary DeiXis* (2010). With Jenz Elze-Volland, he is co-author of *Australian Literature in German Translation: A Catalogue of Titles, Translators and Trends 1789–2010* (2010).

INDEX

Aboriginal people
  in literature 80–81, 167, 179–80
abortion
  in GDR 125–26
Adams, Paul 111
Adelaide Writers Festival 17
Adelaide, Debra 215
Adenauer, Konrad 103
Afterwords 27, 100–2, 104, 188, 190–92,
    197–98, 239, 243–44
Against Hitler and the Boss (Kaufmann) 144
All That I Am (Funder) 232, 235, 237
American Encounter (Kaufmann) – *Begegnungen
    mit Amerika heute* 148–49
Anderson, Amanda 23
Anderson, Benedict 74
Anderson, Edith 212
Appadurai, Arjun 94
Apter, Emily 5, 20, 24, 28n14, 55
archives
  in Eastern Bloc 13, 35
Armstrong, Pauline 94
Ash, Timothy Garton 228, 231, 234
Attridge, Derek 82
Aufbau Verlag (publishing house) 2, 15,
    38–40, 45, 46–47, 82, 211–12
Australasian Book Society 17, 42, 107,
    114, 135, 144, 157
Australian Landfall (Kisch) – *Landung in
    Australien* 2, 40, 47, 59–60, 94
Australian literature
  reception of in GDR 122
  reception of in USSR 19
  reception of in West Germany 3, 109,
    193, 243
  uses of in GDR 122–24
Australian Security Intelligence Organisation
    (ASIO) 94–95, 99, 114, 213

Australian Society of Authors 194
Australian writers
  GDR and 17, 214–15
  international reputation of 19
*Australische Erzähler von Marcus Clarke bis
    Patrick White* (Australian Storytellers
    from Marcus Clarke to Patrick White,
    anthology) 46, 216, 240–42

Bachmann, Sigrid 212–13
Bail, Murray 188, 192, 194
Balibar, Etienne 25
Barck, Simone 15, 25, 75–76, 105
Barnard, Marjorie 44
Bates, Daisy 181–82
Bathrick, David 75
Baynton, Barbara 44
Bebel, August 127
Becher, Johannes R. 5, 14–15, 25, 101
Becker, Wolfgang 229
Beckett, Samuel 44, 199, 201,
    208n78
Beedles, Russell 194, 203
Benedict, Barbara M. 198
Benjamin, Walter 85
Bennett, Tony 98
Berger, Karl-Heinz 48n16, 195, 201
Berghahn, Daniela 234
Berlin Wall 4, 37, 46, 56, 139, 147, 153,
    163, 178, 182, 204, 221, 224–25,
    227–28
Berliner Illustrierte (periodical) 147
Berliner Zeitung (periodical) 8, 103,
    107, 147
Biermann, Wolf 150, 160–61, 188, 198,
    201
biopolitics 80–81, 89
Bird, Delys 130

Birns, Nicholas 19, 27
Bitterfelder Weg 21, 165, 169, 174, 176, 183
Black Lightning (Cusack) – *Wie ein schwarzer Blitz* 120, 131, 214
Blainey, Geoffrey 230
Blake, William 105, 211–13
Blockparteien 37
Blütenhölle in Banusta (Floral Hell in Banusta) (Specht) 176
Bobbin Up (Hewett) – *Die Mädchen von Sydney* 26, 43
Bode, Katherine 98, 114
'Bohemian Party' (Johnson/Mudrooroo) 199, 207
Böll, Heinrich 54
Bony and the Mouse (Upfield) – *Gefahr für Bony* 40
book history 1, 22–23
  Cold War 19
  methodologies 24–26
  study of in GDR 25, 36
Borges, Jorge Louis 198
Börsenblatt des deutschen Buchhandels (trade journal) 104, 115
Box, John 194, 203
Brand, Mona 241, 244
Brandt, Willi 191
Braut von Far Away, Die (Prichard) (The Bride of Far Away) 196
Brecht, Bertolt 39–40
Bredel, Willi 5, 145
Brockhaus (publishing house) 8, 37, 178
Brown, Timothy 196
Brüning, Eberhard 27n1, 241, 243–45, 247n9
Brussig, Thomas 229
Bryson, John 42
Buchverlag der Morgen (publisher) 39, 72–73, 81
Buckley, Vincent 79, 88
Budzislawski, Hermann 99
Burchett, Wilfred 2, 41–43, 48n9, 95–98, 100, 102, 105–8
Burnham, John 13
Burnt Ones, The (White) 195, 205n48
Büro für Urheberrechte (Office for Copyright Law) 9

Campbell, Persia 74
canon

'cross-border' 55, 66
East German 62
'off shore' 55
capitalism
  in literature 27, 81
  in *Power without Glory* 101–102
Capricornia (Herbert) 2, 21, 39, 71–75, 79–81, 83–86
Carey, Peter 3, 188, 192, 194, 198, 202
Carter, David 3, 15, 88, 113, 216
Cartload of Clay, A (Johnston) 53
Casanova, Pascale 3–5, 13, 15, 28n15, 98
Castro, Brian 53
Catalogue of Banned Nazi Books and Military Literature 35
censorship 35
  in Australia 7
  in German Democratic Republic 4, 36–38, 105, 153; *see also* Hauptverwaltung für Verlage und Buchhandel, Ministry of Culture, regulation of book trade
  modernization of 38
  of international writing in GDR 39
  Soviet-style 35
centralized planning 36
Chakrabarty, Dipesh 3
Chant of Jimmie Blacksmith, The (Keneally) – *Australische Ballade* 42–43, 46
Chinese Women Speak (Cusack) – *Auf eigenen Füßen* 42
Christesen, C. B. 194, 202
Christophs Abenteuer in Australien: Eine Erzählung aus der Goldgräberzeit (Heyd) (Christoph's Adventures in Australia: A Story from the Gold Diggers' Era) 39
Clark, Maureen 199
Clarke, Marcus 3, 10–12, 19, 42, 44, 47, 52, 55, 57–64, 66, 101, 193, 241
Claudius, Eduard 145
Clean Straw for Nothing (Johnston) 53
Cold War 1, 4, 13, 19, 22, 28, 30, 48, 95, 96, 102, 108, 113–14, 117–18, 123, 134, 145, 157, 192, 213, 216–18
  cultural 3, 7, 13, 28n15, 93, 97, 113
colonial identity 77
Come In Spinner (Cusack and James) 122, 124–25, 131, 214–15

INDEX 255

Communist Party of Australia (CPA) 93, 132, 135, 173, 213, 215
Communist Party of Great Britain 99
community 74, 76
　imagined 75, 76
　literature and 83
　plurality and 85
　singularity and 82–83
comparative literature 4
congresses
　Fourth German Writers' Congress 14, 25, 101
　International Writers' Congress 192
　Tenth Writers' Congress 85
Connewitzer Verlagsbuchhandlung (publishing house) 47
Constabile-Heming, Carol Anne 75, 87n16
Coonardoo (Prichard) 120, 122, 128, 135n22
Copperheads, The (Blake) 211–12
Coronation Press 107
Cotters' England (Stead) 212–13
Cowan, Peter 192, 194, 202
Crabbe, Chris Wallace 198, 206n29
crime fiction, 3, 21, 79, 87
Crown Jewel (de Boissière) – *Kronjuwel* 42–43, 107
cultural exchange 1, 16–17
Culture in the Age of Three Worlds (Denning) 4–6
Cunningham, Laurel 196, 202
Curse of Maralinga, The (Kaufmann) 147
Cusack, Dymphna 3, 17–18, 21, 42, 44, 119–24, 127, 133–34, 173, 180, 190, 205n13, 214–17
　GDR and 216
Customs
　in Australia 7
　in GDR 37
Czollek, Walter 106, 109, 111

Daily Worker (periodical) 99, 173
Damned Whores and God's Police (Summers) 129
Damrosch, David 4, 28n15, 67, 97, 114
Daniels Weg in die Steinzeit (Daniel's Path to the Stone Age) (Specht) 180
Das demokratische Dorf (periodical) 103, 115
de Boissière, Ralph 42–43, 107, 144, 152

Death in Fremantle (Kaufmann) 150
'Deep Well' (Venn) 200
Deery, Philip 14
Democracy with a Tommy Gun (Burchett) – *Sonnenaufgang über Asien* 2, 42
Denning, Michael 4–6
'Der Buschbrand' (The Bushfire) (Specht) 167
Der Kontinent des Känguruhs (Lockwood) – *Continent of the Kangaroo, The* 181
Der Monat (periodical) 107
Dessaix, Robert 54
'Die Begegnung' ('The Encounter') (Specht) 172
Die Frau von Heute (periodical) 103
Die Gejagten (The Hunted) (Specht) 170–71, 174, 179
'Die Kinder von Broom Tank' (The Children from Broom Tank) (Specht) 168
'Die Langeweile von Minsk' ('The Boredom of Minsk') (Heym) 17, 188–89
Die neuen Leiden des jungen W. (*The New Sorrows of Young W.*) (Plenzdorf) 197
Dietz Verlag (publishing house) 14
Dimock, Wai Chee 4, 28, 67
distant reading 1, 23
Dixon, Robert 3, 79, 204n2
Druckgenehmigung: *see* regulation of book trade; *see also Hauptverwaltung Verlage und Buchhandel*, Ministry of Culture
During, Simon 26, 69
Dyson, Edward 242

Eastern Bloc 1, 14, 18, 26, 233
　archives in 2, 13, 35
　censorship in 7, 21, 36–37
　collapse of 4, 224
　literature in 7, 113
　readers in 4, 95, 112
　Western writers in 17, 22, 105, 108, 214, 219; *see also* Soviet Bloc
Ellis, Cath 132
Encounter (periodical) 107
English literature
　in GDR 59

Erkundungen (book series) 43–44, 188, 192, 204
  Australian volume 41, 43–47, 188–89, 192, 195, 199, 201–2, 239
  Irish volume 44, 188, 208n78
  West German volume 44
Eulenspiegel-Verlag (publishing house) 39
Europäische Verlagsanstalt (EVA, publishing house) 223, 225, 227
Evergreen (Blake) – *Späte Liebe* 212
Express (periodical) 95

feminism 117, 119, 215–16, 230–31
  in GDR 129–30
Ferrier, Carole 98, 107
Festival and Other Stories (Buckley and Hamilton) 193, 207
'Fig Tree, The' (Wright) 197
Findeisen, Helmut 190, 205n11
Flight (Kaufmann) – *Flucht* 148
For Love Alone (Stead) 212–13
For the Term of His Natural Life (Clarke) – *Lebenslänglich* 10, 19–21, 30, 42–43, 47, 52, 55, 57–58, 101, 112, 245
Forshaw, Thelma 200–202, 206, 208
Fortunes of Richard Mahoney, The (Richardson) 53
Forum (periodical) 74
Four-Legged Lottery, The (Hardy) – *Die vierbeinige Lotterie* 55, 110
Frankfurt Book Fair 196
Frankfurter Allgemeine Zeitung (periodical) 3
free reading 23
freedom of speech 96
Freehill, Norman 135, 214–15
Freie Deutsche Jugend (FDJ) 76
Friedländer, Paul 84, 89
Frow, John 22, 31, 98, 111, 116
Funder, Anna 22, 218, 221, 224, 229, 235–37
Für Dich: Illustrierte Zeitschrift für die Frau (periodical) 120

Garner, Helen 222, 227
Gärtner-Scholle, Carola 39, 48n4, 123
Geertz, Clifford 112
Gefahr für Bony (*Bony and the Mouse*) (Upfield) 40
Gelbin, Gertrude 15–18, 30–31, 109

gender 117
  in GDR 118–19
  publishing and in GDR 21
German Democratic Republic 1
  and world literature 3–4
  family and 118
  women and 117
global literature 3
global turn 4
globalization 1
Goethe, Johann Wolfgang von 14, 28n15, 40
'Gold Bride, The' (Stead) 213
Golden Miles (Prichard) – *Die goldene Meile* 43, 55, 119, 122, 125, 131
Good Bye, Lenin! 22, 229–30, 235
'Grand Passion, The' (Forshaw) 200
Granin, Daniil 242
Green, H. M. 79
Greene, Graham 166
Greifenverlag (publishing house) 38
Grieshaber, HAP 180, 186
Gronke, Erich 239, 247n1
Grossmann, Henryk 211–12
Gruner, Jürgen 194, 206, 208
Gustav Kiepenheuer (publishing house, FRG) 37
Gustav Kiepenheuer Verlag (publishing house, GDR) 39

Half-Burnt Tree, The (Cusack) *Der halbverbrannte Baum* 120, 214
Hard Way, The (Hardy) 95, 104, 107, 110
Hardy, Frank 3, 7, 17–18, 29, 31, 41, 43, 55, 93, 97–98, 100–102, 109, 112–16, 135, 144, 157, 190, 212, 216–17, 220, 241, 247
  citizenship and 108
  in Europe 99
  trial of 18, 111
Hasluck, Paul 190
Hauptverwaltung für Verlage und Buchhandel (Main Administration for Publishing and the Book Trade) 8–9, 48n2, 123, 160n61; *see also* Ministry of Culture
Heatwave in Berlin (Cusack) 18, 214
Hein, Christoph 85
Heisler, Renee, 172–73
Hench, John 13
Hensel, Jana 222, 229

INDEX

Herbert, Xavier 2–3, 17, 21, 39, 42–43, 46, 71–74, 79–81, 187, 190
Hewett, Dorothy 3, 17, 26, 42–43, 46, 94, 99, 119, 134n12, 216–17
Heyd, Kurt 39
Heym, Stefan 8, 15–17, 43, 145, 188–89, 201
Hiener, Judy 194, 203
Hinstorff Verlag (publishing house) 38, 147
HMT *Dunera* 142–43, 156n8
Honecker, Erich 4, 187–88, 190, 201, 233
Horst Erdmann Verlag (publishing house) 193, 200
Hughes, Robert 77
Hume, Fergus 3, 21, 71–72, 77
Hunt, Helen 197

ideology 25, 26
I'm Dying Laughing (Stead) 212–13
immigration 52
In den Mangrovensümpfen (In the Mangrove Swamps) (Specht) 177
Insel Verlag (publishing house) 8
International Confederation of Free Trade Unions (ICFTU) 96

James, Ian 83, 89
Jany, Rebecca 16
Johnston, George 53
Jolley, Elizabeth 204
Journey into the Future (Hardy) – *Reise in die Zukunft* 43, 107, 110, 216
Jouvenel, Renaud de 98
Jungfrau (Cusack) 130
Jurgensen, Manfred 31n70, 152, 161, 171, 173

Kabbarli (Specht) 182
Kafka, Franz 192
Kahlschlagsplenum 38
Kaufmann, Walter 3, 8, 17, 21, 39, 42, 94, 108, 139–55, 177, 217, 219
  GDR and 145–46
Keneally, Thomas 3, 42–43, 46
Kiepenheuer und Witsch (publishing house, Federal Republic) 45
Kiernan, Brian 75, 79
Kinderbuchverlag Berlin (publishing house) 27n1

Kisch, Egon Erwin 2, 40, 47, 59, 62, 94, 166
Koch, Hans 74
Koehler, Wolf 54
Kohl, Katrin 225
Korallen-Joe (Coral Joe) (Specht) 177
Kreuzwege (Kaufmann) 147, 158–60, 179
Kultureller Beirat für das Verlagswesen (Cultural Advisory Committee for the Publishing Trade) 8, 48n4
Kulturpolitik 75–76, 80
Kulturpolitisches Wörterbuch 14
Kunze, Reiner 74

Lambert, Eric 107
Lamond, Julieanne 118
Land der Verheißung (*New Life in the New Look*) (Burchett) 43
Langermann, Martina 15, 25, 75–76, 105, 115, 135
Laurie, Werner 99
Lawson, Henry 6, 198
Leane, Jeanine 199
Lefevere, André 225
Leichhardt, Ludwig 45, 243–44, 247n9
Leipzig 12, 37, 45, 47, 182, 211, 222, 232, 239, 240, 244
  publishers 8, 16, 39, 43, 99, 148, 178
  Book Fair 172, 223, 240
  University of 20, 22, 27, 181, 190, 211, 239–40, 246–47
Leseland 26, 75–76, 85, 100; *see also* Literaturgesellschaft
Lessing, Doris 214
Lessing, Gottfried 214
Letty Fox (Stead) 212–13, 219
Leuchtfeuer Eastern Reef (Lights of Eastern Reef) (Specht) 176
Lindsay, Jack 173, 246
Links, Christoph 14, 30n48
literary criticism
  in GDR 38, 238–47
Literary Gazette (periodical) 99
Literaturarbeitsgemeinschaft 45
Literaturgesellschaft 14, 25, 75–76, 85, 101; *see also Leseland*
Literaturnaja Gazeta (periodical) 103, 115
Lives of Others, The 22, 231, 234

Lockwood, Rupert 181
Lokatis, Siegfried 2, 9, 15, 25, 48, 75–76, 105
'Lost Causes' (Stead) 213
Luhmann, Niklas 54, 67–68

Macherey, Pierre 25
Malouf, David 52, 67
Man Who Loved Children, The (Stead) 212, 216
Mann, Thomas 40, 244
Marshall, Alan 17, 44, 144, 190, 197, 217, 247n7
Martens, Lorna 127, 137
Martin, David 144, 149–50, 157n23, 216–17
Maurice Guest (Richardson) 47
McLeod, Jessica 109
McQueen, Humphrey 98
Mead, Phillip 3
Meanjin (periodical) 17, 193–94
Merkel, Ina 197
Merker, Paul 122
Middleton, O. E. 194
Ming Xie 24
Ministerium für Staatssicherheit 8, 9, 15, 29n34; *see also* Stasi
Ministry of Culture (GDR) 7–8, 10–11, 16, 24m 27n2, 42, 48n2, 73, 76, 78, 100, 112, 119, 122–23, 159n52, 160n61, 163, 183, 192–95
Mitchell, Kate 222
Mitteldeutscher Verlag (publishing house) 39, 148, 155, 166
Mittman, Elizabeth 76
Monahan, Sean 81
Monthly, The (periodical) 235
Montrose, Louis 26
Moore, Nicole 29n25, 31n60, 136n44, 206n32, 219n9
Moorhouse, Frank 3, 188, 194, 200, 202–3
Moretti, Franco 98
Morning Sacrifice (Cusack) 215
Morrison, John 144
Mudrooroo 188, 196, 199, 203
My Brother Jack (Johnston) 53
Mystery of a Hansom Cab, The (Hume) – *Das Geheimnis des Fiakers* 3, 21, 71–73, 77–78

Namatjira, Albert 179–80
Nancy, Jean-Luc 21, 76, 82–83, 85–86, 89n43
nation building 80–81
national identity 118
  in GDR 118
national literature 51
  in German Democratic Republic 14
nationalism 6–7, 217
  communism and 113
Naumann, Manfred 82–3, 205n11
neue deutsche literatur (periodical) 75, 169, 171, 184
Neues Deutschland (newspaper) 76, 103, 127, 139, 147, 201, 243, 246
New Life in the New Look (Burchett) – *Land der Verheißung* 43
Ng, Lilian 53
Night Letters (Dessaix) 54
Noble, Jenny 128
Nonveiller, Heinz 199, 203, 206
North, Marilla 214–15

obscenity 7
'On the Tightrope' (Kaufmann) 154
Orwell, George 199, 201, 218, 240
Ossikovska, Vessa 95
Ostalgie 22, 228–30, 235–36
Overland (periodical) 217

Pacific Paradise (Cusack) 215
Palmer, Helen 108
Palmer, Vance 44
Panther Books 15–16, 43, 93, 97–98, 109–10
Paraipagold (Paraipa Gold) (Specht) 177
Paris Review (periodical) 30, 107, 114
Park, Ruth 215, 217
Paul List Verlag (publishing house) 15, 43, 93, 97, 99, 110
Pavlin, Helen 197, 202
Peitzker, Tania 131
People with the Dogs, The (Stead) 212
'Person of Accomplishment, A' (Moorhouse) 200
Peterborough Story (Specht) 166, 169–70, 172–75, 184–85
Petersen, Hans 15, 19, 30, 41, 44–45, 48n15, 122, 169, 178, 187–88, 190–99, 201, 204, 216, 239–40, 242, 244–45

Peterson, Bruno 98
Petrov Royal Commission 20, 178
Phillips, A. A. 144
planetary literature 3
Plenzdorf, Ulrich 9, 197
Porter, Hal 192, 194, 200, 202, 241
postcolonialism 1, 3, 6, 168
Power without Glory (Hardy) – *Macht ohne Ruhm* 7, 17, 21, 43, 55, 93, 94–104, 107, 109, 111–12, 217
  criminal libel and 7, 18, 93
  in USSR 7
  Melbourne and 94
  publication of 98
  reception in GDR 100
Price, Leah 198
Prichard, Katharine Susannah 3, 6–7, 17, 20–21, 41, 43–44, 55, 94, 119–23, 125, 127–28, 130–34, 135n22, 169, 190, 196, 200, 212
  East German theses about 243, 246
  Soviet context 7
print runs
  fraudulent deflation of in contracts 19, 46–47, 116n62
  Australische Erzähler 46
  Clarke 68n37
  Erkundungen, Australian volume 46
  Hardy 108–10
  Herbert 46
  Hewett 46
  Kaufmann 140, 160n67
  Keneally 47
  Specht 177
  Upfield 40
  Wright 47
  Wongar 46
Probyn-Rapsey, Fiona 80–81
proletarian literature 4
proletarian movements 5
proletarian novel 5
propaganda 4, 14, 16, 19
  American 13, 108
  Soviet 8
provincialism 3
publishing houses
  Christian 37
  in Eastern Bloc 36
publishing relations
  between East and West 37

Quadrant (periodical) 107, 217–18

Raddatz, Fritz 4, 57, 60, 65–66, 125
Realist Writers Group 17, 95, 99
  Melbourne 144
  Sydney 99
Reception (periodical) 22
reception
  history 23
  theory 82–83, 205n11
Reclam Verlag (publishing house) 8, 37, 39, 45–46, 110, 239, 243
regimes of reading 22–24
regionalism 3
regulation of book trade
  in Eastern Bloc 36
  in GDR 8–10, 75
  permission to print 8–12, 27n2, 46, 116n62
Renft, Klaus 201, 221, 224
Renn, Ludwig 145
republic of letters 15, 201
  GDR and 15
Richardson, Henry Handel 44, 47, 49, 52, 239, 247
Riemann, Harald 223
'Rightangled Creek, The: A Sort of Ghost Story' (Stead) 216
Roaring Nineties, The (Prichard) – *Goldrausch* 119, 122, 131
Rooney, Brigid 3
Rose, Frederick 20, 177–79
Rubin, Andrew 107
Rum und Coca Cola (de Boissiere) – *Rum und Coca Cola* 42
Rusch, Claudia 222
Rütten & Loening (publishing house) 181

Said, Edward 78
'Sale, The' (Porter) 200
Salzburg Tales, The (Stead) 20, 212–13
Sartre, Jean-Paul 98, 192
Saunders, Frances 13
Say No to Death (Cusack) 119, 123, 125, 135, 180, 214

Scheller, Bernhard 181, 186, 201, 206, 208, 238–47
Schlesinger, Klaus 9, 159
Schlösser, Anselm 57, 59, 60–66, 101, 193
Schreyer, Wolfgang 177
Schroeder, Edith 212–13
  Max 211–12
Schulze, Cornelia 198
Schweigen zwischen Wort und Wort (Silence between Word and Word) (Wright) 42, 44
sedition 93
Segelflug unterm Kreuz des Südens (Gliding under the Southern Cross) (Specht) 177
Seghers, Anna 39–40, 145
Seven Emus (Herbert) – *Der vertauschte Traumstein* 42–43, 46, 187
Seven Poor Men of Sydney (Stead) 212
Seven Seas (publishing imprint) 15–18, 27, 30n53, 31n62, 43, 97, 110, 134n12, 135n22, 147–48, 159n48, 178, 240, 245
Shakespeare, William 59, 87n17, 112, 240–42, 247n8
Sharrad, Paul 3
Shelley, Percy Bysshe 86
Sheridan, Susan 118
Simon, Sherry 86
'Simple Things, The' (Kaufmann) 144
Sinn und Form (periodical) 75
Smith, Stephen Murray 95
socialist realism 4, 62, 88, 122, 130–31, 140, 190, 193
Southern Steel (Cusack) 120
Soviet Bloc 216, 218; *see also* Eastern Bloc
Sozialistische Einheitspartei Deutschlands (SED) 14, 38–39, 46, 74, 79, 81, 87, 96, 123, 127, 226
Specht, Joachim 20, 27, 31, 39, 48, 163–83, 184, 186
  socialism and 176
  speaking engagements 174–75
Spittel, Christina 31n60, 87n17, 206n32
Stade, Martin 9
Stasi 21, 39, 76, 146, 148, 152–54, 158–60, 218, 221, 223, 225–27, 229–31, 233–34, 236–37, 245; *see also* Ministerium für Staatssicherheit
Stasiland (Funder) 22, 218, 221–24, 226–35
  creative nonfiction and 225–28
  genre and 222
  reception of in Germany 223–25
  translation and 232
Stead, Christina 20, 44, 105, 115, 120, 198, 211–12, 219–20
  publication in GDR and 216
  reception of in GDR 212–13
Steinberg, Werner 166, 182, 184, 186
Stivens, Dal 187–88, 191, 194, 203, 205
Summers, Anne 129, 137
Sun Is Not Enough, The (Cusack) 18, 120
Sun, The (periodical) 193
Sunderland, Jane 132
Syson, Ian 98, 107
systems theory 54

Tabloid Story (periodical) 193
Tauchnitz (publishing house) 16
Tennant, Kylie 202, 207–8, 215, 217
Teo, Tsu-Ming 53
Teychenné, Maree 196, 202, 207
'That Part of the World' (Nonveiller) 199
Thürk, Harry 176, 177
Tippet (Specht) 177
'To the Mountain' (Stead) 213
Track to Bralgu, The (Wongar) – *Der Pfad nach Bralgu* 45
Tribune (periodical) 108, 145, 147
'Triskelion, The' (Stead) 213
Twenty Thousand Thieves, The (Lambert) 107

Ulbricht, Walter 103, 127, 174, 185, 187, 233
Union of Soviet Socialist Republics (USSR) 7, 19, 36, 40–41, 42, 43, 99, 107, 110, 118, 190, 214, 215, 216
Union-Verlag (publishing house) 39
Universal-Bibliothek (*Universal Library*) 45
Upfield, Arthur W. 3, 40
Ureinwohner, Känguruhs und Düsenclipper (Indigenous People, Kangaroos and Jet Planes) (Specht) 178

Venn, Victor 194, 200, 202, 208
Verlag der Nation (publishing house) 39, 109, 121, 128, 166, 171–73, 175–77, 179–83
Verlag Kultur und Fortschritt (publishing house) 40
Verlag Neues Berlin (publishing house) 39
Verlag Neues Leben (publishing house) 38, 179
Vesela, Pavla 127, 130, 137
Viidikas, Vicki 188, 194, 198, 203
Voices in the Storm (Kaufmann) 108, 145, 157
Volk und Welt (publishing house) 4, 15, 19, 21, 26, 43–44, 55, 57–58, 60, 94, 98, 105, 106–7, 109, 134n12, 169, 187–88, 190, 194–96, 199, 242, 247n7
  as key publisher 40
  structure of 40–41
  Frank Hardy's praise for 109
  contract with Frank Hardy 100
Voss (White) – *Voß* 45, 239, 243–44, 247n9

Walg: A Novel of Australia (Wongar) – *Der Schoß* 45
Wandlungsliteratur 166
Waten, Judah 44, 88, 190, 216
Waters, Joe 94
Watkin, Christopher 82
Weimarer Beiträge (periodical) 75
Welskopf-Henrich, Lieselotte 177
Welz, Stefan 69n40, 240
Wende 22, 26, 47, 232

Wendt, Erich 16
West-Pavlov, Russell 27n2, 66n2, 67n23
White, Patrick, 3, 15, 20, 42, 44–45, 54, 187, 195–96, 215–17, 219, 240–44, 246; *see also Voss*
Whitlam, Gough 191
Whitlock, Gillian 53
Whoring Around: Short Stories (Bryson) – *Melodram für eine Heldin aus Plast* 42
Wilcox, Maxwell 194–95
Wild Cat Falling (Johnson/Mudrooroo) 199
Wilding, Michael 194
William Heinemann 18, 115
'Windmill in the West, A' (Carey) 198, 202
Winged Seeds (Prichard) 120, 122
Wolf, Christa 17, 28n15, 40, 43, 74, 160n68, 188, 197
Wolf, Volker 201
Woman and Socialism (Bebel) 127
women
  socialism and 127
Wongar, Bahumir, 45–46, 242
Working Bullocks (Prichard) 6, 29, 120, 128
World Federation of Trade Unions (WFTU) 95–97
world literature
  publishing of in GDR 40–41
World Trade Union Movement (periodical) 95
Wren, Dennis 193
Wright, Judith 3, 42, 44, 47, 194, 197, 202, 245

www.ingramcontent.com/pod-product-compliance
Lightning Source LLC
Chambersburg PA
CBHW021822300426
44114CB00009BA/282